THE ROUGH GUIDE TO
DORDOGNE
& THE LOT

This eighth edition updated by
Anna Richards

Contents

INTRODUCTION 4

Where to go	5	Things not to miss	12
When to go	10	Itineraries	18
Author picks	11	Sustainable travel	20

BASICS 22

Getting there	23	Sports and outdoor activities	34
Getting around	25	Shopping and markets	35
Accommodation	28	Travelling with children	36
Food and drink	30	Travel essentials	36
Festivals	33		

THE GUIDE 44

1 Périgueux and the north	45	4 The Upper Dordogne valley and Rocamadour	155
2 Bergerac and around	83	5 The Lot valley and around	181
3 Sarlat and the Périgord Noir	111	6 South of the River Lot	227

CONTEXTS 260

History	261	French	281
Books	279	Glossary	289

SMALL PRINT & INDEX 291

COLLONGES-LA-ROUGE

Introduction to
Dordogne & the Lot

The green, secluded valleys of the Dordogne and the Lot have long attracted artists and lovers of the good life. In the many caves that tunnel into the honey-coloured limestone cliffs, prehistoric peoples painted some of the world's earliest masterpieces, depicting the pot-bellied ponies, mammoths and muscular bison that once lived in the region's woodlands. Later occupants expressed their faith by building the delicate Romanesque churches found on many a hilltop, as well as an array of abbeys and towering cathedrals, while the legacy of a less refined and more bellicose era lies in the medieval fortresses perched on craggy pinnacles of rock.

In addition to this richly layered history, the Dordogne and Lot are endowed with a tremendous variety of scenery, from the dry limestone plateaux of the *causses*, sliced through with narrow gorges, to densely wooded valleys and the serried ranks of gnarled grape vines which yield the region's fabulous wines. Through these landscapes slide the great rivers that unify and define southwest France: running swiftly through its deeply cloven valley, the **Vézère** hurtles into the **Dordogne**, which in turn flows placidly out to the Atlantic coast.

Further south the serpentine **Lot** writhes its way across the country to join the mighty **Garonne**, which along with its tributaries, the **Tarn** and **Aveyron**, mark this region's southern border. This peaceful corner of France is best savoured at its own unhurried pace. There is always some forgotten corner to stumble upon, a market or a village *fête* to enjoy, or something to catch the eye, from the postcard-perfect villages of blue-shuttered stone houses to fields of luminous sunflowers and gurgling willow-lined rivers. The Dordogne and the Lot are certainly not undiscovered – indeed, some sights are numbered among the most visited in the country – but the region's heartland is still steeped in what the French call the *douceur de vivre*, the gentle way of life, where there's

CANOEING ON THE DORDOGNE RIVER

FOOD AND DRINK IN THE DORDOGNE AND THE LOT

The Dordogne and the Lot are blessed with some of the most sought-after delicacies in the culinary world, including the celebrated **black truffle**. Deep in the oak forests, *cèpes* cluster in generous numbers and hordes of wild *sangliers* (boars) roam. On the high limestone *causses* lie secluded dairy farms, where **goat's cheese** reaches its apogee in the creamy *Cabécou*, while swathes of delicate violet flowers – the **saffron crocus** – thrive in the harsh conditions. Between the neatly combed vineyards (*Cabécou*), **walnut** plantations provide barrels of precious walnut oil and the region's famous dessert, *tarte aux noix*. Accompanying this copious feast are the rich, dark **wines** of Cahors and the fragrant, golden Monbazillac of Bergerac. South of the Lot valley the landscape changes to the baking fields of the Quercy Blanc and temperatures shift up a gear to ripen acres of yellow sunflowers, heaps of **melons** and orchards dripping with **peaches**, **plums** and **apricots**.

plenty of time for a long, lazy lunch, be it a picnic of market-fresh produce beneath the shade of a riverbank tree or a restaurant spread of the region's classic dishes.

Where to go

The principal northern gateway to the Dordogne and the Lot is the charming city of **Brive-la-Gaillarde** (usually shortened to Brive), whose cosy café culture exudes the spirit of the south, a hint of pleasures to come. West lies **Périgueux**, where an extraordinary Byzantine-style cathedral stands above a tangle of medieval lanes. The city is the capital

FACT FILE

- The area covered by this Guide amounts to some 22,000 square kilometres, approximately the size of Wales, but has a population of around 600,000, one of the lowest population densities in metropolitan France.
- The French Air Force has special permission to perform occasional low-level flying practice in the Lot valley, on the premise that there is less chance of tragedy should an accident occur.
- The economy is based on tourism and agriculture, primarily **wine** production. Bergerac has 120 square kilometres of vines while the Cahors' vineyards amount to about 43 square kilometres. Originally planted by the Romans in 50 BC they are said to be the oldest in France.
- The region boasts three **World Heritage Sites** – the Vézère valley, with its prehistoric cave art, the entire Causses du Quercy and a dozen or so sites listed under the pilgrims' route to Santiago de Compostela.
- The iconic French **jam**, Bonne Maman, with its distinctive red-checked lid, is made in Biars, in the northern Lot.
- During a *fête*, when the soup course comes to a close, it is *de rigueur* for gentlemen to tip a glass of Cahors wine into the empty bowl, swill it round and drink it down in one, to the boisterous cheers of their companions.
- The Causses du Quercy is known to **astronomers** the world over as the "black triangle" because it has the lowest light pollution in France.
- **Pigeonniers** – vernacular structures originally built as pigeon lofts and often highly ornamental – encapsulate the Quercy landscape. The oldest were constructed on stilts to facilitate the collection of manure. They are still built as architectural features today and nearly every sizeable house has one.

of a broad sweep of rolling pasture and woodland known as **Périgord Vert** (Green Périgord). This region's loveliest river is the Dronne and its most appealing town, water-bound **Brantôme**, known for its rock-cut sanctuaries and plethora of restaurants. East of here is castle-country: **Château de Puyguilhem** stands out for its elegant Renaissance architecture, while the **Château de Hautefort** is one of the grandest castles in the Dordogne and Lot.

South of Périgueux, in an area known as **Périgord Pourpre** (Purple Périgord) thanks to its wine production, vines cloak the slopes of the lower Dordogne valley around the pleasant riverside town of **Bergerac**. The star of this area is the river itself, which loops through two immense meanders near **Trémolat** to create a classic Dordogne scene.

East of Trémolat the colour scheme changes again as you enter the **Périgord Noir** (Black Périgord), named for the preponderance of evergreen oaks with their dark, dense foliage. Here you'll discover the greatest concentration of Périgord cottages with their steep, stone-covered roofs, and dramatic fortresses perched high above the river. This, too, is where you'll find the walnut orchards and flocks of ducks and geese, the source of so much of the produce featured in the region's markets. Of these the most vivid is that at **Sarlat-la-Canéda**, held among the fine medieval and Renaissance houses built in honey-coloured stone. Close by, the beetling cliffs of the **Vézère valley** are riddled with limestone caves where prehistoric artists left their stunning legacy.

Upstream from Sarlat, the abbey-church of **Souillac** offers remarkable Romanesque carvings, while the nearby pilgrimage town of **Rocamadour**, set halfway up a cliff face, is equally compelling. Further east is the **Château de Castelnau**, a supreme example

THE GLORIOUS GARDENS OF THE MANOIR D'EYRIGNAC

of medieval military architecture, and the Renaissance **Château de Montal**, with its exquisite ornamental detailing.

Shadowing the Dordogne to the south, the Lot flows through comparatively wild country where, even in high summer, it's possible to find quiet corners. The departmental capital, **Cahors**, is home to France's best surviving fortified medieval bridge, **Pont Valentré**, while upstream the perched village of **St-Cirq-Lapopie** provides the valley's most dramatic sight. From near here the pretty Célé valley cuts northeast to **Figeac**, which boasts a highly rewarding museum, dedicated to Champollion, the man who unravelled the mystery of hieroglyphics. West of Cahors, atmospheric **Monflanquin** and **Monpazier** represent outstanding examples of *bastide* villages, poignant echoes of a violent past. South of the river, temperatures (see box) ramp up a gear to ripen the sunflowers, vineyards and orchards of the **Quercy Blanc**. You have only to glance at an empty field, bleached by the sun, lavishly dusted with white stone and perhaps decorated with a vernacular *borie* (dry-stone hut), to understand its sobriquet.

The highlights of the Garonne valley to the south are the Romanesque carvings of the abbey-church at **Moissac** and the river's dramatic gorges around the attractive old town of **St-Antonin-Noble-Val** and the evocative ruined fortress of **Najac**.

When to go

Winters are variable in this diverse region. In the north they are generally wet, while in the southern regions they can be short and very dry indeed – on sunny days it's possible to sit outside even in December. January and February, however, can see temperatures plummeting to well below zero. **Spring** is usually the wettest period, although some years see glorious weather. Temperatures begin to pick up around April and can reach the mid-30s in high **summer**, though usually hover in the high 20s. **Autumn** is longer and drier than spring, bringing sunny weather until the end of October.

The most important factor in deciding when to visit is the **holiday seasons**. In July and August (particularly the first two weeks of August), hotels and campsites burst at the seams and top-rank sights are absolutely heaving. Conversely, from November to Easter many places close down completely. Overall, the **best time to visit** is September and early October, with May and June coming a close second.

AVERAGE MONTHLY TEMPERATURES AND RAINFALL

	Jan	Feb	Mar	Apr	May	Jun	Jul	Aug	Sep	Oct	Nov	Dec
CAHORS												
Max/min (°C)	9/2	10/2	14/4	16/6	21/9	24/12	27/14	27/14	23/12	18/9	12/5	9/3
Rainfall (mm)	39	33	34	60	58	47	42	41	58	54	53	43
SARLAT												
Max/min (°C)	9/2	10/2	14/4	16/6	21/9	24/12	27/14	30/14	25/12	18/9	12/5	9/3
Rainfall (mm)	40	35	35	60	60	47	42	41	58	55	52	41

Author picks

Our authors have admired prehistoric caves and charming villages, consumed far more cheese and wine than is strictly necessary and developed excellent canoeing skills – it's a hard job, but someone's got to do it. Here are their favourite things to do, see and eat:

Truffle markets Between December and March, the area's countless wonderful town and village markets are given an exotic foodie twist with the arrival of the delicious, and expensive, fungi (see page 72).

River trips The Dordogne and Lot's many rivers offer superb water-bound activities, though it's hard to beat a gentle canoe paddle along the Vézère river, and in particular the stretch between Montignac and Les Eyzies (see page 126).

Must-see medieval With its solid, soaring towers and graceful arches, the all-powerful Pont Valentré (see page 190) in Cahors is a masterpiece of medieval architecture.

Underground church The Dordogne's most unique ecclesiastical treasure, the Église St-Jean (see page 64) in Aubeterre-sur-Dronne is a stupendous 20m-high chamber carved into the rock face.

Black tipple So-named because of its dark colour and strong taste, the black wine of Cahors (see page 193) is harvested from what are reputedly some of the oldest vineyards in the country, and is worth sampling any time of the year.

Cool cave Glittering stalactites, prehistoric cave paintings and child-friendly activities are three good reasons to make a beeline for the Grotte de Villars (see page 68), hidden away amid the lush Périgord Vert.

Lace up The GR6 hiking trail from Lacave to Rocamadour (see page 161) spans some 1100km but the most spectacular section is right at the end, the arrival at the pilgrimage town of Rocamadour.

Cracking castles The fairytale Château de Beynac (see page 145) lords it over the Dordogne river, while Hautefort (see page 72) is an example of French Renaissance architecture at its best.

> Our author recommendations don't end here. We've flagged up our favourite places – a perfectly sited hotel, an atmospheric café, a special restaurant – throughout the Guide, highlighted with the ★ symbol.

TRUFFLES, AN EXPENSIVE DELICACY

CAHORS WINE

15 things not to miss

It's not possible to see everything that the Dordogne and Lot has to offer in one trip – and we don't suggest you try. What follows is a selective and subjective taste of the region's highlights: spectacular castles, quaint villages and eye-catching architecture. All highlights are colour-coded by chapter and have a page reference to take you straight into the Guide, where you can find out more.

1 ST-CIRQ LAPOPIE
See page 195
Tumbling down a sheer cliff towards the River Lot, this higgledy-piggledy village of half-timbered old houses is one of the most picturesque in the region.

2 ABBAYE DE CADOUIN
See page 108
The astonishing abbey at Cadouin was once a major pilgrimage site, with a richly decorated cloister and a fine Romanesque church.

3 CANOEING
See page 34
A gentle paddle along the region's serpentine rivers gives a unique perspective on the changing scenery.

4 CHÂTEAU DE NAJAC
See page 257
The crumbled ruins of Najac's château afford a startling panorama over the Aveyron valley.

5 PARC NATUREL RÉGIONAL DES CAUSSES DU QUERCY
See page 182
Explore swathes of wild limestone plateau, carved by imposing rivers and dotted with grazing sheep.

6 MONPAZIER
See page 224
One of the region's best-preserved *bastide* towns, in the typical grid-style, with many buildings dating from the thirteenth century.

7 ROCAMADOUR
See page 163
Cliff-side pilgrimage town which will take your breath away – if you avoid the peak-season crowds.

8 PREHISTORIC CAVES
See page 124
The caves and rock shelters around Les Eyzies conceal stunning examples of prehistoric art.

9 SARLAT-LA-CANÉDA
See page 115
Lose yourself in Sarlat's intriguing maze of narrow medieval lanes, and try to coincide your visit with the fantastic Saturday market.

10 LOCAL PRODUCE
See page 30
Famous gastronomic treats from the region include foie gras, walnut oil, goat's cheese and truffles. The winter truffle market in Lalbenque is a highlight of the culinary season.

11 GOUFFRE DE PADIRAC
See page 172
Sign up for a boat ride through this expansive cave system, which shelters stalagmites taller than the average house.

12 VINEYARD VISITS
See page 193
From grand châteaux such as Lagrezette to tiny, family-run concerns, a visit and tasting session at a wine château provides a memorable experience.

13 CORDES-SUR-CIEL
See page 254
Pearl of the *bastides*, this picturesque hill-town was named France's favourite village in 2014.

14 ST-ANTONIN-NOBLE-VAL
See page 252
This handsome town, huddled beneath towering limestone cliffs, boasts a hoard of medieval houses from its glorious heyday.

15 CAHORS
See page 184
Trapped in a tight meander of the Lot river, glorious Cahors is steeped in history, from the richly decorated double-domed cathedral to the fortified Pont Valentré.

Itineraries

These itineraries are designed to lead you up, down and round about the enduringly beautiful Dordogne and Lot – picking out the prettiest towns and villages, finest medieval architecture and food and drink.

LE GRAND TOUR

❶ **Aubeterre-sur-Dronne** Two marvellous churches – one a remarkable subterranean cavern – are the highlights of this gorgeous little hillside town on the Charente border. See page 64

❷ **Périgueux** A rich confection of Roman remains, old-town Renaissance buildings and grand ecclesiastical architecture makes a visit to Périgueux imperative. See page 49

❸ **Bergerac** Hop aboard a traditional *gabare* for a scenic river cruise before heading to one of the town's many excellent bars to indulge in a glass or two of Bergerac wine. See page 87

❹ **Trémolat and Limeuil** Defined by the two dramatic bends at Trémolat and Limeuil, this is the prettiest stretch of the Dordogne river. See page 104

❺ **Les Eyzies** Prepare to be dazzled by some of the world's finest prehistoric cave art, most impressively at the Font-de-Gaume and Abri du Cap Blanc caves. See page 123

❻ **Sarlat-la-Canéda** Run through with handsome medieval houses and honey-stoned Renaissance buildings, Sarlat is perhaps the Dordogne's most alluring town. See page 115

❼ **Rocamadour** Not only is Rocamadour possessed of a breathtaking cliff-top location, but it's one of the country's most important pilgrimage sites. See page 163

❽ **Figeac** Straddling the River Célé, this town boasts a raft of splendid medieval architecture and a superb museum of writing. See page 202

❾ **Moissac** The Romanesque carvings of the abbey-church of St Pierre rate among the most impressive in the country, not least those on its magnificent tympanum. See page 238

GASTRONOMIC ODYSSEY

❶ **Truffles, Sorges** Evocatively known as the "black diamonds of the Périgord", these expensive black fungi crop up in all sorts of dishes, from rich Périgourdin sauces to the humble omelette – head to the museum in Sorges for the lowdown. See page 72

❷ **Monbazillac** Taste a drop of this sumptuously sweet white wine at the eponymous château, just outside Bergerac, or in any number of the surrounding wineries. See page 93

❸ **Cèpes, Monpazier** These plump, brown mushrooms can be sampled just about anywhere in the Dordogne, but you'll find an

---

Create your own itinerary with Rough Guides. Whether you're after adventure or a family-friendly holiday, we have a trip for you, with all the activities you enjoy doing and the sights you want to see. All our trips are devised by local experts who get the most out of the destination. Visit **www.roughguides.com/trips** to chat with one of our travel agents.

abundance of them around Monpazier and Villefranche-du-Périgord. See page 224

❹ Le Bugue market Most towns and villages in the Dordogne and Lot put on terrific markets once or twice a week, but the extravaganza at pretty Le Bugue is one of the best. See page 115

❺ Walnuts, Beynac Though traditionally used to make oil, the humble walnut can also be found in breads, cakes and desserts. For more nutty kicks, follow the Route de la Noix between Argentat and Beynac. See page 150

❻ Cabécou cheese, Rocamadour The region boasts few speciality cheeses, but this is a beauty; a little flat medallion of goat's cheese, typically served on toast or a bed of lettuce with walnut oil. See page 167

❼ Saffron, Cajarc Numerous farms in the region produce this age-old spice, but your best bet is to make a beeline for the marvellous saffron fair in Cajarc at the end of October. See page 198

MEDIEVAL DORDOGNE

❶ Château de Jumilhac Nestled amid thick woodland in the lush Périgord Vert region, Jumilhac is a classic fairy-tale castle, complete with requisite towers, turrets and ramparts. See page 70

❷ Châteaux Beynac and Castelnaud Situated on opposing sides of the Dordogne river, these two magnificent semi-ruined castles are pre-eminent among the region's many châteaux. See pages 145 and 148

❸ Cadouin Attractive village known for its twelfth-century Cistercian abbey, though it's the adjoining cloister, with stunningly carved capitals, that is the real show-stealer. See page 108

❹ Monpazier The most complete of the *bastide* towns, with intact medieval gates, a fine church and a perfect central square. See page 224

❺ Eymet Laid out on a classic *bastide* chequerboard plan, Eymet is centred on a handsome, arcaded main square lined with half-timbered houses. See page 97

❻ Pont Valentré Straddling the Lot in Cahors, this is perhaps the finest example of a fortified medieval bridge in France. See page 190

❼ St-Antonin-Noble-Val Set against a stunning backdrop of white limestone cliffs, St-Antonin's medieval heritage is writ large throughout the village. See page 252

❽ Cordes-sur-Ciel Heavily fortified in its heyday, this charming hilltop village is now an artisanal hub of craftspeople. See page 254

Sustainable travel

Travel can be incredibly damaging to the environment, but done right, it can be used as a force for good, enriching local communities who rely on tourism as vital revenue.

The Dordogne and the Lot are experiencing the effects of climate change firsthand. In parts where much of the industry is agriculture, it's impossible to ignore. Weather extremes are becoming more frequent: floods in the winter and early spring, followed by droughts in the summer. By 2050, it's expected that this area will be two degrees warmer, giving it a Mediterranean climate, and meaning that many of the crops that the region is known for will be difficult to grow. The higher temperatures and increasing droughts are also giving rise to more frequent forest fires. The population across France is ageing, and this is more pronounced in the Dordogne and the Lot than in urban areas. A quarter of residents are over 65 years old, and many young people are forced to leave their hometowns in search of work. Overtourism is a significant problem across the country; a country which sees around a hundred million foreign visitors a year. It's important to tread lightly, consider how you travel and respect the land you're exploring.

TAKE THE SLOW ROAD

With the number of passengers flying to or from France in 2023 reaching pre-Covid levels, air travel shows no signs of slowing down, even though the French government banned domestic flights where there was a suitable equivalent by train of under two hours. Although the Lot and Dordogne have two commercial airports (in Brive-la-Gaillarde and Bergerac), try to travel by train (see pages 24 and 25) or bus (see page 26) instead to limit your CO2 emissions. A car is needed to explore much of the region (see page 26), but if you're driving alone or in a couple, consider posting your ride to BlaBlaCar (http://blablacar.fr). France's largest lift-sharing platform is used by twenty million people, and by taking extra passengers, you're not only opting for greener travel, but you'll be offsetting high fuel costs too.

AVOID AIRBNB

The tourism industry in both the Dordogne and the Lot suffered heavily as a result of Covid-19, particularly in rural areas, where many hotels and restaurants closed their doors for good, or were bought up by big chains. The Dordogne in particular has a high number of second homes (over fourteen percent); many are used as holiday rentals solely during the summer season via booking platforms such as Airbnb. This creates ghost towns, where entire villages empty come winter. Consider opting for small, independent hotels or campsites to avoid buying into the problem.

RESPECT THE TRAILS

As one of the main routes to pilgrimage centre Santiago de Compostela runs through the Lot (from Le Puy-en-Velay), as well as numerous GR (*grande randonnée*) long-distance hiking routes, both the Dordogne and the Lot welcome flocks of walkers each summer. It's important not to deviate from the marked trails, as by doing

SUSTAINABLE TRAVEL

LEAVE NO TRACE ON LONG-DISTANCE HIKING ROUTES

so, you could damage fragile local flora. Wild camping isn't illegal in France, but it is subject to several restrictions (no pitching on public footpaths and protected areas, among them). It should always be done responsibly, following the principles of 'leave no trace'.

ZOOS AND AQUARIUMS

Zoos are a controversial topic. It can be argued that they serve to educate and to protect endangered species. However, France's animal welfare act states that zoos must be run 'under conditions which aim to satisfy the biological and conservation requirements of the individual species', which allows for significant variation. At Rough Guides, we've chosen to include zoos and aquariums, as we believe that it's down to the reader to make an informed choice. We'd encourage anyone planning a visit to read a selection of the most recent online reviews prior to their trip.

FOIE GRAS

It is impossible to visit Dordogne and not notice the proliferation of foie gras on restaurant menus and market tables, particularly in the Périgord region. While foie gras is considered a

luxury delicacy in France, it is in fact the fattened liver of ducks or geese which have been overfed via a long tube forced down their throats. This process, known as 'gavage', causes the birds' livers to swell to up to ten times the original size. Animal activists express concerns over the cruelty of the production process, which is banned in many countries, including the UK.

ALFRESCO DINING IN LE PUY-EN-VELAY

Basics

- **23** Getting there
- **25** Getting around
- **28** Accommodation
- **30** Food and drink
- **33** Festivals
- **34** Sports and outdoor activities
- **35** Shopping and markets
- **36** Travelling with children
- **36** Travel essentials

Getting there

The Dordogne and Lot is easy to reach by plane, with several airlines flying to the region from numerous UK airports. Travelling overland is another, possibly more attractive option, with the Eurostar making the journey from London to Paris, from where you can connect to fast and efficient TGV services. Alternatively, both the Channel Tunnel and cross-Channel ferries allow you to make the journey by car. From the US, Canada, Australia, New Zealand and South Africa, you'll have to fly to Paris, and take an onward connection from there, be it by plane or train.

Fares often depend on how far in advance you can book: earlier is often, but not always, cheaper. Much depends on the **season**, with the highest prices generally from June to August, and around Christmas and the New Year; fares drop during the "shoulder" seasons – roughly September to October and April to May – and you'll get the best prices during the low season, November to March, although much of the accommodation and restaurants in the area close during the winter.

It's invariably cheaper to **book tickets online**, though bear in mind that most of the budget airlines charge extra for checked baggage and for ticketing changes, and may not refund cancelled flights. It's always best to book via the company's own website; using a third-party site usually makes ticket changes more complicated and expensive.

Flights from the UK and Ireland

Flying time to the Dordogne and the Lot from the UK or Ireland is between one and a half and two hours, depending on your departure airport. There are currently three **airlines** flying directly to the region from the UK, almost all of which fly **to Bergerac**: Ryanair (http://ryanair.com) from Bournemouth, Bristol, East Midlands, Edinburgh, Liverpool and London Stansted; Jet2 (http://jet2.com) from Leeds Bradford and Manchester; and British Airways (http://ba.com) from London City and Southampton.

Flying **to Bordeaux** is another option, being just a short train or car journey from the Dordogne: easyJet (http://easyjet.com) links Belfast, London Gatwick, Glasgow, Luton, Liverpool and Bristol with the city; Ryanair offers services from Birmingham, Cork, Edinburgh, Manchester and Stansted; British Airways (http://ba.com) runs daily direct flights from London Gatwick. **From Dublin**, Aer Lingus (http://aerlingus.com) also has direct flights to Bordeaux.

Flights from the US and Canada

The only **direct flights from the US or Canada** to the region is the summer-only Montréal–Bordeaux service offered by Air Transat (http://airtransat.com). However, most major airlines operate scheduled flights to Paris, from where you can take a domestic flight (check there's no inconvenient transfer between Charles de Gaulle and Orly airports) or transfer to the rail network. Air France (http://airfrance.com) has the most frequent and convenient service, with daily flights from more than half a dozen US cities, but its fares tend to be pricey. Other airlines offering services **to Paris from US cities** include American Airlines (http://aa.com) from New York, Chicago, Dallas, Charlotte, Miami and Philadelphia; Delta (http://delta.com) from over a dozen cities including Atlanta, Chicago, Cincinnati, Houston and New York; and United (http://united.com) from Chicago, New York, Washington and San Francisco. Air Canada (http://aircanada.ca) offers direct services to Paris **from Montréal and Toronto**. Thanks to such intense competition, transatlantic **fares** to France are fairly reasonable.

Flights from Australia, New Zealand and South Africa

Travelling **from Australia or New Zealand**, there are scheduled flights to Paris from Sydney, Melbourne, Brisbane, Perth and Auckland. The only direct flight between Australia and Paris is with Qantas (http://

> **A BETTER KIND OF TRAVEL**
>
> At Rough Guides we are passionately committed to travel. We believe it helps us understand the world we live in and the people we share it with – and of course tourism is vital to many developing economies. But the scale of modern tourism has also damaged some places irreparably, and climate change is accelerated by most forms of transport, especially flying. We encourage all our authors to consider the carbon footprint of the journeys they make in the course of researching our guides.

quitus.com), four times a week from Perth. All other options involve at least one stop en route. Alternatively, you can fly via another European hub and catch a connecting flight to Bordeaux from there. Flights via Asia or the Gulf States with a transfer or overnight stop in the airline's home port are generally the cheapest option.

From South Africa, Air France operates direct flights from Johannesburg and Cape Town to Paris, from where you can pick up a connecting flight to Bordeaux. With other airlines you'll likely be routed through another European hub such as London, Amsterdam, Madrid or Frankfurt, and again pick up a connecting flight.

By train

Eurostar (http://eurostar.com) operates high-speed passenger trains daily from St Pancras International to the Continent via the **Channel Tunnel**. Services depart roughly every hour for Paris Gare du Nord (2hr 20min). There are also roughly eight trains a day to Lille (1hr 30min). You can connect with TGV trains to the southwest at either station.

There are three classes of travel: standard, standard premier and business premier. Tickets are generally cheaper mid-week and booked at least a month before travel, and fares are often significantly lower for those under 26. Keep a look out for flash sales (the Eurostar app sends alerts), which generally happen every one to two months.

Note that Interrail and Eurail **rail passes** entitle you to discounts on Eurostar trains. It's possible to take folding bikes on Eurostar. No fully assembled bikes are allowed.

Rail passes

Rail Europe (http://raileurope.com) issues a number of **rail passes** for travel within France and for trips combining France with other European countries. Note that these passes must be purchased in your home country.

If you plan to visit several countries and are a European resident, the best bet is an **Interrail Pass** (https://interrail.eu), which entitles you to unlimited travel within the specified period and geographical area. The passes (Global and One Country) come in over-26 and (cheaper) under-26 versions, and cover thirty European countries.

The France Rail Pass version allows between three and eight days of unlimited travel within a month; first-class passes and cheaper passes for children, those under 26 and seniors are also available. For non-European residents there are various **Eurail passes** (http://eurail.com), covering either several countries or just France.

By car from the UK

If you have the time and inclination, then travelling to the Dordogne **by car** – a distance of some 850km from London – is certainly an attractive proposition. Given the distance, it's well worth going slow and turning the drive into a part of the holiday, with lots of breaks and perhaps an overnight stop en route.

Ferries from the UK and Ireland

The ferries plying the waters **between Dover and Calais** offer the cheapest means of getting to the other side of the Channel, and are particularly convenient if you live in southeast England, from where the quickest crossings take 1hr 30min. Operators on this route include P&O Ferries (http://poferries.com) and DFDS Seaways (http://dfdsseaways.com). If your starting point is west of London, it may be worth heading to one of the south-coast ports and catching a **ferry to Brittany or Normandy**; the quickest crossing from Portsmouth is around three hours.

Brittany Ferries (http://brittany-ferries.co.uk) runs plentiful services from Portsmouth to Caen, Cherbourg, Le Havre and St Malo, from Poole to Cherbourg, and from Plymouth to Roscoff. Condor Ferries (http://condorferries.co.uk) also connects Portsmouth and Cherbourg, and several ports in northern France via the Channel Islands. If you're travelling from the north of England or Scotland, you could consider the overnight crossing **from Hull to Zeebrugge** (Belgium) operated by P&O Ferries, though it'd be quicker just to drive down to the south coast and take a ferry there.

Another option is to take a ferry from Portsmouth **to Santander or Bilbao** (Brittany Ferries) in northern Spain. Crossing times are long (24–32hr), and once you touch dry land in Santander you've still got a six-hour drive north into the Dordogne or five hours from Bilbao.

From Ireland, Irish Ferries (http://irishferries.com) runs from Dublin to Cherbourg or Rosslare (near Wexford) to Roscoff or Cherbourg.

Most ferry companies also offer **fares for foot passengers**; accompanying bicycles can usually be carried free in the low season, though there may be a small charge during peak periods.

An easy way to compare ticket prices and see an overview of possible boat routes is via Ferry Savers (http://directferries.co.uk) and EuroDrive (http://eurodrive.co.uk), both of which offer cut-price fares;

though note that the latter caters only for people taking their cars across the Channel.

Eurotunnel

Drive-on drive-off shuttle trains operated by **Eurotunnel** (http://eurotunnel.com) run continuously between Folkestone and Coquelles, near Calais, with up to four departures per hour at peak times (one every two hours from midnight to 6am) and take 35min (slightly longer at night), though you must arrive at least 30min before departure. It is possible to turn up and buy your ticket at the check-in booths, but you'll pay the highest rate on the day.

Agents and tour operators

There are a vast number of **travel agents** and **tour operators** offering holidays in the Dordogne and Lot, the majority of which are geared to providing trips centred around outdoor activities such as cycling and canoeing, or food and wine.

AGENTS AND OPERATORS

Cycling for Softies http://cycling-for-softies.co.uk. An easy-going cycle-holiday operator offering a seven-day Dordogne and Garonne trip. Accommodation and restaurants tend to be top-end, including the occasional Michelin-starred restaurant.

Cyclomundo France http://cyclomundo.com. Defining itself as the "bike rider's travel agency", and specializing in custom-made "biking à la carte" trips for serious cyclists. Guided and self-guided trips including six different Dordogne and Lot tours.

Equestrian Escapes UK http://equestrian-escapes.com. Five-day horseback holidays in the northern part of the Dordogne, catering to all levels, from beginners to advanced.

Eurocamp UK http://eurocamp.co.uk. Self-drive, go-as-you-please holidays with tent or mobile home.

France Afloat UK http://franceafloat.com. UK-based French canal- and river-cruising specialist leading trips on the Garonne Canal around Moissac and Agen, and the Canal du Midi.

Headwater UK http://headwater.com. Self-guided holidays, often with an active focus, such as walking and cycling. Trips are tailor-made, with plenty of accommodation options available.

The International Kitchen US http://theinternationalkitchen.com. "Cooking school vacations" in a Bordeaux wine château, or in the Dordogne and the Quercy.

Getting around

France has the most extensive train network in Western Europe. The nationally owned French train company, the SNCF (Société Nationale des Chemins de Fer), runs fast, modern trains between all the main towns in the Dordogne and Lot, and even between some of the minor ones. In rural areas where branch lines have been closed, certain routes (such as Agen to Villeneuve-sur-Lot) are covered by buses operated by the SNCF or in partnership with independent lines. It's an integrated service, with buses timed to meet trains and the same ticket covering both. However, as so many of the region's highlights are out in the countryside and in little villages, you'll need your own transport to fully explore the Dordogne and Lot.

By rail

SNCF has pioneered one of the most efficient, comfortable and user-friendly railway systems in the world. Pride and joy of the French rail system is the high-speed **TGV** (*train à grande vitesse*; http://sncf.com). The quickest way to reach the Dordogne by train is to take a TGV from Paris Montparnasse to Bordeaux (3hr); some of these services continue on along the main line to Agen and Montauban, or you can take an Intercité train across to Périgueux. Alternatively, take a TGV from Paris to Libourne or Limoges, with an onward connection to Périgueux. Brive, meanwhile, is served by a handful of direct Intercité trains each day from Paris Austerlitz. Elsewhere, the majority of trains you will use here are designated TER (*Train Express Régional*) which cover shorter distances and stop at more and smaller stations. A scenic branch traces much of the Dordogne valley linking Bordeaux with Bergerac and Sarlat, while three north–south axes cross the Dordogne and Lot valleys (Périgueux–Agen, Brive–Cahors–Montauban and Brive–Figeac–Toulouse). In all these cases, schedules are thin, with often big gaps between trains, so it's imperative to check timetables in advance. Paper copies of **timetables** are available free at most stations, or check http://snf-connect.com. *Autocar* (often abbreviated to *car*) at the top of a column means it's an SNCF bus service, on which rail tickets and passes are valid.

Tickets

Tickets for all SNCF trains can be bought online with a credit card through http://sncf.com, which has an English-language option, or by phone and at any train station (*gare SNCF*). Here you can buy tickets at the ticket office, or one of the yellow touch-screen machines (in English). You can also buy tickets via the SNCF application. All paper tickets – but not passes or internet tickets printed out at home – must be **validated** in the orange machines located at the entrance to the platforms; it is an offence not to follow the instruction *Compostez votre billet* (Validate your ticket).

Fares

Fares are cheaper if you travel off-peak (*période bleue*; blue period) rather than during peak hours (*période normale* or *période blanche*; normal or white period) – in general, peak period means Monday mornings and Friday and Sunday evenings. A leaflet (*le calendrier voyageurs*) showing the blue and white periods is available at train stations. For longer journeys it's worth checking the advance special discounts, known as *tarifs Prem's*, on the SNCF website. A limited number of these are available on some main lines and can be bought online between two months and two weeks in advance. Even cheaper internet-only TGV fares can be purchased through http://ouigo.com on services from Paris to Bordeaux and Toulouse; tickets go on sale four months before departure. Try to book in advance for all TGV trains, as **seat reservations** are obligatory, and are included in the ticket price, though note that you will have to pay extra for them if you are travelling on an Inter-Rail pass. Anybody under 26 is entitled to a discount of 25 percent off all blue-period trains in France.

By bus

Travelling around the Dordogne and Lot region by bus is not particularly recommended. A very limited timetable serves a few routes, and those services that do exist are usually governed by the needs of schoolchildren rather than tourists, running once or twice a day in term-time only – and hence hardly a practical option for most visitors.

The most convenient **bus services** are those operated as an extension of rail links by SNCF, which run between train stations and serve areas not accessible by rail. In addition to SNCF buses, private, municipal and departmental buses can be useful for local and some cross-country journeys, though be prepared for early starts and careful planning if you want to see much outside the main towns.

Timetables for SNCF services are available at http://sncf-connect.com but times for services run by private companies can be frustrating to track down. If you can read French then a trawl through the website http://dordogne.fr will reveal a downloadable PDF of main timetables, but frankly it's easiest just to ask at local tourist offices.

Larger towns usually have a *gare routière* (**bus station**), often next to the *gare SNCF*, though this is often little more than just a couple of bus stands. However, the private bus companies don't always work together, and you'll frequently find them leaving from an array of different points (here, too, the local tourist office should be able to help).

One final thing to note is that many rural bus services only operate *sur réservation* or "on demand". This means that you will need to phone the operating company by 6pm the day before you wish to travel (or by 6pm on Friday for travel on Monday). Such limited services are usually indicated by a telephone icon in the bus timetable.

By car

Driving in the Dordogne and Lot can be a real pleasure, and is often the only practical means of reaching the more remote sights. There are three **autoroutes** in the area: the A20 cuts south from Limoges to Toulouse via Cahors; the A62 runs along the Garonne from Bordeaux to Toulouse; and the A89 links Bordeaux with Périgueux and Brive. Motorway **tolls** are payable in cash or by credit card (lane marked CB) at the frequent tollgates (*péages*). The Michelin website (http://viamichelin.fr) details the cost of tolls on any particular journey. Slower and more congested are the toll-free **national roads** (marked, for example, N21 or RN21 on signs and maps). The smaller **routes départementales** (marked with a D) are generally uncongested and make for an even more scenic drive; as with N or R roads, they offer easier access to lunch stops in the small towns en route.

For up-to-the-minute **information** regarding traffic jams and roadworks on *autoroutes*, consult http://vinci-autoroutes.com; for other roads, visit http://bison-fute.gouv.fr. You can also tune into the radio on 107.7FM to listen to live traffic updates for main routes or download a free app such as Waze (http://waze.com).

At the time of writing, petrol prices were hovering around €1.40 a litre for unleaded (*sans plomb*) and €1.43 a litre for diesel (*gazole* or *gasoil*); you'll find prices lowest at out-of-town hypermarkets. Note that in rural areas most petrol stations close at night, on Sundays and on bank holidays, and some may also close on Mondays. The majority of fuel stations have card machines on the pump meaning they can be used even when the station is unstaffed.

If you run into **mechanical difficulties** you'll find garages and service stations in the Yellow Pages of the phone book under *"Garages automobiles"*; for **breakdowns**, look under *"Dépannages"*. If you have an accident or theft, you should contact the local police – and keep a copy of their report in order to file an insurance claim. Within Europe, most vehicle **insurance** policies cover taking your car to France; check with your insurer. However, you're advised to take out extra cover for motoring assistance in case your vehicle breaks down; contact your insurer or motoring organizations such as the AA or RAC for a quote.

Rules of the road

US, Canadian, Australian, New Zealand and all EU **driving licences** are valid in France, though an International Driver's Licence makes life easier. The minimum driving age is 18 and you must hold a full (not a provisional) licence. Drivers are required to carry their licence, insurance papers and vehicle registration document (*carte grise*) with them in the car.

Since the French drive on the right, drivers of right-hand-drive cars must adjust their **headlights** to dip to the right. This is most easily done by sticking on black glare deflectors, which can be bought at motor accessory shops and at the Channel ferry ports or the Eurostar terminal. Motorcyclists must drive with their headlights on, and must also wear a **helmet**.

All non-French vehicles must display their **national identification letters** (GB, etc), either on the number plate or by means of a sticker, and all vehicles must carry a red warning triangle, two fluorescent jackets and a single-use breathalyzer. **Seat belts** are compulsory front and back, and children under 10 years are not allowed to sit in the front of the car. It is illegal to use a hand-held **mobile phone** while driving.

The law of *priorité à droite* – **giving way** to traffic coming from your right, even when it is coming from a minor road – was mostly phased out years ago. However, it still applies on a very few roads in built-up areas, so it pays to be vigilant at junctions. A sign showing a yellow diamond on a white background gives you right of way, while the same sign with a diagonal black slash across it warns you that vehicles emerging from the right have priority. *Stop* signs mean you must stop completely; *Cédez le passage* means "Give way".

Unless otherwise indicated, **speed limits** are: 130kph (80mph) on *autoroutes*; 110kph (68mph) on dual carriageways; 80kph (50mph) on other roads; and 50kph (31mph) in towns. In wet weather, and for drivers with less than two years' experience, these limits are 110kph (68mph), 100kph (62mph) and 80kph (50mph) respectively, while the town limit remains constant. **Speed cameras** have become much more common in the past few years: if you speed you will almost certainly get caught and fined – and don't think that having foreign plates will mean you can get away without paying a fine, as nowadays you will be chased up. The legal blood **alcohol limit** is 0.05 percent alcohol (0.5 grams per litre), and police frequently make random breath tests, as well as saliva tests for drugs. There are stiff **penalties** for driving violations, ranging from on-the-spot fines for minor infringements, to the immediate confiscation of your licence and/or car for more serious offences.

Car rental

To rent a car in France you must be over 21 and have driven for at least one year. **Car rental** in France costs upwards of €50 for a day and €200 for a week for the smallest car, but is usually cheaper if arranged online before you leave home. You'll find the big firms represented in most of the bigger towns, while a few of these also have desks at Bergerac and Brive airports. Local firms can be cheaper, but most don't offer one-way rentals. Unless you specify otherwise, you'll be given a car with manual transmission.

The **cost** of car rental includes the minimum car insurance required by law. Under the standard contract you are liable for an excess (*franchise*) for any damage to the vehicle. This starts at around €500 for the smallest car and can be covered by credit card.

By bicycle

Bicycles (*vélos*) have high status in France, where cyclists are given respect both on the roads and as customers at restaurants and hotels. In addition, local authorities are actively promoting cycling, not only with urban cycle lanes but also with comprehensive networks in rural areas (frequently using disused railways). Tourist offices can usually provide maps of local routes. Note that all cyclists are required by law to wear a **reflective safety jacket** at night outside urban areas and in the daytime during periods of poor visibility, or risk being fined up to €38.

Most towns have well-stocked retail and **repair shops**, where parts are normally cheaper than in Britain or the US. However, if you're using a foreign-made bike with nonstandard metric wheels, it's a good idea to carry spare tyres.

The **train** network runs various schemes for cyclists, all of them covered online at http://velo.sncf.com. It's possible to take your bike for free on all trains – make sure you arrive in good time to secure a slot in the bike rack. To take bikes for free on TGV and Intercité services, they must be dismantled or folded and placed in a cycle bag; if not, you'll pay an €10 fee. You'll also need to make a bike reservation on TGV/Intercité services, or you may incur a €35 fine and will be asked to leave the train at the next station.

Eurostar will carry all folding bicycles for free, as long as they're smaller than 85cm when folded.

> ### ACCOMMODATION PRICE CODES
>
> Throughout the Guide, accommodation is categorized according to a code, which roughly corresponds to the following price ranges. Price categories reflect the cost of a double room, without breakfast, in peak season.
>
> €̄ = under €100
> €̄€̄ = €100–150
> €̄€̄€̄ = €150–250
> €̄€̄€̄€̄ = over €250

Ferries usually carry bikes free (though you may need to register them), as do some **airlines** such as British Airways, while others charge – check when booking.

Bikes – either mountain bikes (*vélos tout-terrain* or VTT) or hybrid bikes (*vélos tout-chemin* or VTC) – are widely available to **rent** from campsites and hostels, as well as from specialist cycle shops and some tourist offices; rental costs are usually €15–20 per day. As for **maps**, a minimum requirement is the IGN 1:100,000 series (see page 40) – the smallest scale that carries contours. The UK's national cyclists' organization, the CTC (http://ctc.org.uk), can suggest routes. Companies offering specialist bike touring **holidays** are listed on page 25.

By boat

Boating is a leisurely way to explore the Lot and Garonne valleys. From April to September the **River Lot** is navigable for motorboats from St-Cirq Lapopie downstream to Luzech (65km), and from Fumel down to its confluence with the Garonne (78km). From October through to March the current is too swift and the river too high to be safe. But the Lot is a capricious river at any time, so it pays to follow the guidelines provided by rental companies carefully.

The other option is to potter along the **Garonne Canal**, which tracks the Garonne eastwards from Castets-en-Dorthe, near Langon, to Toulouse (190km), where it joins the Canal du Midi. You can also combine the Garonne Canal with the River Lot and the **River Baïse** south to Nérac.

Boats are usually rented by the week, though shorter periods are also available outside the July and August peak. **Rates** range from €800 to €2500 per week for a four- to ten-person boat, depending on the season and level of comfort. No licence is required, but you'll receive instruction before taking the controls. You should also be given a **carte de plaisance**, guaranteeing that the boat is insured and in good working order.

BOAT RENTAL COMPANIES IN THE LOT

Babou Marine http://baboumarine.com.
Locaboat Plaisance http://locaboat.com.
Nicols http://nicols.com.

Accommodation

Throughout the Dordogne and Lot, there's an excellent spread of hotels and chambres d'hôtes, which are complemented by some smart campsites and a smattering of hostels. In general, you'll be able to book a simple double for around €55, though sometimes with shared facilities, while €60 should secure a reasonable level of comfort. At most times of the year, you can turn up in any town and find a room or a place in a campsite, but it's best to book in advance, especially if you have your heart set on a particular place.

Problems may arise between mid-July and the end of August, when the French (and Germans, Spanish, Dutch and others) take their own vacations en masse. During this period, hotel and hostel accommodation can be hard to come by – particularly in the most popular towns, such as Sarlat – and you may find yourself falling back on local tourist offices for help. Some offer a **booking service**, though they can't guarantee rooms at a particular price, and all provide lists of hotels, hostels, campsites and bed-and-breakfast possibilities. With **campsites**, you can be more relaxed about finding an empty pitch somewhere for a tent, though it may be more difficult with a caravan or camper van.

Hotels

Most French hotels are **graded** from zero to five stars. The price more or less corresponds to the number of stars, though the system is rather simplistic, having more to do with ratios of bathrooms-per-guest and so forth than genuine quality.

What you get for your money varies enormously between establishments. Paying under €50, you take your chances somewhat: there won't be soundproofing and the showers (*douches*) and toilets (WC or *toilettes*) may well be communal (*sur le palier*). However, you should have your own bidet and washbasin (*lavabo*), often partitioned off from the rest of the room in an area referred to as a *cabinet* de toilette. Over €50 should get you a room with its own bath or shower though not necessarily toilet and, though the decor may not be anything to write home about, comfortable furniture. For around €100 you can expect a decent en-suite room with smart furnishings, while anything over €150 should give you something approaching luxury. **Single rooms** – if the hotel has any – are only marginally cheaper than doubles, so sharing always slashes costs, especially since most hotels willingly provide rooms with **extra beds** for three or more people at good discounts.

Breakfast, which is not normally included, will add between €9 and €16 per person to a bill, sometimes more – though there is no obligation to take it. Unless otherwise stated, all hotels listed in this guide offer free **wi-fi**, although it doesn't always reach every room.

Note that many family-run hotels close for two or three weeks a year. In smaller towns and villages, they may also shutter for one or two nights a week, usually Sunday or Monday. Details are given where possible in the Guide, but dates change from year to year and some places will close for a few days in low season if they have no bookings. The best precaution is to phone ahead to be sure. Many hotels also close for the entire winter season (November to March).

A useful option, especially if you're driving and looking for somewhere late at night, are the modern **chain hotels** located at motorway exits and on the outskirts of major towns. Among the cheapest (from around €70 for a three-person room with communal toilets and showers) are the one-star Formule 1 chain (http://hotelf1.accor.com) and the slightly more comfortable Ibis Budget (formerly Etap; http://all.accor.com).

There are also a number of well-regarded **hotel federations** in France, the biggest and most useful of which is **Logis** (http://logishotels.fr), an association of over three thousand hotels nationwide; standards are generally good, though they can sometimes come across as a bit dated. Two other, more upmarket federations worth mentioning are the Relais & Châteaux brand (http://relaischateaux.com) and The Originals (http://theoriginalshotels.com), both of which offer very high-class accommodation in beautiful older properties, often in rural locations.

Chambres d'hôtes, Airbnb and self-catering

Predominantly in country areas, but increasingly found in towns, **chambres d'hôtes** offer bed-and-breakfast accommodation in someone's house, château or farm. Though the quality can vary, on the whole the standards are very high, and in many cases, the properties are blessed with an abundance of charm and character. Moreover, the owners may also provide traditional home cooking and a great insight into French life. In general, prices range between €50 and €100 for two people including breakfast; payment is almost always expected in cash. Some offer meals on request (*tables d'hôtes*), usually evenings only, while others are attached to *fermes auberges*, farm-restaurants serving local produce. All things considered, a well-run *chambre d'hôte* is very often a vastly more enticing place to stay than a hotel.

If you're planning to stay a week or more in any one place it might be worth considering renting **self-catering accommodation**. This will generally consist of self-contained country cottages known as *gîtes* or *gîtes ruraux*, many in converted barns or farm outbuildings. While some can be quite grand, quite a few *gîtes* can be a bit dowdy.

You can find lists of both *gîtes* and *chambres d'hôtes* from **Gîtes de France** (http://gites-de-france.com). It also publishes annual guides such as *Nouveaux Gîtes Ruraux*, *Chambres et Tables d'Hôtes* and *Chambres d'Hôtes de Charme*, and more comprehensive regional or departmental guides that include photos. All these guides are available online or from departmental offices of Gîtes de France, as well as from local bookshops and tourist offices. Tourist offices will also have lists of places in their area that are not affiliated to Gîtes de France.

You'll also find self-catering accommodation, much of it foreign-owned, on http://frenchconnections.co.uk and http://cheznous.co.uk; or try one of the agents listed in the Travel Shop section of the official French tourist office website, www.france.fr.

Hostels, foyers and gîtes d'étape

At around €20–40 per night for a dormitory bed, usually with breakfast thrown in and the opportunity to prepare your own meals in a shared kitchen, **youth hostels** – *auberges de jeunesse* – are invaluable for single travellers on a budget.

Most hostels are run either by the municipality or by the French **hostelling association**, the Fédération Unie des Auberges de Jeunesse (FUAJ). Many can be reserved online through the FUAJ website, http://hifrance.org. To stay at FUAJ hostels you normally have to show a current HI (Hostelling International) **membership card**, which you can buy at http://hihostels.com. It's usually cheaper and easier to join before you leave home, provided your national Youth Hostel association is a full member of HI.

Unfortunately, there aren't that many youth hostels in the Dordogne and Lot region. Sometimes, as is the case. In Villefranche-de-Rouergue and Périgueux, hostel accommodation is provided in workers' hostels (**Foyers de Jeunes Travailleurs**). These tend to be functional and centrally located, with good canteens. Other hostels, most notably that at Cadouin, are more beautifully sited, though you might have to factor in the cost of a taxi in order to get there.

In the countryside, hostel-style **gîtes d'étape** are aimed primarily at hikers and long-distance bikers. Often run by the local village or municipality, they are less formal than hostels and provide bunk beds, primitive kitchen and washing facilities from around €15. They are marked on the large-scale IGN walkers' maps and listed in the individual Topo-guides. For more information check out the Gîtes de France booklet *Gîtes d'Étapes et de Séjours*, and *Gîtes d'Étape et Refuges*, published by Rando Éditions, downloadable at http://gites-refuges.com.

Camping

The French are great campers and practically every village and town in France has at least one **campsite** to cater for the thousands of people who spend their holiday under canvas. Most sites open from around Easter to September or October. The vast majority are graded into four **categories**, from one to four stars, by the local authority. One- and two-star sites are very basic, with toilets and showers (not necessarily with hot water), but little else, and standards of cleanliness are not always brilliant. At the other extreme, four-star sites are far more spacious, have hot-water showers and electrical hook-ups, swimming pools – sometimes several and sometimes heated – as well as washing machines, a shop, sports facilities and children's activities, and will provide refreshments or meals in high season. At three-star sites you can expect a selection of these facilities and less spacious plots. A further designation, **Camping Qualité** (http://campingqualite.com), indicates those campsites with particularly high standards of hygiene, service and privacy, while the Clef Verte (http://laclefverte.org) label is awarded to sites (and hotels and hostels) run along environmentally friendly lines. For those who really like to escape it all, **camping à la ferme** – on somebody's farm – is a good, simple option. Facilities will be minimal, but the setting is often blissfully rural, with lots of space plus peace and quiet – things often missing from the fancier campsites. Lists of farm sites are available at local tourist offices.

Though **charging systems** vary, most places charge per pitch and per person, usually including a car, while others apply a global figure. As a rough guide, two people with a tent and car might pay as little as €12 at a simple municipal site to as much as €50 at a four-star in a prime location. In peak season and if you plan to spend a week or more at one site, it's wise to book ahead, and note that many of the big sites have caravans and chalet bungalows for rent, though there's often a one-week minimum stay for these in high season.

The **Fédération Française de Camping et de Caravaning** (http://ffcc.fr) has some 1200 affiliated sites and publishes an annual guide covering ten thousand campsites, details of which can also be found on the excellent http://campingfrance.com. If you'd rather have everything organized for you, a number of companies specialize in **camping holidays**, including Eurocamp (see page 25).

Lastly, a word of **caution**: never camp rough (*camping sauvage*, as the French call it) on anyone's land without first asking permission. If the dogs don't get you, the guns might – farmers have been known to shoot first and ask later. On the other hand, a politely phrased request for permission will as often as not get positive results. Camping on public land is not officially permitted, but is widely practised by the French, and if you are discreet and pack up first thing in the morning (and leave no litter) you're not likely to have problems.

Food and drink

The cuisine of the Dordogne and Lot region is predominantly simple, country cooking (cuisine de terroir), revolving around duck and goose, garlic, a host of mushrooms, walnuts and whatever else the land has to offer. It's the sort of cuisine best sampled in little family-run places, where it's still possible to eat well for €20 or less. That said, every restaurant worth its salt offers a menu du terroir, featuring local specialities. Expensive gastronomique restaurants throughout the region, and most mid-priced establishments, also offer a smattering of fish dishes. The food glossary is on page 284.

Breakfast and light meals

For most locals, **breakfast** is a quick no-frills affair consisting of a chunk of baguette with jam or a croissant and coffee. In hotels, though, it's often a different story and the standard hotel breakfast comprises cereals, yoghurt, bread and/or pastries, jam, orange juice and a jug of coffee or tea, and usually costs €9–15. More expensive hotels typically offer fresh fruit, cheeses and hot and cold meats in addition to the above. If you're not staying in a hotel (or don't want to fork out that much), head to a café-bar and grab a croissant or *pain au chocolat* with coffee or hot chocolate, which will cost around €4.

Traditionally, the big meal of the day for the French is **lunch**, still long, leisurely and the cornerstone service in rural areas. Most restaurants offer a weekday lunchtime **plat du jour** (daily special) and/or a **menu du jour** (menu of the day), a three-course meal with wine for €18–25. *Menus* are great value – the multiple courses mean you may only need a light snack in the evening. At the lower end of the price scale the offerings are often very traditional but good, while at the upper end you're likely to be served much more inventive and unusual food.

More popular for lunch with foreign tourists than most French are snacks such as *croques-monsieur* and *croques-madame* (variations on the toasted-cheese sandwich), along with *frites*, *gaufres* (waffles) and fresh-filled baguettes. You could also try a **crêpe** (pancake with a filling): the savoury buckwheat variety (*galettes*) are the main course; sweet, white-flour crêpes are dessert. **Pizzerias**, usually *au feu de bois* (wood-fired), are also very common, though more popular with the French in the evening.

For **picnics**, local markets or supermarkets will provide you with almost everything you need. Cooked meat, prepared snacks, ready-made dishes and assorted salads are also available at charcuteries (delicatessens), which you'll find in some villages, and in most supermarkets. You'll find boulangeries (bakeries) just about everywhere – often several in one village – and it's here you can pick up delicious breads and, usually, a mouthwatering array of cakes and pastries too, though a pâtisserie is more of a specialist cake shop. Look for the word *artisanal(e)* after the name of a boulangerie or pâtisserie – this means its bread or cakes are home-made.

Restaurant meals

There's no difference between restaurants (or *auberges* or *relais* as they sometimes call themselves) and brasseries in terms of quality or price range. The distinction is that **brasseries**, which resemble cafés,

EATING OUT PRICE CODES

Each restaurant and café reviewed in this Guide is accompanied by a price code, which roughly corresponds to the following ranges. Price categories are based on the cost of a two-course meal (or similar) for one, with a non-alcoholic drink.
€ = under €25
€€ = €25–35
€€€ = €35–60
€€€€ = over €60

serve quicker meals at most hours of the day, while **restaurants** tend to stick to the traditional mealtimes of noon to 2pm, and 7pm to 9pm or 9.30pm. In touristy areas in high season, and for all the more upmarket places, it's wise to make reservations – easily done on the same day in most cases.

When hunting for places to eat, don't forget that **hotel restaurants** are open to non-residents, and can be very good value. In country areas keep an eye out for **fermes auberges**, farm-restaurants where the majority of ingredients are produced on the farm itself. These are often the best places to sample traditional local cuisine at very reasonable prices; a four-course meal for between €20 and €40 is the norm, including an apéritif and wine, but reservations are a must.

Prices, and what you get for them, must be posted outside. Normally there's a choice between one or more **menus fixes** – with a set number of courses and a limited choice – and choosing individually from the *carte* (menu). *Menus fixes*, often referred to simply as *menus*, are normally the cheapest option, especially at lunch but going **à la carte** offers greater choice and, in the better restaurants, unlimited access to the chef's inventiveness – though you'll pay much more for the privilege. **Wine** (*vin*) or a drink (*boisson*) is sometimes included in the cost of a *menu fixe*. Otherwise, the cheapest option will be the house wine, usually served in a jug (*pichet*) or carafe; you'll be asked if you want *un quart* (0.25 litre), *un demi* (0.5 litre) or *un litre* (1 litre).

One final note is that you should always call the waiter or waitress *Monsieur* or *Madame* (*Mademoiselle* if a young woman), never *Garçon*.

SERVICE CHARGES AND TIPPING

Tipping is not expected in France, although always appreciated. Many French leave just a couple of euros in loose change, though something more substantial is customary in upmarket places; in general, though, tipping is not deemed as important here as in the US.

Vegetarian food

On the whole, **vegetarians** can expect a fairly lean time in the Dordogne and Lot region. That said, in the very best restaurants you'll often find one or two fantastically creative vegetarian dishes on the menu, typically featuring *cèpes* (mushrooms) as the star ingredient. Otherwise, your best bet is to head for a crêperie or pizzeria, while Chinese or North African restaurants (though these are normally only found in the bigger towns) can be good standbys. Occasionally, they'll be willing to replace a meat dish on the fixed-price menu (*menu fixe*); at other times you'll have to pick your way through the *carte*. Remember to ask "*Je suis végétarien(ne); est-ce qu'il y a quelques plats sans viande?*" (I'm a vegetarian; are there any non-meat dishes?). **Vegans**, however, should probably forget about eating in regular restaurants and stick to self-catering, although there are a few vegan restaurants starting to spring up around the region. Expect blank looks if you try to ask if restaurant dishes are gluten- or dairy-free.

Drinks

In France **drinking** is done at a leisurely pace whether it's a prelude to food (*apéritif/apéro*), or a sequel (*digestif*), and cafés are the standard places to do it. Every bar or café has to display its full price list, including service charges. You normally pay when you leave, and it's usually perfectly acceptable to sit for hours over just one cup of coffee. Note that the minimum age for buying alcohol is 18, though younger teenagers may drink wine in a restaurant if with their parents. Public displays of drunkenness are very much frowned upon.

Wine

French wine (*vin*), drunk at just about every meal or social occasion, is unrivalled in the world for its range, sophistication, diversity and status. The house wine served in restaurants can be very good value in this wine-producing region, or opt for a bottle of AOP (*appellation d'origine protégée*) wine if you want a more sophisticated taste. You can buy a very decent bottle of wine for €6 in a shop or from the producer, while €10 and over will get you something worth savouring. A glass of wine in a bar will typically cost €3 to €5.

The best way of **buying wine** is directly from the producers (*vignerons*) at their vineyards, or at Maisons or Syndicats du Vin (representing a group of wine-producers) and Coopératives Vinicoles (producers' co-ops). At all of these you can usually sample the wines first. The most interesting option is to visit the

> **TOP 5 RESTAURANTS**
> **Déjeuner sur l'Herbe**, St-Léon-sur-Vézère see page 136
> **Le Gindreau**, St Médard see page 212
> **Jehan de Valon**, Rocamadour see page 168
> **La Table d'Olivier**, Brive-la-Gaillarde see page 78
> **Vieux Logis**, Trémolat see page 104

vineyard itself, where the owner will often include a tour of the *chais* in which the wine is produced and aged. The most economical method is to buy *en vrac*, which you can do at some wine shops (*caves*), filling a plastic five- or ten-litre container (generally sold on the premises) straight from the barrel. Supermarkets often have good bargains, too.

There are strict limitations on the extent to which winegrowers can interfere in the natural process – it's illegal even to water vines. The result is that, far more than in other countries, French wines are the product of a very specific bit of land and *terroir*, and there will often be significant differences in taste between the wines of two neighbouring producers. This makes tasting wines a real joy, and even if you're not an expert, it's well worth trying to establish which grape types you particularly like or dislike, and whether you like your wine fruity or dry, light or heavy. Waiters and wine producers are usually delighted to give you advice in making a choice.

For basic wine vocabulary, see page 288.

Beer

Light Belgian and German **beers**, plus various French brands from Alsace, account for most of the beer you'll find. Draught beer (*pression*) – very often Kronenbourg – is the cheapest drink you can have next to coffee and wine; *une pression* (usually 0.33 litre) will cost around €4. For a wider choice of draught and bottled beer you need to go to special beer-drinking establishments such as the English- and Irish-style pubs found in larger towns and cities, or to one of a sprinkling of artisan breweries now dotted around the Dordogne and Lot. A small bottle at one of these places can cost up to twice as much as a *demi* in an ordinary café-bar. Buying bottled or canned beer in supermarkets is much cheaper.

Spirits and liqueurs

Strong alcohol, including **spirits** (*eaux-de-vie*), such as cognac and armagnac, and **liqueurs** such as locally made walnut liqueurs (*vins de noix*), are always available. Refreshing *pastis* – the generic name for aniseed drinks such as Pernod or Ricard – is served diluted with water and ice (*glace* or *glaçons*). Among less familiar names, try Poire Williams (pear brandy), or Marc (a spirit distilled from grape pulp). Measures are generous, but they don't come cheap: the same applies for imported spirits such as whisky (usually called Scotch). Two drinks designed to stimulate the appetite – *un apéritif* – are Pineau (cognac and grape juice) and Kir (white wine with a dash of cassis – black-currant liqueur – or with champagne instead of wine for a Kir Royal). For a post-meal *digestif*, don't miss out on armagnac, oak-aged brandy from the south of the Garonne but available in bars and restaurants throughout the region.

Soft drinks

On the **soft drink** front, you can buy cartons of unsweetened fruit juice in supermarkets, although in cafés, the bottled (sweetened) nectars such as apricot (*jus d'abricot*) and blackcurrant (*cassis*) still hold sway. Fresh orange or lemon juice (*orange/citron pressé(e)*) is a much more refreshing choice on a hot day. More soft drinks to try are syrups (*sirops*) of mint, grenadine and other flavours mixed with water. The standard fizzy drinks of lemonade (*limonade*), Coke (*coca*) and so forth are all available. Bottles of **mineral water** (*eau minérale*) and spring water (*eau de source*) – either sparkling (*gazeuse*) or still (*plate*) – abound. But there's not much wrong with the tap water (*l'eau du robinet*), which will always be brought free to your table if you ask for it.

Coffee, tea and hot chocolate

Coffee served after a meal is always espresso: small, black and very strong. You can also order it with a dash of milk (*noisette*), or a long, black coffee, halfway between an espresso and an Americano (**allongé**). *Un café* or *un express* is the regular version. The French only drink milky coffee in the morning with breakfast, when you could ask for *un café au lait* – espresso in a large cup or bowl filled up with hot milk; at other times of the day ask for *un crème* (*grand crème* for a large cup). *Un déca* is decaffeinated, and is available everywhere. Ordinary **tea** (*thé*) – Lipton's nine times out of ten – is normally served black (*nature*) or with a slice of lemon (*au citron*); the French never add milk to tea but if you prefer it like that then ask for *un peu de lait frais* (some fresh milk), but expect the result to be a dishwater-weak brew. *Chocolat chaud* – **hot chocolate** – lives up to the high standards of French food and drink and is available at any café and at some specialist chocolate shops, where it's invariably superb. After meals, **herb teas** (*infusions* or *tisanes*), are offered by most restaurants: most commonly *verveine* (verbena), *tilleul* (lime blossom), *menthe* (mint) and *camomille* (camomile).

Festivals

It's hard to beat the experience of arriving in a small French village, expecting no more than a bed for the night, to discover the streets decked out with flags and streamers, a band playing in the square and the entire population out celebrating the feast of their patron saint. As well as the country-wide Fête de la Musique (June 21) and Bastille Day (July 14), there are any number of festivals – both traditional and of more recent origin – throughout the Dordogne and Lot.

The region's cathedrals, churches and châteaux make superb venues for festivals of **music** and **theatre**. All the major towns, and many of the smaller ones, put on at least one such festival a year, usually in summer, when you can often catch free performances in the streets. Anyone interested in contemporary theatre should make a beeline for Périgueux in early August, when international mime artists gather for Mimos, one of France's most exciting and innovative festivals.

Popular local culture is celebrated in the **Félibrée**, a festival established in 1903 to promote and safeguard the local *Occitan* (or *Oc*) language and culture. The **Félibrée** takes place on the first Sunday in July, when there is a procession, an *Occitan* Mass and – of course – a blow-out Périgordin meal. Nowadays, the celebrations also continue for around ten days either side of the Félibrée itself in the form of folk concerts, crafts demonstrations, theatre and so forth. It takes place in a different town in the Dordogne *département* each year; contact the tourist office in Périgueux (see page 56) for the latest information.

More recent introductions are the **historical spectaculars** hosted at places such as Castillon-la-Bataille, where the final battle of the Hundred Years' War is re-enacted by hundreds of local budding

> ### TOP 5 FOODIE TREATS
> **Monbazillac wine** see page 92
> **Rocamadour cheese** see page 167
> **Truffles** see page 72
> **Walnuts** see page 150
> **Cèpes** see page 225

thespians. Such events may be touristy, but the atmosphere – most are held at night – and general enthusiasm more than compensate.

In such dedicated **wine** country, there are inevitably festivals coinciding with the grape harvest, when each village stages its own celebrations.

For details of the region's most important and interesting festivals, see the boxes at the beginning of each chapter of the Guide.

Sports and outdoor activities

The Dordogne and Lot region offers a terrific range of sports and outdoor activities, including hiking, cycling, trekking and waterborne diversions such as canoeing and kayaking. By far the most popular spectator sport in the region is rugby, particularly in Brive, but you'll find a team of some description in just about every town.

Walking

Walking is undoubtedly the best way to enjoy this region of France. Well-maintained long-distance paths known as *sentiers de grande randonnée*, or simply **GRs**, cut across country, signed with red and white waymarkers and punctuated with campsites and *gîtes d'étape* at convenient distances. Some of the main routes in the region are the GR6, linking Ste-Foy-la-Grande in the west to Figeac; the GR36, which wanders southeast from Périgueux via Les Eyzies and Cahors to the Gorges de l'Aveyron; and the GR65, the great pilgrimage route passing through Figeac, Cahors and Moissac on the way to Santiago de Compostela in Spain.

The entire GR65 and parts of the GR36 and GR6 are described in a **Topo-guide** (available outside France in good travel bookshops), which gives a detailed account of the route, including maps, campsites, refuges, sources of provisions, etc. In France, the guides are available from bookshops and some tourist offices, or direct from the principal French walkers' organization, the Fédération Française de la Randonnée Pédestre (http://ffrandonnee.fr).

In addition, many tourist offices produce guides to their local footpaths; where there is no tourist office, try asking at the *mairie*. For recommendations on walking **maps**, see page 40.

Cycling

The region's minor roads and demarcated **cycling** routes provide plenty of opportunities for cyclists; it's best to avoid main roads if you want to enjoy yourself, particularly in the high season. Among the long-distance routes, there's the "Grande Traversée du Périgord" running 180km from Mareuil in the far northwest via Brantôme, Périgueux and Les Eyzies to Monpazier. In the Lot-et-Garonne, the "Véloroute" follows the River Lot 80km from Aiguillon northeast to Fumel and Bonaguil. Many tourist offices can provide details of cycle paths in their area, while the French Federation of Cycling has lots of useful information on its website (http://ffct.org). For recommendations on cycling **maps**, see page 40.

Canoeing and kayaking

Canoeing is hugely popular in the Dordogne and Lot region, and in the summer months every navigable river has outfits renting canoes and organizing excursions, which we've listed throughout the Guide. Those along Dordogne itself are the busiest, particularly the stretch between La Roque-Gageac and Beynac, where you pass beneath some of the region's most dramatic castles; and the Vézère, where you can stop off at various points to visit the valley's prehistoric sights. Other, quieter options include the River Lot, through the Aveyron gorges and the smaller Dronne, Dropt and Célé rivers.

You can **rent** two- to three-person canoes and single-seater kayaks on all these rivers; every tourist office also stocks lists of local operators. Although it's possible to rent by the hour, it's best to take at least a half-day and simply cruise downstream. The company you book through will provide transport as required. Prices vary according to what's on offer, but you can expect to pay from €20 per person for a day's canoe rental, and from €25 for a kayak.

On the Dordogne and Lot rivers you can make **longer excursions** of up to two weeks, either accompanied or on your own, sometimes in combination with cycling or walking. Various tour operators (see page 25) offer canoeing packages or you can book

> **TOP 5 BEAUTIFUL VILLAGES**
>
> **St-Cirq Lapopie** see page 195
> **Cordes-sur-Ciel** see page 254
> **Limeuil** see page 105
> **St-Jean-de-Côle** see page 66
> **St-Léon-sur-Vézère** see page 135

direct with the local company. Two of the biggest along the Dordogne valley are Canoës Loisirs (http://destination-perigord-loisirs.com) and Copeyre Canoë (http://canoes-dordogne.fr).

The length of the canoeing **season** depends on the weather and the water levels. Most operators function daily in July and August, on demand in May, June and September, and close between October and April when the rivers are too high for inexperienced canoeists. One or two, however, stay open throughout the year. All companies are obliged to equip you with lifejackets (*gilets*) and teach you basic safety procedures. You must be able to swim, and children under 5 years old are not allowed aboard.

Horseriding

Horseriding is an excellent way of enjoying the countryside. Practically every town in the Dordogne and Lot, and many farms, have equestrian centres (*centres équestres*) where you can ride with a guide or unaccompanied – depending on your level of experience – on the marked riding trails that span the region. Local and departmental tourist offices can provide details, or you can contact the Comité National du Tourisme Équestre (http://ffe.com).

Rock climbing and caving

In the limestone regions of the Dordogne and the Lot **rock climbing** (*escalade*) and **caving** (*spéléologie*) are popular activities. Several local canoe-rental outfits, such as Couleurs Périgord (http://ladordogneencanoe.com) and Kalapca (http://kalapca.com) offer beginners' courses and half-day or full-day outings in the region. Further information is available from tourist offices or the national federations: Fédération Française de la Montagne et de l'Escalade (http://ffme.fr) for rock climbing, and Fédération Française de Spéléologie (http://ffspeleo.fr) for caving.

Swimming

Several pebbly beaches give access to the water along the Dordogne and Lot rivers, but it's often too shallow or fast-flowing to be ideal for **swimming**. An alternative is to head for one of the natural or man-made lakes which pepper the region. Many have leisure centres (*bases de plein air*) at which you can rent pedaloes, windsurfing equipment and dinghies, as well as larger boats and jet-skis (on the bigger reservoirs). It's worth noting, however, that in high summer, when the water is at its lowest, pollution warnings have been issued on rivers and lakes in the region. Check with local tourist authorities for the current situation. Many hotels and campsites also have their own swimming pools for guests to make use of. One thing to be aware of is that some impose strict rules on what sort of swimming costumes can and can't be worn: for men, long or baggy swimming shorts are often outlawed.

Rugby

Despite the influence of France's footballing prowess, **rugby** remains the most important and closely followed field game throughout this region. In season (mid-September to mid-May) virtually every town worth its salt boasts a team and if you head to a match you'll soon find yourself swept up in the camaraderie; unless it's a final, tickets are easy to buy at the gate and are reasonably priced (€10–15).

Boules

Once the preserve of elderly men in berets, **boules**, and its variant *pétanque* (in which contestants must keep both feet on the ground when throwing), has been growing in popularity in recent years and broadening its appeal to include more young people and women. There is even a world championship and talk – not all of it in jest – of getting *boules* recognized as an Olympic sport.

Shopping and markets

The quickest and most convenient places to shop are the hypermarkets and supermarkets you'll find in and around every major town; even some villages have a "supérette". But more interesting by far are the specialist food shops and, of course, the markets, which are still held at least once a week in towns throughout the region.

Many of these **markets** have been held on the same day for centuries. One of the region's biggest and best is that at Sarlat, but the competition is fierce and it's worth including several market days in your itinerary. Other terrific markets are held in Brantôme, Brive, Cahors, Le Bugue, Périgueux and Ribérac, among many other towns and villages. In recent years the hordes of visitors in summer have meant an inevitable increase in the volume of generic tack sold at the biggest markets, but they still boast more than enough enticing local produce and genuine craftsmanship to be unmissable.

For a list of the region's most important and interesting markets, see the boxes at the beginning of each chapter of the Guide.

Travelling with children

The Dordogne and Lot region is one of the most appealing parts of France for family holidays. There are lots of child-friendly activities and sights that will appeal to kids, from visiting castles to exploring some of the caves.

In the summer season, almost every tourist town and sight of note puts on special **children's activities**, which can range from kid-oriented guided tours to pottery and art classes, face-painting and more. Ask at tourist offices for details of what's on.

In terms of **accommodation**, most hotels have a couple of family rooms and can provide cots. *Chambres d'hôtes* are less predictable and it's best to ask in advance; we've highlighted family-friendly places throughout the Guide. Camping is very popular with French families, and for good reason: most of the better sites offer swimming pools, activity centres and sometimes even kids' clubs.

With the exception of some gourmet places (where you probably wouldn't want to eat with kids in tow anyway), most **restaurants** have children's menus and highchairs, and in general, the French take a laidback approach to eating out with children.

Baby-changing facilities can be found at all the bigger tourist sights, while at smaller, less frequented places, space will be made available for you to change a baby if you ask. Most restaurants, however, don't have dedicated changing facilities.

Formula milk, **baby food**, nappies and other necessities are available in all supermarkets, chemists and most small shops.

Travel essentials

Accessible travel

The French authorities have been making a concerted effort to improve facilities for **disabled travellers**. Though haphazard parking habits and stepped village streets remain serious obstacles for anyone with mobility problems, ramps and other forms of access are gradually being added to hotels, museums and other public buildings. All but the oldest hotels are required to adapt at least one room to be **wheelchair-accessible**, and a growing number of *chambres d'hôtes* are doing likewise. Accessible hotels, sights and other facilities are gradually being inspected and, if they fulfil certain criteria, issued with a "Tourisme & Handicap" certificate. Listings produced by Logis (see page 29) and Gîtes de France (see page 29) indicate places with specially adapted rooms. It's essential to double-check when booking that the facilities meet your needs.

Most **train stations** now make provision for travellers with reduced mobility. Spaces for wheelchairs are available in first-class carriages of all **TGVs** for the price of the regular, second-class fare; note that these must be booked in advance. For other trains, a wheelchair symbol in the timetable indicates services offering special on-board facilities, though it's best to double-check when booking. SNCF also runs a scheme called Accès Plus, through which it assists

---

THE DORDOGNE AND LOT FOR KIDS

Caves The Grotte de Villars (see page 68) boasts rock formations, wall paintings, a garden of cavemen and lots of children's activities. At the Grotte de Rouffignac (see page 130) you can ride a miniature train underground and admire ancient wall art, while the Gouffre de Padirac (see page 172) offers a boat ride along a subterranean river and spectacular stalagmites.

Castles The region's châteaux are often a delight for kids, with child-friendly activities in the holidays: at Château de Castelnaud (see page 148), kids can even have a go at firing a trebuchet siege engine.

Boating Keep a lookout for kingfishers and damsel flies while riding a silent electric boat down the Dronne from Montagrier (see page 62).

Gardens Check out the giant maze, fountains, playground and craft activities for children at the Jardins Suspendus de Marqueyssac (see page 146).

travellers with disabilities, including ticket reservations, baggage assistance and a full reception service. You must, though, get in contact with them 48 hours in advance. Full details are on the website http://groupe-sncf.com, which also includes a downloadable guide.

Drivers of **taxis** are legally obliged to help passengers in and out of the vehicle and to carry guide dogs. Ask at the local tourist office or *mairie* for further information on specially adapted taxis. All the big **car rental** agencies can provide automatic cars if you reserve sufficiently far in advance, while most agencies should also be able to able to offer cars with hand controls on request – again, make sure you give them plenty of notice.

If you can read French, there are some other excellent guides to make use of. The association Vacances Accessibles (www.vacances-accessibles.apf.asso.fr) produces the *Handi-plus Aquitaine* (http://handiplusaquitaine.fr) booklet, which outlines suitable itineraries across the whole region. *Handi-tourisme*, published annually by Petit Futé (http://petitfute.com), covers the whole of France.

For general **information** about accessibility, special programmes and discounts, contact one of the organizations listed below before you leave home.

CONTACTS FOR TRAVELLERS WITH DISABILITIES

Access Tourisme Service http://access-tourisme.com. Organized and customized holidays for disabled people, including adapted vehicle rental, accessible hotels and travel companions.
Accessible Journeys http://disabilitytravel.com. Well-established travel agent offering both group tours and advice on independent travel for disabled travellers.
APF (Association des Paralysés de France) http://apf.asso.fr. National association that can answer general enquiries and put you in touch with its departmental offices.

Costs

Although **prices** have been rising steadily in recent years, the Dordogne and Lot is not an outrageously expensive place to visit, especially compared to the regions further south towards the coast, and east towards the Alps. When and where you go, however, will make a difference: in prime tourist spots, hotel rates can increase by a third during July and August.

For a reasonably comfortable existence, including a double room in a mid-range hotel, lunch and dinner in a restaurant, plus moving around, café stops and museum visits, you need to allow a **daily budget** of around €150/£130/US$165 per person based on two people sharing a room. But by counting the pennies, staying at youth hostels or camping, and being strong-willed about extra cups of coffee and doses of culture, you could manage on around €70/£60/US$80 a day each, to include a cheap restaurant meal.

Youth and student discounts

Once obtained, various official and quasi-official youth/student ID cards soon pay for themselves in savings. Full-time students are eligible for the **International Student ID Card** (ISIC; http://isic.org), which entitles you to special air, rail and bus fares, and discounts at museums, theatres and other attractions. It also gives you access to a free 24-hour helpline to call in the event of a medical or legal emergency. You have to be 25 or under to qualify for the **International Youth Travel Card**, while teachers are eligible for the **International Teacher Card**, offering similar discounts. Both are available through universities and student travel specialists such as USIT and Travel CUTS.

Taxes

The majority of goods and services in France are subject to **value-added tax** (*taxe sur la valeur ajoutée* or *TVA*), usually at a rate of 20 percent, which is included in the price. Most local authorities also levy a **tourism tax** on hotel and *chambre d'hôte* accommodation – called a *taxe de séjour* – of up to €3.30 per person per night for the highest-end hotels; in some areas this tax only applies in peak season. While the tax is not included in room rates, it must be clearly indicated as a separate item.

Crime and personal safety

In the more rural parts of the Dordogne and Lot region, crime is extremely rare. However, it obviously makes sense to take the normal **precautions**: don't flash wads of notes around; carry your bag or wallet securely; never leave cameras, mobile phones or other valuables lying around; and park your car overnight in a monitored parking garage or, at the very least, on a busy and well-lit street. It's wise to keep a separate record of bank card numbers, and the phone numbers for cancelling them. Finally, make sure you have a good travel insurance policy.

There are two main types of **police** in France: the Police Nationale and the Gendarmerie Nationale. The former deals with all crime, parking and traffic affairs

> ### EMERGENCY NUMBERS
> Police 17; Ambulance 15; Fire 18 or call 112 for all emergencies.

within large and mid-sized towns, where you will find them in the Commissariat de Police. The Gendarmerie Nationale covers the rural areas.

If you need to **report a theft**, go to the local Gendarmerie or Commissariat de Police (addresses of commissariats are given in the Guide for the major towns), where they will fill out a *constat de vol*. The first thing they'll ask for is your passport, and vehicle documents if relevant. Although the police are not always as cooperative as they might be, it is their duty to assist you if you've lost your passport or all your money. As in most European countries, the police generally won't do more than a cursory investigation into car break-ins.

If you have an **accident** while driving, you must fill in and sign a *constat d'accident* (declaration form) or, if another car is also involved, a *constat à l'amiable* (jointly agreed declaration); these forms should be provided with the car's insurance documents. The police can impose on-the-spot fines for minor **driving offences** and take away your licence for anything more serious.

Drugs

Drug use is just as prevalent in France as anywhere else in Europe – and just as risky. People caught smuggling or possessing drugs, even just a few grams of marijuana, are liable to find themselves in jail. Should you be **arrested** on any charge, you have the right to contact your consulate, though don't expect much sympathy.

Electricity

The **electricity** supply in France is almost always 220V, using plugs with two round pins. If you need a transformer, it's a good idea to buy one before leaving home, though you can find them in big department stores.

Entry requirements

Citizens of the European Union (EU), and most of those from European countries not in the EU, can travel freely in France, while those from the UK, Australia, Canada, New Zealand and the United States, among other countries, do not need a visa for a stay of up to ninety days out of 180.

All non-EU citizens who plan to remain in France longer than ninety days should apply for a **long-stay visa**, for which you have to show proof of – among other things – a regular income or sufficient funds to support yourself and medical insurance. For further information about up-to-date visa regulations, consult the Ministry of Foreign Affairs website: http://diplomatie.gouv.fr.

From mid-2025, UK visitors will need to apply for an ETIAS visa waiver (https://etiasvisa.com), which can be used any number of times during its validity (three years). Note, however, that if you change your passport during that period, the ETAIS waiver becomes invalid.

Health

In general, visitors to the Dordogne and Lot region have little to worry about as far as **health** is concerned. No vaccinations are required, there are no nasty diseases to be wary of and tap water is safe to drink. The worst that's likely to happen is a case of sunburn or an upset stomach from eating too much rich food – or a hangover from all that wonderful wine. If you do need treatment, however, you should be in good hands: the French healthcare system is rated one of the best in the world.

Under the French health system, all services, including doctor's consultations, prescribed medicines, hospital stays and ambulance callouts, incur a charge which you have to pay upfront. **EU citizens** are entitled to a refund (usually between 70 and 80 percent), providing the doctor is government registered (*un médecin conventionné*), on presentation of a **European Health Insurance Card** (EHIC; *Carte Européenne d'Assurance Maladie*; http://nhs.uk). Note that everyone in the family, including children, must have their own cards, which are free. British citizens are still covered by the EHIC scheme until the date of expiry on their card; after this, they can access the new UK **Global Health Insurance Card** (GHIC; http://nhs.uk).

While the EHIC and GHIC guarantee free or reduced-cost medical care in the event of minor injuries and emergencies, maternity care or flare-ups of pre-existing conditions, it won't cover every eventuality – you'll have to pay for X-rays, lab tests and the like, as well as hospital stays, so travel insurance is also essential. If you don't have an EHIC/GHIC card, you'll be charged for everything and will have to claim it back from your insurance, so obtain receipts. All visitors should also ensure they have adequate medical coverage as part of their insurance cover.

For minor complaints visit a **pharmacie**, signalled by an illuminated green cross. You'll find at least one in every small town and even some villages. They keep normal shop hours (roughly Mon–Sat 9am–noon and 3–6/7pm), though some stay open late and, in larger towns, at least one (known as the *pharmacie de garde*) is open 24 hours according to a rota; details are displayed in all pharmacy windows (although you might actually have to phone the pharmacy to ask someone to come and open up).

For anything more serious you can ask for the name of a **doctor** from a pharmacy, local police station, tourist office or your hotel. Alternatively, look under "Médecins" in the Yellow Pages (*Pages Jaunes*) phone directory. A consultation fee is in the region of €25–27. You'll be given a statement of treatment (*Feuille de Soins*) for later insurance claims. Any prescriptions will be fulfilled by a pharmacy and must be paid for; little price stickers (*vignettes*) from each medicine will be stuck on the *Feuille de Soins*.

In serious **emergencies** you will always be admitted to the nearest general hospital (*centre hospitalier*). Phone numbers and addresses are given in the Guide for all the main cities. The national number for calling an ambulance is 15.

Insurance

Even with an EHIC or GHIC card, it's advisable to take out a **travel insurance** policy to cover against theft, loss and illness or injury. Before paying for a new policy, however, it's worth checking whether you are already covered: some all-risks home insurance may cover your possessions when overseas, and many private medical schemes include cover when abroad. In Canada, provincial health plans usually provide partial cover for medical mishaps overseas. Students will often find that their student health coverage extends during the vacations and for one term beyond the date of last enrolment.

A typical travel insurance **policy** will provide cover for the loss of baggage, tickets and – up to a certain limit – cash or cheques, as well as cancellation or curtailment of your journey. Most policies exclude so-called dangerous sports unless an extra premium is paid: in the Dordogne and Lot this would include rock climbing and pot-holing and sometimes such apparently benign activities as canoeing, so it's best to check the small print carefully. Many policies can be chopped and changed to exclude coverage you don't need.

If you need to **make a claim**, you should keep receipts for medicines and medical treatment, and in the event you have anything stolen, you must obtain an official statement from the police (called *un constat de vol*).

Internet

Wi-fi is available in even the cheapest French hotels and *chambres d'hôtes* as well as the majority of campsites (bar basic farm sites), and is almost always free; all accommodation listed in this Guide has wi-fi unless otherwise stated. Most cafés also have wi-fi available free to customers.

Laundry

Laundries are still reasonably common in French towns – just ask in your hotel, or the tourist office, or look in the phone book under "*Laveries automatiques*" or "*Laveries libre-service*". They are usually unattended, and while some have machines for changing notes, it's prudent to come armed with small change. Washing powder (*la lessive*) is always available on site. Machines are graded in different wash sizes, costing in the region of €4 to €5 for 7kg. Most hotels forbid doing any laundry in your room, though you should get away with just one or two small items.

LGBTQ+ travellers

In general, France has a more liberal attitude to homosexuality than many other European countries. The legal age of consent is 15 and civil unions between same-sex couples were made legal in 1999; gay marriage and adoptions by same-sex couples were legalized in 2013. On a day-to-day level, the French mostly consider sexuality to be a private matter.

ROUGH GUIDES TRAVEL INSURANCE

Looking for travel insurance? Rough Guides partners with top providers worldwide to offer you the best coverage. Policies are available to residents of anywhere in the world, with a range of options whether you are looking for single-trip, multi-country or long-stay insurance. There's coverage for a wide range of adventure sports, 24-hour emergency assistance, high levels of medical and evacuation cover and a stream of travel safety information. Even better, roughguides.com users can take advantage of these policies online 24/7, from anywhere in the world – even if you're already travelling. To make the most of your travels and ensure a smoother experience, it's always good to be prepared for when things don't go according to plan. For more information go to roughguides.com/bookings/insurance.

USEFUL CONTACTS

Spartacus International Gay Guide http://spartacusworld.com. An extensive section on France, with some info for lesbians.
Têtu http://tetu.com. France's best-selling gay/lesbian magazine, with events listings and contact addresses; you can buy it in bookshops, newsagents or through its website, which is also an excellent source of information.

Mail

French **post offices**, known as La Poste and identified by bright yellow-and-blue signs, are generally open from around 9am to 5pm or 6pm Monday to Friday, and 9am to noon on Saturday. Those in smaller towns and villages usually also close from noon to 2pm.

Stamps (*timbres*) are sold at *tabacs* and newsagents as well as post offices. Visit http://laposte.fr for information on postal rates. **Postboxes** are bright yellow; make sure, where necessary, to put your letter in the box marked *étranger* (abroad).

Maps

In addition to the **maps** in this guide and the various free town plans you'll be offered along the way, the one extra map you might want is a good, up-to-date road map of the region. The best are the regional maps produced by Michelin (http://viamichelin.fr) and IGN (http://ign.fr). To cover the area encompassed by this guide, IGN's Dordogne map (1:200,000), and Michelin's Aquitaine and Midi-Pyrénées maps (1:200,000) are all worth seeking out. Alternatively, both companies issue large spiral-bound road atlases covering the whole of France at around the same scale.

If you're planning to walk or cycle, it's well worth investing in the more detailed IGN maps. The Carte de Randonnée (1:25,000) series is specifically designed for walkers, while the Carte de Promenade (1:100,000) is ideal for cyclists.

Money

France's currency is the **euro** (€), which is divided into 100 cents (also called *centimes*). There are seven notes – in denominations of 5, 10, 20, 50, 100, 200 and 500 euros – and eight different coins: 1, 2, 5, 10, 20 and 50 cents, and 1 and 2 euros. It's very rare to see anything larger than a €50 note; staff in shops and restaurants may refuse to accept larger denominations. Consult http://xe.com for up-to-date **exchange rates** with the euro.

The best way to access money in France is to use your **credit** or **debit card** to withdraw cash from an **ATM** (known as *un distributeur de billets* or *un point argent*); most machines give instructions in several European languages. Note that there is often a transaction fee, so it is more efficient to take out a sizeable sum of money each time rather than making lots of small withdrawals.

Credit and debit cards are widely accepted in shops, hotels and restaurants, though some smaller establishments don't accept cards, or only for sums above a certain threshold. Visa – called Carte Bleue in France – is almost universally recognized, followed by MasterCard (also known as EuroCard). American Express ranks a lot lower.

You can **change cash** at most banks and main post offices. There are money-exchange counters (*bureaux de change*) at French airports, major train stations and usually one or two in city centres as well, though they don't always offer the best exchange rates.

Newspapers and radio

The large number of Brits living in France has led to an active English-language press in the country. The main monthly **newspaper** in English is *The Connexion* (http://connexionfrance.com), available from newsagents (*maisons de la presse*) and, in larger towns, from street-side kiosks.

Opening hours and public holidays

Basic **hours of business** are 9am to noon and 2 to 6pm. Small food shops often don't reopen till halfway through the afternoon, closing around 7.30 or 8pm, just before the evening meal. Supermarkets also tend to stay open to at least 7.30pm.

The standard **closing day** is Sunday, though some food shops, particularly bakeries (*boulangeries*) and newsagents are open in the morning. Many

---

PUBLIC HOLIDAYS

January 1 New Year's Day
March/April Easter Monday
Ascension Day (forty days after Easter)
Pentecost or Whitsun (seventh Sunday after Easter)
May 1 Labour Day
May 8 Victory in Europe (VE) Day 1945
July 14 Bastille Day
August 15 Assumption of the Virgin Mary
November 1 All Saints' Day
November 11 Armistice Day 1918
December 25 Christmas Day

CALLING HOME FROM ABROAD

Note that the initial zero is omitted from the area code when dialling the UK, Ireland, Australia and New Zealand from abroad.
Australia international access code + 61
New Zealand international access code + 64
UK international access code + 44
US and Canada international access code + 1
Republic of Ireland international access code + 353
South Africa international access code + 27

---

independent shops and businesses, particularly in the rural areas, also close on one other day a week.; it's often a Monday but this varies from town to town.

Core **banking hours** are Monday to Friday 9am to noon and 2 to 6pm. Some branches close on Monday, while others stay open at midday and may also open on Saturday morning. All are closed on Sundays and public holidays.

Most **tourist offices** are open all day every day throughout July and August, but hours outside these months vary considerably. **Museums** tend to open around 9.30 or 10am, close for lunch from noon until 1 or 2pm, and then run through to 5 or 6pm. In summer some stay open all day and close later, while in winter, many open only in the afternoon. Museum closing days are usually Monday or Tuesday, sometimes both. Many state-owned museums have one day of the week or month when they're free or half price.

Churches are generally open from around 8am to dusk, but may close at lunchtime and are reserved for worshippers during services (times of which will usually be posted on the door). Country churches are increasingly kept locked; there may be a note on the door saying where to get the key, usually from the priest's house (*le presbytère*) or someone else living nearby, or from the *mairie*.

France celebrates eleven **public holidays** (*jours fériés*), when banks and most shops and businesses (though not necessarily restaurants), and some museums, are closed.

Phones

French **telephone numbers** have ten digits. Those beginning 0800 or 0805 are free-dial numbers; 081 and 086 are charged as a local call; and anything else beginning 08 is premium-rated. Numbers starting 06 and 07 are for mobiles.

Mobile phones

If you have a non-European mobile phone and want to use it in France, contact your phone provider before leaving home to check whether it will work locally, and what the call charges are.

French mobile phones operate on the European GSM standard, so many **US cellphones** won't work in France unless they are "tri-band". The quickest and cheapest option is probably to change your phone and/or service provider.

As of 2021, when the UK lost the guarantee of free roaming in EU countries, most UK network providers applied roaming charges in France. Check with your service provider.

Smoking

Smoking is banned in all enclosed public spaces, including museums, hotels, restaurants, bars and nightclubs, but widely accepted in outdoor spaces, including restaurant patios.

Time

France lies in the **Central European Time Zone** (GMT+1): one hour ahead of the UK, six hours ahead of Eastern Standard Time, and nine hours ahead of Pacific Standard Time. Between April and October France is eight hours behind eastern Australia and ten hours behind New Zealand; from November to March, it is ten hours behind southeastern Australia and twelve hours behind New Zealand.

Daylight Saving Time (GMT+2) in France lasts from the final Sunday of March to the last Sunday of October.

Tourist information

The **French Government Tourist Office** (Maison de la France, http://france.fr) increasingly refers you to its website for information, though it still produces a number of useful brochures. For information specific to the Dordogne and Lot region, contact the regional or departmental tourist offices before you leave home.

Tourist offices

In the Dordogne and Lot region you'll find a tourist office – usually an **Office du Tourisme** (OT) but sometimes a **Syndicat d'Initiative** (SI) – in practically every town and many villages (addresses, contact details and opening hours are detailed in the Guide). For the practical purposes of visitors, there is little difference between them; sometimes they share premises and call themselves an OTSI. In small villages where there is no OT or SI, the *mairie* (town hall) will offer a similar service.

All these offices are well stocked with information, both locally and regionally, including hotels and restaurants, leisure activities, bike rental, markets and festivals, while those in the wine regions will provide information on local vineyards, and in peak season may also conduct vineyard tours; many can also book accommodation for you.

Most offices can provide a town/village plan and/or walking leaflets, while an increasing number now provide audioguides (with English language) for self-guided town or village walks, though there will be a charge for this. Most, too, have maps and local walking guides on sale.

REGIONAL AND DEPARTMENTAL TOURIST OFFICES

Aquitaine http://nouvelle-aquitaine-tourisme.com.
Corrèze http://tourismecorreze.com.
Dordogne www.dordogne-perigord-tourisme.fr.
Lot http://tourisme-lot.com.
Lot-et-Garonne http://tourisme-lotetgaronne.com.

Work and study in the Dordogne and Lot

EU citizens are free to work in France on the same basis as a French citizen, so don't have to apply for a residence or work permit. Most **non-EU citizens**, however, including those from UK, will need a work permit (*autorisation de travail*) and a residence permit along with a whole host of other papers; contact your nearest French consulate or, if already in France, your local *mairie* or *préfecture* to check what rules apply in your particular situation. Whatever your nationality, once you have a work permit, you are entitled to exactly the same conditions as French workers, including the national **minimum wage** (SMIC), currently set at €11.65 per hour.

When **looking for a job**, a good starting point is to read one of the books on working abroad published by Vacation Work (http://vacationwork.co.uk). You could also try the websites http://monster.fr and http://jobs-ete.com; the latter focuses on summer jobs for students. Once in France, you'll find "Offres d'Emploi" (Job Offers) in the national and regional papers, or there's the national employment agency, *pôle emploi* (http://pole-emploi.fr), with offices all over France and which advertises temporary jobs in all fields. Non-EU citizens will have to show a work permit to apply for any of their jobs.

A degree and a TEFL (Teaching English as a Foreign Language) or similar qualifications are normally required for **English-language teaching** posts. The online *EL Gazette* newsletter (http://elgazette.com) is a useful source of information, as is the annual *Teaching English Abroad* (available from online retailers). The TEFL website (http://tefl.com) has a good database of English-teaching vacancies.

Foreign students pay the same as French nationals to enroll for a course and you'll be eligible for subsidized accommodation, meals and all the student reductions. French **universities** are fairly informal, but there are strict entry requirements, including an exam in French for undergraduate degrees, but not for postgraduate courses. For full details and prospectuses, contact the Cultural Service of any French embassy or consulate.

FURTHER CONTACTS

AFS Intercultural Programs http://afs.org. Opportunities for high-school students to study in France for a term or full academic year, living with host families.
Campus France http://campusfrance.org. Government-run agency set up to promote French higher education abroad.
Erasmus http://britishcouncil.org. EU-run student exchange programme enabling students at participating universities in Britain and Ireland to study in one of 31 European countries. UK students will need a visa.
Language Courses Abroad http://languagesabroad.co.uk. Long- or short-term language courses throughout France, some combined with other activities such as cookery and skiing.
Workaway http://workaway.info. Volunteering opportunities, family exchanges, working holidays and farmstays around France.
World Wide Opportunities on Organic Farms (WWOOF) http://wwoof.fr. Volunteer to work on an organic farm in return for board and lodging.

Périgueux and the north

- 49 Périgueux
- 58 Brantôme
- 61 The lower Dronne valley
- 65 La Double
- 66 The Northern Périgord Vert
- 70 Jumilhac-le-Grand
- 71 Excideuil
- 72 Hautefort and around
- 74 Brive-la-Gaillarde
- 78 Arnac-Pompadour
- 80 Turenne
- 81 Collonges-la-Rouge

PÉRIGUEUX AND ITS CATHÉDRALE ST-FRONT

Périgueux and the north

The north of the Dordogne *département* is its least known and most rural corner, a land with few people and large tracts of pasture and woodland, its intimate green valleys lending it the name of the Périgord Vert. It's a region that will appeal to those who love peace and quiet, picnics in flower meadows, somnolent villages and gentle countryside ambles. But there is some urban excitement to be found here. With its searing-white old town, pineapple-capped cathedral and superb Roman remains, Périgueux – capital of both Périgord Blanc and of the whole *département* – is an easy city to fall for, but really it's the countryside around that holds the region's best attractions.

One of the loveliest parts of the entire Dordogne is the **Dronne valley**, which shadows the River Isle to the north of Périgueux. At **Brantôme** the Dronne's still, water-lilied surface mirrors the limes and weeping willows along its banks, before flowing on past the twin fortresses of **Bourdeilles** to **Ribérac**, a market town beloved by the British, and **Aubeterre-sur-Dronne** just over the border in the Charente region. As at Brantôme, the river-carved cliffs at Aubeterre were hollowed out into primitive churches by twelfth-century monks. Others built dozens of little Romanesque churches on the sunny hills around, while south of the Dronne their successors helped tame the marshy, insalubrious plateau of **La Double**. In doing so they created the pine and chestnut forests that blanket the area today.

Upstream from Brantôme, two tributaries of the Dronne lead northeast through woodlands and butterfly-speckled pastures to the tiny village of **St-Jean-de-Côle** and the decorative, Renaissance pile of **Château de Puyguilhem**. Further northeast, there's no mistaking the warlike nature of the hulking granite castle at **Jumilhac-le-Grand**. As a break from the châteaux trail, truffle-lovers might like to press on to **Sorges**, where there's a marked path through truffle country and another small museum to explain it all. This town is close to the southeast border of the Périgord Vert, where the scenery becomes softer towards the lovely Auvézère valley. Here, in a spectacular spot high over the river, the **Château de Hautefort** reveals the elegance of past lives.

East of Hautefort, across the border in the Corrèze *département*, **Brive-la-Gaillarde** lies on an important crossroads and provides an alternative to Périgueux as a gateway to the region. For such a large city, Brive has a surprisingly compact and enjoyable old centre with more than enough to detain you for a day or two. The countryside around also holds a few surprises, from the National Stud at **Arnac-Pompadour** to the appropriately named **Collonges-la-Rouge**, a village built with rich red sandstone, and neighbouring **Turenne**, another absurdly pretty village capped by the substantial remains of its eponymous fortress.

GETTING AROUND   PÉRIGUEUX AND THE NORTH

Both Périgueux and Brive are major transport hubs, the latter especially so now that there are **flights** to the UK to and from Brive-Vallée de la Dordogne airport. In addition, both cities have frequent flights to Paris. Périgueux and Brive also have reasonable **train** connections, both to other towns in the region (such as Les Eyzies, Thiviers, Bergerac and Sarlat-la-Canéda) and to destinations beyond the Dordogne. Local **bus** services throughout the region, however, are very sporadic – we've detailed those that do exist at the relevant points in the text, but as many of these are geared towards schoolchildren to tie in with drop-off and pick-up times, they're not much of an option for visitors – a car is pretty much essential if you wish to explore the more remote areas.

BRANTÔME

Highlights

❶ **Périgueux** From prehistoric and Gallo-Roman remains via Renaissance-era mansions to the cathedral's Byzantine extravagance, Périgueux has something for everyone. See page 49

❷ **Brantôme** Stroll the tree-shaded waterways, bridges and parks of this handsome town, then paddle a kayak along the lily-strewn Dronne. See page 58

❸ **Bourdeilles** Perched precariously over the Dronne, the château of Bourdeilles guards one of the prettiest villages in the Dordogne. See page 61

❹ **Église Souterraine Saint-Jean** Explore the cool, dark cavern of Aubeterre's mysterious subterranean church. See page 64

❺ **Grotte de Villars** A rare opportunity to see displays of stalagmites and stalactites alongside prehistoric wall paintings in these wonderful caves. See page 68

❻ **Château de Hautefort** Built to rival the châteaux of the Loire, Hautefort stands out for its elegance and architectural harmony. See page 72

❼ **Brive-la-Gaillarde** Vibrant, energetic and with a beautifully restored city centre, rugby-loving Brive is worth a day's exploration. See page 74

HIGHLIGHTS ARE MARKED ON THE MAP ON PAGE 48

FESTIVALS, EVENTS AND MARKETS

The list below comprises some of the biggest and most interesting of the **festivals** and **events** in this region. Where we haven't given a specific phone number or website, contact the relevant tourist office.

First weekend in May Bertric Burée, near Ribérac: Snail Festival. Locals celebrate snails by preparing and cooking them in their thousands; they are then consumed throughout the village by locals and tourists alike.

Second weekend in May St-Jean-de-Côle: Les Floralies (http://floralies-saintjean.fr). Longstanding and highly rated festival, where the streets and squares of this pretty village are packed with flower stalls.

Mid-July and August Brive and around: Festival de la Vézère (http://festival-vezere.com). Operas and classical concerts in the open air (bring a picnic) or in various châteaux and churches, including Arnac-Pompadour and Turenne.

Late July Périgueux: Mimos, the International Festival of Mime (http://mimos.fr). One of the most exciting and innovative contemporary art festivals in France, with more than 150 artists performing in over fifty shows; mostly street performances but also some ticketed events.

Second week in August Périgueux: New Orleans Music Festival (http://mnop.fr). Jazz, gospel and blues concerts in a different area of the city each night.

Last week of August Périgueux and around: Sinfonia en Périgord (http://sinfonia-en-perigord.com). A five-day celebration of Baroque and Renaissance music, with concerts in various venues in Périgueux, as well as the nearby abbeys of Chancelade and Brantôme and the Château de Bourdeilles.

First weekend in November Brive: La Foire du Livre (http://foiredulivredebrive.net). One of the country's most prestigious literary gatherings. Held in Brive's market hall, it attracts some three hundred authors and artists presenting their new works, and around ten thousand book-lovers keen to snap up signed editions.

Mid-November Périgueux: Salon International du Livre Gourmand (http://livregourmand.perigueux.fr). Book fair dedicated to wine and gastronomy. Events take place over four days in the theatre (1 allée d'Aquitaine), and include book exhibitions, cooking demonstrations and opportunities to sample the results.

MARKETS

The main weekly **markets** in this region are: Brantôme (Fri); Brive (Tues, Thurs & Sat); Excideuil (Thurs); Périgueux (Wed & Sat); Ribérac (Fri); and Thiviers (Sat). In winter many local towns hold foie gras, truffle and walnut markets, generally on the same day as their weekly market. In summer 'marchés nocturnes' (night markets) are popular events, offering a chance to sample regional produce and typically accompanied by live entertainment.

Périgueux

PÉRIGUEUX, capital of the Dordogne, might be the biggest urban centre in the Dordogne, but at heart it's just an attractive market town for a province made rich by tourism and specialized farming. Its name derives from the Petrocorii, the local Gaulish tribe, but it was the Romans who transformed it into an important settlement. While a few **Roman remains** survive, it is the city's **medieval and Renaissance core** that gives Périgueux its particular appeal. Pretty, sun-bleached stone-flagged squares and a maze of narrow alleys harbour richly ornamented merchants' houses, while above it all rises the startlingly white spire of St-Front cathedral, flanked by its cluster of pinnacled, Byzantine domes. It looks best at night – particularly from across the river – when floodlights soften the sharper edges and accentuate its exotic silhouette.

Périgueux's compact **historic centre** – much of it pedestrianized – sits on the west bank of the River Isle, occupying a rough square formed by the river, the tree-shaded

PÉRIGUEUX AND THE NORTH | PÉRIGUEUX

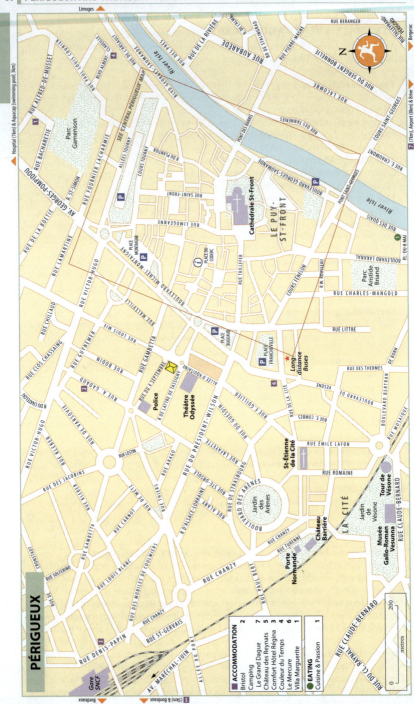

cours Tourny to the north, boulevard Michel Montaigne to the west and cours Fénelon to the south. Though the hilltop **Cathédrale St-Front** provides a natural magnet, the surrounding streets hide some particularly fine Renaissance architecture as well as the **Musée d'Art et d'Archéologie du Périgord**, with its collection of Paleolithic tools, and a remnant of **medieval wall**. The main commercial hub is concentrated around rue Taillefer, running from the cathedral west to place Bugeaud, and along pedestrianized rue Limogeanne to the north. At the southwest corner of the old town lies the wide place Francheville, from where rue de la Cité leads westwards towards Périgueux's other principal area of interest, **La Cité**, centred around a rather mutilated church. This is where you'll find the smart Gallo-Roman Museum, **Vesunna**, featuring the foundations of a Roman villa. Everything is within easy walking distance, making it possible to explore the city comfortably in a day or two.

Brief history

Périgueux began life some time after the fourth century BC as a fortified settlement inhabited by the **Petrocorii** ("Four Tribes"), whose craftspeople were noted for their ironwork. After 51 BC, however, the area came under Roman rule and a thriving town known as **Vesunna** (Vésone in French) began to develop, complete with amphitheatre, temples and luxurious villas. By the first century AD its population had reached an estimated twenty thousand, but the glory was shortlived. Vesunna, like many other towns, had neglected its defences under the *pax romana* and was caught unprepared by a succession of **barbarian invasions** in the third century. When Germanic tribes swept through the area in 275 AD, the population used stone from the surrounding civic monuments to construct defensive walls that helped the town survive, but in a much reduced state. As it faded it became known as La Cité des Pétrocores, then simply **La Cité**.

La Cité and Le Puy-St-Front

St Front arrived on the Périgueux scene some time in the fourth century to convert the local population to Christianity. After giving La Cité a new breath of life by founding what eventually became St-Étienne-de-la-Cité cathedral, the saint was later buried on a neighbouring hilltop, or *puy*, where his tomb became a pilgrimage centre. By the thirteenth century it had spawned a small but prosperous town of merchants and artisans known as **Le Puy-St-Front**, which began to rival La Cité, now the seat of the counts of Périgord. Though the two communities were joined by an act of union in 1240, they continued to glare at each other over their encircling walls – indeed, at the start of the **Hundred Years' War** La Cité sided with the English and Le Puy with France. For a while following the Treaty of Brétigny in 1360, Périgueux, as it was now known, fell under English rule, but the loyal burghers of Le Puy soon rallied to Charles V, and by 1369 Périgueux had been liberated by Bertrand du Guesclin, who then chased the English back towards the coast. Even so, by the early fifteenth century the city was in ruins, its population decimated by war, plague and famine and its buildings crumbling through neglect.

With peace, however, came renewed prosperity and a building boom that left Périgueux its wonderful legacy of **Renaissance** architecture, though much was lost or damaged during the **Wars of Religion**: despite being predominantly Catholic, Périgueux was held by the Protestants for six years after 1575, during which time they vandalized many religious buildings, among them St-Étienne-de-la-Cité cathedral. This proved to be the final blow for La Cité, which fell into slow decline, culminating in the transfer of cathedral status to St-Front in 1669.

Modern Périgueux

La Cité and Le Puy-St-Front remained firmly inside their respective walls, separated by open space, up until the beginning of the eighteenth century, after which Périgueux began to expand into today's **modern city**. In the process the medieval walls gave way to wide boulevards, while in the nineteenth century the canal and railway brought further development to what was by then the capital of Périgord. The old city centre was left largely untouched, so that in 1979 some twenty hectares were designated a preservation district. Nevertheless, Périgueux is still the *département*'s most industrialized town: its biggest current claim to fame – a result of 1970s decentralization policies – is the printing works where all French postage stamps are produced.

Le Puy-St-Front

There's still a slight medieval air to **Le Puy-St-Front**, the city's old quarter. Its confined and cobbled alleys harbour Périgueux's oldest buildings – the former homes of wealthy merchants – as well as the last remaining fragment of the medieval fortifications. Le Puy was originally surrounded by 28 defensive towers, of which only stout, circular **Tour Mataguerre**, protecting the southwest corner, remains. According to legend, it was named after an English captain imprisoned here during the Hundred Years' War, but the present structure dates from the late fifteenth century, when it was rebuilt using leper labourers. Although there's little to see inside – just the prison and a simple guardroom above – the views from the roof are worth the climb.

Maison des Dames de la Foi
6 rue des Farges

From beside Tour Mataguerre, rue de la Bride runs into rue des Farges, where you'll find Périgueux's most venerable building, **Maison des Dames de la Foi**, dating from the late twelfth century. The name, "House of the Ladies of Faith", refers to a convent established in the seventeenth century for young Protestant women wishing to convert to Catholicism. Two hundred years earlier, during the Hundred Years' War, it's said that du Guesclin stayed here while preparing to liberate nearby Chancelade Abbey from the English. Nowadays, it's a private residence, and you'd be forgiven for walking straight past: the only evidence of its illustrious history is the blocked-in window arches on the ground floor.

Musée Militaire
32 rue des Farges • Charge • http://museemilitaire-perigord.fr

At the top of rue des Farges, the **Musée Militaire** contains a vast and rather chaotic array of military memorabilia, one of the foremost such collections in France. Covering everything from the Franco–Prussian War to the Gulf War and today's UN peacekeeping missions, the exhibits are of rather specialized interest, but there are some noteworthy pieces including some poignant sketches of trench life in World War I and memorabilia dating back to the French colonial wars in Indochina (today's Vietnam, Laos and Cambodia), among them a couple of tattered Viet Minh flags.

Rue de l'Aubergerie

Rue de l'Aubergerie is known for its fortified fifteenth-century houses, of which **Hôtel d'Abzac de Ladouze** at no. 16, a typically dour building with an octagonal defensive tower, is the most interesting. The massive blind arch on the wall is evidence of much older foundations, while the incongruous ornamental balustrade above is a Renaissance addition. Note also the cockleshell carving on the side of the tower, indicating that the house once received pilgrims en route to Santiago de Compostela. Further down the street, at no. 6, **Hôtel de Saltgourde** sports an impressive tower complete with a machicolated parapet.

Rue St-Roch to place de la Clautre

Rue St-Roch leads east from below Hôtel d'Abzac past several interesting houses, one retaining its wood-timbered upper storey, others their overhanging latrines or decorative arcaded windows, to **rue du Calvaire**. This was the road that criminals in

DAUMESNIL: THE PEG-LEG GENERAL

A devoted follower of Napoleon Bonaparte, **Baron Pierre Daumesnil** (1776–1832) was fiery, impetuous, loyal, patriotic and, above all, brave. He first distinguished himself during the Italian campaign (1796–97) when he rescued the drowning Napoleon from a river during the Battle of Arcole; then, at Acre in 1799, Daumesnil threw himself in front of his hero when a bomb landed at Napoleon's feet. It failed to explode, but Daumesnil, by now a major, was less lucky at the **Battle of Wagram** in Austria in 1809, when his left leg was so badly mutilated that it had to be amputated. Three years later he was promoted to general and made **governor of the Château de Vincennes** – the country's largest arsenal – which he twice refused to hand over to the allied European armies fighting Napoleon. The second time, in 1815, he declared: "I will give up Vincennes when you give me back my leg." Nevertheless, Daumesnil was forced to retire a few months later following Napoleon's defeat at Waterloo, and he eventually died of cholera in 1832, though his wooden leg was preserved and is now on display in Paris's Musée de l'Armée. In Périgueux you'll find a statue of him towards the south end of boulevard Michel Montaigne.

---

the Middle Ages climbed on their way to the courthouse, identifiable by its studded Renaissance door. The condemned would then continue to the gallows on **place de la Clautre**, which also served as an execution ground during the Revolution. Nowadays it provides a more peaceful setting for a twice-weekly produce **market** (Wed & Sat mornings) against the backdrop of the cathedral.

Cathédrale St-Front
Place de la Clautre • **Cathédrale** Free • **Cloister** Charge

The domed and coned **Cathédrale St-Front** began life in the sixth century as a simple chapel over the tomb of St Front. Seven hundred years later – by then an important abbey – it was rebuilt after a fire and in the process the architects created one of the most distinctive Byzantine churches in France, modelled on St Mark's in Venice and on Constantinople's Church of the Holy Apostles. Multi-language leaflets available at the cathedral entrance give a concise run-down of its points of interest, and in July and August the tourist office run daily tours of the cathedral in French at 3pm.

From outside, the cathedral is the very picture of exotica (despite some over-enthusiastic nineteenth-century restoration work). The Byzantine influence is evident in the interior's Greek-cross plan – unusual in France – and in the massive, clean curves of the domes. The bell tower also survived largely intact and is one of the few vestiges of the twelfth-century reconstruction. The adjoining **cloister** has two sides constructed in the Gothic style, and the other two in Romanesque.

North of the cathedral

North of the cathedral crowd the renovated buildings of the **Renaissance** city. The longest and finest street in this part of town is narrow **rue Limogeanne**, leading north from place de la Clautre via rue Salinière. Among the proliferating souvenir shops stand elegant mansions, now turned into swish boutiques, confectioners and delicatessens; its most notable facade belongs to **Maison Estignard** at no. 5, whose elaborate architecture – mullions, dormer windows and ornamental columns – is typical of the Renaissance. It's also worth popping into the more sober courtyard of no. 3 to see a salamander carved above the inner door; this was the insignia of Francis I (reigned 1515–47), who brought Italian Renaissance style to France. Opposite, impasse Limogeanne leads into a series of courtyards and passageways known as **galerie Daumesnil** after the famous general born at 7 rue de la Clarté in 1776.

Though nearby place du Coderc and place de l'Hôtel-de-Ville are both strong contenders, **Place St-Louis**, to the west of rue Limogeanne, is probably the prettiest of

Périgueux's squares. In its southeast corner stands the handsome, turreted **Maison du Pâtissier** – built by a man who made his fortune from *pâté en croûte* (pâté in a pastry crust) – with a lovely Renaissance door bearing a fearsome warning on its lintel. There are more fine houses over to the east of rue Limogeanne on rue de la Constitution; from here the lanes begin to drop steeply to the river, where you'll find the semi-fortified fifteenth-century **Maison des Consuls** with the sixteenth-century **Maison Lambert** next door.

Musée d'Art et d'Archéologie du Périgord
22 cours Tourny • Charge • http://perigueux-maap.fr

Set in a grand, nineteenth-century building at the top of rue St-Front, overlooking the broad, tree-lined allées de Tourny is the **Musée d'Art et d'Archéologie du Périgord**. First and foremost, the museum houses an extensive **prehistoric collection**, among its most prized exhibits a partially complete 90,000-year-old human skeleton, the oldest yet found in France, and a delicate engraving of a bison's head. However, many of the more fragile items on display are copies, and the museum's old-fashioned layout makes it hard to appreciate what's on offer: the ethnographic exhibit is particularly poorly displayed and looks as if it hasn't been touched since 1897. Of the fine and **decorative arts section** the display of sculpture by the Transylvanian-born French sculptor Étienne Hajdu (1907–96) is worth musing over; his striking, bright-white aluminium structures are loosely based on the work of renowned Romanian sculptor, Constantin Brancusi. Elsewhere, the **cloister** is packed with carved stones and decorative sculptures, some taken from the Cathédrale St-Front, as well as some beautiful Gallo-Roman mosaics.

Look out, too, for the **temporary exhibitions**, often innovative and challenging in their outlook.

La Cité

Remnants of the Roman town of Vesunna, now known as **La Cité**, lie southwest from place Francheville along Le Puy-St-Front's rue de la Cité. Named after a local divinity, Vesunna was an important and prosperous town: by the first century AD it extended over some seventy hectares, complete with a forum, basilica, thermal baths and a 7km-long aqueduct. Today the most visible vestiges – a ruined amphitheatre, the remains of a temple complex and an excavated villa – lie scattered around the hulk of Périgueux's first cathedral, **St-Étienne-de-la-Cité**.

St-Étienne-de-la-Cité
Place de la Claustre • Free

Approaching from the east, the domes of **St-Étienne-de-la-Cité** dominate the surrounding area. The cathedral was founded by St Front in the fourth century, then rebuilt in its present form, with a Romanesque nave comprising big square bays, some six hundred years later. The original building comprised four bays but two were destroyed, along with the bell tower, by Huguenots in 1577, leaving the church's west facade roughly truncated. The first bay you enter is the older of the two, dating from the eleventh century: the dome is more massive, the windows smaller and fewer and the stone less regular. The second bay was added a century later, then restored as an exact copy in the 1600s. Apart from being lighter and higher, its main feature is the line of decorative columns along the walls which stand out in the otherwise unornamented church.

Jardin des Arènes
Bd des Arènes • Free

The pretty **Jardin des Arènes**, a circular garden a few paces northwest of St-Étienne-de-la-Cité, conceals a few remnants – comprising an entrance arch and traces of the foundations – of an enormous **amphitheatre** capable of holding twenty thousand people or more. Built in the first century AD, it was dismantled two hundred years later to construct defensive walls, of which you can see a fragment, the **Porte Normande**, along nearby rue Turenne. In the panic, the walls were cobbled together

> **FOLLOW THE RIVER**
>
> Once you've had your fill of tramping the streets, you might like to explore Périgueux's greener side. If you're on a bicycle, or on foot, take to **La Voie Verte** (see page 66), a 15km path winding from Marsac in the west of the city to Trélissac in the east. With car parks, picnic areas and information points along the way, it's popular with both locals and tourists. **La Voie Bleue** is the water-based alternative – a 21km paddle down the River Isle by canoe. For more details on both routes ask at the tourist office; for canoe hire contact **Canoë Marsac** (http://canoemarsac.fr).

with whatever came to hand: a column, some capitals, a carved lintel, all pilfered from neighbouring monuments.

For most locals, though, history plays second fiddle to parklife, and the biggest attraction (particularly for children) is the large fountain and kids' paddling pool that stand at the heart of the park.

Tour de Vésone
Jardin de Vésone • Free

Southeast of the Jardin des Arènes, past the empty carcass of the twelfth-century **Château Barrière** and across the train lines, you reach the neatly manicured **Jardin de Vésone**, within which stands Périgueux's most imposing Roman monument, the **Tour de Vésone**. This high, hulking circular tower was once the sanctuary of a temple dedicated to Vesunna's eponymous guardian goddess. The gaping breach on the north side is said to have been created when St Front exorcized the pagan gods; more prosaically, the bricks and stones probably went into local building works.

Musée Gallo-Romain Vesunna
Jardin de Vésone • Charge • http://perigueux-vesunna.fr

Concealed within a magnificent modern glass building a few paces from the Tour de Vésone is the **Musée Gallo-Romain Vesunna**, an outstanding museum built around the well-preserved remains of a grand Roman villa, which were discovered by chance in 1959. Superbly conceived wooden walkways (note how the layout is cleverly mirrored in the ceiling painting) take you over the walls and into the heart of the site, which is dominated by the garden, ornamented with peristyles of varying height. Indeed, this villa was no humble abode. It was complete with at least sixty rooms, an underfloor central-heating hypocaust, thermal baths and colonnaded walkways. Around the walls you can see the remains of first-century murals of river and marine life, the colours still amazingly vibrant, and here and there, graffiti of hunting scenes, gladiatorial combat and even an ostrich – perhaps the work of some bored Roman teenager. The best views of the site are from the two balconies, which are otherwise laid out with exquisitely crafted pilasters and funerary monuments.

On Thursday evenings in July and August, the museum stages special tours and various family-friendly activities (conducted in French).

ARRIVAL AND DEPARTURE — PÉRIGUEUX

By train The *gare SNCF* is on rue Denis-Papin, a 10min walk from the centre, or you can take bus #3, #4 and #NSe to the city centre (€1.30).

Destinations Bordeaux (17 daily; 1hr–1hr 30min); Brive (12 daily; 1hr); Neuvic (16 daily; 20–30min); St-Astier (22 daily; 10–15min); Thiviers (13 daily; 20–30min).

By bus Long-distance buses leave from the bus stop on rue de la Cité, behind place Francheville. Most routes are operated by CFTA (http://cftaco.fr), which has an information office close to the rue de la Cité bus stop. Tickets are available on board.

Destinations Angoulême (1hr 45min); Bergerac (1hr); Brantôme (40min); Excideuil (1hr); Hautefort (40min); Neuvic (40min); Ribérac (1hr).

By car You can park for free along the river below St-Front Cathedral (these car parks often close during the summer holidays), or there's plenty of pay-parking along allées de Tourny, to the north of the centre, in place Montaigne to the east and underneath place Francheville.

GETTING AROUND

Car rental Near the train station, try: Ada Location 24, 4 bis avenue Henri-Barbusse (http://ada.fr); Europcar, 7 rue Denis-Papin (http://europcar.fr); or Avis, 11 rue Denis-Papin (http://avis.fr). You can also arrange to pick up cars at the airport.

Taxis Call Allo Taxi Périgueux (05 53 09 09 09; http://taxiperigueux.com). There are also taxi stands outside the train station and another on place Bugeaud.

INFORMATION

Tourist office 9bis place du Coderc (Jan–June & Oct–Dec Mon–Sat 9am–12.30pm & 2–6pm; July & Aug Mon–Sat

9am–7pm, Sun 10am–6pm; Sept Mon–Sat 9am–12.30pm & 2–6pm, Sun 10am–1pm, 05 53 53 10 63, http://tourisme-grandperigueux.fr). They offer themed city tours (April to mid-Sept; €6) covering medieval and Renaissance Périgueux, the Gallo-Roman city or with a focus on music or food and drink. Though the tours are predominantly in French, some guides also speak English; ask in advance.

ACCOMMODATION   SEE MAP PAGE 50

Bristol 37 rue Antoine-Gadaud, http://bristolfrance.com. Now part of the Citotel chain, this welcoming place looks pretty bland from the outside, but inside it's another story with airy, bright and bold part-painted, part-wallpapered en-suite rooms. €€

Camping Le Grand Dague Route du Grand Dague, Atur, http://sandaya.fr. Lost in the hills 7km southeast of Périgueux, this spacious and immaculate four-star site is worth seeking out if you have your own transport. A wealth of facilities, including TV lounge, shop, launderette, playground, swimming pools and slides, a restaurant, plus bike hire. Mobile homes available too. €

Château des Reynats 15 av des Reynats, http://chateau-hotel-perigord.com. In the village of Chancelade, roughly 5km northwest of central Périgueux, this nineteenth-century château has plush, immaculately turned-out rooms both in the château itself and the orangerie annexe, with those in the latter fashioned in more contemporary style. There's a top-class restaurant too. Closed Jan. €€€

Comfort Hôtel Régina 14 rue Denis-Papin, http://hotelregina-perigueux.fr. The only hotel in the vicinity of the train station worth considering, a pleasant place offering cheerful en-suite rooms with high ceilings with spotlights, and windows to match (double-glazed on the front). Triple rooms are available too. €

★ **Couleurs du Temps** 20 bd Albert-Claveille, http://couleursdutempsdordogne.blogspot.fr. Easily the most imaginatively decorated hotel in town. The two huge attic rooms in this gracious town-house are a masterpiece of creative thinking, with quirky touches such as lamps made from bike lights and chains, crimson Louis XV-style chairs, curved Perspex mirrors and fabulous photo art. Rooms have small fridges, microwaves and coffee-making facilities – and breakfast is included, served to your room. Best of all, though, are the two very helpful owners. €

Le Mercure 7 place Francheville, http://mercure.accor.com. Located on the corner of the city's most prominent square, *Le Mercure* is by some distance the smartest hotel in the centre. The classic facade conceals a fairly typical business-style chain hotel with impeccably kept rooms decorated in cream and beige tones, and with a few extras like tea- and coffee-making facilities. €€

Villa Marguerite 7 rue du Parc, http://chambres-hotes-perigueux.com. Five *chambres d'hôtes* bursting with character, each with its own theme (from a New York-style loft to a cottagecore attic suite). There's a sheltered, walled garden, and breakfast is sumptuous. Two-night minimum stay. €€

EATING   SEE MAPS PAGES 50 AND 54

l'Atelier 2 rue Voltaire, http://restaurant-perigueux-atelier.com. A high-end restaurant with multi-course menus on the edge of the old town. Chef Cyril Haberland worked with Thierry Marx for years, and his experience in Michelin-starred restaurants shows in the beautifully presented menu, which uses the finest local produce, including truffles and foie gras. The walled patio is bedecked with plants. €€€€

Café Louise 10 place de l'Ancien Hôtel de Ville, 05 53 08 93 85. Family-friendly bistro serving a mixture of Italian and French cuisine in cosy surroundings. There are plenty of pasta dishes and regional specialties, and the wine list also spans both countries. Save room for dessert, notably the panna cotta. €€

Le Clos St-Front 5 rue de la Vertu, http://leclossaintfront.com. This elegant, brick-walled restaurant has a well-earned reputation for its inventive *menus*. The dishes are beautifully presented, the *menu* changes approximately every six weeks and could include delights such as pigs' feet in garlic cream, which is actually a lot tastier than it sounds, or octopus with a saffron and mussel cream. €€€

Le Comptoir du Tourny 6 Cour Tourny, 05 53 13 92 99. Dishes are presented as they would be in a far pricier establishment, but in much more generously sized portions. Although based on classic French cuisine, the flavour combinations used are far from traditional (miso hake or guinea fowl cooked in yellow wine, for instance). The terrace is a great spot for people-watching. €€

Cuisine & Passion 7 place du 8-Mai, http://cuisine-et-passion.fr. Chef Yoann has trained under a string of Michelin-starred chefs and his flair for creative gourmet cuisine shines through at this modern restaurant. Grab a table on the terrace and save space for one of the decadent desserts with options like raspberry and pistachio pavlova. €€€

L'Essentiel 8 rue de la Clarté, http://restaurant-perigueux.com. As the city's sole Michelin-starred restaurant, *L'Essentiel* is, as you'd expect, a high-class and pretty expensive affair. The service and cooking here, by supremo chef Eric Vidal, are outstanding, and you'll have a tough time choosing from the seasonal menu which includes the likes of spit-roasted pigeon stuffed with foie gras. €€€

Hercule Poireau 2 rue de la Nation, http://restaurant-perigueux-hercule-poireau.fr. One of Périgueux's best-known restaurants, located down in a gorgeous, sixteenth-century stone-vaulted room with soft lighting and cheerful

MARKETS IN PÉRIGUEUX

Périgueux has some great **markets**: the biggest are the fresh-produce markets in the centre of Le Puy-St-Front around **place de la Claultre**, **place du Coderc** and **place de l'Hôtel-de-Ville** (Wed & Sat mornings), and the clothes and household goods market just to the southeast on **place Bugeaud** (Wed morning). There's also a daily fresh-food market (mornings only) in place du Coderc's covered **halle**. In winter (mid-Nov to mid-March), stalls selling foie gras and truffles set up just north of the Cathédrale St-Front in place St-Louis for the annual **marchés au gras** (Wed & Sat morning).

red-check fabrics. This is rich fare: house speciality is the luxurious *rossini de canard* (duck with a slice of foie gras in a truffle sauce). €€

IZBA 19 rue Aubergerie, http://restaurant-izba.com. Serving organic vegetarian cuisine (with a few vegan and gluten-free options thrown in for good measure), this humble restaurant is a rare gem amid Périgueux's meat-heavy dining options. Choices are limited but change weekly and everything on the menu is homemade, seasonal and locally sourced. A highlight is the desserts, which are often as surprising as they are delicious, like the dairy-free crème brûlée made with silken tofu. €

DRINKING SEE MAP PAGE 54

★ **Le Chai Bordin** 8 rue de la Sagesse, http://lechaibordin.com. Ostensibly a shop, *Le Chai Bordin* is actually a delightful little wine bar that makes for a terrific place to linger for an hour or two. Some six hundred varieties of both French and foreign wines are available, many of these by the glass.

The Silver Owl 4 rue Saint-Front, http://the-silver-owl-perigueux.eatbu.com. A seductive-looking cocktail bar with dim lighting and a seemingly endless menu, though the owl-themed decor seems a little kitsch in its sophisticated environs. Warm service, knowledgeable staff, and rib-sticking pub-grub-style food to soak up the excesses.

THEATRE AND CINEMA

CGR Cinema Place Francheville, http://cgrcinemas.fr/perigueux. The multiscreen CGR Cinema is the place to catch a Hollywood blockbuster as well as some art-house films, screened in the original language.

Théâtre Odyssée (NTP) 1 allée d'Aquitaine, http://odyssee-perigueux.fr. Cultural centre which puts on a varied programme of theatre, dance, concerts and variety shows.

SHOPPING SEE MAP PAGE 54

Boukie's Bookshop 32 rue Taillefer, http://boukiesbookshop.com. English-language bookshop with a café (which also serves wine and cocktails), which hosts regular events from live music to knitting workshops and English conversation exchanges.

La Grange du Périgord 10 rue Limogeanne, 05 53 53 31 72. Vaulted delicatessen selling local produce, including wine, truffles and foie gras.

Librairie Marbot 15 bd Michel-Montaigne, 05 53 06 45 20. Capacious bookshop which stocks a few English-language novels.

DIRECTORY

Hospital Central Hospitalier, 80 av Georges-Pompidou (05 53 45 25 25, http://ch-perigueux.fr), to the north of the centre off bd Michel-Montaigne.

Police Commissariat de Police, rue du 4-Septembre (05 53 06 44 44, http://masecurite.interieur.gouv.fr); Police Municipale, 2A cours Fénelon (05 53 08 49 33).

Post office The central post office is at rue du 4-Septembre.

Swimming pool Aquacap (http://aquacap.agglo-perigueux.fr; currently closed for renovations, due to reopen late 2025/early 2026) at Champcevinel, northeast of the city centre, just after the main hospital, is Périgueux's watersports centre, with space for serious swimmers as well as slides, aquagym, swimming for babies, hot tub, sauna and hamam.

Brantôme

Thirty kilometres north of Périgueux, the beautiful town of **BRANTÔME** is often described in tourist literature as the "Venice of Périgord". Of course, it's nothing of the sort, though the river walks and the waterside, along with a Benedictine **abbey** and some **troglodyte caves**, certainly help to make it one of the more attractive towns in a region blessed with an overabundance of pretty competitors.

Handsomely located on an almost circular island, which was created around a thousand years ago when local monks dug a mill-stream across a tight meander of the Dronne, Brantôme's **old centre** is seemingly tethered to the surrounding bank by its bridges and is surrounded by leafy gardens and parks such as the waterfront **Jardin Public**, from which you can take in the lively waterborne **jousting competitions** staged on Friday evenings (from 9pm) in July and August. All this scenic beauty attracts masses of tourists, and even though a modern bypass takes the worst of the traffic, in summer it's still a bottleneck along the main road, **rue Gambetta**, which cuts north across the island to place de Gaulle on the far bank of the Dronne. The modern bridge directly in front of the abbey leads into **rue Puyjoli de Meyjounissas**, Brantôme's main shopping street, where you'll find a variety of attractive **shops**, while the **café-bars** on place du Marché are a popular spot for a drink. A good day to visit is Friday, when the waterfront and surrounding streets are given over to the weekly **market**, which has been doing a roaring trade for some 450 years. Between December and March, the stalls are augmented with truffles, foie gras and walnuts. It's also worth coming here to take to the river: Brantôme is one of the most popular places in the region to hop in a **canoe** or **kayak** for a couple of hours (see page 60). The Dronne is especially pretty here, with its narrow width and overhanging trees, and at times it can feel like you're paddling through an Amazonian rainforest.

Abbaye St-Pierre-de-Brantôme
Bd de Charlemagne

Brantôme owes its existence to some rock-shelters – where the first hermits set up home around the fifth century – and a **spring**, whose waters are said to be able to cure sick children and treat infertility. The spring is now behind the church and convent buildings of the **Abbaye St-Pierre-de-Brantôme**, standing on the river's far north bank. The first church was built under the cliffs here sometime before 817 – according to local tradition, it was Charlemagne (742–814) who founded the abbey with the endowment of St Sicaire's relic, one of the infants massacred by Herod. It had a rocky start, but by its twelfth-century heyday the abbey supported 24 parishes and had spawned a thriving town. Nevertheless, things started going downhill again with the Hundred Years' War and, after being rebuilt on several occasions, the abbey was finally abandoned after the Revolution. The present buildings, which date from the seventeenth century but were heavily restored two hundred years later, house the **Hôtel de Ville**, whose staring, serried windows still hint at ascetic institutional life.

The abbey **church** recalls some of this history. The death of St Sicaire is the subject of a stained-glass window behind the altar, while bas-reliefs to either side depict the Massacre of the Innocents and Charlemagne offering Sicaire's relic to the church.

Grottes de l'Abbaye de Brantôme and the Musée Desmoulin
Bd de Charlemagne • Charge

After a quick look at the palm-frond vaulting in the chapterhouse, adjacent to the Benedictine Abbey, head to the **Grottes de l'Abbaye de Brantôme**. At the time of writing, the caves were closed for security reasons, following rockfalls and fallen trees, but are due to reopen in 2025. Despite being used as a quarry over the years, there's still considerable evidence of the monks' earlier troglodytic existence here. The most interesting of the caves contains a large, rather crude **sculpture** of the Last Judgement, believed to date from the fifteenth century, in the aftermath of the Hundred Years' War. Look out, too, for the *pigeonniers*, identifiable by several rows of niches carved into the rock face; not only were pigeons a valuable source of meat, but their droppings were traded as fertilizer.

ACTIVITIES IN BRANTÔME

In summer, **boat trips** around Brantôme's island depart from beside the town's old bridge in the Jardin Public. From Brantôme you can also embark on a **canoe** or **kayak** expedition, from a full-or half-day paddle downriver to a spin around the town's waterways for an hour or so. Either way, reservations are recommended in high season: try Allo Canoës, on the road to Bourdeilles (http://allocanoes24.com) or Brantôme Canoë, just out of the centre on the road east to Thiviers (http://brantomecanoe.com); both rent canoes and kayaks and are open from April to October or thereabouts, depending upon the weather. Brantôme Canoë also rents stand-up paddleboards.

The surrounding area is also a good bet for **cycling**. Bikes can be rented from L'Hermitage in Saint-Julien-de-Bourdeilles (http://gitehermitageperigord.fr), 4km west of Brantôme, though they can deliver bikes (extra charge).

In the same complex as the caves, the **Musée Desmoulin** is dedicated to the eponymous illustrator and painter. Much of Desmoulin's work was heavily influenced by spiritualism, hence his well-known (if slightly spooky) medium drawings, many of which are on display here – typically pencil or charcoal portraits of women, or more specifically, women's faces. The artist later went on to paint more orthodox impressionist works, in particular, landscapes.

ARRIVAL AND INFORMATION BRANTÔME

By bus Buses on the Périgueux–Angoulême route, timed to connect with TGV trains in Angoulême, stop on the Champs de Foire, at the south end of rue Gambetta.
Destinations Angoulême (1hr); Périgueux (35min).
Tourist office Église Notre-Dame, 2 rue Puyjoli (April & May daily 10am–1pm & 2–6pm; June & Sept daily 10am–6pm; July & Aug daily 10am–6.30pm; mid-Feb to March & Oct–Dec Mon & Wed–Sun 10am–noon & 2–5pm; 05 53 05 80 63, http://perigord-dronne-belle.fr). Family-friendly guided tours of the town can be organized through the tourist office; reserve in advance.

ACCOMMODATION

Camping Peyrelevade Av André-Maurois, http://camping-dordogne.net. Shady and sunny site just 1km east of town beside the River Dronne, with private beach, fishing and heated swimming pool. Children's playground, shop, snack bar and campervan emptying facilities, as well as chalets for rent. €

Camping Puynadal 186 Imp. De Puy Nadal, http://camping-puynadal.com. Small, family-run site offering around thirty pitches, but it's well equipped with bar, restaurant, children's playground, sports facilities and swimming pool, plus chalets to rent. Closed Sept–April. €

Charbonnel 57 rue Gambetta, http://hotelrestaurantcharbonnel.com. One of Brantôme's most popular hotels, in a superb location by the Pont des Barris, offering quality rooms decked out in lots of pretty florals combined with fine wood-carved furnishings. The more expensive rooms have river views. €€

Coligny 8 place Charles-de-Gaulle, http://hotel-coligny.fr. This friendly hotel is the cheapest option in Brantôme, with eight good-sized, a/c rooms painted in strong violet and mauve colours and with marshmallow-puffy sofas and wooden floorboards. Some rooms have partial river views. Downstairs is an inexpensive and popular restaurant. €

Le Jardin des Chouchoux 37 rue Pierre de Mareuil, http://lejardindeschouchouxbrantome.fr. Seven rooms, all unique in style, in a renovated barn. There's a courtyard garden, an outdoor swimming pool and a great restaurant serving local produce and dishes, with plenty of outdoor seating. The well-travelled hosts are extremely obliging. €€

Le Moulin de l'Abbaye 1 rue de Bourdeilles, http://moulinabbaye.com. If you're feeling self-indulgent, treat yourself to a night of unbridled luxury in this beautiful old mill to the west of the abbey. Twenty rooms are spread between three buildings, though there's little to distinguish between them in terms of comfort offered. Sumptuous, but perhaps a little overpriced. €€

Villa Medicis 17 Avenue Dr Devillard, http://medicisvilla.com. Pint-sized B&B with just three rooms in a historic manor house, 300m from the centre of town. The rooms are positively opulent, as is the breakfast spread. Great value for money. €

EATING AND DRINKING

★ **Charbonnel** 57 rue Gambetta, http://hotelrestaurantcharbonnel.com. The restaurant of the *Charbonnel* hotel is in the gourmet class, but still has good value *menus*; expect sumptuous dishes like pigeon in smoked milk. The elegant

dining room looks fantastic, as does the adjacent stone terrace – and the views across the water are even better. €€
Cô 'Thé-Café Salon de Thé 30 rue Victor-Hugo, 05 53 06 93 17. With a shady rear courtyard lined with pot plants and guarded by a soft-toy farmer, this little tea shop is a fun place to relax and recharge with one of its huge range of teas as well as various coffees, milkshakes, juices and snacks. €
Côté Rivière 13 Bd Colingy, http://cote-rivier-brantome.eatbu.com. With a dining room overlooking the River Dronne, there are few places with more enviable views. Plenty of meat and fish options; vegetarians have a thin selection. €€

SHOPPING

Oscar Simonin Souffleur de Verre 6 bd Charlemagne, http://oscarsimonin.com. Son of the famous glassblower Éric Simonin, Oscar has followed in his father's footsteps. Expect to part with over two hundred euros for one of his stunning glass jellyfish or mushrooms, though there are also some far less expensive options.

The lower Dronne valley

The country west of Brantôme and along the **River Dronne** remains largely undisturbed. It's tranquil, very beautiful and restoring, best savoured at a gentle pace, perhaps by bike or, even better, by canoe along the river. Delightful **Bourdeilles**, the first real settlement downstream from Brantôme, was the seat of one of Périgord's four baronies, as its great tower testifies, while the Renaissance château next door contains a marvellous collection of furniture. From the foot of the castle, the Dronne meanders through water-meadows to one of the Dordogne's most famous market towns, **Ribérac**. Though Ribérac itself holds little else of interest, it makes an agreeable base from which to visit a crop of Romanesque churches scattered in the countryside around. **Aubeterre-sur-Dronne**, with another extraordinary troglodyte church and a splendid position, represents the final stop along the river.

Bourdeilles

BOURDEILLES, 16km southwest of Brantôme via the pretty D106, is at its best when approached for the first time by canoe. Many visitors only come here on a day-trip from Brantôme, but this sleepy backwater, clustered round its **château** on a rocky spur above the river, is also a good option for an overnight stay, with some enticing accommodation and eating options; the river around Bourdeilles offers some delightful **canoeing** and **kayaking** (see page 62), too.

Château de Bourdeilles
Place de la Halle • Charge • www.chateau-bourdeilles.fr

The **Château de Bourdeilles** essentially comprises two buildings, the first of which is a thirteenth-century **fortress**. Entered via a heavily cobbled yard, it consists of a now empty banqueting hall – though the two enormous, unadorned fireplaces are worth a peek – and a sturdy octagonal **keep**, the top of which offers lovely views over the town and river below.

The other building, and the main reason for visiting, is the sombre-looking **Renaissance château** begun by the lady of the house, Jacquette de Montbrun, wife of André de Bourdeilles, as a piece of unsuccessful favour-currying with Catherine de Médici – unsuccessful because, though she passed through the area, Catherine never came to stay and so the château remained unfinished. The Renaissance residence is now home to an exceptional collection of **furniture** and religious statuary. Among the more notable pieces are some splendid Spanish dowry chests; the gilded bedroom suite of a former Yugoslav king; and a sixteenth-century Rhenish *Entombment* whose life-sized **statues** embody the very image of the serious, self-satisfied medieval burgher. The showpiece room, however, is the overly elaborate **salon doré** (the room Catherine de Médici was supposed to sleep in), which has retained its original decor, notably a fine oak-panelled wainscot comprising over sixty painted panels depicting the various

> **BOATING WITH DAMSELFLIES**
>
> Safety precautions mean that children under 5 aren't allowed on the canoes and kayaks available for rent throughout the Dordogne and Lot, but there is an alternative for kids who desperately want to glide down the rivers on a boat. The Maison de la Dronne, 14km southwest of Bourdeilles along the D106 in the village of Montagrier, offers river trips open to all ages aboard silent little **electric paddle boats**, which seat up to four. An hour's motoring will take you up a jungly, narrow river channel where masses of damselflies dance and herons perch like statues on the riverbanks, and there's a deeper part where you can stop for a swim. You can either go it alone or with an experienced nature guide.

properties owned by the Bourdeilles family, and the coffered ceiling bearing a riot of paintings, from flowers and insects to sphinxes.

Throughout summer, the château offers **children's activities** such as calligraphy and coin-making; book ahead.

INFORMATION AND ACTIVITIES — BOURDEILLES

Tourist office Place de la Mairie (June 15–30 & Sept 1–15 daily 10am–noon & 2–5pm; July & Aug daily 10am–noon & 2–6pm; 05 53 05 62 43, http://perigord-dronne-belle.fr).

Canoe & kayak rental Canoës Bourdeilles Loisirs (http://canoesbourdeilleloisirs.fr), by the bridge, offers an array of different routes that range from a gentle 1hr downstream paddle back to Bourdeilles (you'll be driven upstream to the starting point) to a full-day trip from Brantôme.

ACCOMMODATION AND EATING

★ **l'Ambroisie** Grand Rue, 06 64 89 82 73. At the top of the hill leading into the village, this charming *chambre d'hôte* is a place for idle living. Its four rooms (one of which sleeps four) have high ceilings with eighteenth-century wooden beams and elegant furnishings. Add to all this a chatty lady owner, big breakfasts made using local market produce (included in the price) and a little hidden garden and you get a sure-fire winner. €€

Hostellerie le Donjon Place de la Halle, 05 53 04 07 50. A sweet little family-run residence, directly opposite the tourist office, offering seven modestly sized rooms fitted out in nicely carved wooden furnishings. Whether you're staying here or not, the courtyard restaurant to the rear of the hotel is a top place to eat, with a menu that's heavily skewed towards North African influences, from Moroccan chicken with herbs to duck tagine. The courtyard really comes alive on Thursday evenings throughout the summer, when there's free live music, either blues, jazz or folk. Breakfast included. €

Hostellerie les Griffons Grand Rue, http://griffons.fr. About 200m down from *Le Donjon*, the more upmarket *Griffons* occupies a fabulously picturesque spot in a sixteenth-century house beside the humpback bridge. The ten rooms are plushly carpeted in anthracite grey, which looks great set against the partially exposed brickwork and occasional stone fireplace; all have a view of the river, though some are better than others. A small, kidney-shaped pool enclosed within a flowery walled garden rounds things off beautifully. €€

Moulin du Pont Route de Grand Brassac, Lisle, www.moulin-du-pont.com. If you don't fancy eating in Bourdeilles, head 8km downstream to the *Moulin du Pont*, near the village of Lisle, and grab a seat on a terrace with the river on one side and the restaurant's trout ponds on the other. Three-course *menus* feature duck, walnuts, truffles and, of course, trout. There are also three *gîtes* on site. €€

Ribérac and around

Surrounded by an intimate, hilly countryside of woods, hay meadows and drowsy hilltop villages, **RIBÉRAC**, 30km downstream from Bourdeilles, is a pleasant if unremarkable town whose greatest claim to fame is its Friday **market**, bringing in producers and wholesalers from all around. The town lies on the south bank of the Dronne: its main street starts in the south as rue Jean Moulin, runs through the central **place Nationale** and then continues northwards as rue du 26 Mars 1944. From place Nationale, rue Gambetta heads east to **place Général-de-Gaulle** and the vast market square beyond.

There's nothing really in the way of sights, but the country here is dotted with numerous **Romanesque churches** that provide a focus for leisurely wandering – the tourist office (see page 63) has a leaflet detailing these. A couple of hundred metres from Ribérac's centre on the hill to the east of town, the **Collégiale Notre-Dame** (free), now an exhibition and concert hall, makes a good place to start exploring. It's a pleasing building, with its squat tower and semi-circular apse designed on a grander scale than its country cousins, but the west end and interior have been extensively altered; if it's open, it's worth popping in to see the recently restored seventeenth- and eighteenth-century frescoes.

The Romanesque churches

Nowadays many of the **Romanesque churches** in the villages around Ribérac are kept locked, but the route described here takes in a representative sample of those that are more likely to be open – hours tend to be 9am to 6/7pm daily. The **Église St-Pierre** in the village of **FAYE**, 1km west of Ribérac on the D20, has great charm even though it's no architectural beauty: its diminutive single nave seems barely able to carry the fortress of a tower above. There's more reason to stop at **BOURG-DU-BOST**, 6km further downstream, where the significantly chunkier **Église Notre-Dame** possesses a similarly haphazard mix of architectural styles and an almost identical tower. It also harbours some very faded twelfth-century **murals**: the four Evangelists inside the dome, and the twelve Apostles around the choir.

From here the route cuts north and climbs to an undulating plateau with good views back over the Dronne's river meadows, then meanders through a string of villages. The first one to aim for is **ST-MARTIAL-VIVEYROL**, roughly 15km due north of Ribérac. Its church more resembles a castle keep; the windows are reduced to narrow slits, there's just a single, simple door at ground level and the belfry doubles as a watchtower with, behind it, a guardroom along the length of the nave big enough to hold the whole village. Looping southeast from St-Martial-Viveyrol, the **Église St-Pierre-et-St-Paul** in **GRAND-BRASSAC** is unusual in that sculptures were added over its north door. They show Christ in majesty flanked by St Peter and St Paul above a frieze of the Adoration with traces of earlier paintwork.

The last of the Romanesque churches, **St-Pierre-ès-Liens**, is also one of the most prettily sited. It lies in wooded country 6km south of Ribérac and is best approached from the west with the roofs of **SIORAC-DE-RIBÉRAC** clustered behind. From the hastily erected rubble walls it's easy to see where, in the fourteenth century, the nave was raised a couple of metres and a guard tower added at the west end. Again, there are almost no windows, and the walls are up to 3m thick – which explains why the nave is so surprisingly narrow.

ARRIVAL AND INFORMATION — RIBÉRAC

By bus Buses for Périgueux and Angoulême stop on place Debonnière, a few paces north of the tourist office.
Destinations Angoulême (1hr); Périgueux (1hr).
Tourist office Inside the Palais de Justice on place Général-de-Gaulle (July & Aug daily 9.30am–12.30pm & 2–7pm, Sept–June Mon–Fri 10am–12.30pm & 2–5pm, Sat 9.30am–12.30pm; 05 53 90 03 10, http:// perigordriberacois.fr). The office doubles as a ticket office for SNCF, and in July and August it organizes guided walks and farm visits.
Canoe rental Beside the entrance to Camping de la Dronne, Canoës Ribérac (mid-June to mid-Sept; 06 77 30 89 63, http:// daviddessaigne.wixsite.com) rents out canoes and pedal-boats, and also organizes guided day-trips along the Dronne.

ACCOMMODATION

Camping de la Dronne Rte d'Angoulême, 06 41 71 99 61. Inexpensive, mid-sized but quite basic site just across the Dronne on the Angoulême road, with reasonable facilities, including shower blocks, laundry and play area. €
Chambres Florence 5 place Général-de-Gaulle, http:// chambres-florence.com. In a spacious and elegant townhouse just across the square from the tourist office, this enthusiastically run chambre d'hôte has two rooms and a suite variously accommodating exposed stone walls, lovingly polished parquet floors and roll-top baths, plus there's a gorgeous conservatory for breakfast and a small pool. Elsewhere, the boldly painted walls clearly take their cue from the in-house art gallery. Breakfast included. €
Rev'Hôtel Rte de Périgueux, http://rev-hotel.fr. Some 1km east of town, this single-storey, two-star hotel won't win any awards for class, but it does offer inexpensive, convenient and comfortable rooms (two wheelchair accessible) and helpful service. Triples and quads available, too. €

EATING AND DRINKING

Café des Colonnes 17 place Général-de-Gaulle, 05 53 90 01 39. You can't beat sitting under the trees with a coffee on the terrace of this venerable café, which has been keeping locals fuelled since 1832 – alternatively, head inside to park yourself on one of the leather seats and admire the old posters and photos dotted around the walls. The food is classic bistro fare with well-priced mains. €

L'Escapade Gourmande 2b av de Verdun, 05 24 14 11 62. With decor that could be seen as quaint or threatening depending on your take (think pitchforks on the whitewashed walls and heavy wooden beams), it's nonetheless one of the best options in Ribérac. Meals are good value and hearty, but won't necessarily stick in your memory. €

Aubeterre-sur-Dronne

Hanging on a steep hillside above the river, some 30km west of Ribérac (and technically just inside the Charente region rather than the Dordogne), **AUBETERRE-SUR-DRONNE** is a beautiful town of steep, cobbled streets, its ancient galleried and turreted houses overlooking the lazy River Dronne. The town's attractions – including two interesting churches – haven't gone unnoticed, however, and the place can be absolutely packed to the gills with visitors in summer. For a cooling break, head down the hill to the river where you will find a man-made **beach** with swimming area.

Église Souterraine Saint-Jean

Rue St-Jean • Charge • http://aubeterresurdronne.com

Aubeterre-sur-Dronne's principal curiosity is the cavernous **Église Souterraine Saint-Jean**, in the lower town northeast of the village's lime-shaded central square, **place Trarieux**. Carved out of the soft rock by twelfth-century Benedictine monks, it's the largest subterranean church in Europe – it took at least a century to excavate the astonishing 20m-high chamber and gallery above. Accessed via some eighty steps, the gallery offers the best views over the capacious baptismal font, designed for total immersion, and the two-tiered, hexagonal structure, possibly a reliquary, cut from a single piece of rock – its precise arches seem strangely out of place against the rough walls. The side-chapels are riddled with eerie, rock-hewn tombs, while a now blocked-off tunnel connects the gallery with the château on the bluff overhead. The chilly crypt, meanwhile, was discovered by chance after a lorry accidentally demolished this part of the square in 1961.

Église St-Jacques

On the southwestern hillside, the upper town of Aubeterre-sur-Dronne consists of a single street of houses culminating in the **Église St-Jacques**, where only the beautiful, sculpted west facade remains of the original twelfth-century church. The great tiered and decorated arch around the main door is lovely, but don't overlook the frieze of zodiacal signs on the smaller arch to the left: Taurus, Aries and Pisces are easy enough to recognize, then come Capricorn, Aquarius and Sagittarius. The other half of the frieze is missing. The remainder of the exterior is rather humble by comparison. Inside, the cold, but light-coloured brickwork is devoid of ornamentation, though the smooth circular arches separating the nave and aisles, and timber-beamed ceiling, are worth a look.

ARRIVAL AND INFORMATION — AUBETERRE-SUR-DRONNE

By train There's no train station at Aubeterre-sur-Dronne, but Chalais, which is on the Angoulême–Bordeaux train line, is 12km to the west; call Chalais-Taxi on 05 45 98 18 53 if you need a taxi into Aubeterre.
Tourist office Facing the town's main car park on place du Champ de Foire (Jan–June & Sept–Dec Mon–Sat 9.30am– 12.30pm & 2–6pm; July & Aug daily 9.30am–1pm & 2–6.30pm; 05 45 98 57 18, http://sudcharentetourisme.fr).
Canoe hire On weekends in May and June and daily in July and August, there's canoe rental down by the bridge (http://canoe-aubeterre.com).

ACCOMMODATION AND EATING

Camping Aubeterre-Sur-Dronne Rte de Ribérac, http://camping-aubeterre-sur-dronne.fr. Just across the

bridge, and adjacent to the river, this three-star site has some good amenities; snack bar and grill, a kids' play area, and a small sandy beach for volleyball and sunbathing. Mobile homes for rent, too. €
Crêperie de la Source 4 rue St-Jean, 05 45 98 61 78. On the corner of the main town square, this endearing little crêperie has fab views down onto the plains far below, and an inexpensive three-course *menu* consisting of a melon or charcuterie starter, a savoury *galette* for the main and a crêpe or other dessert to finish up. €
Du Périgord Quartier Plaisance, http://hotelduperigord.fr. An appealing low-rise building down by the bridge on the Ribérac road, the *Périgord* offers bright (though not particularly inspiring) rooms, with the occasional floral wallpaper and wicker furniture, and there's a pool, hot tub and sauna for good measure. The in-house restaurant hosts occasional cookery courses. €
Grange Bleuet 1 Square Gaillardon, http://grangebleuet.com. Blue shuttered windows masked by abundant foliage, these *chambres d'hôtes* couldn't look any more quintessentially French. The rooms are old-fashioned but pretty, there's a generous breakfast, and the owners are friendly and hands-on. €€

La Double

South of the Dronne valley the landscape and atmosphere change dramatically as you enter the region known as **La Double**. This high, undulating plateau is strewn with lakes and brooding **forests** of oak, chestnut and pine, interspersed with pockets of vines, scattered farmhouses and an abbey at **Échourgnac**. The larger lakes, such as the **Étang de la Jemaye**, have been developed for tourism, and in summer the Double is a popular destination for walkers, cyclists and nature lovers; the best place to pick up information is Ribérac tourist office (see page 63).

GETTING AROUND   **LA DOUBLE**

While there is no public transport in the Double itself, several services on the Périgueux to Bordeaux train line stop daily at Neuvic, to the east of the region.

Échourgnac and around

Until the late nineteenth century, when Napoléon III decreed that the region should be drained and planted with maritime pines in similar fashion to the great Landes forest further south, La Double was largely uninhabited thanks to its poor soils and malarial marshes. The drainage work was partly carried out by Trappist monks who arrived from Port-Salut in 1868. They settled near the only village of any size, **ÉCHOURGNAC**, plumb in the middle of the plateau and nearly 20km southwest of Ribérac, where they founded the **abbey** which still dominates the village today.

Abbaye Notre-Dame de Bonne-Espérance
La Trappe • http://abbaye-echourgnac.org

Since 1923 the walled **Abbaye Notre-Dame de Bonne-Espérance** has sheltered a small community of Cistercian sisters – these days numbering about thirty, some under a vow of silence – who not only continued in the monks' spiritual footsteps but also in their role as local cheesemakers. But the enterprising and energetic sisters didn't stop there. In their well-stocked **shop** opposite the church entrance, you'll find the original Le Trappe Échourgnac, a firm, orange-crusted cheese with a smoky flavour, and a newer version laced with walnut liqueur, as well as jams, pâté, jellied sweets and handicrafts from missions around the world; you can also watch a video about the convent here. You can peek inside the abbey's **church**, which was given a very modern renovation in 2016.

Étang de la Jemaye

The large, scythe-shaped and forest-fringed **Étang de la Jemaye**, a few kilometres to the northeast of Échourgnac, offers lots of summertime fun, with its beaches and swimming, watersports, children's playgrounds, fishing and forest walks.

EATING AND DRINKING

ÉCHOURGNAC

Auberge de la Double Échourgnac, 05 53 80 06 65. To fortify yourself before setting off to explore the area, you can eat at this little village inn which serves good-value weekday lunches and a fixed price *menu* (Fri & Sat eves & Sun lunchtime). €

Ferme du Parcot

Free • http://parcot.org

Some 5km east of Abbaye de Notre-Dame de Bonne-Espérance, on the D41 from Échourgnac, the **Ferme du Parcot** has been preserved as a typical example of the architecture of La Double. With walls of mud and straw on latticed timber frames, protected by a limestone plaster, these farm buildings are quite unlike the sturdy stone houses found elsewhere in the Dordogne. They date from 1841 and, from the grandeur of the barn, it seems the farmer was relatively affluent. In true rural style, however, the house itself, which was inhabited up to 1990, consists of just two very spartan rooms containing a few bits and pieces of furniture and old implements. The farm also marks the start of a gentle **nature trail** (2.5km; accessible all year) through the fields and forest to a fishing lake.

The Northern Périgord Vert

North of Brantôme lies a peaceful, little-populated region with one or two classic tourist attractions (including the superb **Grotte de Villars**), but as much as anything this area is about exploring quiet lanes and picnicking in the countryside. **St-Jean-de-Côle**, a tiny sun-soaked village dominated by its château, makes a good base for exploring nearby attractions such as the ruined Cistercian **Abbaye de Boschaud** and the French Renaissance **Château de Puyguilhem**, while quiet **Thiviers** is another good bet for an overnight stay.

St-Jean-de-Côle

Twenty kilometres northeast of Brantôme, **ST-JEAN-DE-CÔLE** ranks as one of the loveliest villages in the Périgord Vert, and with a couple of restaurants, it makes a good lunchtime stop. Tiny and very picturesque without being twee, St-Jean's unusually open, sandy square is dominated by the charmingly ill-proportioned **Église St-Jean-Baptiste**, dating from the late eleventh century. The view as you approach is harmonious enough – layers of tiled roofs from the low, square market hall to the steeply pitched belfry – but on entering the single, lofty bay it becomes apparent that the nave was never completed, due to a lack of funds. Beside the church stands the rugged-looking **Château de la Marthonie** (no public access), which dates from the twelfth century, but has since acquired various additions in a pleasingly organic fashion. Apart from a huddle of houses round the square, the rest of the village consists

> **LA VOIE VERTE**
>
> One of the lesser-known walking and cycling routes in the region is **La Voie Verte** ("Green Way"), an 18km footpath and cycleway that follows a disused train line from Thiviers into the heart of the Périgord Vert. On a warm summer's day it's a delightful outing, taking in pretty villages like St-Jean-de-Côle and Milhac-de-Nontron, as well as rivers and viaducts, before winding up at Saint-Pardoux-la-Rivière. Local tourist offices can provide a handout illustrating the route and can organize bike rental (regular or electric). Call in advance. Trailer-buggies and child seats are available too.

of a line of pastel-plastered cottages stretching west to a humpbacked bridge over the River Côle and the inevitable water mill. The whole ensemble makes a perfect backdrop for the Floralies **flower festival**, held on the second weekend in May.

INFORMATION — ST-JEAN-DE-CÔLE

Tourist office 19 rue du Château (mid-June to mid-Sept daily 10am–1pm & 2–6.30pm; mid-Sept to Oct & March to mid-June Wed–Sun 10am–1pm & 2–6pm; Nov–Feb Mon–Fri same times; 05 53 62 14 15, http://ville-saint-jean-de-cole.fr). The office runs guided tours of the village (in French) daily at 11am in July and August (charge) or you can go it alone with a multi-language audioguide.

ACCOMMODATION, EATING AND DRINKING

★ **Parenthèses Imaginaires** Fontaine de Cardissou, http://parentheses-imaginaires.com. A couple of kilometres outside the quiet village of Milhac-de-Nontron, this is a small, shady and fun glamping site. Accommodation is in a series of pre-erected tents (sleeping 2–4) that are more wooden chalet than canvas, equipped with beds and kitchenettes. The pricier ones are built right beside a carp-filled lake, and you can jump straight from your private terrace into the water. With a nature cabin where children are encouraged to make art from pinecones, shells and driftwood, as well as a shallow swimming pool and crazy golf, this is one of the best sites around for families. One-week minimum stay in high season. Closed Nov–March. €

La Perla Café Place de l'Église, 05 53 52 38 11. Take a seat at this welcoming outdoor café overlooking the church and fill up with one of their light lunches, for example duck salad or flambéed prawns, or just kick back with a coffee. €

Le St Jean Le Bourg, http://le-stjean.fr. The menu is almost as extensive as its generous terrace, where patrons feast on classic local dishes such as *magret de canard* and foie gras with out-of-the-ordinary touches (such as mango compote). €€

Le Temps des Mets 1 place du Vieux Pont, 09 67 78 25 72. With big, puffy paper lampshades hanging from the branches of trees and lime-green chairs on a lawn surrounded by hot pink flowers, Le Temps des Mets is a stylish place to eat treats such as roasted cod with a seasonal veg sauce or duck kebab with goats' cheese cream. €€

Château de Puyguilhem

Charge • http://chateau-puyguilhem.fr

About 10km west of St-Jean, just outside the attractive village of **VILLARS**, the **Château de Puyguilhem** is a perfect example of early French Renaissance architecture. It was erected at the beginning of the sixteenth century by the La Marthonie family of St-Jean-de-Côle on the site of an earlier and more military fortress. The lake that once filled the foreground has long gone, but the château still makes an enchanting prospect, with its steep roofs, stone balustrades, mullion windows, carved chimney stacks and an assortment of round and octagonal towers reminiscent of contemporaneous Loire châteaux. Though the **interior** suffered more from neglect and pillaging, it too has been beautifully restored and contains some noteworthy pieces of furniture and Aubusson tapestries; the most impressive of the latter are located in the Great Hall, one tapestry depicting a rhinoceros, and another, a lion fighting a leopard.

Its most remarkable features, however, are two magnificent fireplaces: the first, in the guardroom, depicts three Greek soldiers, while upstairs in the banqueting hall the theme is continued with six of the twelve Labours of Hercules. Both are heavily restored, but no less remarkable for that. The sculptors also went to work on the entrance hall and main staircase, leaving a wealth of oak, vine and acanthus leaves, thistles, fleur-de-lis and a few salamanders for good measure. Right at the top, it was the turn of the master carpenters, whose superb hull-shaped roof timbers have lasted five hundred years. Once done in the château, peek at the **pigeonnier** among the trees to the rear of the castle; it's a fine example of a French medieval pigeon house, this one consisting of hundreds of *boulins* (pigeon holes), each typically lodged a pair of birds.

ACCOMMODATION AND EATING — VILLARS

Le Petit Château de Villars Rue du Moulin, http://chateaudevillars.com. This glamorous, American-owned grand residence dating back to 1862 sits in five hectares of parkland on the southern fringe of Villars. With five regal rooms, a classy dark wood panelled bar and an excellent restaurant serving local classics as well as more international dishes, from curries to southern US-style barbeque, it offers a taste of rather royal living. €€

Abbaye de Boschaud

Unrestricted access • Free

The ruined Cistercian **Abbaye de Boschaud**, 3km from Villars in the next valley south of the Château de Puyguilhem, merits a quick visit while you're in the area. Standing in the middle of a field, it's reached by a lane not much bigger than a farm track. Though the pure, stark lines of the twelfth-century architecture hold a certain appeal, the abbey's real charm rests in the fact that it is – for once – unfenced and unpampered, and you can explore its tumbledown walls and lifeless shell at will.

Grotte de Villars

Charge • http://grotte-villars.com

In 1953 speleologists discovered an extensive cave system in the hills 3km north of Villars, now known as the **Grotte de Villars**. To date, around 13km of the system has been explored, and some 600m of caves are open to the public via a guided tour. Villars is unusual in that it boasts a combination of both concretions and paintings. As impressive as these few paintings are – notably of horses and a still-unexplained scene of a man and bison – the main reason for coming here is the variety of **stalagmites** and, in particular, **stalactites**. Some are almost pure white and as fine as needles, others ochre-yellow or tainted red from the soil, and there are also cascades, semicircular basins and hanging curtains of semi-translucent calcium carbonate. The final cave contains the **paintings**, dating from 17,000 years ago, though they're only just discernible under the thick layer of calcite.

Look out, too, for the claw marks further back from the entrance, where generations of tiny bear cubs have left their imprints – there are a handful of cave-bear bones, including part of a jaw, on display near the reception area. There's a good chance, too, that you'll encounter one of the many resident pipistrelle bats as they swoop around the caves.

The **parkland** surrounding the cave holds models of prehistoric wildlife and people alongside information panels about life on the hillside then and now; and with a variety and range of activities laid on for children, from making your own "cave painting" to spear-throwing, Villars is arguably the most family-friendly cave complex in the whole of the Dordogne.

Thiviers

Eight kilometres east of St-Jean-de-Côle, and linked by the pleasant Voie Verte cycle route (see page 66), the small market town of **THIVIERS** sits on the main road and rail links between Périgueux, 40km to the south, and Limoges. The peaceful old centre comprises a clutch of pretty, aged houses round the church and along pedestrianized rue de la Tour. Thiviers is at its most lovely during the Saturday **market**, when the streets present a lesson in local agriculture: walnuts, apples, Limousin beef, pork, duck and goose and all manner of associated foodstuffs. From mid-November to mid-March the *foies* come out in force at the *marché au gras*, some of them destined to go into the local speciality, *L'autre fois de Thiviers*, consisting of duck- or goose-liver robed in pâté.

Up until the 1920s, Thiviers was an important centre for **faïence** (tin-glazed pottery), a hundred or so pieces of which are displayed in the town hall (free). But the pretty blue-and-white faïence plays second fiddle to the town's prime concern: the history and production of **foie gras**, the subject of the small **Maison du Foie Gras** museum (charge) accessed via the tourist office (which also houses a specialist foie gras shop), though it's expensive for what it is, not particularly stimulating and doesn't provide a balanced perspective of the controversial force-feeding production process (see box), especially as there's nothing by way of English explanation.

ARRIVAL AND INFORMATION | THIVIERS

By train The *gare SNCF* is located on rue Pierre-Sémard, just a few minutes' walk north of Thiviers' centre.
Destinations Bordeaux (10 daily; 2hr); Limoges (13 daily; 45min); Périgueux (13 daily; 25min).

Tourist office 8 place du Maréchal Foch (July & Aug Mon–Fri 9.30am–1pm & 2–6pm, Sat & Sun 9.30am–12.30pm; April–June, Sept & Oct Mon–Fri 9.30am–12.30pm & 2–5.30pm, Sat 9.30am–12.30pm; Nov, Dec, Feb & March

FOIE GRAS: A CONTROVERSIAL TOPIC

You can't help but notice foie gras on restaurant menus and market tables across Dordogne, particularly in the Périgord region. Foie gras is the fattened liver of ducks or geese, which have been forcibly overfed via a long tube inserted down their throats. This process, known as 'gavage', causes the birds' livers to swell to around ten times the original size. Its production is banned in many countries, including the UK. Despite the controversy surrounding the food item, it is considered a luxury delicacy in France. It is a huge part of the country's culinary heritage: nearly eighty percent of the world's foie gras is made there, with ninety percent of producers in Dordogne. From November to March, Thiviers holds numerous Marché au Gras where stalls sell locally produced liver, pâtés and mousses, and Sarlat even hosts a three-day festival, Fest'oie, dedicated to the food item.

PÉRIGORD PRODUCERS

Foie gras is produced throughout southwest France and also in Alsace, Brittany and the Vendée. However, the yellowish-hued livers from the Périgord, where the birds are traditionally force-fed local yellow (as opposed to white) maize, and where producers jealously guard their methods of preparation, are particularly sought after. Périgord farmers now favour hybrid Mulard or Barbary ducks over the more traditional geese for a variety of reasons: they fatten more quickly, are easier to raise and force-feed, and the liver is easier to cook with. The softer goose livers, on the other hand, are said to have a more delicate flavour and smoother texture. They are also larger – 600g to 700g for an average goose liver (*foie gras d'oie*) as opposed to 500g for duck (*foie gras de canard*).

PRODUCTION

The young birds are raised outside to the age of four months, after which they are kept in the dark and forcibly fed over one kilo (2lbs; the equivalent of a bag of sugar) per day of partly cooked maize for between two and three weeks. This gavage, or force-feeding, was traditionally carried out using a funnel to tip the grain into the bird's throat and then forced down the neck by hand. Modern techniques follow the same principle but use a mechanized feeder.

TYPES OF FOIE GRAS

If you do decide you want to try foie gras, it is possible to buy fresh liver or the ready-prepared preserved version, of which there is a huge variety. The majority is de-veined, seasoned and then sterilized by cooking briefly (*mi-cuit*) before being vacuum-packed or sealed in jars or cans. On the label, it will state *foie gras entier*, consisting of one or more whole lobes; *foie gras*, which is composed of smaller pieces; or *bloc de foie gras*, made up of reconstituted liver (sometimes *avec morceaux*, visible pieces of lobe) pressed together. Then there are all sorts of *mousses*, *parfaits*, *pâtés* and so forth. It's said to be best to buy from small family concerns, either direct from the farm – local tourist offices can advise – or from the region's many *marchés au gras*, though this doesn't change the nature of the production process.

Tues–Fri 9.30am–12.20pm & 2–5.30pm, Mon 9.30am–12.30pm; 05 53 55 12 50, http://perigord-limousin-tourisme.com), also known as La Maison du Foie Gras on account of it housing the foie gras museum.

ACCOMMODATION AND EATING

De France et de Russie 51 rue du Général Lamy, http://thiviers-hotel.com. A warm welcome is assured at this ever-so-relaxing English-run hotel, set in a former eighteenth-century coaching inn and popular with pilgrims travelling the route to Santiago. Its rooms retain a pleasingly timeworn ambience, though the whole place is run through with the owner's personal, and occasionally quirky, touch – you can even play chess in the reception area or tinkle on the ivories in the lounge. In the building to the rear, two rooms have been specially adapted for wheelchair users. €€

Le Repaire http://camping-le-repaire.fr. A well-run three-star campsite beside an artificial lake on the D707 road towards Lanouaille, with lounge bar, pool and playground, plus chalets to rent. Closed Nov–March. €

La Sablière 25 Promenade de la Sablière, 06 14 21 02 22. Classy *chambre d'hôte* located around 1km north of town. There are four rooms, basically mini-suites (three of them sleep four): fantastically comfortable beds, fine white linen and brilliant power showers are just some of the little luxuries that await. It's a little tricky to find as there are no signs; head north along the road towards Jumilhac-le-Grand and take a left at the turning for the abattoir. €€

Jumilhac-le-Grand

In its upper reaches the Isle valley narrows down between steep, wooded banks to become a mini-ravine. One of its rocky bluffs, some 20km northeast of Thiviers, is home to the vast Château de Jumilhac, centrepiece of attractive **JUMILHAC-LE-GRAND** village. For more than two centuries Jumilhac has been closely associated with **gold**, and though the nearby mines closed in 2001, you can learn more about the history of gold here and further afield in the **Galerie de l'Or** (charge), a succinct but well-presented museum, next to the tourist office and overlooking the grassy square in front of the château. Visit in summer and you can even try your luck **panning for gold** in the River Isle (July & Aug; call the tourist office to reserve a half-day session; charge); it's not uncommon to find tiny specks, but don't expect to make your fortune.

Château de Jumilhac

Place du Château • Charge • http://chateaudejumilhac.com

While elements of the original thirteenth-century **Château de Jumilhac** remain – such as the stone-paved ground-floor rooms and the family chapel – the present structure largely owes its existence to an ironmaster, Antoine Chapelle, later count of Jumilhac, who made his fortune manufacturing arms for the future Henry IV during the Wars of Religion. The body of the château is suitably uncompromising: the hard, grey stone allowed for little decorative detail, and what windows there are mostly consist of narrow slits. But the roof is another matter, adorned with no fewer than eight different **towers**, from great grey-slate wedges to pinnacled turrets and a jaunty pepper-pot, topped off with delicate lead statues depicting the angels of justice or more mundane pigeon-shaped weathervanes.

Inside, however, austerity reigns once again. This is particularly so in the cramped, ground-floor rooms, which date back to the thirteenth century, but also extends to the medieval rooms above, of which the much-vaunted **spinner's room** provides the focus of the tour. Not so much for its architecture – it's a small vaulted chamber decorated with naive frescoes of animals and flowers – but for the story attached. The spinner in question was **Louise de Hautefort**, wife of the then count of Jumilhac, who was imprisoned here for thirty years (1618–48) for her alleged infidelity. Not one to mope, Louise took to painting the walls and spinning to occupy her time – or so it seemed. The shepherd who regularly called under her window, and from whom she bought her wool, was of course her lover in disguise, and the spindles were used to carry secret messages between them. According to one legend, the story ended in the lover being killed in a duel, while another has him retiring to a monastery. To give you some idea what all the fuss was about, there's a portrait of Louise, supposedly painted at the time of her release, defiantly holding her spindle aloft.

The two wings enclosing the courtyard were added later in the seventeenth century and are gradually being restored by the château's present owners, descendants of Antoine Chapelle, who bought it back from the state in 1927. The interior is demonstrably lighter in tone, thanks to the prevailing use of limestone – witness the handsome staircase – while the flooring is a pebble and stone mosaic encrusted in sand. The outstanding features here are two wooden fireplaces at opposing ends of the **Grand Hall**, which is otherwise dominated by paintings of various hunting scenes. Crossing the balustraded stone balcony to the opposite wing gives you superb views of the steeply sloping tree-lined square straight ahead.

The castle is opened up for **evening visits** in the summer, when the candle-lit gloom adds a suitably spooky aspect, while the beautiful and very formal flower **gardens** are well worth a look, with display panels to identify the plants.

INFORMATION — JUMILHAC-LE-GRAND

Tourist office Place du Château (April–June & Sept Mon–Fri 9.30am–12.30pm & 2–5.30pm; July & Aug Mon–Sat 9.30am–1pm & 2–6pm, Sun 9.30am–1pm; 05 53 52 55 43, http://pays-jumilhac.fr).

ACCOMMODATION

La Chatonnière www.chatonniere.com. Beside the Isle just over 1km north of Jumilhac, the three-star *La Chatonnière* campsite is a small, family-oriented affair, with extensive play spaces and a sandy river beach to keep the little ones amused. Closed mid-Sept to June. €

Excideuil

The old route between Périgueux and Limoges used to run up the Isle and Loue rivers to **EXCIDEUIL**, 17km southeast of Thiviers, where two huge medieval keeps still dominate the little market town. The **castle** was one of the region's most heavily fortified and for a while the viscounts of Limoges held court here. Following the Hundred Years' War, however, the fortress lay in ruins until relatively recently, when restoration was carried out. It is now privately owned, so you can enter only the (fairly uninteresting) precinct, but it's an impressive sight from afar, particularly if you approach from the west. From the castle, rue des Cendres leads north into the tight knot of streets concentrated around lovely **place Bugeaud**, with its stone duck fountain and the much-restored church, with its Gothic portal. This square and the nearby *halle* are the venue for a lively farmers' **market** on Thursday mornings, augmented in winter (Nov to early March) by a *marché au gras et aux truffes*, dedicated to foie gras and truffles. The tourist office can provide a leaflet outlining a walking tour of the village which, even at an easy pace, should take no more than an hour.

ARRIVAL AND INFORMATION — EXCIDEUIL

By bus Buses stop beneath the castle on place du Château. Destinations Périgueux.
Tourist office 1 place du Château, which lies on the main road through town (June–Sept Mon–Sat 10am–1pm & 2–6pm, plus July & Aug Sun 9.30am–1pm; Oct–May Thurs–Sat 10am–1pm & 2–6pm; 05 53 52 29 79, http://naturellementperigord.fr).

ACCOMMODATION AND EATING

Hostellerie du Fin Chapon Place du Château, 05 53 62 42 38. Next to the tourist office, the *Hostellerie du Fin Chapon* offers rather plain but comfortable rooms in stock *Logis* chain-style fashion. Some have views over the castle that will leave lasting memories. €

Le Patio Café 10 rue Jean Jaurès, 05 53 55 17 74. Cheerful little place with a walled patio serving coffee, home-made cakes and light lunches. €

THE BLACK DIAMONDS OF PÉRIGORD

The **black truffle** of Périgord, *tuber melanosporum*, is one of those expensive delicacies that many people find overrated. This is mainly because it's usually served in minute quantities or combined with such strong flavours that its own subtle, earthy taste and aroma are completely overwhelmed. Truffle is best appreciated if eaten in a salad, omelette or simple pastry crust.

The truffle is a **fungus** that grows entirely underground, and a fussy one at that. It prefers shallow, free-draining limestone soils rich in organic matter, a sunny position and marked seasonal differences, and requires the presence of certain species of oak, or occasionally lime or hazelnut, around the roots of which it grows. It's greedy, too, absorbing so much of the nutrients and water available that the vegetation overhead often dies. This tell-tale ring of denuded earth is just one of the clues truffle-hunters are on the lookout for. Others include small, yellow truffle-flies hovering just above the soil, and the distinct smell – which is where the pig, or generally these days the more amenable dog – comes in.

Even now the **life cycle** of the Périgord truffle – the most prized out of more than forty different varieties – is not completely understood, and attempts to cultivate them artificially have so far proved unsuccessful. What is clear is that the spores are released in the spring and mature truffles are ready for harvest between December and early March. When ripe, the skin of a Périgord truffle is a deep purple-brown or black, while the lighter-coloured flesh is flecked with fine white veins. It should be firm to the touch and give off a pleasantly earthy aroma; an overripe truffle stinks.

The principal **truffle markets** take place at Périgueux, Sorges, Sarlat and Brantôme, and at Labenque near Cahors in the Quercy, and the truffles cost extortionate amounts per kilo. In the past, however, truffles were so common that they were considered a pest by vine growers. Ironically, the fungus proved a lifesaver for many local farmers when phylloxera hit in the late nineteenth century, ushering in the truffle's "golden age". Since the 1950s, the harvest has declined dramatically for a number of reasons – deforestation and rural depopulation among others – although a revival is well underway with up to ninety hectares of truffle trees being planted each year in the Dordogne since 2000.

If you want to learn more about truffles, then head to Sorges, 17km west of Excideuil, where the **Musée de la Truffe** (charge) offers detailed explanations (in French only) of the truffle-growing process – from how the fungus forms to how to create your own truffle-oak orchard. There are also many preserved specimens for sale in the downstairs shop, which doubles as the tourist office.

Hautefort and around

Southeast of Excideuil you cross the pretty Auvézère valley and enter the limestone plateaux of the Périgord Blanc. The views are magnificent, and nowhere more so than around **HAUTEFORT** and its eponymous **château**, standing on a south-facing promontory some twenty kilometres from Excideuil and forty kilometres northeast of Périgueux. Bustling with tourists during the day, Hautefort is a peaceful backwater come evening and is an enjoyable place for an overnight stay, with swallows and cicadas providing the only background noise.

Château de Hautefort

Charge • http://chateau-hautefort.com

The **Château de Hautefort** is a stunning sight from whichever direction you approach, a magnificent example of blue-blood living on a grand scale, endowed with an elegance that's out of step with the usual rough stone fortresses of Périgord. Indeed, when the then marquis de Hautefort rebuilt it in the mid-seventeenth century, his ambition was to create a château worthy of the Loire.

The original fortress was built some time around 1000, and in the twelfth century it belonged jointly to the famous troubadour **Bertran de Born** (see page 269) and his brother Constantin, until Bertran persuaded his overlord, Henry II of England, to grant him sole ownership in 1185. The following year Constantin took his revenge and left the place in ruins – at which point Bertran went off to become a monk. The château's recent history has been no less troubled. After decades of neglect, in 1929 Hautefort was bought and meticulously restored by the rather unfortunately named Baron Henri de Bastard and his wife. Then in August 1968, just three years after the work was completed, a **fire** gutted everything except the chapel in the southeast tower. A year later the indomitable baroness – her husband having died before the fire – set about the whole task again, and master craftsmen were called in to recreate everything from the staircases to the ornate chimneypieces. There's no disguising the fact that it's all brand new, but the quality of work is superb – and if you visit in summer you might coincide with various **special events** (mainly aimed at children), from nature and art workshops to a special film-set experience; see the website for details.

The approach to the château lies across a wide esplanade, flanked by immaculate topiary gardens, and over a drawbridge to enter a stylish Renaissance **courtyard** opening to the south. The two wings end in a pair of round towers, whose great bulk is offset by grey-slate domes topped with matching pepper-pot lanterns; the southwestern tower, nearest the entrance, is the only part of the medieval château still standing. While the main building is equally symmetrical, the overall impression is one of rhythm and harmony rather than severity.

About the only furnishings saved from the fire were four sixteenth-century tapestries, now on display inside, but the real highlight is the **great hall**, a monumental room which provides the perfect setting for two huge chimneypieces. Exact copies of the originals and carved from local walnut, each took five thousand hours' work. The **chapel**, meanwhile, is worth a look for its pebble mosaic flooring, representing the family coat of arms, and the trompe l'oeil ceiling.

With open lawns and plenty of grand old trees, the undulating **park** surrounding the château also holds a formal garden and a maze.

Musée de la Médecine

Place du Marquis J-F de Hautefort • Charge • http://musee-hautefort.com

The **Musée de la Médecine** lies in the midst of an open square and is accessed via Hautefort's tourist office. It occupies part of a hospice for the poor founded in 1669 by Marquis Jacques-François de Hautefort, who also built the Château de Hautefort, as its architecture – particularly the domed central chapel – suggests. One of the ground-floor rooms presents an early-nineteenth-century ward (complete with silly-looking mannequins under the ministration of the Sisters of Charity). Here you'll find a reconstruction of a so-called *tour*, essentially a revolving cupboard in which abandoned children would be placed by mothers who could not, or did not wish to, care for their child – they would then ring the bell to inform the hospice of the new arrival; these could be found in hospices all over the region, including here at Hautefort, until their removal in 1847. As if this wasn't sobering enough, things get worse upstairs among the displays of brutal-looking medical implements through the ages (the gynaecological stuff doesn't bear thinking about), culminating in examples of dental surgeries up to 1970. There's also a section devoted to Louis Pasteur, inventor of the rabies and anthrax vaccines, among many other notable achievements. However, the absence of any English captioning ultimately renders this a rather frustrating visit if you don't read French.

ARRIVAL AND INFORMATION **HAUTEFORT**

By bus Public transport to Hautefort is almost non- existent, the only possibility being to catch a late afternoon

bus from Périgueux with the return service departing from Hautefort early the following morning.
Tourist office In the north wing of the old hospice on Place du Marquis J-F de Hautefort (Jan–March, Nov & Dec Mon–Fri 9.30am–12.30pm & 2–6pm; April, May & Oct daily 9.30am–12.30pm & 2–6pm; June–Sept daily 10am–7pm; 05 53 50 40 27, http://vezere-perigord.fr).

ACCOMMODATION AND EATING

Auberge du Parc 05 53 50 88 98, http://aubergeduparc-hautefort.fr. The *Auberge du Parc*, right under the castle walls, has five rooms, which are basic at best and rather on the dowdy side – though they're pleasingly inexpensive. The on-site restaurant has good value *menus* and all-inclusive deals are available for guests. €€

Le Camping du Coucou http://campingducoucou.com. A lakeside campsite, less than 2km to the south of Hautefort in Nailhac, with superb facilities including a grocery shop, TV lounge, playground, boulodrome and swimming pool, plus chalets to rent. Closed Sept to Easter. €

Le Troubadour 1 place Eugène le Roy, http://letroubadour-hautefort.fr. Comfort food served with flair, such as burgers and chips on the most beautiful ceramic platters. Save room for home-made cakes for dessert. €

Abbaye de Tourtoirac

Museum Free

Some 8km west of Hautefort, the village of **Tourtoirac** is best known for its caves, but you can also visit the **Abbaye de Tourtoirac**, parts of which date from the tenth century, and which houses an **archeological museum** containing weapons and tools found during the course of excavations at the site.

Grotte de Tourtoirac

Charge • http://grotte-de-tourtoirac.fr

Some 2km south of Tourtoirac village along the D5, the **Grotte de Tourtoirac** cave system was only discovered in 1995, and opened to the public in 2010. The caves were never inhabited, but contain a rich array of stalactites and stalagmites, and have the advantage of offering access to for those with limited mobility via a lift. Entrance is by guided tour only (around one hour), which are held around eight times a day. Temperatures in the cave hover around 13°C, so you might want to bring something warm.

Brive-la-Gaillarde

A major road and rail junction, **Brive-la-Gaillarde** is the nearest thing to an industrial centre for miles around. That said, its largely pedestrianized old centre, enclosed within a circular boulevard shaded by plane trees, comes as a pleasant surprise after its sprawling suburbs. The town's cultural highlights include the much-restored **Collégiale St-Martin de Brive**, the wide-ranging **Musée Labenche** and the local Resistance museum, the **Musée Edmond Michelet**, along with a handful of very smart restaurants. However, this is very much a town for locals rather than tourists.

It's thought that Brive earned its nickname **la Gaillarde** during the Hundred Years' War when, for much of the time, it was a lone French stronghold surrounded by English. Opinions are divided, but the name "la Gaillarde" (meaning strong, sprightly or bawdy) refers either to its fortifications or – the generally preferred option – the spirited, valiant nature of its people. The ramparts disappeared after the Revolution to make way for today's gardens and ring road, but the "Brivistes" themselves haven't changed, as they will happily tell you, citing past glories on the rugby field as the prime example. Brive also makes a convenient base for exploring the beautiful towns and villages around, and it's not that far to Lascaux and the upper reaches of the River Dordogne.

BRIVE-LA-GAILLARDE **PÉRIGUEUX AND THE NORTH** | 75

Collégiale St-Martin de Brive

Place du Général-de-Gaulle • Free

As a focus for wandering Brive's compact old streets, head first to the **Collégiale St-Martin de Brive**, plumb in the middle of town on a square dotted with handsome turreted and towered houses, some dating back to the thirteenth century. The church was originally Romanesque in style; now only the transept, apse and a few comically carved capitals survive from that era. The most striking aspect of the church **interior**, however, is its outwardly slanting columns, which have supposedly given way in this manner due to the sheer weight of the central vault. It's said that St Martin, a Spanish aristocrat, arrived in pagan Brive in 407 AD on the feast of Saturnus, smashed various idols and was promptly stoned to death by the outraged onlookers. Supposedly, St

> **RUGBY IN BRIVE**
>
> Southwest France is without question the heartland of French **rugby**, and Brive one of its major centres. Founded in 1910, **Club Athlétique Brive Corrèze Limousin** (or CA Brive) enjoyed only moderate success until the 1990s, when, somewhat surprisingly, it emerged as a major European force. The club's greatest moment came in 1997, when it won the European Cup, beating Leicester Tigers in Cardiff. The following year they reached the final again, this time narrowly losing to Bath, and in 2000 contested the final of the French Cup, though this proved to be their last taste of success, as that same year they were relegated, following financial mismanagement. Since then, they've yo-yoed between the top two divisions, currently sitting in division two. CA Brive games take place at the **Stade Amédée Domenech**, twenty minutes' walk east of the centre, usually on a Saturday or Sunday; tickets cost a pittance (http://cabrive-rugby.com).

Martin's unmarked tomb is among those in the tiny crypt, which is otherwise crammed with archeological remnants, reliquaries and other religious artefacts.

Musée Labenche

26 bd Jules-Ferry • Charge • http://museelabenche.brive.fr

The most impressive of the buildings on or just off place du Général-de-Gaulle is the sixteenth-century **Hôtel de Labenche**, now housing the enlightening **Musée Labenche**, whose prime focus is local art and history. As you enter, note the busts of the Labenche family leaning forward over each window. The museum's exhaustive collection encompasses wide-ranging geological and archeological finds, including stalagmites and cave-bear bones, some delightful Gallo-Roman bronzes complete with moulds, and a superb ethnographic section featuring a beautiful display of multicoloured accordions made in Brive by the Dedenis factory prior to 1939. The highlight, though, is a rare collection of **Mortlake tapestries**. The Mortlake workshop, under the supervision of Dutch weavers, was founded by James I of England in 1620, and though they were only in business until the end of that century, they produced a number of important, highly prized works. The most interesting of the ten tapestries presented here are *Fête de Nuit*, and *La Chasse au Loup*, the latter depicting a fox-hunting scene – both are still in exceptional condition and have retained their vibrant colours.

Denoix Distillery

9 bd du Maréchal Lyautey • Free • Tours (charge) by reservation only • http://denoix.com

Founded in 1839, the **Denoix Distillery** is renowned throughout the region for its walnut-flavoured **liqueurs**, notably a very mellow tipple called Suprême Denoix, of which you can have a free taste here. It has also been busy resurrecting a local **mustard**, Moutarde Violette de Brive, which is made with grape must and spices and was first devised in the fourteenth century for Pope Clément VI, a native of Corrèze. Not surprisingly for this area, it goes very well with duck. Guided visits last an hour and include a free tasting.

Chocolaterie Lamy

5 rue de l'Hôtel-de-Ville • Charge • http://chocolaterie-lamy.com

Those with a sweet tooth won't want to miss the **Chocolaterie Lamy**. Though just a chocolate shop at heart, it's nonetheless a hive of Wonka-style creativity, where you can watch demonstrations of the delectable chocolates being made during the summer, and even learn how to make them yourself on half-day courses. The shop itself is well worth a browse, too.

Musée Edmond Michelet

4 rue Champanatier • Free • http://museemichelet.brive.fr • To get here take the main rue de la République west from St-Martin church as far as the ring road, from where the museum is signed straight ahead along avenue Émile-Zola

A short way west of central Brive, the **Musée Edmond Michelet** occupies the former home of Edmond Michelet, one of Brive's leading *résistants*, who was arrested here in 1943 and deported to Dachau, where he remained until the camp was liberated in April 1945. Not long after, Michelet became a minister in de Gaulle's postwar government, rising to the post of Minister of Justice in 1959. Spread over three floors, the rooms portray the Resistance and deportations during World War II through personal effects, posters and objects of the time, though most affecting are the chilling photographs taken in the concentration camps. A free audioguide in English is available.

Jardins de Colette

Charge • http://lesjardinsdecolette.com

Ten minutes' drive west of Brive, at **Varetz**, are the lovely **Jardins de Colette**, named after the eponymous and controversial French writer, and generally at their best in June and early July. Between 1912 and 1923, Colette lived next door in Château de Castel Novel (now a hotel) with her second husband, Henry de Jouvenel. By means of plants and landscaping, the gardens aim to represent the places she lived, from her native Burgundy through to the Palais Royal in Paris. There are six in all, the most impressive of which is the **Brittany garden**, distinguished by its various rock formations, and the **Provence garden**, bursting with the typically distinctive colours of the region. The highlight – for kids at least – is an immense butterfly-shaped **maze** (a nod to Colette's beloved butterfly collection), made from double-plaited willow and dotted with educational signs outlining aspects of the writer's life. Once you're done wandering, take a cool drink on the terrace of the *salon de thé* overlooking the gardens.

ARRIVAL AND DEPARTURE   BRIVE-LA-GAILLARDE

By plane Brive airport (Brive-Vallée de la Dordogne; 05 55 22 40 00, http://aeroport-brive-vallee-dordogne.com) is around 18km to the south of town in Nespouls. There is no public transport into Brive. If there aren't any taxis waiting outside, you can call the local company (05 55 24 24 24) or ask at the airport information desk; Uber is also available. There are few other facilities to speak of here, save for a small café.

By train The *gare SNCF*, on the Paris–Toulouse and Bordeaux–Lyon main lines, is located on the south side of Brive, a 10min walk along avenue Jean-Jaurès from the centre. Alternatively, bus #3 makes the trip into the centre of town.

Destinations Arnac-Pompadour (3–4 daily; 1hr); Bordeaux (10 daily; 2hr 30min); Cahors (10 daily; 1hr 10min); Paris Austerlitz (13 daily; 4–5hr 30min); Périgueux (12 daily; 1hr); Souillac (10 daily; 25min); Toulouse (10 daily; 2hr–2hr 30min).

By bus Buses depart from various spots round town, including the *gare SNCF*, though many buses around the *département* leave from place du 14-Juillet, just across from the tourist office; for information on timetables contact CFTA buses (http://transdev.com).

Destinations Arnac-Pompadour (2hr); Beaulieu-sur-Dordogne (1hr–1hr 30min); Collonges-la-Rouge (25min–1hr); Meyssac (30min–1hr 5min); Turenne (20–40min).

GETTING AROUND AND INFORMATION

Car rental Avis, 56 av Jean-Jaurès (http://avis.fr); Europcar, 52 av Jean-Jaurès (http://europcar.fr); National, 59 av Jean-Jaurès (http://nationalcar.fr). All of these companies also have desks at the airport.

Taxis Allô Brive (05 55 24 24 24; http://taxibrive.fr).

Tourist office Place du 14-Juillet (April–June & Sept Mon–Sat 9am–12.30pm & 1.30–6.30pm; July & Aug Mon–Sat 9am–7pm, Sun 11am–5pm; Oct–March Mon–Sat 9am–noon & 2–6pm; 05 55 24 08 80, http://brive-tourisme.com). It occupies an old pumping station and water tower built in the form of a lighthouse, so you can't miss it; for €0.50 you can pop up to the top of the tower and enjoy the views of the marketplace below.

ACCOMMODATION   SEE MAP PAGE 75

Le Château de Lacan Rue Jean-Mace, http://hotelchateaulacan.com. Hidden away, somewhat incongruously, in a residential area north of the centre, this superbly renovated twelfth-century mansion is the place for a splurge, offering

BRIVE'S MARKETS AND FAIRS

The modern **Marché Brassens**, behind the tourist office on place du 14-Juillet, is the venue for a huge **market** on Tuesday, Thursday and Saturday mornings, though the Saturday one is by far the biggest; the hall itself is usually reserved for foodstuffs, while the square itself is taken over with stalls selling clothes, textiles and other knick-knacks. On the first Saturday of each month between December and March, the *foires grasses* – for foie gras and truffles – are held in the same place. During the first weekend in November, the fruit and veg gives way to one of the country's most important book fairs, **La Foire du Livre** (see page 49), which attracts a number of well-known authors and artists.

thirteen rooms and two suites of the highest order, each beautifully and thoughtfully integrated into this ancient building. And as well as going that extra mile – bottled water, fresh fruit and pastries in the rooms – the place is impeccably staffed, too. €€

Le Collonges 3 place Winston-Churchill, http://hotel-collonges.com. Easily the best value in the centre, offering impressive rooms with smart, dark furniture and impeccable bathrooms. Despite its position on a busy road junction, it's just a few paces from the old centre, and there are a couple of cafés and bars close by as well as pay parking. €€

Le Quercy 8 bis quai Tourny, http://hotelduquercy.com. Super-slick hotel owned by Best Western in a central location overlooking the marketplace. Each floor is colour themed, so if you really have a preference, there's black and white, lime green and beige, or silver and rose. There are some neat little touches like reading lights on bed headboards. €€

La Truffe Noire 22 bd Anatole-France, http://la-truffe-noire.com. Rather dated both in and out, this nineteenth-century pile could quite easily be transformed into a stupendous boutique hotel, but as it is the rooms are rather forgettable. It does have a quirky charm that some guests might enjoy, but it's undeniably expensive for what it offers. €€

EATING   SEE MAP PAGE 75

Chez Francis 61 av de Paris, http://chezfrancis.fr. A favourite haunt of writers, actors and artists during Brive's book festival, with its walls, ceilings and lampshades covered with messages of appreciation, which add to the mildly bohemian, occasionally eccentric, flavour of the place. The imaginative seasonal menus feature the best of local ingredients for reasonable prices. €€

L'Instant Basque 21 Promenade des Tilleuls, http://linstantbasque.com. For a taste of the far southwest corner of France (and of northern Spain), head to this inexpensive, simple and characterful place, with stone walls and dangling hams. The food is classic Basque all the way: *axoa* (made from mashed veal, onions, tomato and lots of red Espelette pepper), and cod scorched on the *plancha* (hot plate). Tapas (*pintxos* in Basque) are also big here. €€

★ **La Table d'Olivier** 3 rue St-Ambroise, 05 55 18 95 95. Locals speak about the Michelin-starred *La Table d'Olivier* in tones of awe, and when you sit down to enjoy finely presented dishes like salmon with a white cheese sorbet or summer truffles you'll understand why. €€€€

Arnac-Pompadour

Some 30km northeast of Brive, among the green fields and apple orchards of the southern Limousin, **ARNAC-POMPADOUR** is a must for anyone remotely interested in horses. The town is dominated by its massive, turreted château – from where Madame de Pompadour got her name – a fitting and stately backdrop to a national **stud farm** and one of the most picturesque **racecourses** in France.

Château de Pompadour

Charge • http://chateau-pompadour.fr

Although there was a fortress of sorts here as far back as the eleventh century, the present **Château de Pompadour** largely dates from the fifteenth century. When the Pompadour line died out in 1745, it was ceded to Louis XV who promptly bestowed the title on his mistress, the **Marquise de Pompadour**. Though she never bothered to visit, the marquise started breeding horses on her estate before being forced to sell for financial reasons in

1760; she nevertheless kept the title. On regaining possession of the castle the following year, Louis founded the Royal Stud, which became a **National Stud** in 1872, and which is open to visitors (see box). In between, the horses were sold off during the Revolution, but Napoleon I soon re-established the stud to keep his cavalry supplied. He sent four Arab stallions, booty from his Egyptian campaign, which were crossed with English thoroughbred mares to produce the first **Anglo-Arabs**. Although historically bred for military purposes, today these magnificent horses are ideally suited to eventing, owing to their powerful combination of speed, stamina and jumping ability.

The **château** was gutted by fire in 1834 and now houses the stud's headquarters. If you want to visit the château itself (albeit just three rooms), you must do so on a **guided tour** organized by Trois Tours de Pompadour. Otherwise, you can explore the formal gardens and parkland independently.

Chapelle St-Blaise
45min guided tours (in French only) • Free

In the centre of Arnac-Pompadour, just behind the château, lies the town's own parish church, the **Chapelle St-Blaise**. Since its restoration in 2008, the chapel is home to over three hundred square metres of paintings depicting Old and New Testament scenes by the contemporary artist, André Brasilier, worth seeing for the scale of the work alone. You're free to explore independently if you don't fancy the guided tour.

Église Prieurale d'Arnac
Rue des Écoles • Free

Some 2km northwest of Arnac-Pompadour, in the village of Arnac itself, the Romanesque **Église Prieurale d'Arnac** (part of the Pompadour *domaines*) is chiefly of interest for its carved capitals, which sit atop the inwardly leaning columns, just about perceptible if you stand at the back of the church. Though the columns are exceptionally high, enlarged photos beside each one help identify the striking images, including Daniel in the lions' den.

ARRIVAL AND INFORMATION   ARNAC-POMPADOUR

By train Arnac-Pompadour lies on a minor train line between Brive and Limoges; the *gare* SNCF is 500m southeast of town on the D7 to Vigeois. **Destinations** Brive (45min); Limoges (1hr 15min).

VISITING THE NATIONAL STUD

The **stallions** of Pompadour's National Stud are housed in the **Écurie du Puy Marmont** (charge), across the chestnut-shaded esplanade from the château. During the spring breeding season (March–June) there are fewer stallions in the *écurie*, but this is the best time to visit the **mares** (*juments*) at the **Jumenterie de la Rivière** (afternoons only, charge), 4km southeast, near the village of Beyssac. In late spring (May & June) the fields around are full of mares and foals, the best being kept for breeding, the rest sold worldwide as two-year-olds. To visit both the Écurie du Puy Marmont and the Jumenterie de la Rivière, you have to join a **guided tour** organized by Trois Tours de Pompadour, located inside the gatehouse of the château. Times of the visits vary, so check first. It also sells tickets to the château and a "passport", with which you can visit all of the three sites for €15.

At any time of year, you will see horses being exercised round the magnificent oval track in front of the château. On numerous Sundays between May and September, there are **race meetings** (as well as dressage and driving events; charge) and open days. A calendar of events is available from Trois Tours de Pompadour. A good time to be here is August 15, when the Pompadour *fête du cheval* takes place, with various races, dressage and jumping events.

By bus Buses from Brive (1hr 15min) stop by the château.
Tourist office In the gatehouse of the château (April, May & mid-Sept to Oct daily 10am–12.30pm & 2–5.30pm; June daily 10am–12.30pm & 2–6pm; July to mid-Sept daily 10am–6.30pm; Nov–March Mon–Sat 10am–12.30 & 2–5.30pm; 05 55 98 55 47, http://pompadour-tourisme.fr).

ACCOMMODATION

Auberge de la Marquise 4 av des Écuyers, http://auberge-de-la-marquise.com. Arnac-Pompadour doesn't have much in the way of hotel accommodation, but this friendly place on the southeast edge of town is a good bet, with smallish, somewhat old-fashioned, rooms and a decent restaurant down below. €

Camping Les Étoiles Allée du Stade, Saint-Sornin-Lavolps, http://campingpompadour.ellohaweb.com. Spruce, well-shaded campsite by a small lake 2km south of town, with places for both tents and campervans; there are also a handful of chalets sleeping between two and five. €

Turenne

TURENNE, 16km south of Brive, is the first of two very picturesque villages in the vicinity. In this case, slate-roofed, mellow stone houses crowd under the protective towers of a once-mighty fortress. At their peak during the fifteenth century, the viscounts of Turenne ruled over a vast feudal domain containing some 1200 villages. Virtually autonomous, it was one of the most powerful estates in France. The viscounts retained the right to raise taxes and mint their own coins, amongst other privileges, up until 1738 when Louis XV bought the viscountcy in the aftermath of the Fronde rebellion.

Château de Turenne

Charge • http://chateau-turenne.com

Although Louis XV ordered that the **Château de Turenne** be demolished, two towers still sprout from the summit, one of which is occupied by the present owners of the château. From this first tower (known as the **Tour de l'Horloge**, or Clocktower), you walk along a gravel pathway through the neatly manicured **gardens** – which is where the main body of the castle once stood – to the round **Tour César**, where a further 64 steps await. It's well worth climbing for the vertiginous views away over the ridges and valleys to the mountains of Cantal. Although it's a stiff fifteen-minute climb up to the castle entrance, you do pass a number of elegant Renaissance houses and the all-important salt store, as well as a **church** hurriedly thrown up in 1662 during the Counter-Reformation to bring the local populace back to Catholicism; take a peek inside at the gilded altar and unusual mosaic ceiling.

ARRIVAL AND INFORMATION — TURENNE

By bus Buses from Brive (25min) stop on the main road near the tourist office booth.
Tourist office Place Belvedere (May & June daily 10am–12pm & 2–6pm, closed Wed & Sat mornings; July & Aug daily 9.30am–12.30pm & 2.30–6.30pm; April & September Fri–Wed 10am–12pm & 2–6pm; 05 55 85 59 97, http://brive-tourisme.com). You can pick up walking maps of the village here; they are also available at the souvenir shop next to the lane that leads up to the castle. The office runs guided walks around Turenne in July and Aug (charge).

ACCOMMODATION AND EATING

Le Bisrot de Turenne Place de la Halle, 09 88 49 29 96. Copious portions made from fresh, seasonal produce, and a slap-up brunch at the weekend. The courtyard garden is a delight. €€

Le Clos Marnis Place de la Halle, 05 55 22 05 28, http://closmarnis.online.fr. Quiet and homely bed and breakfast just a stride or two from the main square, housed within a barn-like building erected by the Guild of White Penitents in 1771. While the five rooms won't set the pulse racing, they're of a decent size and tidily furnished with low-slung beds, and there's a large open garden to chill in. €

La Maison des Chanoines Rue Joseph-Rouveyrol, http://maison-des-chanoines.com. Along the path leading up to the church, this handsome sixteenth-century house has retained many of its fine Gothic flourishes, some of which have been incorporated into the four rooms and three suites (the latter in the building opposite). There are plenty of thoughtful touches too, like tea- and coffee-making facilities, while all the rooms offer either a castle or countryside view. There's also a pleasant little courtyard garden and a superb restaurant, offering solid French country fare, sometimes featuring truffles. €

Collonges-la-Rouge

There's a great view back to Turenne as you head southeast from the village on the D20 before cutting eastwards on pretty back lanes through meadows and walnut orchards to reach **COLLONGES-LA-ROUGE**, some 10km on; alternatively, you can walk between the two on the GR446 footpath. The village is the epitome of bucolic charm, with its rust-red – even verging on mauve – sandstone houses, pepper-pot towers and chestnut trees, although it's arguably more touristy than Turenne and crammed with artisan shops and souvenir stalls; it's best to arrive earlier or later in the day if possible. Though small-scale, there is grandeur about Collonges, for this is where the nobles who governed Turenne on behalf of the viscounts built their mini-châteaux, each boasting at least one tower – there's a wonderful view of the bristling roofs as you approach from the west.

On the main square, the twelfth-century **Église St-Pierre** is unusual in having two naves, of which the shorter, north nave – the one used today – was a later addition. They came in handy during the sixteenth century when Turenne supported the Huguenot cause; here at least, Protestants and Catholics conducted their services peacefully side by side. Outside, the timber-framed covered **market hall** still retains its old-fashioned baker's oven, which is fired up just once a year for the annual **Bread Festival** on the first Sunday of August.

Maison de la Sirène

Rue de la Barrière • Reserve in advance, charge • 07 82 27 41 39, http://tourismecorreze.com

Diagonally opposite the Collonges tourist office, the sixteenth-century **Maison de la Sirène** is named after the little mermaid sculpted above the entrance. Though battered, she's still charming as she preens herself, comb in one hand and mirror in the other. The only house in the village open to visitors, it contains a small **museum** with archeological remains including a Merovingian sarcophagus, tools relating to local trades, and rooms arranged with typical rural furniture from the eighteenth and nineteenth centuries. The curator is a mine of information on the village and also gives guided tours; book through the tourist office.

ARRIVAL AND INFORMATION   COLLONGES-LA-ROUGE

By bus Buses from Turenne (15min) and Brive (25min) pass Collonges on their way to the terminus at Meyssac, stopping on the main road at the northern entrance to the village.
Tourist office Rue de la Barrière (April–June, Sept & Oct Mon–Sat 10am–12.30pm & 2–6pm; July & Aug daily 9.30am–1pm & 2–7pm; Nov–March Mon–Sat 10am–12.30pm & 2–5pm; Nov–Feb Mon–Sat 2–5pm; 05 65 33 22 00, http://vallee-dordogne.com).

ACCOMMODATION AND EATING

Camping de Collonges-la-Rouge http://aquadis-loisirs.com. Just off the main road, halfway between Collonges and Meyssac, this is a large, sunny site with comprehensive facilities, among them a snack bar, lounge, laundry, tennis courts and heated pool with slides, as well as chalets for rent. €

Relais de St-Jacques de Compostelle Rue de la Barrière, http://hotel-stjacques.com. The village's most prominent hotel, located just around the corner from the Maison de la Sirène, though it's not quite as grand as it sounds. There are ten rather sparsely furnished guest rooms, though the views of the narrow streets are lovely and it's fairly priced. There's also a good restaurant; expect combinations such as tandoori breast of guinea-fowl with lemon juice. €

Relais du Quercy http://relaisduquercy.fr. Some 2km east of Collonges towards the village of Meyssac is this pleasant *Logis* hotel, which has two categories of room, both in a clean modern style, as well as a brightly coloured garden with swimming pool. €

Bergerac and around

- **87** Bergerac
- **93** Monbazillac and around
- **95** Pécharmant
- **95** South of Bergerac
- **100** West of Bergerac
- **102** East of Bergerac

PICTURESQUE ISSIGEAC

Bergerac and around

In its lower reaches the Dordogne slides wide and slow through a landscape of vine-planted hills where the scent of wine is thick and heady. This is the heart of the Périgord Pourpre, a major wine-growing region that blends seamlessly into the Bordelais vineyards to the west. For centuries the region's most important market town, port and commercial centre has been Bergerac, the second largest city in the Dordogne *département*, but still a pleasantly provincial place with a clutch of worthwhile sights tucked away among its twisting lanes. While lacking the sheer concentration of big-ticket tourist attractions to be found in other parts of the Dordogne, the outlying areas do offer a rich complement of stately châteaux, attractive *bastide* towns and some outstanding natural heritage.

The foremost sight in the wine region is the Renaissance **Château de Monbazillac**, clearly visible on the ridge to the south of Bergerac and surrounded by its prestigious vineyards, originally planted by monks in the Middle Ages, which produce a very palatable sweet white wine. The high country further south of Bergerac, where the gentle River Dropt marks the border of the Dordogne and Lot-et-Garonne *départements*, wasn't always such a bucolic scene, as a glance at the remaining fortifications of **Issigeac** and **Eymet** – the ramparts built in the run-up to the Hundred Years' War – goes to show. The prevailing sense of unease following more than a century of war, plague and famine is caught in the fifteenth-century frescoes of the Last Judgement in the little **Église St-Eutrope** at Allemans-du-Dropt. Further downstream at **Duras**, another semi-ruined château dominates the valley.

To the west of Bergerac, the Dordogne valley becomes wider, busier and less attractive. Nevertheless, there are one or two appealing sights, notably the Gallo-Roman remains at **Montcaret** and the nearby **Château de Montaigne**, where the eponymous philosopher wrote his original, wide-ranging *Essais*. North of here, the **Forêt du Landais** stretches north across the top of the Périgord Pourpre. It's a pretty region of wooded hills, meandering streams and sparse habitation, good for wandering, though without any particularly compelling sights.

Upstream of Bergerac, the pure waters of the River Couze, a tributary of the Dordogne, have spawned a paper-making industry at **Couze-et-St-Front**, where traditional, handmade paper is still produced to this day. Further east, the Dordogne has carved two gigantic meanders at **Trémolat** and **Limeuil**, which also happen to be two of the prettier villages in the region. Here also the Périgord Pourpre gradually gives way to wooded hills on the western edge of the Périgord Noir.

The change is perhaps most obvious in the landscapes unfurling south of the river, where the *bastide* town of **Beaumont** and the nearby abbey of **St-Avit-Sénieur** stand isolated on the edge of a high, open plateau. Just a few kilometres to the northeast, however, **Cadouin**'s abbey church is cradled in a hidden valley deep among the chestnut forests.

GETTING AROUND — BERGERAC AND AROUND

Overall, exploring this region solely by public transport is not easy. While the main towns and villages along the Dordogne valley are reasonably well served by train services on the Sarlat–Bordeaux railway line, anywhere inland requires your own vehicle. What limited bus services do exist are planned around the needs of schoolchildren rather than travellers, and in school holidays many services simply don't operate.

ABBAYE DE CADOUIN

Highlights

❶ Bergerac Surrounded by vineyards, this sleepy provincial town of cobbled squares and half-timbered facades makes for an atmospheric day's wander. See page 87

❷ Bastides The fortified towns of Issigeac, Eymet and Beaumont, with their arcaded central squares, retain a heady medieval atmosphere. See pages 97 and 107

❸ Église Saint-Eutrope, Allemans-du-Dropt Fifteenth-century frescoes depict the Last Judgement in spine-tingling detail. See page 98

❹ Montcaret The elaborate mosaics in a fourth-century villa unearthed here provide ample evidence of luxury living, Roman-style. See page 101

❺ Cingle de Trémolat A classic Dordogne river meander, best viewed from the limestone cliffs to the north. See page 104

❻ Canoeing the Dordogne Don a lifejacket and take to the waters at Limeuil for a leisurely trip down either the Vézère or Dordogne rivers. See page 105

❼ Cadouin An exceptionally pretty village with unusual accommodation options and the main draw of an austere twelfth-century Cistercian abbey. See page 108

HIGHLIGHTS ARE MARKED ON THE MAP ON PAGE 86

FESTIVALS, EVENTS AND MARKETS

The list below comprises some of the biggest and most interesting of the **festivals** and **events** in this region. Where we haven't given a specific information number or website, contact the relevant tourist office.

July and August Bergerac: Les Mercredis du Jazz (http://bergerac.fr). Free concerts by French jazz artists on Wednesday evenings on place de la Myrpe and the Cloître des Récollets.

Third weekend in July Duras: Fête de la Madeleine (http://paysdeduras.com). The castle grounds in Duras play host to inexpensive or free concerts, a firework display on the Monday night and plenty of wine tasting.

Third Sunday in July Issigeac: Foire aux Paniers. Unique basket-weavers'fair held on the place du Château. Some sixty artisans from all regions of France demonstrate their different techniques and styles.

Late July to mid-August Bergerac and around: Été Musical en Bergerac (http://festivalbergerac.com). Performances of classical music, jazz and ballet in Bergerac, the Château de Biron, Monpazier, St-Avit and Cadouin.

Mid-July to mid-August Castillon-la-Bataille: La Bataille de Castillon (http://batailledecastillon.com). Locals stage a spectacular floodlit re-enactment of the battle that ended the Hundred Years' War. Some four hundred actors and forty cavaliers take part, performing for around six weeks each Friday and Saturday evening (plus Thursdays in the first half of August); tickets are €24 per performance (€12 for children).

August Dropt valley: Itinérance Médiévale en Vallée du Dropt. This four-week festival sees all kinds of events – gastronomic markets, parades in medieval costumes, joustings and concerts by torchlight – laid on in towns and villages along the Dropt valley, including Duras, Eymet, Issigeac and Cadouin.

Second or third Sunday in August Duras: Fête du Vin (http://vins-bergeracduras.fr). A one-day wine-fest held beside the château with free tastings (you have to buy a refillable glass at the entrance). The festival features some good music too, with live jazz/blues on the Sunday afternoon.

MARKETS

The main **markets** in this region are at Bergerac (Wed & Sat); Le Buisson-de-Cadouin (Fri); Cadouin (Wed); Eymet (Thurs); Issigeac (Sun); Lalinde (Thurs); Ste-Foy-la-Grande (Sat) and Trémolat (Tues).

Bergerac

Lying mostly on the Dordogne's north bank overlooking its wide flood plain, **BERGERAC** is a rather sleepy place for much of the year, but bursts into life for the summer tourist season, when cafés and restaurants spill out into the cobbled squares and alleyways. It suffered particularly badly during the Wars of Religion, but in recent years the old streets fanning out from the former port have been carefully restored to bring out the best in the rows of half-timbered cottages and more bourgeois stone-built residences; main sights are a surprisingly rewarding **museum** devoted to tobacco and a former **monastery** which now houses an information centre on the local wines.

The best place to start exploring is beside the old port where, in season, replica *gabares* (barges) pick up passengers for leisurely **river trips**. A short hop east of the port, the narrow lanes of the **vieille ville** spread gently uphill. A calm and pleasant area to wander, with numerous late-medieval houses and perfect pavement cafés, its main artery is the Grand Rue, which runs north from the central **Église St-Jacques** to join rue de la Résistance, the old town's northern perimeter; these two form Bergerac's principal shopping streets. Just beyond their junction, across the wide place de Lattre-de-Tassigny, stands another useful landmark, the **Église Notre-Dame**.

Brief history

The largest town in the Dordogne valley, Bergerac owes its existence and prosperity to the **river**. By the twelfth century it was already an important bridging point and port, controlling the trade between its Périgord hinterland and Bordeaux, particularly the burgeoning **wine trade**. Things began to take off after Henry III of England sought to keep the townspeople sweet by giving them certain privileges in 1254: they were exempted from local taxes, given the right of assembly and allowed to export their wines to Bordeaux unhindered. Local burghers took advantage of the new dispensations to ship their own wines first, while the less privileged were forced to sell later, at disadvantageous prices, and were also charged a tax of five *sous* per barrel. Bergerac's wine aristocracy were thus able to corner the lucrative foreign market until the seventeenth century, when the technique of ageing wines was discovered.

The town's heyday came in the decades preceding the Wars of Religion (1561–98), when Bergerac was among the foremost centres of **Protestantism** in southwest France. One of many truces between the warring factions was even signed here in 1577, but in 1620 the Catholic Louis XIII seized the town and ordered that the ramparts and fortress be demolished. Worse was to come when Catholic priests arrived to bring Bergerac back into the fold. They met with mixed success – the majority of the

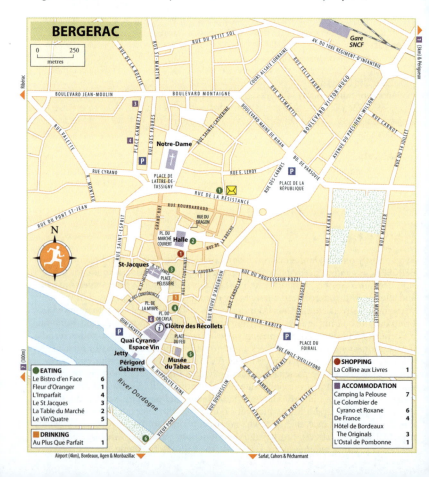

Protestant population fled, principally to Holland, where they soon established a long and mutually profitable business importing Bergerac wines.

Since then, wine has continued to be the staple of the local economy. Up until the railway arrived in the 1870s, the bulk of it was transported by river, leading to a thriving **boat-building** industry all along the Dordogne. Though most have long disappeared, a few sturdy *gabares* are still being built to cater to the tourist trade.

Musée du Tabac
Place du Feu • Charge • http://bergerac.fr

Rue de l'Ancien Pont leads northwards from portside rue Hippolyte Taine to the splendid seventeenth-century Maison Peyrarède, which houses the unexpectedly absorbing **Musée du Tabac**. Tobacco used to be a major crop in the Bergerac region (and is still grown hereabouts today), and Europe's major tobacco research centre is based here. While inevitably glossing over the more dire medical effects of smoking, this is nevertheless an impressive collection of pipes, tobacco jars and various tools of the trade, garnered from all over the world. There are wooden graters etched with religious scenes, snuffboxes engraved with the busts of Napoleon and Marie Antoinette, blushing young beauties adorning porcelain pipe-bowls and hunting scenes fashioned out of meerschaum. Among many rare and beautiful pieces, the museum's prize possessions are an incredibly ornate Viennese meerschaum-and-amber cigar holder depicting a Sicilian wedding, and an intriguing machine, invented in the 1860s, for carving fourteen brier pipes at once. Look out, too, for the clay pipe in the ominous form of a skull with glittering glass eyes. The cool 1960s and 70s-era Gitanes posters, meanwhile, hark back to a time when smoking was regarded as a somewhat more glamorous activity.

Cloître des Récollets
Rue des Récollets

Just north of the Musée du Tabac stands the **Cloître des Récollets**. This simple, galleried cloister dates from the early seventeenth century when, in the aftermath of the Wars of Religion, Louis XIII dispatched five monks of the Franciscan Récollets order to bring Protestant Bergerac back to the faith. They were not warmly welcomed – it took a visit by Louis himself, in 1621, to assure their authority – but by the end of the decade the Récollets had succeeded in founding a new chapel and monastery. Not that they

---

CYRANO DE BERGERAC

In 1897, the poet and playwright Edmond Rostand penned his most successful play, **Cyrano de Bergerac**. It tells the story of a guardsman and poet, renowned for his bravery and intellect, who falls in love with his cousin Roxane, but feels unable to declare his feelings because of his unattractive looks – in particular his large, protruding nose. Instead, he writes letters to her on behalf of one of his cadets, the handsome but dim-witted Christian, who has also fallen for her charms. First attracted by Christian's looks, Roxane falls in love with the soul revealed in the letters – not discovering until it is too late that it is in fact Cyrano's soul. Rostand's play has since been the subject of numerous adaptations, perhaps most famously the much-loved 1990 French film version starring Gérard Depardieu.

The lead character was inspired by a seventeenth-century soldier, playwright and free-thinking philosopher called **Savinien de Cyrano**, who was born in Paris and only decided to embellish his name while serving in a Gascon company. It seems Cyrano was well able to match the Gascon reputation for swaggering boastfulness and impetuosity. Not only was he a famous duellist, but many of his works were so outspoken that they had to be withheld from publication until after his death.

had the last word. After the Revolution, Bergerac's remaining Protestant congregation bought the chapel and re-established a temple on the site, which is still used for regular Sunday-morning worship. The monks' vaulted grain and wine cellars now form an unusual setting for Bergerac's **Espace Vins**, which can be entered through the cloister.

Quai Cyrano – Espace Vin

1 rue des Récollets • Free • http://vins-bergeracduras.fr

Accessed either through the Cloître des Récollets or at street level on the riverfront, the purpose-built **Quai Cyrano** is home to Bergerac's Tourist Office, as well as an Espace Vin devoted to the region's wines. Oenophiles can enjoy various **exhibitions** on the history of the Bergerac *appellation*, and pick up the *Route des Vins de Bergerac*, a handy guide to visiting the vineyards around the town. There's also a chance to sample wines and regional produce, and a shop selling over 140 wine varietals. Between mid-June and mid-September, the Espace Vin hosts daily special events, tasting sessions and presentations from regional growers.

Place de la Myrpe

On its north side the Cloître des Récollets opens onto Bergerac's most picturesque square, the cobbled, tree-shaded **Place de la Myrpe** (also spelt Mirpe), lined with stone and half-timbered labourers' cottages looking onto a badly weathered statue, erected in 1977, honouring Edmond Rostand's fictional hero **Cyrano de Bergerac** (see box) in typically haughty pose.

Église St-Jacques

Rue St-Jacques

Uphill from place de la Myrpe stands the patchwork **Église St-Jacques**. A stop on the route to Santiago de Compostela, the church has had a chequered past, founded in the twelfth century but plundered and destroyed in the Hundred Years' War and the Wars of Religion – only the campanile and balcony remain from the original structure. Today's church is fairly modest, but has a certain grandeur in its narrow, high nave, topped by a precise rib-vaulted ceiling and lit by stained-glass windows.

Rue St-James to the market square

Rue St-James runs east from the Église St-Jacques across the top end of pedestrianized **place Pélissière**, the old tanners' quarter but now dotted with cafés and ice cream parlours. Like the place de la Myrpe, place Pélissière also boasts a statue of **Cyrano de Bergerac** (see box), this one a recent incarnation from 2005 and bearing an uncanny (and somewhat cartoonish) resemblance to Gérard Depardieu. From here, pretty **rue des Fontaines** continues uphill past prosperous fourteenth- and sixteenth-century houses – no. 29 on the corner with rue Gaudra is particularly noteworthy, with its large, arched windows and carved capitals – to the market square. The covered **Halle** is the focus of a vast market on Wednesday and Saturday mornings, with more stalls on the square outside the Église Notre-Dame.

Église Notre-Dame

Place de Lattre de Tassigny

The **Église Notre-Dame** was built in 1865 as the town's congregation grew too large for the church of St-Jacques. Designed by Paul Abadie of Sacré-Coeur fame, it does impress for the resolutely neo-Gothic style of its architecture, though the twee miniature columns and Nativity-scene sculptures on its main facade verge on greeting-card kitsch. The long, high and grey interior does little to inspire, though it's worth a look to view two large oil paintings in the east chapel: *The Adoration of the Shepherds*, attributed to a pupil of Leonardo de Vinci, and *The Adoration of the Magi* from the Venetian School.

ARRIVAL AND DEPARTURE — BERGERAC

By plane Bergerac's airport is in Roumanière (http://bergerac.aeroport.fr), 5km southeast of the city on the Agen road. There's a restaurant and an ATM here but nothing else. Moreover, there's no public transport to the centre and taxis are often in short supply. If there aren't any outside, you can call Abeilles Bergerac Taxis (05 53 23 32 32).
Airlines Jet2 (http://jet2.com); Ryanair (http://ryanair.com); British Airways (http://britishairways.com); Transavia (http://transavia.com).
By train The *gare SNCF* is located at the north end of cours Alsace Lorraine, a 10min walk from the old town.
Destinations Bordeaux (15 daily; 1hr 15min–1hr 30min); Le Buisson (6 daily; 55min); Castillon-la-Bataille (15 daily; 40–50min); Couze (4 daily; 15min); Lalinde (6 daily; 25min); Lamothe-Montravel (4 daily; 35–40mins); Libourne (15 daily; 45min–1hr); St-Émilion (14 daily; 40min); Ste-Foy-La-Grande (15 daily; 20min); Sarlat (4–6 daily; 1hr 20min–1hr 30min); Trémolat (6 daily; 30min).
By bus Most buses around the region depart from outside the *gare SNCF*.
Destinations Eymet (50min–1hr 20min); Issigeac (45min); Lalinde (40min); Périgueux (1hr); Port de Couze (30min).
By car You'll find free parking in the cobbled area beside the old port and on place du Foirail, a short walk east of the town centre.

GETTING AROUND

Bike rental The friendly and helpful Apolo Cycles, 31 bd Victor-Hugo (http://apolo-cycles.com), rents bikes and offers drop-offs at your hotel.
Car rental Near the train station, try Avis, 42 rue d'Agen (http://avis.fr), and Europcar, 3 av du 108e Régiment d'Infanterie (http://europcar.fr); also at the airport is Hertz (http://hertz.fr).
Taxis There's a taxi stand outside the station; otherwise, call Abeilles Bergerac (05 53 23 32 32).

INFORMATION AND TOURS

Tourist office Quai Cyrano, 1 rue des Récollets (http://pays-bergerac-tourisme.com). Bergerac's Tourist Office is located in the purpose-built Quai Cyrano complex in the Cloître des Récollets. It organizes guided tours of the old town twice a week in high season (charge). There's also an Espace Vin (see page 90) and a boutique selling regional wines, foods and gifts.
River trips Périgord Gabarres, Le Quai Salvette (http://gabarres.fr), operates replica *gabares* which depart from the old port for leisurely 50min river trips (charge) along the Dordogne to a nature reserve that is home to herons, cormorants and kingfishers, among other wildlife; commentary is bilingual. Departures are at least four times daily, or up to once an hour in July and Aug.

ACCOMMODATION — SEE MAP PAGE 88

For a modestly sized town, Bergerac has a fairly broad range of **accommodation**, offering an appealing mix of hotels and *chambres d'hôtes*, many of the latter clustered in or around lovely place de la Myrpe, as well as some excellent options just a short drive out of town. There's no hostel in Bergerac, though there is a well-located **campsite** very close to the centre.
Camping la Pelouse 8 bis rue J-J Rousseau, http://night-and-day.fr. In a beautiful position on the peaceful south bank of the river, a short walk west from the Vieux Pont, this is an inexpensive and friendly municipal site but with fairly basic facilities. As well as tent pitches, there are mobile homes for rent. €
Le Colombier de Cyrano et Roxane 17 rue du Grand Moulin, http://lecolombierdecyrano.com. This lovely if rather eccentric little *chambre d'hôte* in a flagstone sixteenth-century cottage is adorned with blue shutters, flower boxes and a tiny blue wooden door. Bursting with colour, the two en-suite rooms offer touches of Baroque extravagance, while one – only a touch more expensive – has its own private terrace with wicker chairs and a hammock. €€
De France 18 place Gambetta, http://hoteldefrance-bergerac.com. This three-star hotel has an unpromising modern exterior, but don't let that put you off; the twenty rooms are pleasing on the eye and there's a high level of comfort on offer. In addition, there's an open-air pool at the back to enjoy. Front rooms overlook the road but are more colourful than those at the quieter rear. €€
Hôtel de Bordeaux The Originals 38 place Gambetta, http://hotel-bordeaux-bergerac.com. Set in the middle of the new town, this hotel boasts a retro Art Deco exterior that gives an immediate sense of character. Inside, though,

THE WINES OF BERGERAC

The **Bergerac wine region** extends along the north bank of the Dordogne from Lamothe-Montravel in the west to Lalinde in the east, and south as far as Eymet and Issigeac. It comprises no fewer than thirteen different *appellations*, of which over half the total output is red wine, although the region's most famous wine is the sweet white Monbazillac.

There is evidence of wine production around Bergerac since Roman times, but the vineyards really began to develop in the thirteenth century to supply the English market. Demand from Holland, for sweet white wines in particular, triggered a second spurt in the sixteenth century and then again after the Wars of Religion, when Protestant émigré merchants virtually monopolized the market in Monbazillac wines. By the nineteenth century vines covered 100,000 hectares around Bergerac, only to be decimated by phylloxera in the 1870s; the area under AOP wines today covers a mere 12,000 hectares.

Pre-eminent among the Bergerac wines is **Monbazillac**. This pale golden, sweet white wine is blended from Sémillon, Sauvignon and Muscadelle vines grown on the chalky clay soils of the valley's north-facing slopes. As with Sauternes, a key element is the cold, autumn-morning mists which lead to the development of *Botrytis cinerea*, or "noble rot", on the grapes. The result is an intensely perfumed, concentrated wine best consumed chilled with desserts or as an apéritif. Though they can't compare to the finesse of Sauternes, even a top-quality Monbazillac is eminently affordable.

Pécharmant, the best of the local reds, is often compared unfavourably to Bordeaux wines, though some now rival a number of less prestigious St-Émilions. Pécharmant wines are produced from Cabernet Sauvignon, Cabernet Franc and small quantities of Malbec or Merlot grapes, grown on the most favourable pockets of sand and gravel soils found to the north and east of Bergerac. They are thus far more complex and full-bodied than other Bergerac reds, and some will age well up to seven years.

You can sample the range of local AOP wines at Bergerac's Espace Vin. Alternatively, many producers offer **tastings and visits** to their *chais* – for a full list see the brochure *Route des Vins de Bergerac* available at the Espace Vin (see page 90) or Bergerac tourist office (see page 91).

---

the rooms are disappointingly identikit business-chain-like, but even so in terms of facilities, comfort and price it's arguably Bergerac's top choice, and boasts a sizeable pool and plush bar. Rooms at the back are quieter and have views of the pool and small garden. €

★ **L'Ostal de Pombonne** 19 rue du Bourg de Pombonne, http://ostaldepombonne.fr. Set in the village of Pombonne, some 4km northeast of central Bergerac, this is a delightful four-room *chambre d'hôte* in an old stone-walled farmhouse with a pretty garden. Named after plants and trees found in the garden, the rooms have cool, clean modern accents, while the garden has a swimming pool and children's toys (which make this a perfect base for young families). Breakfast is taken at a communal table. €€

EATING
SEE MAP PAGE 88

When it comes to places to eat, Bergerac offers a temptation of tasty treats – you'll find a bunch of terrific **restaurants** clustered around place du Marché Couvert, and several more located further down towards the river.

Le Bistrot d'en Face 1 rue Fénelon, 05 53 61 34 06. There's nothing out of the ordinary about the restaurant menu, which is staunchly French and, predictably for the Dordogne, duck-heavy, but the dishes are beautifully presented and burst with colour. Save room for *café gourmand*. €€

Fleur d'Oranger 30 rue de la Résistance, 05 53 63 40 36. Plenty of fresh fruits, veggies and vegetarian dishes at this tearoom-cum-restaurant in the heart of Bergerac, where dishes can also be ordered to go. There's a positive library of different herbal teas on offer. €

L'Imparfait 8 rue des Fontaines, http://imparfait.com. Bergerac's longest-standing and most refined traditional restaurant is an attractive high-ceilinged stone dining room complete with fireplace and a somewhat out-of-place fish tank. In summer diners migrate outside to the well-shaded terrace. The menu changes daily, but revolves around fresh fish and meat, subtly flavoured by a talented chef; the veal sweetbreads are a house speciality. €€€

Le St Jacques 30 rue St-James, http://restaurant-saintjacques-bergerac.com. This place has a charming shaded garden at the back, complete with outdoor fireplace and stone walls strewn with lanterns and candles. The menu is small but varied, from beef in a truffle sauce to *dorade* (bream). €€

★ **La Table du Marché** 21 place du Marché Couvert, http://table-du-marche.fr. If you've only time for one meal in Bergerac, then make it *La Table du Marché*, where chef Stéphane Cuzin oversees dazzlingly market-fresh dishes (which are limited to a choice of one meat and one fish main a day). The black-and-white decor gives the venue a sharp, contemporary feel, as does the open kitchen where you can watch your food being prepared. €€€

Le Vin'Quatre Rue Saint-Clair, http://levinquatre-restaurant.fr. Although this little place is in the heart of the old town, it's somewhat tucked away down a side-alley, with just a couple of tables inside and three more out on the terrace. Most of the patrons are locals in search of quality, highly creative dishes such as slow-cooked lamb with hummus or a white cream and pineapple piña-colada dessert. There are also a few British-inspired dishes on the menu and the chefs are happy to cater for vegetarians, vegans and gluten-free guests. €€

DRINKING   SEE MAP PAGE 88

Bergerac is hardly your typical party town, hence the paucity of **drinking** establishments, though there are one or two bars and cafés where you can linger over a morning coffee or a beer at sundown.

Au Plus Que Parfait 12 rue des Fontaines, 05 53 61 95 11. Great-looking pub across the street from *L'Imparfait*, where you'll receive a warm welcome and a choice of seven or eight Belgian beers on tap and dozens more by the bottle. There's plenty of entertainment too, from games nights and salsa to occasional live music on Saturday evenings.

SHOPPING   SEE MAP PAGE 88

As well as the individual **shops** picked out below, Bergerac also has some excellent **markets**. The main event (Wed & Sat morning) spreads out from the central *halle* into the surrounding streets and squares; the *halle* also has a fresh-produce market (Mon–Sat mornings). There's a small organic market (Tues morning) in front of the town hall, and a flea market on place de la Myrpe on the first Sunday of the month.

La Colline aux Livres Place Louis-de-la-Bardonnie, 05 53 57 90 97. This fantastic independent bookshop has a small selection of books in English.

DIRECTORY

Hospital Central Hospitalier Samuel-Pozzi, 9 bd du Professeur Albert-Calmette, the eastern extension of rue du Professeur Pozzi (05 53 63 88 88).

Police Commissariat de Police, 37 bd Chanzy (05 53 74 74 17).
Post office The main post office is at 36 rue de la Résistance.

Monbazillac and around

Six kilometres south of Bergerac, **MONBAZILLAC** is the name not only of a village but also, more famously, of a château and a sweet white wine (see page 92) similar to those of the Sauternes in the Bordeaux region. After whetting your appetite at Monbazillac, investigate some of the area's private **vineyards**. There are two good options to the east of Monbazillac near the village of **Colombier**.

Château de Monbazillac

Charge • http://chateau-monbazillac.com

Visible from miles around, the handsome sixteenth-century **Château de Monbazillac** sits invitingly atop a low hill, surveying the gentle slopes of its long-favoured vineyards below. An eye-catching blend of Renaissance residence and mock-medieval fortress, its corners reinforced by four sturdy towers, the château was a Protestant stronghold during the Wars of Religion. Surprisingly, it has survived virtually intact and now contains many richly furnished rooms; although few original furnishings remain, it is nevertheless an impressive collection. The pick of the rooms are located on the **ground floor**, notably the *grand salon* with its beautifully decorated ceiling, herringbone parquet flooring of oak, pine and cherry wood and a Renaissance fireplace with heraldic sculptures. There's another fine fireplace in the adjoining *petit salon*, this one clad in walnut and featuring an unusual triptych. The so-called **Library Tower**, meanwhile, is just that, well-stocked with books as well as a family tree of the

D'Aydies', the founders of the castle. Better still is the superbly vaulted **cellar** with its many wine-related displays including a cabinet full of antique bottles specially labelled for the Dutch market, the oldest of which dates from 1920.

Cave de Monbazillac

Free • http://chateau-monbazillac.com • The cave is 2km west of Château de Monbazillac on the D933 Bergerac–Marmande road

The Château de Monbazillac and its vineyards have been under the ownership of the local wine producers' co-operative, the **Cave de Monbazillac**, since 1960. You can taste its famous velvety sweet white wine both at the château or at the main **showroom**, where the helpful staff can offer expert advice on what to buy, too.

Maison de Tourisme

Free • 05 53 58 63 13, http://pays-bergerac-tourisme.com

Just 500m up the road from the Château de Monbazillac, you can sample (and purchase) a variety of local wines at the **Maison de Tourisme**, which also has a small but interesting exhibition on the local vineyards. Staff can help to arrange château tours, too.

Château de la Jaubertie

Free • http://chateau-jaubertie.com

Some 4km southeast of Monbazillac via the D14E is the sixteenth-century **Château de la Jaubertie**, which was supposedly built by Henry IV for his mistress, Gabrielle d'Estrée, and later belonged to a doctor of Marie Antoinette. Now owned by an English family, the Rymans, the estate produces a variety of very reasonable wines under the Bergerac *appellation*, the most prominent of which is the *Bergerac Blanc Sec*.

Domaine de l'Ancienne Cure

http://domaine-anciennecure.fr

The **Domaine de l'Ancienne Cure** in the village of **COLOMBIER**, overseen by Christian Roche, has won any number of awards for its high-quality, and mostly organic, Monbazillac, Bergerac and Pécharmant wines – its three *cuvées*, namely the Jour du Fruit, L'Abbaye and the highly concentrated L'Extase are all fantastic; a bottle of the latter, which is harvested only in vintage years, will set you back around €20. You can visit the *chais* by appointment, but tastings are available at any time at its shop just below the village on the main N21 Bergerac–Agen road, right by the Issigeac turning.

Château de Bridoire

http://chateaudebridoire.com

Four kilometres west of Monbazillac, in Ribagnac, the **Château de Bridoire** has undergone a fabulous partial renovation, and is one of the more interesting – and certainly most family-friendly – of the châteaux around here. Of the restored rooms, the **grand salon** is a magnificent example of upper-class eighteenth-century living while the **Salle des gardes** (guardroom) comes complete with a knight in armour mounted on a horse. Other rooms to look out for include the so-called King's bedroom and the main dining room.

There's also lots of fun to be had in the surrounding **grounds**, where dozens of medieval and traditional French games and activities have been laid out, from *Jeu de l'Oie* (similar to snakes and ladders, with wooden geese rather than serpents) to archery, croquet and an enormous chess board, as well as the **Vallée Mystérieuse** fantasy maze of twisting pathways and obstacle courses, with a few surprises thrown in. Between mid-July and the end of August the château is open on Thursday and Saturday nights for torchlit visits, musical events and medieval food tastings; see the website for more details.

ARRIVAL AND GETTING AROUND

MONBAZILLAC AND AROUND

By bus Very infrequent buses run between Monbazillac and Bergerac, which are normally timed only to get children to and from school. Once in Monbazillac you'll need your own transport to get to and from sites of interest.

ACCOMMODATION

Le 1500 315 rue du Château, Saussignac, http://le1500.rocks. A restored twelfth-century house run by two artists, where the stay is as much about the experience as the (admittedly beautiful) accommodation. Michael and Lee run art workshops, yoga sessions, and art and wine retreats, and even the food in the on-site restaurant is served with creative flair. There's a lovely sheltered pool too. €€

The Wine Lodge at Château Feely 326 rue du Pressoir, Saussignac, http://chateaufeely.com. A self-catering lodge in the heart of an organic wine estate, *The Wine Lodge at Château Feely* has panoramic views that take in the woodland, vineyards and hills. There's a saltwater swimming pool on site, and the property is solar-powered. Sleeps four. €

EATING

Tour des Vents http://vieux-logis.com. Some 3km west from the Cave de Monbazillac, the Michelin-starred *Tour des Vents* sits beside the Moulin de Malfourat, a ruined windmill perched on the highest point for miles around. Though it's not an attractive building, the views from the restaurant's picture windows and terrace are superb, and the ever-changing menu might include veal with cashew nuts and panna cotta or turbot with Espelette peppers. €€€€

Pécharmant

East of Bergerac, if you leave the river valley at Creysse and head north, you're soon back among vine-striped hills. Some of this region's best red wines are produced around the village of **PÉCHARMANT**, 6km northeast of Bergerac; indeed, the wines here are certainly a cut above the surrounding Côtes de Bergerac and Bergerac *appellations*.

Domaine du Haut-Pécharmant

Signposted north off the D32 between Bergerac and Ste-Alvère • Free tours • http://haut-pecharmant.com

Just to the northeast of Pécharmant, the family-run **Domaine du Haut-Pécharmant** stands in the thick of fields of vines, with views across to Monbazillac. It produces a typically full-bodied, aromatic wine, which ages well. Short but informative tours are available in English (call ahead to be sure an English-speaker is available) that finish with a tasting and the chance to buy.

Château de Tiregand

Charge • http://chateau-de-tiregand.com

Opposite the turnoff from the D32 to Domaine du Haut-Pécharmant, at the end of a long alley, the much grander **Château de Tiregand** offers free tastings, as well as guided tours (in French) of the estate. Its star wine is the delicious Cuvée Grand Millésime.

South of Bergerac

South of Bergerac, you gradually leave the vines behind as you cross an area of high, rolling country, featuring several picturesque small towns and villages that have a low-key but undeniable charm. The region is off the standard Dordogne tourist trail but is very popular with British ex-pats – in fact, some towns can seem to have almost as many British residents as French. The first stop, **Issigeac**, is perhaps the most rewarding, with its pretty medieval centre situated on a tributary of the Dropt. From here you can follow quiet backroads southwest along the **Dropt valley** to **Eymet**, a particularly satisfying *bastide* with a well-preserved central square and an abandoned castle, and on to Allemans-du-Dropt, where the focus of interest is a remarkable series of frescoes in its otherwise unassuming **Église St-Eutrope**. Last but not least comes **Duras**, the town from which the twentieth-century novelist Margaret Duras took her penname after spending part of her childhood in the region. Duras's semi-ruined but still forbidding castle holds a commanding position on Périgord's southwestern border and is easily the most impressive in the Bergerac region.

GETTING AROUND — SOUTH OF BERGERAC

Public transport is almost non-existent. Buses do link Bergerac with Eymet and Issigeac, and Eymet with Allemans, but there are only one or two in each direction daily, none of which allows for a day-trip from Bergerac.

Issigeac

An almost perfectly circular huddle of houses in the midst of pastureland and orchards 8km southeast of Colombier along the D14, **ISSIGEAC** owes its prosperity to the bishops of Sarlat who established a residence here in 1317. Only fragments of the outer walls remain, and in recent years the village has been considerably tarted up, but otherwise its core of half-timbered medieval buildings is largely unspoilt and the narrow streets mercifully traffic-free. On Sunday mornings an animated **market** takes over much of the centre.

The seventeenth-century **bishop's palace**, now containing various administrative offices, and the **Maison des Dîmes**, the former tax office, with its immense roof, command the village's north entrance. Behind the palace, and not much larger, the Gothic **Église St-Félicien** contains little of interest beyond some polychrome statues. Better instead to wander the old streets, starting with the **Grand Rue**, leading south to Issigeac's most famous building, known as the **Maison des Têtes** for its roughly carved, almost grotesque crowned and grimacing heads. It stands on the corner with rue Cardénal, at the east end of which a house with a half-timbered upper storey on a narrow stone pedestal – allowing carts to pass on either side – resembles nothing so much as a toadstool. From here, take rue Sauveterre circling southwest past more medieval houses and then cross over the southern end of the Grand Rue to find the rue de l'Ancienne Poste, which meanders generally back northwards to the Maison des Dîmes.

ARRIVAL AND INFORMATION — ISSIGEAC

By bus Infrequent buses from Bergerac stop on the main road on the southwest side of Issigeac.

Tourist office The office is set in a vaulted cellar beneath the bishop's palace (June–Sept Mon–Sat 10am–12.30pm & 2–6pm, Sun 10am–12.30pm; 05 53 58 79 62, http://pays-bergerac-tourisme.com). As well as holding temporary exhibitions, which allow you to explore a few rooms of the palace, the office can provide you with a walking guide to the village.

ACCOMMODATION AND EATING

La Brucelière Place Capelle, http://labruceliere.fr. Located by the roundabout on the road to Beaumont, the cheery, family-run *Brucelière* offers five light and airy rooms with polished floors, beige curtains, wicker chairs, and crisp white bedlinen. Whether you're staying here or not, it'd be remiss not to give its handsome, yellow and cream stone restaurant a try. *Menus* feature devilishly tempting dishes like crayfish and mushrooms in ravioli parcels with shellfish sauce, and crème brûlée with spiced pineapple. €€€

★ **Passé & Présent** 14 Grand Rue, 05 53 63 35 31. You could quite easily miss this wonderful *chambre d'hôte*, such is the mass of pretty foliage enveloping its little grey door. The interior is similarly winsome, with four gorgeous, parquet-floored rooms possessing lots of homely detail: ornamented fireplaces, handmade textiles and linens, black-and-white wall prints and shelves of antiques, many of which are for sale. All rooms, one of which sleeps four, offer views of the pretty garden below. €

Thénac

Take a drive through the vine-combed countryside southwest of Bergerac, close to the blink-and-you'll miss it hamlet of **THÉNAC**, and you may well come across rather incongruous-looking groups of people wearing the maroon robes of Buddhist monks. They're residents of **Plum Village** (aka Les Pruniers; http://plumvillage.org), a commune established by two Vietnamese monks in 1982 to provide Buddhist **retreats** (€300–550 weekly per person, including accommodation), as well as shorter stays and **meditation classes** and "Days of Mindfulness" (donation expected), which have become very popular over the years. Even if you're not in search of enlightenment, Thénac itself makes for a lovely, quiet rural base from which to explore the countryside south of Bergerac.

ACCOMMODATION — THÉNAC

Château de Panisseau http://chateaudepanisseau.com. Built by the English during the twelfth century, this château just outside Thénac is a good option for families, with well-equipped four- to eight-bedroom *gîtes* and very comfortable rooms with shared kitchen facilities; guests can make use of the heated pool, gym and sauna. Tastings of the estate wines and vineyard tours are also available. €€

Eymet

In contrast to Issigeac's meandering medieval streets, **EYMET**, 15km to the southwest, is laid out on a typical *bastide* chequerboard plan around a well-preserved arcaded central square, **place Gambetta**. Founded in 1270 by Alphonse de Poitiers, Eymet changed hands on several occasions – not always by force – during the Hundred Years' War and later joined Bergerac as a bastion of Protestantism. Indeed, locals are still proud of the fact that in 1588 Henry of Navarre, the then leader of the Protestant armies and future King Henry IV, wrote a letter from Eymet to his mistress, Diane d'Andouins. With its distinctive sloping roof, corner tower and trefoil windows, the house in which he supposedly set pen to paper is the grandest on **place Gambetta**; naturally, it's called the **Maison d'Amour**. Otherwise, the square – also known as place des Arcades – is a wonderful confection of rough-hewn stone buildings and timbered medieval houses, their thick beams creaking and curving with age. Three sides of the square shelter broad arcades, variously concealing cafés and shops – the only thing rather spoiling the whole ensemble is the proliferation of cars.

Once you've soaked up the atmosphere here – which will take longer if you chance to be here for the Thursday-morning **market** – head to Eymet's ruined **castle**, north of the centre. It hasn't been developed as a tourist sight at all, so you're free to wander inside the curtain wall and right up to the largely intact thirteenth-century keep, built shortly before the *bastide* itself. The **riverfront** plays a surprisingly low-key role in town life, but it's worth a quick walk along it; look out for the communal village laundry sinks here, which were still in use until surprisingly recently.

ARRIVAL AND INFORMATION — EYMET

By bus Buses from Bergerac and Issigeac stop on the main boulevard, east of the central square.
Destinations Allemans-du-Dropt (15min); Bergerac (45min); Issigeac (25min).
Tourist office 45 place Gambetta, under the arcades on the square's southeastern corner (May–Sept Mon–Sat 10am–12.30pm & 2–6.30pm, plus Sun 10am–12.30pm in July & Aug; Oct–April Tues–Sat 10am–12.30pm & 2–5.30pm; 05 53 23 74 95, http://eymet-dordogne.fr).

ACCOMMODATION AND EATING

52 Eymet 52 rue du Temple, http://52eymet.com. Just back from place Gambetta, the four gorgeous rooms at this English-run *chambre d'hôte* are individually decorated in antiques, dainty china, gold-rimmed chairs and mirrors, and each has its own balcony. It also opens up to non-guests for a lovely home-made afternoon tea. Two-night min stay. €€
Camping du Château Rue de la Sole, 05 53 23 80 28. A modest, peaceful little site north of place Gambetta between the château and the river; facilities include decent shower blocks, laundry and wi-fi, plus bike and boat rental. €

★ **La Cour d'Eymet** 32 bd National, http://lacourdeymet.com. Set inside an elegant old building with a shady summer courtyard, this is the locals' choice when it comes to eating out in Eymet. The food is based on local products used in a refreshingly modern way and includes dishes like prawn crumble with a carrot and celery fondant, and white truffles or beef cooked for seven hours in a chocolate sauce. €€€

Maison 20 20 rue Traversière, http://maison20.com. On a quiet street one block west of place Gambetta and running parallel to bd National, is this very stylish French/Kiwi-run boutique *chambre d'hôte*. The two rooms are a cool mix of contemporary and antique; there's also a self-contained apartment that sleeps up to four. €€€

La Maison d'Amour 37 place Gambetta, 05 53 22 34 64. Place Gambetta has plenty of places to eat, the best of which is this always-busy crêperie and *salon de thé*. You'll have a tricky time choosing from a mouth-watering menu of stuffed *galettes* like *canard à la Royale* (duck breast with honey and vinegar) and *Normande* (chicken with mushrooms and cider), but there are also some decent veggie options and salad platters. The interior is nicely done, but you can't beat sitting out on the colourful terrace. €

Église Saint-Eutrope

Free

Some 10km downstream from Eymet lies the tiny village of **ALLEMANS-DU-DROPT**, not much more than a central square and the **Église Saint-Eutrope**. The church's top-heavy lantern tower (topped with a carp as opposed to a cock) and grand west door are both nineteenth-century additions to this much-altered tenth-century building. The interior, meanwhile, would be unremarkable were it not for some recently restored fifteenth-century **frescoes** depicting the Crucifixion and Last Judgement. A number of scenes have been lost or damaged over the years, but on the whole the paintings, which were only rediscovered in 1935, are unusually complete. They read from left to right as you enter, starting with the Last Supper and ending with a particularly graphic view of Hell. Despite the best efforts of St Michael, clad in medieval armour, a mere two souls seem bound for heaven while the damned are being carried off by the basket-load, or skewered on a spit, to be thrust into a boiling cauldron.

ARRIVAL AND INFORMATION　　　　　　　　　　　　　　　　　　　ALLEMANS-DU-DROPT

By bus Buses stop on place de la Mairie, which is located southwest of the church.

ACCOMMODATION AND EATING

Camping Municipal 05 53 20 23 37. Allemans-du-Dropt has a tiny, low-key municipal campsite beside the river, north across the old stone bridge from the village. Closed mid-Oct to March. €

L'Étape Gasconne Place de la Mairie, http://letapegasconne-hotel.com. Just across from the market hall, this is a peaceful hotel whose comfortable rooms rather belie the dowdy, old-fashioned bar downstairs. Three rooms have balconies looking onto the outdoor pool, and in the absence of anywhere else to eat in the village, there's a reasonable restaurant serving traditional cuisine. €

Duras and around

From Allemans, the Dropt winds its way northwest for 10km to where the castle-town of **DURAS** lords it over the valley from its rocky outcrop. The château towers were truncated during the Revolution, but they still afford fine views beyond the Dropt to an enchanting region of rolling hills topped with windmills, of pasture, orchards, woods and, particularly to the north, of vines. The town of Duras sits at the heart of an interesting **wine region**, worthy of its own *appellation*. Sandwiched between Bergerac and the Entre-Deux-Mers region, Duras wines come in all shades: reds, dry whites, and some sweet whites that are lighter than those of Monbazillac.

Château des Ducs de Duras

Charge • http://chateau-de-duras.com

The chequered history of Duras is evident in the mix-and-match architecture of the **Château des Ducs de Duras**, which dominates the town. The château was founded in

1137, but then rebuilt after 1308 by Bertrand de Goth, nephew of Pope Clément V; it is said he used money confiscated from the Templars. Rebuilt again after the Hundred Years' War, it was then extensively remodelled during the more peaceful and prosperous late sixteenth and seventeenth centuries. The finishing touches were added in 1741, just in time to be ransacked during the Revolution, after which the château was left to crumble until the commune bought it in 1969. Since then, it has been thoroughly restored, allowing you to visit almost the whole building, from the basements, where the bakery is still recognizable, to the panoramic ramparts at the top. On your way round, look out for wells cut straight through the bedrock and freshwater tanks in case of siege, and a kitchen fireplace big enough to roast a whole ox. The dukes obviously liked to build on a grand scale – across a wide, open courtyard the entrance hall is impressive enough, and the ceremonial hall above has no fewer than eleven chimneys.

The château is probably the single best day out for families in the Bergerac area (where so many of the attractions are aimed more at adults). In summer it also stages occasional **medieval shows** with jousting, sword fights and knights in armour.

Moulin de Cocussotte
Charge • http://moulin-de-cocussotte.fr

Three kilometres southeast of Duras, back on the banks of the River Dropt just north of the town of St-Pierre-sur-Dropt, the **Moulin de Cocussotte** and its surrounding garden are a haven of bucolic calm. As well as the ivy-covered thirteenth-century mill and its slowly turning waterwheel, the garden has a wide variety of trees and plants and a shop-cum-café selling some rustic local produce including wine and honey.

Maison des Vins
Free • http://paysdeduras.com

The best place to find out more about the local wines is the tremendously innovative **Maison des Vins**, just downhill from Duras. As well as the standard opportunity to taste and buy, this showcase also has interactive displays on the history of the local wine region, and its own small sample vineyard, planted with different types of vine.

ARRIVAL AND INFORMATION — DURAS AND AROUND

By car Sadly, Duras is pretty much inaccessible without your own transport – the closest station is at Ste-Foy-la-Grande (see page 100), which is 27km to the north.
Tourist office 14 bd Jean-Brisseau (July & Aug daily 9am–12.30pm & 2–5.30pm, Sun 10am–1pm; Sept–June Mon–Fri 9am–12.30pm & 2–5.30pm; 05 53 93 71 18, http://paysdeduras.com).

ACCOMMODATION AND EATING

Camping Municipal 05 53 83 70 18. The only campsite in Duras is this extremely basic municipal site right under the château's north wall; the sole facilities are showers and toilets. Closed Sept–June, although pitches/van spaces are still accessible if you don't mind the lack of washroom facilities. €̄
Hostellerie des Ducs Bd Jean-Brisseau, http://hostellerieducs-duras.com. A few paces back along from the tourist office, this rather grand-looking building, complete with ostentatious turret hovering near the entrance, makes for a most comfortable stay; variously priced rooms are available, either with a shower or bath, and some with a/c. In addition to a pool, spa/sauna and flower-filled terrace, there's also an excellent conservatory restaurant serving upmarket regional cuisine; ox-cheek in belly of pork and local duck prepared in "different ways". There's also a small selection of vegetarian dishes. €€€

West of Bergerac

Downstream from Bergerac, the steep north slopes of the Dordogne valley are clothed in vines all the way along to the more illustrious vineyards of St-Émilion. The valley here is flat and uninteresting, dominated by a major road and rail line, but there are a few worthwhile diversions en route. First is **Ste-Foy-la-Grande**, which – with its excellent Saturday market and medieval traces – is the most interesting town on this stretch. From here, it's a short drive to the well-preserved mosaics at **Montcaret**'s Gallo-Roman villa, which is by far the biggest draw in these parts; and to the **Château de Montaigne**, where the influential Renaissance thinker and confirmed sceptic, Michel de Montaigne, wrote most of his famous *Essais*.

GETTING AROUND — WEST OF BERGERAC

Public transport along this stretch of the Dordogne is limited to trains on the Sarlat–Bordeaux line. With just a couple of services a day between some of these towns, it requires careful planning and a fair bit of walking to reach the area's more interesting sites.

Ste-Foy-la-Grande

Heading west from Bergerac along the River Dordogne, the first place of any size is the prosperous town of **STE-FOY-LA-GRANDE**. The central **place Gambetta** retains some of its original arcades, now shading lively café terraces, while **rue de la République** also boasts several fine, timbered medieval houses, the most grandiose of which, with its corner tower, now houses the tourist office. However, it's the soaring, jagged spire of the **Église Notre-Dame** that marks this particular building out as the street's most prominent edifice. The bulk of this present incarnation dates from the mid-seventeenth century, its beautifully proportioned interior pure Gothic, with tall, slender pillars reaching upwards to a fine rib-vaulted ceiling. Take a look, too, at the stained-glass windows, depicting characters from the Old and New Testaments.

Also worth a wander is the riverside esplanade a short walk to the north, from where you can cross the river via the pont Michel-Montaigne to visit Ste-Foy's modest museum, the **Maison du Fleuve et du Vin** (charge), covering the role played by river trade in the town's history and providing information on the wine produced around Ste-Foy. Even if that doesn't tempt you, it's definitely worth timing your visit to Ste-Foy to catch the Saturday-morning **market**, one of the region's biggest and most important, when the whole town centre is closed to traffic.

ARRIVAL AND INFORMATION — STE-FOY-LA-GRANDE

By train The *gare SNCF* is a 5min walk south of Ste-Foy; from the station, turn left along av de la Gare then walk north along av Paul Broca and then rue Victor-Hugo, the town's major shopping street.

Destinations Bergerac (15 daily; 20min); Bordeaux (15 daily; 1hr); Castillon-la-Bataille (15 daily; 15–20min); Lamothe-Montravel (1–3 daily; 15–20min); St-Émilion (15 daily; 30min).

Tourist office 102 rue de la République (Jan–June & Sept–Dec Mon–Sat 9.30am–12.30pm & 2–5.30pm; July & Aug Mon–Sat 9.30am–1pm & 2–6.30pm, Sun 10am–1pm & 2–5.30pm; 05 57 46 03 00, http://tourisme-dordogne-paysfoyen.com).

Canoe rental In July and Aug you can rent canoes from Canoë Kayak (http://canoe-kayak-port-ste-foy.com), on the north side of the river opposite *Camping de la Bastide*.

ACCOMMODATION AND EATING

Au Fil de l'Eau 3 rue de la Rouquette, http://aufildeleau-33.fr. A carnivore's paradise, featuring a duck-heavy menu with plenty of red meat and poultry thrown in. The wine list is vast with lots of organic options. Vegetarians should make their dietary requirements known at the time of booking. €€€

Camping de la Bastide Allée du Camping, http://camping-bastide.com. Just 500m east of town along the river's south bank on av Georges-Clemenceau – the extension of rue de la République – this is a small and comfortable three-star site, with modern shower blocks, a laundry, play area, games room and pool; mobile homes are also available to rent. €

Grand Hôtel 117 rue de la République, http://grandhotel-sainte-foy.com. Not nearly as grand as its name implies, this is nevertheless a decent enough hotel, with airy, high-ceilinged rooms, albeit slightly frayed around the edges. Still, it's handily located bang in the centre and fairly priced. €

Le Victor Hugo 101 rue Victor-Hugo, 05 57 41 35 43. Just on the edge of the old centre as you're coming in from the train station, the ten spotlessly clean, generously sized rooms here are painted in warm colours, and come with beautifully styled wood-carved furnishings. There's also an excellent restaurant serving classic French dishes. €€€

Around Ste-Foy-la-Grande

The area **around Ste-Foy-la-Grande** holds several worthwhile excursions, though in order to reach any of them, you will require your own wheels. One attractive option, particularly if you don't have a car, would be to rent a bike in Ste-Foy and then follow the flat, quiet side roads running parallel to the D936.

Jardins de Sardy
Charge • http://jardinsdesardy.com

West from Ste-Foy on the D936, you can make a brief detour after about 10km up into the hills north of the river to visit the **Jardins de Sardy** in Vélines. The entry fee is a bit steep, but the gardens – a combination of English and Italian style – occupy a pretty, sheltered spot overlooking the Dordogne. The centrepiece is an informal pond garden set against the wisteria-covered farmhouse.

Villa Gallo-Romaine de Montcaret
Charge • http://villa-montcaret.fr

Twelve kilometres west of Ste-Foy-la-Grande, in the tiny village of **MONTCARET**, the remains of the fourth-century **Villa Gallo-Romaine de Montcaret** lie randomly scattered around the village church. The first mosaic of this Gallo-Roman villa was discovered in 1827, but it wasn't until the early twentieth century that major excavation works took place, carried out by local villager Pierre-Martial Tauziac. Still, only about one-tenth of the villa has been fully excavated, but it's more than enough to demonstrate the occupants' affluent lifestyle, from underfloor heating and a variety of hot and cold baths to a grand reception room measuring 350 square metres. The floors, baths and covered walkways were laid with elaborate mosaics, of which large areas have survived relatively intact, most notably in the **cold bath**, which is superbly decorated with shellfish, dolphins and octopuses – the only figurative decorations remaining. No less impressive is the "dining room", or **Cruciform Room**, housed within a glass building adjoining the reception; here, you can see the more abstract pattern of shields and fish scales, alongside a couple of skeletons; note, however, that from mid-November to mid-April those mosaics outdoors are covered to protect them from frost and are therefore not on view. The reception area houses a small **museum** displaying some of the many objects found on the site, such as pottery fragments, bits of axes, amphorae and oil lamps.

ACCOMMODATION	MONTCARET

À l'Olivier 7 rue de la Villa Gallo-Romaine, 05 53 61 65 87. Right opposite Montcaret's village church and Roman villa, this child-friendly *chambre d'hôte* has large, peaceful gardens and comfortable but rather plain rooms, and offers a very relaxed place to stay. Dog-friendly. €

Château de Montaigne
Charge • http://chateau-montaigne.com

Back lanes lead 3km northwest from Montcaret to the sleepy village of **ST-MICHEL-DE-MONTAIGNE**, where Montaigne (1533–92) wrote many of his chatty, digressive and influential essays on the nature of life and humankind. Even if you haven't read any of his works, it's worth making the pilgrimage to the **Château de Montaigne**, just beyond the village to the north, to learn more about this engaging, if somewhat quirky and complex, character. Montaigne's castle residence burned down in 1885, and its modern reconstruction is closed to the public. You can, however, sign up for a guided tour (in French only) of the fourteenth-century **tower** where Montaigne closeted himself away after 1571 to work on his three volumes of essays. On the ground floor was his private chapel, the first floor is the room where he died, and the final storey held the library. Unfortunately, his priceless collection of more than a thousand books, all carefully annotated, was dispersed immediately after his death, but some traces of his thought can still be found in the Greek and Latin maxims he inscribed on the beams.

THE LORD OF MONTAIGNE

The third son of a Catholic father and a mother from a wealthy Spanish-Portuguese Jewish family, Michel Eyquem, **Lord of Montaigne**, had an unusual education which involved everyone, including the servants, speaking to him in Latin, and being woken by a musician to ensure "his brain not be damaged". It certainly seems to have caused no harm, since Montaigne went on to become a councillor and later mayor of Bordeaux, and was highly respected for his tolerance, wisdom and diplomacy. There is evidence that he also possessed a mischievous sense of humour – throughout the bitter Religious Wars, the Catholic Montaigne apparently took pleasure in ringing his chapel bell as loudly and as often as possible to annoy his Protestant neighbours. On the other hand, it must also be said that Montaigne, who held the Protestant leader Henry of Navarre in great esteem, played an important role in resolving the conflict, though he didn't live to see peace restored in 1598.

Though he attended Mass regularly before his death, and received the last sacrament, Montaigne's **writings** are renowned for their scepticism; in a typical outburst he declares, "Man is insane. He wouldn't know how to create a maggot, and he creates Gods by the dozen." His philosophical standpoint was essentially an argument for introspection – "if man does not know himself, then what can he know?" While it is criticized as being inconclusive, his legacy is rather his great originality of thought and his essays' wide-ranging questioning of generally accepted truths.

East of Bergerac

The real interest and beauty of the Bergerac region lies upstream of the city, where the Dordogne river makes two great meanders near **Trémolat** and **Limeuil**: here, castles, abbeys and pretty villages of soft stone crowd the hilltops and valley floors. There are two main tourist routes: along the Dordogne river itself, or looping inland up the heavily wooded **Couze valley** to the village of **Cadouin**, with its austere abbey church and elaborately carved cloister.

GETTING AROUND   EAST OF BERGERAC

Transport along the Dordogne valley is provided by trains on the Bergerac–Sarlat line, with the stations at Lalinde, Trémolat and Le Buisson served fairly regularly. To reach the towns and churches on the inland route, you'll need your own car or bike – though it's hilly country for cycling.

Along the Dordogne

Following the Dordogne east from Bergerac, the first sight of any interest is the half-completed **Château de Lanquais**, as much for the story behind its architecture as for its somewhat dilapidated interiors. The working paper mills at **Couze-et-St-Front** also merit a quick stop, while **Lalinde** provides hotels, transport and other tourist facilities, before you meet the first of the Dordogne's great loops, the **Cingle de Trémolat**. At the top of the second meander, the feudal village of **Limeuil** marks where the River Vézère flows into the Dordogne and where you pass into the Périgord Noir, while the final destination, **Le Buisson-de-Cadouin**, sits on an important rail junction on the Bergerac–Sarlat and Agen–Périgueux lines.

Château de Lanquais
Charge • http://chateaudelanquais.fr

Some 15km east of Bergerac and just outside the village of the same name, the **Château de Lanquais** is described in tourist literature as "Périgord's unfinished Louvre", and its isolation and rugged charm make for an enjoyable little excursion; come in July or August and you might coincide with regular special events such as medieval fairs, night markets and antique roadshows.

In the mid-sixteenth century, when Bergerac and much of the surrounding country was under Protestant sway, Lanquais was owned by a Catholic, Isabeau de Limeuil, cousin to Catherine de Medici. In a brave – or foolhardy – move, Isabeau commissioned the architects of the Louvre in Catholic Paris to add a wing in similar style to her castle. Before the work could be completed, however, the Protestant armies besieged the château in 1577 and left the facade pitted by cannonballs. They didn't destroy it, though, and you can still discern the change in styles where the Renaissance wing, with its dormer windows and ornamentation, was grafted onto the medieval fortress. It's an imposing rather than an attractive building and some of the **interiors** are in need of restoration. As in many Périgord châteaux, it's the fireplaces that steal the show, notably that occupying one whole wall of the "blue salon" with its two enigmatic bulls'-skull carvings. The difference between medieval and Renaissance styles is perhaps most discernible in the kitchen, where the large stone slabs of the former give way to the Italian *pisé* style of mosaic flooring, whereby stones are dug into the earth. Underneath the kitchen are the extensive cellars, part of which once functioned as a prison – as evidenced by the one remaining gloomy cell. The adjoining pavilion, meanwhile, was a nineteenth-century addition by a local abbot.

Couze-et-St-Front

Two kilometres east of Lanquais, the road drops down to the Dordogne again at what was once an important paper-making centre, **COUZE-ET-ST-FRONT**. Head down a side street in the northwest corner of the town to see a series of beautiful old mill buildings, some cut into the cliff face itself, all profiting from the source of power provided by the River Couze. During the industry's heyday in the late fifteenth century – when some thirteen mills were in operation here – *gabares* would carry the paper along the river to Bordeaux, from where it would be exported abroad, principally to the Netherlands.

Moulin de la Rouzique
Charge • http://moulin-de-la-rouzique.com

The only waterwheel still turning in Couze-et-St-Front is that of the fifteenth-century **Moulin de la Rouzique**, where you can see how paper is made in time-honoured fashion, using rags. Note that it is only possible to visit on a **guided tour**, for which there are no set times, so you'll just have to turn up and wait until there are enough people for a small group. Tours begin inside the *chiffonnerie* (rags room), itself hewn into the rock face, where the rags were stored to make the paper pulp – a mix of plant fibres and water. Here, the crushing machine would set to work, its hammers crushing the material, which would eventually soften and decompose following several weeks in large vats of water. Today, though, a far more efficient Dutch machine is used, which is able to convert around 30kg of rags into paper pulp in around ten hours, a process so powerful that it renders decomposition unnecessary. The metal waterwheel still turns at quite a lick, having replaced the old wooden wheel (still on view) some years ago. The tour concludes in the drying room, where you can examine a beautiful collection of antique watermarked papers.

In July and August, there's a free daily paper-making workshop for children (and adults, if they want to, too) at 10am.

Lalinde

The only town of any size along this stretch of the Dordogne, **LALINDE** guards an important river-crossing 3km upstream from Couze and 23km from Bergerac. In 1267 Henry III of England chose the little settlement on the river's north bank to become the first English *bastide*. The central square, grid plan and fragments of wall remain, but Lalinde today is mainly of interest as a place to stay or have a bite to eat, and to visit its **market** (Thursday is the main trading day, and there's also a smaller farmers' market on Saturday), though the **Église Sainte-Colombe** and gardens on its balustraded riverfront and a large canal basin immediately to the north are worth a quick stop. The **canal** was built in the nineteenth century to bypass a dangerous set of rapids, made more hazardous in legendary times by the presence of a dragon, La Coloubre, which lurked in a cave on the opposite bank. According to legend, St Front got rid of the monster in the fourth century by burning it on an enormous bonfire on the hill above its lair – grateful citizens later erected the tiny clifftop **Chapelle de St-Front** in his honour. You can reach the chapel in ten minutes on foot by crossing the bridge and then scrambling up the steep marked path in the hillside.

ARRIVAL AND INFORMATION   LALINDE

By train The *gare SNCF* is a 5min walk across the canal on av du Général Leclerc.
Destinations Bergerac (6 daily; 25min); Couze (3 daily; 5min); Les Eyzies (2–6 daily; 1hr–2hr 45min); Sarlat (7 daily; 45min); Trémolat (7 daily; 10min).
By bus Buses to Bergerac depart from the central place de la Halle.

Destinations Bergerac (40min); Port de Couze (15min).
Tourist office In the Jardin Public, by the old bridge (Nov–March Thurs 9am–12.30pm & 2–5.30pm; April–June, Sept & Oct Mon–Fri 9am–12.30pm & 2–5.30pm; July & Aug Mon–Sat 9am–1pm & 2.30–6pm, Sun 9am–1pm; 05 53 61 08 55, http://ville-lalinde.fr).

ACCOMMODATION AND EATING

La Closerie de Baneuil 182 rue du Donjon, Baneuil, https://lacloseriedebaneuil.fr. *Chambre d'hôtes* and *gîtes* in a gorgeous old manor house, set amid vast, gated gardens. There's a heated outdoor swimming pool, spa, a gourmet restaurant, tennis court, ping-pong table, and even *pétanque* sets on request. €€

★ **Côté Rivage** Badefols-sur-Dordogne, http://cote-dordogne.com. Some 3km east of Lalinde, on the south side of the river in Badefols-sur-Dordogne, this refined hotel offers seven beautifully thought-out rooms, each styled according to a different theme: wine, chocolate, the *bastide* and so forth. The restaurant is a joy too; it not only looks superb, with fantastic views across the river, but the food is first-class; melon gazpacho, prawn risotto or slow-cooked lamb are typically tantalizing dishes. €€

Trémolat

Some 8km upstream from Lalinde the Dordogne snakes its way through two huge loops, of which the first you come to, the **Cingle de Trémolat**, is the tighter and therefore more impressive. A bend in the river might not sound like a very worthwhile sight, but this is where one of the most beautiful rivers in France puts on its prettiest face. The best views are from the limestone cliffs to the north of the village – follow signs to the Panorama de Trémolat, or on upwards to the Belvédère de Rocamadour – from where the whole meander is visible. Over to the east, a heavily fortified church tower pinpoints the village of **TRÉMOLAT**, one of the more picturesque in the area and home to one of the finest hotel-restaurants in the Dordogne, as well as a boulangerie and small supermarket where you could stock up on picnic supplies.

ARRIVAL AND INFORMATION   TRÉMOLAT

By train The *gare SNCF* is located just over 1km to the south of the village.
Destinations Bergerac (7 daily; 45min); Couze (3 daily; 25min); Lalinde (7 daily; 15min); Sarlat (7 daily; 35min).

Tourist office Tucked away in one corner just behind the church (July & Aug Mon–Thurs 9am–1pm & 2.30–5.30pm, Sun 2.30–5pm; May, June, Sept & Oct Mon–Fri 9am–12.30pm & 2–5.30pm; 05 53 22 89 33, http://tremolat.fr).

ACCOMMODATION AND EATING

★ **Bistrot de la Place** Le Bourg, http://vieux-logis.com. Operated by the *Vieux Logis* (see below), the sprightly *Bistrot de la Place*, just on the corner of the main square, is the less expensive version of the hotel's upscale restaurant, but it doesn't scrimp on quality. This apparently simple, workaday place offers a superb take on old Périgord classics: expect dishes such as cream of asparagus with prawn curry or guineafowl with leek and hazelnut crumble. €€€
Camping de Trémolat http://camping-tremolat.com. On the banks of the Dordogne, this is a good-sized campsite, also with mobile homes to rent. There's a restaurant/bar, pool and excellent sports facilities, including canoeing and kayaking. €
★ **Vieux Logis** 81 rue des Écoles, http://vieux-logis.com. Having served as a place of worship and a tobacco farm, this

is now one of the best hotels in the Dordogne and one of the original members of the upmarket Relais & Châteaux chain. There are 23 utterly swish rooms with a 1920s feel, and though all differ somewhat, most have carved wooden furnishings and portraits of dour Victorian-era families on the walls. In addition, there are two cosy lounges, a smoking room, large pool surrounded by formal gardens and a lovely terrace for summer dining at the hotel's phenomenal, Michelin-starred gastronomic restaurant where renowned chef Vincent Arnould offers a creative modern take on local classics. €€€

Limeuil

The D31 east from Trémolat takes you over a ridge for a bird's-eye view of the second meander in the Dordogne, the **Cingle de Limeuil**. But this pretty loop is only half the story; the road drops down to the gorgeous honey-stoned village of **LIMEUIL**, which straggles down a steep hillside leading to the confluence of the Vézère and Dordogne rivers. Limeuil reached its first peak in the Middle Ages, thanks to its strategic location, and then another in the nineteenth century when local craftspeople built boats for the booming river trade. Today, the flower-filled village relies on tourism for its bread and butter, and can be over-run in high season, but with an ideal combination of waterborne river activities, pretty streets with an arty, hippy air and good places to eat, it offers something for everyone.

Limeuil's willow-shaded riverbank makes a good picnic spot, and also has a pebbly **beach** from which you can go for a dip in the river. This is also the base for all canoeing and kayaking trips on the river.

Jardins Panoramiques de Limeuil
Rue du Port • Charge • http://jardins-panoramiques-limeuil.com

Passing under Limeuil's old gate and huffing and puffing up the narrow, central and steep rue du Port will bring you to the hilltop **Les Jardins Panoramiques de Limeuil**, where the feudal château once stood. The gardens here are leafy, with pretty water features, and it does monopolize the best river views, but since the entry fee is about as steep as the hill it's on, you might prefer to head for the classic viewpoint of the Cingle de Limeuil near Trémolat (see above).

Atelier du Verre Soufflé
Rue de la Poste • Free • http://nicolas-guittet-verrier.com

Down at the bottom of the village is the **Atelier du Verre Soufflé** glassblowing workshop, where you can marvel as glass vases in a dozen different shades appear like magic out of the flames and, of course, buy one of the beautiful pieces to take home. There are no set opening hours, as these are governed by whenever the owner feels like turning up.

ARRIVAL AND INFORMATION — LIMEUIL

By car As Limeuil isn't on the train line and the bus service is scanty at best, you'll need a car to get here.
Tourist office Jardin de la Mairie, just up rue du Port and through a little gateway on your left (Jan–March & Oct–Dec Tues, Wed & Fri 10am–12.30pm & 2–5pm, Mon & Thurs 10am–12.30pm; April–June Mon–Sat 9.30am–12.30pm & 2–6pm, Sun 9.30am–12.30pm; Sept Mon–Sat 9.30am–6pm, Sun 9.30am–12.30pm; July & Aug daily 9.30am–6.30pm; 05 53 63 38 90, http://limeuil-en-perigord.com).

Informative walking leaflet guide you around the village.
Canoe and kayak rental Canoës Limeuil (http://canoes-limeuil.fr), based on Limeuil's beach, offers a 1hr trip along the Dordogne river to Buisson (6km) by canoe or kayak. You can also hire canoes and kayaks for longer periods.
Horseriding There's an excellent riding centre, La Haute Yerle (http://hauteyerle.fr), a little to the southwest of Limeuil off the D2 road in Alles-sur-Dordogne, which offers treks from half a day up to a week's circuit of the Périgord Noir.

ACCOMMODATION AND EATING

Au Bon Accueil Rue du Port, http://au-bon-accueil-limeuil.com. Small, friendly hotel-restaurant towards the top end of this pretty cobbled street. In a separate building to the restaurant, the hotel has five rooms, though they're rather sparse, with smallish beds and boxy bathrooms. The restaurant, meanwhile, not only looks great – with exposed stone walls and a vine-covered terrace overlooking the valley – but the food is outstanding; sublime dishes like pork in a rich mustard sauce, and rabbit *fricassée*, in addition to half a dozen daily home-made desserts chalked up on a board. €€
★ **Port de Limeuil** Rue du Port, http://leportdelimeuil.com. Campers are very well catered for at this excellent four-

star site across the river from the village. Facilities include shaded pitches, mobile homes, gîtes, glamping tents and lodges, a laundry, restaurant/snack bar, lots of sporting activities, pool and bike/canoe hire. Dogs welcome. €€

★ **Garden Party** Place des Fossés, 06 47 60 22 28. Right by the entrance to the Jardins Panoramiques at the top of town, this is a fun, poppy place to eat and the terrace is the most convivial spot in town for an evening *apéro*. The frequently changing menu is limited to three or four light, creative dishes (one of which is normally vegetarian). €€€

Chapelle St-Martin
Free

One kilometre northeast of Limeuil on the Le Bugue road is the **Chapelle St-Martin**; opening hours can be as up and down as the building's history – if it's locked, you can get the key from the house opposite. A Latin inscription inside this dumpy little Romanesque chapel records that it was dedicated to St Thomas à Becket, the archbishop of Canterbury murdered by Henry II's courtiers in 1170 after the king famously asked who would rid him of "this turbulent priest". The inscription goes on to relate that the chapel was founded in 1194 by Henry's son and successor, Richard the Lionheart, together with Philippe II (Philippe Auguste) of France on their return from the Third Crusade, "to beseech the pardon of God". There are also the remnants of fifteenth-century frescoes in the choir: to the right a Crucifixion scene and the Descent from the Cross; to the left the Flight from Egypt.

Le Buisson-de-Cadouin

LE BUISSON-DE-CADOUIN, 5km south of Limeuil, is the last stop on this stretch of the Dordogne river. Other than the **Grottes de Maxange**, the town is no great shakes when it comes to tourist attractions, but it has convenient transport links and a few other facilities.

Grottes de Maxange
Charge • http://lesgrottesdemaxange.com

Just 1km southeast of Le Buisson-de-Cadouin, the **Grottes de Maxange** were discovered completely by chance in 2000 by the owner of the quarry in which they are located. The caves were opened to the public in 2003, while a newly discovered and equally impressive gallery was revealed in 2009; tours take in around 350m of the cavern. The Grottes de Maxange are particularly unusual in that they hide extensive displays of *excentriques*. These delicate limestone formations, some looping round on themselves, others suddenly veering off in a different direction, are believed to occur where water evaporates from extremely fine fissures in the rock. Here and there the walls glitter with star-like formations known as *aragonites*. Look out, too, for the cave-bear scratches on

> ### GROTTE DE CUSSAC
>
> In September 2000, great excitement broke out among art historians and archeologists when a speleologist nosing around Cussac, near Le Buisson-de-Cadouin, stumbled on a previously unknown decorated cave containing more than one hundred **prehistoric engravings**. So important is Marc Delluc's discovery that it's been dubbed the "Lascaux of engraving", in reference to the famous Vézère-valley cavern (see page 138).
>
> The Grotte de Cussac is particularly significant because of the number and size of the engravings. The biggest is a 4m-long bison, while some scenes comprise as many as forty figures. They are also unusually well preserved, the outlines etched deep into the clay by artists sometime between 25,000 and 30,000 years ago. **Horses**, **bison**, **mammoths**, **rhino** and **deer** all feature strongly, but there are also very rare representations of **birds**, as well as **female silhouettes**, **fertility symbols** and a strange long-snouted animal that has yet to be identified.
>
> Because of the vulnerability of these caves (see page 139), it is unlikely that Cussac will ever be opened to the public, but you can get a glimpse of what all the fuss is about at http://archeologie.culture.fr/fr/a-propos/grotte-cussac.

the walls. Maxange is also one of the more accessible caves in the region, with no stairs or narrow passages to negotiate – and little in the way of queuing for tickets.

ARRIVAL AND INFORMATION | LE BUISSON-DE-CADOUIN

By train Le Buisson-de-Cadouin is a junction on the Bordeaux–Sarlat and Agen–Périgueux train lines; its *gare SNCF* is a couple of minutes' walk north of the town centre; for a taxi call Taxi Morante (05 53 22 06 51).
Destinations Agen (4–6 daily; 1hr 30min); Bergerac (4–6 daily; 30–40min); Le Bugue (7 daily; 8min); Couze (3–4 daily; 25min); Les Eyzies (7 daily; 15min); Lalinde (6 daily; 20min); Périgueux (8 daily; 50min); Sarlat (5–7 daily; 40min); Trémolat (5 daily; 10min).
Tourist office Place André-Boissière, 150m down from the train station (July & Aug Mon–Sat 9.30am–1pm & 2–6pm, Sun 10am–1pm; May, June, Sept & Oct Mon, Tues, Thurs & Fri 9am–12.30pm & 2–5.30pm; Nov–April Fri 9am–12.30pm & 2–5.30pm; 05 53 22 06 09, http://lebuissondecadouin.fr).

ACCOMMODATION AND EATING

Manoir de Bellerive http://bellerivehotel.com. Just under 2km east of town on the road to Siorac, the *Manoir de Bellerive* is an elegant little château, built on the orders of Louis-Napoleon in 1830 and housing a charming luxury hotel set in an English-style park on the banks of the Dordogne. Some of the rooms in the original manor have river views, while those in the quieter *orangerie* annexe have private terraces. There's also a tennis court, pool and a perfect breakfast spot on the terrace overlooking the river. Its restaurant serves meals "inspired by the seasons and the surrounding countryside", which translates as fresh market and farm produce used to create dishes such as scallops in a cream of mushroom sauce or duck with walnut sauce. €€€
Le Pont de Vicq Av de la Dordogne, http://camping lepontdevicq.com. Around 2km beyond the train station, on the road to Le Bugue, this large and tidy three-star campsite has a heated pool, as well as a long river-beach for bathing, cabins for rent and canoe and kayak hire on site; in summer there's also a snack bar where you can drink and eat barbecued food till late. €

The Couze valley

The **Couze valley**, striking southeast of the paper-making town of Couze-et-St-Front, has provided an important thoroughfare since Gallo-Roman times. It's a region of thickly wooded hills and pastoral valleys, interspersed with comely villages, such as **Beaumont**, and hilltop churches, none finer than those at **St-Avit-Sénieur** and **Montferrand-du-Périgord**.

Beaumont

Part of Edward's I's motivation for founding **BEAUMONT** in 1272, on a dominant spur 10km upstream along the Couze from its confluence with the Dordogne, was to guard the trade routes along the valley. As in many such *bastides*, the fourteenth-century **Église Saint-Laurent-et-Saint-Front** was built for military as well as religious reasons – a final outpost of defence in times of attack – hence the two bulky towers either side of the entrance, and the well inside.

The north tower, to the left of the entrance, is the old clocktower; it is lower by some 30m than the south tower, a brooding presence complete with battlements. The largely Gothic interior is a hollow, single-nave structure, and is fairly ordinary save for its impressive vaulted ceiling.

The main focus of the town, however, is the attractive **place Centrale**, which once held sixteen arcades, of which seven now remain. The square's most notable building is **Maison Lafitte**, a fine timbered house on the south side, which used to sit above a covered market; note the cross of St Andrew set between the windows. The modern-day market takes place here on Tuesdays and Saturdays. Off to the west of the square stands the Porte de Luzier, one of the original sixteen town gates.

INFORMATION | BEAUMONT

By car There's no reliable public transport to Beaumont, so you'll need a car to get here.
Tourist office Place Centrale (July & Aug Mon–Sat 10am–12.30pm & 2–6pm, Sun 10am–12.30pm; Sept–June Mon–Fri 9am–12.30pm & 2–5.30pm; 05 53 22 39 12, http://pays-bergerac-tourisme.com). It stocks an impressive selection of English-language history and architecture leaflets on Beaumont, St-Avit and Montferrand.

St-Avit-Sénieur
Church Free

On the other side of the Couze valley from Beaumont, roughly 4km by road, the semi-ruined abbey of **St-Avit-Sénieur** stares across the countryside from another rocky knoll. It grew up around the burial place of a fifth-century hermit, Avitus, who was born at Lanquais and later served in the Visigoth army until taken prisoner in 507 by the Frankish king Clovis, a recent convert to Christianity. At some point during his fourteen years' captivity in Paris, Avitus followed suit, and was then instructed in a vision to return to Périgord, where he lived as a hermit until his death in 570. Tales of his miracles soon attracted pilgrims, and the simple chapel grew into a monastery; the present **church** was founded in the early twelfth century, and an inscription records that the saint's bones were brought here in 1117.

Montferrand-du-Périgord

Upstream of St-Avit-Sénieur, the D26 pushes southeast up the narrowing valley for another 8km to the tiny village of **MONTFERRAND-DU-PÉRIGORD**. With a clutch of typical Périgord houses sheltering beneath a semi-ruined château, this is one of those gorgeous lost hamlets that seems to have stopped moving forward in time about a hundred years ago; and if its looks weren't reason enough to make the minor detour out to Montferrand-du-Périgord, the excellent *Lou Peyrol* restaurant (see below) might sway you. A single street leads up past the village's superb sixteenth-century **market hall** to where a footpath veers west, past the château, its crumbling walls and a panoramic **viewpoint**. If you fancy stretching your legs a bit more then stick with the footpath, which wends its way through the woods. Roughly a kilometre later it emerges near the hilltop **Église St-Christophe**, standing on its own in a cemetery. It used to be the parish church but has been diminished over the years to little more than a stocky bell tower, so it's surprising to find that the twelfth- and fifteenth-century **frescoes** have survived. There's some wonderful detail to admire, not least on the north wall (to your left as you enter), where you can just about make out a sea monster, mouth agape as it readies itself to swallow the damned, next to which is a woman riding a lion, supposedly the symbol of lust. The oldest painting is on the north wall of the choir, portraying St Leonard releasing prisoners (the little building below symbolizing the prison), while St Christopher himself makes an appearance on the west wall, carrying the Infant Jesus on his shoulder.

ACCOMMODATION AND EATING   MONTFERRAND-DU-PÉRIGORD

★ **Lou Peyrol** La Barrière, http://hotel-loupeyrol-dordogne.com. Owned by a friendly English–French couple, this small, creeper-covered country hotel is down on the main road and has five rustic and simple rooms (think wrought-iron beds with floral-patterned bedspreads) and an excellent restaurant serving traditional Périgord cuisine. €

Cadouin

At the same time that Augustinian monks were busy building their church in honour of St Avit, the Cistercians founded a typically austere **abbey** in what is now **CADOUIN**, 8km northeast of Montferrand-du-Périgord, up the D25. Abbey aside, the village's handsome confection of honey-coloured stone buildings is a big draw for tourists, as is the Wednesday morning **market**, which spreads out over much of the town centre. Moreover, there's no shortage of terrific places to sleep and eat here, most on or just off pretty place de l'Abbaye. Leaving Cadouin, most people drop straight down to the Dordogne at Le Buisson and head for the caves around Les Eyzies (see page 124).

Abbaye de Cadouin
Place de l'Abbaye • Charge • http://abbaye-de-cadouin.com

The efforts of the Cistercians were given a boost when, in 1117, crusaders returning from the Holy Land brought them a piece of cloth believed to have been part of Christ's shroud.

For eight hundred years it drew flocks of pilgrims – including Eleanor of Aquitaine, Richard the Lionheart and King Louis IX – until in 1935 the two bands of embroidery at either end were shown to contain an Arabic text from the early eleventh century. The original cloth is no longer kept at the **Abbaye de Cadouin**, but a replica is displayed in the small museum at the entrance to the flamboyant Gothic **cloister**, which is accessed via a separate entrance to the north of the church door. In any case, the cloth plays second fiddle to the finely sculpted but badly damaged capitals around the cloister, most of which are concentrated along the north wall; the first one you come to is of two monks opening a book, beyond which are two merchants squabbling over a goose. Next to this, above the abbot's seat, is a superb bas-relief, showing Jesus carrying the cross while two soldiers dice for his tunic, and a procession of monks alongside a prostrate Mary Magdalene – the remains of a Crucifixion scene. A little further along you can just make out the traces of a fifteenth-century fresco, the only one remaining. Scattered along the east side of the cloister, meanwhile, are some twenty-five pendants, representing prophets and evangelists.

Adjacent to the cloister stands the contrastingly austere Romanesque church, **La Paroisse de Cadouin**, with its stark, monumental west wall and unusual double-tier belfry roofed with chestnut shingles. Inside, the triple nave is equally spartan and so high that the pillars appear to bulge outwards. You can still see the chains above the altar where the shroud was suspended in its casket, but the main point of interest is the stained glass in the north aisle, installed around a century ago, which recounts the story of the shroud's journey from Jerusalem.

ARRIVAL AND DEPARTURE · CADOUIN

By train The only way to travel here by public transport is by train to Le Buisson-de-Cadouin and then a taxi for 6km.

ACCOMMODATION

L'Ancienne Gendarmerie Rue de Beaumont, 05 53 58 39 84. Some 300m from the main square on the Beaumont road, this *chambre d'hôte* is set in Cadouin's former police station. There are four lovely en-suite rooms, each possessing warm stone walls, exposed beams and colourful floor tiling; two have their own balcony overlooking the garden. There's also an elegant communal sitting room, with an open hearth and books aplenty. The Dutch/French breakfast is excellent. €

★ **Auberge de Jeunesse** Abbaye de Cadouin, http://hifrance.org. Adjacent to the cloister, the monks' dormitories have been turned into an excellent and very friendly HI youth hostel, with five-, seven- and ten-bedded dorms, as well as private rooms with shower, basin and mezzanine sleeping area. There's also a well-equipped kitchen and laundry facilities. Picnics and hot evening meals can be provided upon request, though breakfast is included in the price. €

Les Jardins de l'Abbaye Rue de Monpazier, http://jardinsabbaye.com. Out on the Montferrand road just above the village, this is a calm, shady site which also has some attractive mobile homes set above the camping area on a series of picturesque ridges. Snack bar and outdoor pool. €

Les Songes de l'Abbaye Place de l'Abbaye, 05 53 63 94 18. Situated plum on the main square, this charming *gîte* has three exceptionally cool, gloriously colourful rooms (yellow, salmon, mauve and grey), all furnished in gorgeous French oak and chestnut wood. The bathrooms are similarly snappy, featuring huge showers, glass basins and wood-framed mirrors, as is the dining area with its red-painted wooden beams running across the ceiling. €

★ **Villa Marguerite** Place Géraud de Salles, http://villa-marguerite-cadouin.com. One of the Dordogne's most memorable *chambres d'hôtes*, the *Villa Marguerite* is so rammed with antique memories it might as well be a museum. Each of the five rooms is individually styled, one themed on ancient Greece, another the jungles of Central Africa. Everything is immaculately well kept, the owner loves a good chat and there's a cute little garden. It's just back from the main road at the western end of the village. €€

EATING

Les Terrasses de la Côte Rouge 6 rue de la Côte Rouge, http://lesterrassesdelacoterouge.fr. Run by a Dutch-Belgian couple who grow lots of the vegetables used in the colourful, creative dishes on site. Exposed-brick interiors and swing seats make it look more like it belongs in East Paris than the rural Dordogne. €€

Restaurant de l'Abbaye Place de l'Abbaye, 05 53 63 40 93. Cadouin's best restaurant offers tasty, traditional *menus*, from rabbit terrine with chestnuts to a terrific chocolate-nut pie; it's also renowned for its home-made garlic soup. The predominantly bare brick interior, with a beautiful stone fireplace at its centrepiece, looks fabulous, though dining alfresco on the terrace garden looking across to the abbey is no less inviting. €€€

Sarlat and the Périgord Noir

115 Sarlat-la-Canéda and around

122 The Vézère valley and around

141 The middle Dordogne

LA ROQUE-GAGEAC

Sarlat and the Périgord Noir

The central part of the Dordogne valley and its tributary, the valley of the Vézère, form the heart of the Périgord Noir. This is the classic Dordogne countryside of tourist brochures: rivers meandering through deep-cut valleys framed by limestone cliffs; dense, dark oak woods; orchards of walnut trees; and flocks of ducks and low-slung grey geese. This rich, fertile land has provided food and shelter since the earliest times, and the first settlers left behind them the world's greatest concentration of prehistoric sites. Later generations built the beetling medieval castles and huddled villages that now provide the region's iconic images. It is rich fare, best taken at a gentle pace, concentrating on a few sites rather than trying to see everything.

The focal point of the Périgord Noir region is its capital, **Sarlat-la-Canéda**. Though this medieval town boasts no great monuments, Sarlat is not to be missed, with a warren of old lanes, hidden courtyards and fine architecture – the background for many a period drama – not to mention its excellent weekly markets.

Sarlat is within spitting distance of the two iconic river valleys which have come to define the whole region. First up is the **Vézère valley**, cutting diagonally across the region from the northeast. The valley's immense, overhanging cliffs have been worn away by frost action over the millennia to create natural rock shelters where humans have sought refuge for thousands of years, leaving an incredible wealth of archeological and artistic evidence from the late Paleolithic era. The two unmissable highlights are the outstandingly preserved polychrome paintings of the **Grotte de Font-de-Gaume**, which you can still visit in the original, and the reproductions at **Lascaux**, near Montignac. The valley has more than cave paintings to offer, however: several sites show how cliff shelters were lived in throughout the Middle Ages up until relatively recently, while some breathtaking chasms like the **Gouffre de Proumeyssac** are the work of nature alone.

South of Sarlat, in the sublime, château-studded **Dordogne valley**, it's the region's medieval, feudal history that's most palpable. **Beynac** and **Castelnaud**, two semi-ruined fortresses on either side of the river, are without doubt the most spectacular. Closer to river level, **La Roque-Gageac** presents a more homely scene. From a distance, save for its red-tiled roofs, the village is barely distinguishable from the vertical cliff into which it nestles. This is also one of the best spots in the whole country to hop on a **canoe** and take a leisurely trip downstream.

> ### THE DORDOGNE AND LOT'S BEST CAVE ART
>
> **Lascaux IV** Superb replica of the summit of Cro-Magnon art. See page 138
> **Grotte de Font-de-Gaume** Beautifully preserved paintings and engravings in a narrow tunnel. See page 127
> **Abri du Cap Blanc** Sculpted frieze of life-size horses and bison. See page 129
> **Grotte de Pech-Merle** "The chapel of mammoths" stands out among more than five hundred drawings. See page 200
> **Grotte de Rouffignac** Hop on an electric train to view drawings of mammoths and woolly rhinos in a 1km-long cave. See page 130
> **Grotte du Sorcier** Mystifying engraving of a human – the "Sorcier" – among many animals. See page 133

THE GARDENS AT THE MANOIR D'EYRIGNAC

Highlights

❶ **Sarlat-la-Canéda** Wander the cobbled lanes of this beautifully preserved medieval town, which hosts one of the region's best markets. See page 115

❷ **Manoir d'Eyrignac** The formal gardens, with their manicured hornbeam hedges and trompe l'oeil parterre, are as much a work of art as of nature. See page 121

❸ **Vézère valley** Prehistoric artists left moving testimony of their skill in myriad decorated caves here, among them the magnificent friezes of Lascaux and Font-de-Gaume, the bas-reliefs of the Abri du Cap Blanc and the drawings of the Grotte de Rouffignac. See page 122

❹ **La Roque-St-Christophe** Multistorey living medieval-style in these dozens of rock shelters cut into the limestone cliffs. See page 135

❺ **Château de Castelnaud** This archetypal feudal fortress lording it over the Dordogne valley contains a superb museum of medieval warfare and offers lots of summertime family fun. See page 148

❻ **La Roque-Gageac** One of the region's most picturesque villages, with its jumble of roofs and the towering cliffs above mirrored in the slow-moving waters of the Dordogne, which you can explore by boat. See page 149

HIGHLIGHTS ARE MARKED ON THE MAP ON PAGE 114

SARLAT AND THE PÉRIGORD NOIR

With so many first-class sights in such a compact area, it's not surprising that this is one of the most heavily visited inland areas of France, and as a result has all the concomitant problems of crowds, high prices and tat. If you can't come out of season, seek accommodation away from the main centres, visit places first thing in the morning and always drive along the back roads, even when there is a more direct route available. On the plus side, the competition for tourism revenue has resulted in some outstandingly good-value places to stay.

GETTING AROUND THE PÉRIGORD NOIR

By train Though you'll need your own transport for exploring much of the Périgord Noir, two train lines cut through the area. Sarlat is the terminus of a line from Bordeaux via Bergerac, while trains between Agen and Périgueux stop at Le Bugue and Les Eyzies; the best place to change between the two lines is Le Buisson. In addition, the northern Vézère valley can be accessed from Terrasson, on the Brive–Bordeaux main line.

By bus The region is served by a minimal smattering of bus routes, though even these early-morning school services can fizzle out entirely in the school holidays.

By bike In addition to bike rental outfits in Sarlat, Les Eyzies and Castelnaud-la-Chapelle, Bike Bus, based at Castelnaud (http://bike-bus.com), offers a range of bikes, including mountain bikes, tourers and children's bikes. It delivers free to Sarlat, Beynac, La Roque-Gageac, Vitrac and most other towns in the immediate region so long as a minimum rental fee is met. Similarly Aquitaine Bike (http://aquitainebike.com), based in the Périgord Noir at Le Coux-et-Bigaroque, offers free deliveries within 20km, or further afield for a fee.

HIGHLIGHTS
1. Sarlat-la-Canéda
2. Manoir d'Eyrignac
3. Vézère valley
4. La Roque-St-Christophe
5. Château de Castelnaud
6. La Roque-Gageac

FESTIVALS, EVENTS AND MARKETS

The list below comprises some of the biggest and most interesting of the **festivals** and **events** in this region. Where we haven't given a specific information number or website, contact the relevant tourist office.

Late March, April or early May Sarlat: La Ringueta (http://sarlat-tourisme.com). At Pentecôte (Whit Sunday) in even-numbered years, place de la Grande-Rigaudie is the venue for traditional games and sports of the Périgord.

Mid-July to early August Sarlat: Festival des Jeux du Théâtre (http://festival-theatre-sarlat.com). One of the most important theatre fests in France, covering a wide range of material from Shakespeare to the avant-garde Theatre of the Absurd, as well as several productions for children. The open-air performances take place over two weeks in various venues around town.

Mid- to late July Montignac: Festival de Montignac (http://festivaldemontignac.fr). Major arts festival featuring local and international folk groups from as far afield as South America and China. As well as ticket-only events, there are street performances, food stalls, exhibitions and crafts demonstrations during the week.

Late July to late September St-Léon-sur-Vézère and around: Festival du Périgord Noir (http://festivalmusiqueperigordnoir.fr). Baroque and classical music concerts in the atmospheric churches of St-Léon, St-Amand-de-Coly, Sarlat and in other venues throughout the region.

Early August Les Eyzies and around: Festival Musique en Périgord (http://musique-en-perigord.fr). Interesting mix of medieval and classical works alongside jazz and traditional music from around the world. Concerts take place over two weeks in the Romanesque churches of Les Eyzies, Campagne and Audrix, among other venues.

Late July to early August Belvès and Cadouin: Festival Bach (http://festivalbach.fr). Dedicated to the composer and comprising a handful of concerts generally held in Belvès church and the abbey at Cadouin.

Early November Sarlat: Festival du Film (http://festivaldufilmdesarlat.com). One-week festival previewing films from around the world, including special screenings of student productions.

MARKETS

The main **markets** in this region are at Belvès (Sat); Le Bugue (Tues & Sat); Domme (Thurs); Les Eyzies (April–Oct Mon); Montignac (Wed & Sat); St-Cyprien (Sun); St-Geniès (Sun); Sarlat (Wed & Sat); and Terrasson (Thurs).

Sarlat-la-Canéda and around

Very picturesque and very touristy, **SARLAT-LA-CANÉDA** (usually known just as Sarlat) sits in a green hollow between hills 10km or so north of the River Dordogne. You hardly notice the modern suburbs, as it is the mainly fifteenth- and sixteenth-century houses of the old town in mellow, pale ochre-coloured stone that draw the attention. Unless you're here for the Wednesday and Saturday **markets**, Sarlat's main draw is its architectural harmony and its foodie-oriented shops; there's also a large range of **accommodation**, both in and just outside the town, making it the most natural base for exploring the Périgord Noir. The ramparts surrounding old Sarlat were torn down in the late 1800s, at about the same time that the north–south **rue de la République** was cut through the centre to create its main thoroughfare. The streets to the west remain relatively quiet; the east side is where you'll find the majority of interest.

The hills above Sarlat also contain a number of sights, such as the topiary gardens of the **Manoir d'Eyrignac**, with perhaps a detour to the picturesque village of **St-Geniès**. Heading westwards, the still-occupied **Château de Puymartin** tends to be overshadowed by the more famous castles along the Dordogne, but contains some unusual interior decorations, while the nearby **Cabanes de Breuil**, a harmonious group of what were probably shepherds' huts, represent a completely different architectural tradition. With the exception of St-Geniès, which, with an early start, is accessible on the Sarlat–Périgueux bus route, you'll need your own **transport** to reach any of these places.

Brief history
Though it started life as a Gallo-Roman settlement, Sarlat really came to prominence in the late eighth century when Benedictine monks established an **abbey** here, later dedicated to a former bishop of Limoges, St Sacerdos. In 1147 **Bernard of Clairvaux** also left his mark when he preached the Second Crusade – according to legend he miraculously cured the sick by offering them bread he had blessed. In spite of this, the townspeople were keen to gain independence from Church rule, and in 1298 were eventually granted the right to elect their own consuls by Louis VIII. In return, they remained loyal to the French Crown during the Hundred Years' War and staunchly Catholic in the Wars of Religion, when the town suffered considerably at the hands of the Protestants. The fine **Renaissance** facades visible today date from a period of prosperity in between these two wars. That they are so well preserved is largely due to the fact that the town went into slow decline after the late 1700s. By the early twentieth century the centre was in a pretty poor state, but was saved from further decay by the vision of **André Malraux**, the novelist, Resistance hero and politician who launched the concept of the *secteur sauvegardé* ("protected area") in 1962. Sarlat's town centre was a pilot for this initiative, saving it from excessive postwar renovation and providing funds for a huge restoration project. Today, the 65 **protected monuments** in the medieval centre make it the most popular tourist destination in the whole of Dordogne, packed to the gunwales in summer, though still relatively undisturbed during the winter months.

Place de la Liberté
Sarlat's labyrinthine lanes fan out from **place de la Liberté**, the central square where the big Saturday **market** spreads its stands of flowers, foie gras, truffles, walnuts and mushrooms, according to the season; it's mostly foodstuffs in the morning and general goods after lunch.

Hôtel de Maleville
Place de la Liberté • Closed to the public

The finest building on place de la Liberté is the **Hôtel de Maleville**, also known as the Hôtel de Vienne, tucked into its southwest corner. The facade facing onto the square consists of a tall, narrow building in French Renaissance style with ornate window surrounds; turn down the lane beside it to see its more classical Italianate frontage, with a balustraded terrace and two medallions above the door representing Henry IV and, according to popular belief, his mistress Gabrielle d'Estrée.

Maison de La Boétie
Place du Peyrou • Ground floor occasionally open for art exhibitions

The lane beside the *Hôtel de Maleville* continues through a series of passages and geranium-filled courtyards to emerge beneath Sarlat's most famous house, the **Maison de La Boétie**. Though its prominent gables and tiers of mullion windows, each within a sculpted frame, are certainly eye-catching, much of the building's renown derives from the fact that the poet and humanist **Étienne de La Boétie**, a close friend of Michel de Montaigne, was born here in 1530. He went on to study law in Orléans, where he wrote his most famous work, *Discourse on Voluntary Servitude*, though it wasn't published until after his premature death at the age of 33. A treatise on the tyranny of power, and thus a very early expression of anarchism, the *Discourse* later struck a chord with Rousseau and other radical thinkers in the run-up to the Revolution.

Cathédrale St-Sacerdos and around

Opposite the Maison de La Boétie, the former **Bishop's Palace**, with its Renaissance gallery and windows, is now home to the tourist office and is attached to the large and unexciting Cathédrale St Sacerdos, which mostly dates from a seventeenth-century renovation. More interesting are the two pretty courtyards to the south of the cathedral – **cour des Fontaines**, filled with the sound of playing water, and **cour des Chanoines**, surrounded by a pleasing assembly of buildings – and the **Passage des Enfeus** around the chevet, where Sarlat's nobles were laid to rest in arched niches (*enfeux*) let into the wall. Less illustrious mortals were buried in the cemetery above, presided over by a curious bullet-shaped tower, the **Lanterne des Morts**, built in the twelfth century. Its exact purpose remains a mystery. Local tradition maintains that it commemorates St Bernard's visit in 1147.

Further north along the same slope you come to the **Présidial**, the former seat of royal justice, now a restaurant.

Ascenseur Panoramique

Rue des Consuls • Tickets available at the tourist office, or on site by credit card only • http://sarlat-tourisme.com

Just off place de la Liberté, behind the back of the church of Ste-Marie (now a covered market accessed through massive metal doors) lies the entrance to the **Ascenseur Panoramique**, a lift built into the church tower. The glass-sided lift takes you up 35m to peer out of the top of the tower, which was never roofed, for ten minutes, while the guide points out Sarlat's more famous monuments, including some of its 22 towers and remnants of the medieval walls. From up here you also get a bird's-eye view of the town's many *lauze* roofs (see page 123). In July and August, it's also possible to combine an evening visit with a truffle tasting (charge).

Manoir de Gisson

Place du Marché-aux-Oies • Charge • http://manoirdegisson.com

Dominating the north side of the place du Marché-aux-Oies – a delightful corner decorated by three bronze geese in tribute to the square's name – stands the **Manoir de Gisson**. This impressive building, with its hexagonal tower and stone-mullion windows, offers a rare chance to see inside one of Sarlat's noble houses. It dates from the thirteenth century, though was considerably enlarged in the fifteenth by the Gisson family, whose members most famously served as consuls in charge of the town's public order. You'll find their portraits inside, presiding over rooms decked out with furniture from medieval times to the seventeenth century, much of it fashioned in local walnut. At the top of the lovely circular stone staircase don't miss the chance to admire the internal structure of the heavy *lauze* roof (see page 123).

West of rue de la République

It's worth crossing over **rue de la République** to wander the western sector of Sarlat, particularly **rue Jean-Jacques Rousseau**. There's nothing particular to see, beyond more cobbled lanes and ornate doorways or the odd defensive tower, but this side of town is less touristy and quieter.

Gorodka

La Canéda • Charge • http://gorodka.com

Just outside Sarlat, 4km south off the D704 to Gourdon, **Gorodka** provides a complete break from Sarlat's medieval monuments. The home of conceptual artist **Pierre Shasmoukine**, it's a rambling place with various galleries crammed full of inventive pieces of art, enlivened by a strong dose of irony. The extensive grounds serve as an offbeat gallery of the weird and wonderful, including a giant dragonfly made from the body of a helicopter and bizarre, sinister-faced plastic totems that glow in the dark.

ARRIVAL AND DEPARTURE   SARLAT-LA-CANÉDA

By train Sarlat's *gare SNCF* is just over 1km south of the old town on the road to Souillac.
Destinations Bergerac (5–7 daily; 1hr 30min); Bordeaux (5–7 daily; 2hr 50min); Le Buisson (5–7 daily; 30min); Castillon-la-Bataille (5–7 daily; 1hr 40min–2hr); Lalinde (10 daily; 45min–1hr 30min); St-Cyprien (5–7 daily; 15min); Ste-Foy-la-Grande (10 daily; 1hr 20min–2hr 10min); Siorac-en-Périgord (7 daily; 20min); Trémolat (5–7 daily; 20–50min).

By bus Buses from Périgueux and Souillac pull into place Pasteur, immediately south of the centre. Souillac buses also call at the train station. As well as the routes covered below, there are also services to Montignac, Périgueux and St-Geniès, though as these run during school term-time only to coincide with children's pick-ups and drop-offs, they're not really a viable option for visitors.
Destinations Carsac (2–4 daily; 20min); Souillac (2–4 daily; 50min–1hr).

By car It's normally easy to find a metered parking space in central Sarlat, though more difficult on market days and in July and August. Paid parking is also available all around Sarlat's ring road, the most convenient being on place de la Grande-Rigaudie. Prices and the maximum stay vary by season; check the instructions on the meter. Note that Sarlat's medieval core is mostly closed to traffic in July and Aug and at weekends from mid-April to late June and Sept. Free parking is available at any time in most streets just beyond the central part of town.

GETTING AROUND

Car rental Europcar (http://europcar.co.uk), on place de Lattre-de-Tassigny, near the train station.
Taxis Call Allô Taxi (05 53 59 02 43). Uber is also in operation here, although vehicles are often sent from out of town so trips can be expensive.

Bike rental Liberty-cycle at Zone de Madrazes (http://liberty-cycle.com), on the edge of Sarlat and the start of the Voie Verte cycle path, offers bike rental, electric scooters and half-, full- and multi-day guided bike rides around the region.

INFORMATION AND ACTIVITIES

Tourist office In the heart of the old centre at 3 rue Tourny (April–June & Sept Mon–Sat 9am–6pm, Sun 10am–1pm & 2–5pm; July & Aug Mon–Sat 9am–7.30pm, Sun 10am–1pm & 2–6pm; Oct Mon–Sat 9am–noon & 2–5pm, Sun 10am–1pm; Oct Mon–Sat 9am–12.30pm & 2–5pm, Sun 10am–1pm; Nov–March Mon–Sat 9am–noon & 2–5pm; 05 53 31 45 45, http://sarlat-tourisme.com). As well as stocking the *Sortir à Sarlat* leaflet, which gives a run-down of the town's cultural calendar, including its excellent theatre and film festivals (see page 115), the office sells maps of hiking and mountain-bike trails around the Périgord Noir.

Guided tours The tourist office runs a wide array of French-language guided tours in Sarlat, from a straightforward trot through local history to themed tours with a guide in fancy dress; most run from Easter to October only, but check with the office for exact times and tour types. There are also standard Discovery tours in English and the office sells a booklet (€0.50) which lists self-guided tours of Sarlat.
Canoe rental Head to Vitrac, 7km south of Sarlat, where Périgord Aventure et Loisirs (http://canoe-copeyre.com) offers a range of self-guided canoe and kayak excursions.

ACCOMMODATION   SEE MAP PAGE 117

Note that during the peak holiday season (July–Sept) it's advisable to book several weeks in advance and to consider the quieter places outside the town centre. If you arrive without a **reservation**, it's worth asking for help at the tourist office.

IN SARLAT

Au Grand Hôtel de Sarlat 97 av de Selves, http://au-grand-hotel-de-sarlat.com. Impressive five-star hotel just outside the town centre, this is all old-fashioned elegance with grand four-poster beds, soft lighting and bright colours. Other perks include a covered heated pool, sauna and hot tub. Garage parking is extra. Book online in advance for big discounts. €€€

Camping Huttopia Sarlat Rue Jean-Gabin, http://europe.huttopia.com/site/camping-sarlat. Sarlat's closest campsite is on a terraced hillside 1km northeast of the centre up rue Jean-Jaurès. It's small, intimate and well equipped – facilities include heated indoor pool, outdoor pool, washing machines, tennis courts and grocery shop, plus mobile homes to rent. €

Les Cordeliers 51 rue des Cordeliers, http://lescordeliers-sarlat.com. You'll need to book early for this excellent English-run *chambre d'hôte* in an elegant eighteenth-century townhouse just outside the historic centre, decked out with period furnishings (including a floor-to-ceiling hallway mirror). Spacious rooms are equipped with a/c and impeccable bathrooms. Those on the top floor are tucked under the eaves, and one boasts its own roof terrace. €€

La Couleuvrine 1 place de la Bouquerie, http://la-couleuvrine.com. One of Sarlat's more atmospheric hotels, *La Couleuvrine* partly occupies one of the town's defensive towers and has twenty-six comfortable rooms with exposed stone walls and sweet-smelling polished wooden floorboards. Downstairs is a big fireplace and a good restaurant and a lunchtime bistro. €€

Le Jardin Sarlat 14 rue du Jardin-de-Madame, http://lejardin-sarlat.com. A highly rated English-owned *chambre d'hôte* tucked down a quiet backstreet a short walk from the centre. It's set in a lush cottage garden with a vine-covered terrace, fruit trees, a splash-pool and an outdoor hot tub. Inside is a lounge and four cute, airy, en-suite bedrooms. The generous breakfast will set you up for the day. €€

★ La Maison des Peyrat Le Lac de la Plane, http://maisondespeyrat.com. High on a hill, a 10min walk from the town centre, this gorgeous property, parts of which date back to the fourteenth century, has served as a farmhouse, a hospital and place of worship; it's now a unique hotel of higgledy-piggledy corridors, low wooden beams, whitewashed walls and bathrooms big enough for a knight in armour. The surrounding gardens are an idyllic spot for an alfresco breakfast, and there's a nice pool and a friendly dog. It has rooms for families as well as appealing doubles. €€

Montaigne 2 place Pasteur, http://hotelmontaigne.fr. This three-star hotel occupies an imposing building just south of centre. The rooms, in cool creams, have less character than the grand exterior might suggest but are well equipped for the price, including double-glazing and a/c. €€

Hotel des Récollets 4 rue Jean-Jacques Rousseau, http://hotel-recollets-sarlat.com. Offering great value, this budget hotel on a very quiet street has a range of different rooms which retain some unusual features like arched stone doorways. The cheapest are very small and it's worth splashing out for something a little more expensive. Breakfast is served on the patio in fine weather. €

La Villa des Consuls 3 rue Jean-Jacques Rousseau, http://villaconsuls.fr. Neatly positioned on a quiet side street next to a seventeenth-century chapel, this place has taken an old, stone building with wobbly chimneys and converted it into a pleasantly modern hotel complete with a massage centre. The studios and apartments are good for travelling families, while the standard rooms are spacious and bright. €€

AROUND SARLAT

Aux Trois Sources Pech-Lafaille, http://hebergement-sarlat.com. A very well-priced *chambre d'hôte* in a handsome seventeenth-century manor house 3km east of Sarlat on the road to Ste-Nathalène. Five charming but very simple en-suite rooms, with wooden floors, rugs and original hearths, are squeezed into a converted barn, and there are three small studios. It's surrounded by an attractive park, with chestnut trees and pond full of frogs, not to mention the three springs. €

★ La Palombière Ste-Nathalène, http://lapalombiere.fr. A five-star job, this is one of the region's best campsites, roughly 10km east of Sarlat on the D47. In a lovely, peaceful location in an extensive area of mature woodland, it's very well equipped – including restaurant, bar, grocery store, pools and tennis courts – and puts on all sorts of kids' events in summer. Chalets available, too. €

★ La Roche d'Esteil http://larochedesteil.com. Run by a welcoming young family, this magical *chambre d'hôte* is one of the most appealing in all of the Dordogne. Set in a converted old farmhouse of warm, dry-stone walls, rooms are painted in pastel colours and decorated in natural, home-made art. There's lots of space outside, with a large, sun-drenched pool, plenty of shade-giving trees and a whole load of peace and tranquillity. A couple of evenings a week in season, excellent dinners are cooked up by the owner. It's 1km or so outside the hamlet of Ste-Nathalène. €

EATING
SEE MAP PAGE 117

During the main tourist season Sarlat is chock-a-block with **restaurants**. In winter pickings are thinner as many places close up for a few months, but those that do stay open tend to be the better-quality places patronized by locals. You'll find foie gras, duck and walnuts in various guises everywhere, alongside another local staple, *pommes sarladaises*: potatoes crispy-fried in duck fat with lashings of garlic, parsley and, sometimes, mushrooms.

L'Adresse 10 rue Fénelon, http://ladressedesarlat.fr. This small, glass-fronted place on the edge of the old quarter offers an eclectic mix of Asian and Dordogne flavours, including Thai-style wok vegetables with rice noodles and a duck-heavy selection of local dishes. It's a real favourite with locals. €€€

Le Bistro de l'Octroi 111 av de Selves, http://lebistrodeloctroi.fr. A couple of minutes' walk from the town centre, *l'Octroi* sells itself as a simple bistro, but with deer steaks, prawn risotto and duck in walnut sauce on the menu it's clear that it's far from ordinary. €€

★ Chez Les Gaulois 9 rue Tourny, 05 53 59 50 64. Not one for vegetarians, but charcuterie addicts will love this authentic and welcoming restaurant where cured Savoy, Corsican and Spanish hams and sausages hang from the ceiling. They're served, along with Savoy cheeses, on a choice of platters and in salads or you can buy to take away. €€

La Crémerie 4 av Général Leclerc, http://lacremiere-sarlat.com. Cheese shop and restaurant largely only open for lunch, serving the kind of platters that lactose-induced reveries are made from. It also serves sandwiches, quiches, samosas and the like, usually with high dairy content. €

Gueule et Gosier 1 Rue Salamandre, http://gueule-et-gosier.fr. It's refreshing to see a menu not entirely composed of duck and duck liver in Sarlat (although it's still on the menu). Here, vegetarians aren't fobbed off with a lettuce leaf, but rather served watermelon tataki and shitake and seitan skewers. Dishes are a work of art, you can taste the quality of the produce, and service is exemplary. €€€

La Petite Borie 4 rue Tourny, 05 53 31 23 69. Friendly and consistently reliable restaurant offering good service and

classic Périgord cuisine at affordable prices. The majority of ingredients are sourced locally, with *cassoulet* and foie gras featuring strongly. The *menus* offer excellent value for money, each starting with a traditional garlic soup. €€
Le Présidial 6 rue Landry, http://lepresidial24.fr. Classy restaurant in the former court building, with a walled garden and airy, elegant dining rooms. While the setting is more spectacular than the food, especially when floodlit on a summer's evening, it's a reliable choice, offering dishes such as duck breast with blackcurrant sauce. €€€

SHOPPING   SEE MAP PAGE 117

While the **markets** are the best place to buy walnuts, walnut oil, prunes and other local foods straight from the farmer, place de la Liberté, rue de la Liberté and rue des Consuls are full of **speciality shops**.

Distillerie du Périgord Place de la Liberté, http://distillerie-perigord.com. Delectable liqueurs from walnut to plum, as well as fruits in alcohol – try its Guinettes, containing local morello cherries.

DIRECTORY

Hospital The Centre Hospitalier is on rue Jean-Leclaire (05 53 31 75 75) to the northeast of the centre.
Police Sarlat's Gendarmerie is located at 1 bd Henri-Arlet (05 53 29 18 71).
Post office The main post office is on place du 14-juillet.

Manoir d'Eyrignac

Charge • http://eyrignac.com • The gardens are 14km northeast of Sarlat, signed along backroads via Ste-Nathalène

Northeast of Sarlat, the River Enéa rises among oak woods on a plateau to the north of the hamlet of Ste-Nathalène. Though the hills appear scrubby and dry, one of the Enéa's tributaries is fed by seven springs, the same springs that prompted a seventeenth-century noble, Antoine de Costes de la Calprenède, to build a manor house here, the **Manoir d'Eyrignac**. The house itself isn't open to the public, but you can explore the glorious **gardens**.

The gardens aren't huge, but, consisting of lush evergreens – mainly hornbeam, box, cypress and yew – clipped and arranged in formal patterns of alleys and borders, achieve remarkable effects with almost no colour. The regimented lines are softened by the occasional pavilion or fountain and by informal stands of trees framing the countryside around. The original formal garden was laid out by an eighteenth-century Italian landscaper, and later converted to an English romantic garden according to the fashion of the times. What you see today is the work of the last forty years, the creation of the present owner's father in a combination of Italian and French styles.

The complex also contains a small **exhibition hall** next to the ticket office, where you can watch a video about the garden and its history, and a restaurant-cum-snack bar. You can also bring your own food and take advantage of their picnic tables.

St-Geniès

Some 14km north of Sarlat, the cluster of buildings known as **ST-GENIÈS** is worth a detour. It's a typical Périgord Noir village, with its partly ruined château and fortress-like church all constructed from the same warm-yellow stone under heavy *lauze* roofs. Unless it's market day (Sun morning), it won't take long to explore, the only sight being the **Chapelle de Cheylard**, standing on its own on a small knoll to the east. The fourteenth-century frescoes inside have suffered over the years – at one time the chapel served as a dance hall – but a number remain visible, including a particularly manic bunch pelting St Stephen with stones.

Château de Puymartin

Charge • http://chateau-de-puymartin.com

Eight kilometres northwest of Sarlat on the D47, the **Château de Puymartin** stands guard over the headwaters of the Petite Beune River, which flows down to join the

Vézère at Les Eyzies. The castle, which underwent extensive remodelling in the seventeenth and nineteenth centuries, has been in the same family since 1450 and is remarkably well preserved.

Among a large collection of family heirlooms, most noteworthy are the **tapestries**, particularly those in the grand hall, depicting the Siege of Troy. The Classical theme continues in the seventeenth-century trompe l'oeil paintings on the chimneypiece here and in the guest bedroom, where Zeus visits Danaë in a shower of gold – presumably he would have been surprised to find her clothed and holding a cross, a liberty taken in the more puritanical 1800s.

The same sensibilities demanded that a number of naked figures in the **mythological room** also be dressed. To preserve the original, visitors now only see a replica, but it is still an extraordinary sight. The room, though not large, is completely covered in monochrome scenes from mythology: snake-haired Medusa, Argus with his hundred eyes and Althaea murdering her son Meleager by burning a brand. The general consensus is that the room was a place of meditation, though surprisingly it also served as a children's nursery for some time.

Like all good castles, Puymartin also has its **ghost**, in this case La Dame Blanche, who supposedly haunts the north tower. In real life she was Thérèse de St-Clar, the lady of the household during the sixteenth century, who, on being surprised in the arms of a lover, was walled up in the tower until she died fifteen years later. More prosaically, it's worth climbing up into the roof here to admire the elaborate timber framework supporting the *lauzes*.

Cabanes du Breuil

Charge • http://cabanes-du-breuil.com

Located at the opposite end of the architectural scale to Puymartin are the **Cabanes du Breuil**, a couple of kilometres up in the hills to the northwest of the château. You'll find these dry-stone circular huts under conical *lauze* roofs scattered throughout the region, but none so picturesque as this group belonging to a small, working farm. Known locally as *bories*, the huts were originally used for human habitation, then for animals or storage.

In season (June–Sept) there's a video presentation explaining how the huts are made, but really these beautiful structures speak for themselves.

The Vézère valley and around

Billed as the "Vallée de l'Homme", the **Vézère valley** is home to the greatest concentration of **prehistoric sites** in Europe. They are by no means the oldest, but the sheer wealth and variety are quite stunning. It was here also that many important discoveries were made in the nineteenth and early twentieth centuries.

Now listed by UNESCO as a World Heritage Site, and for many the top attraction in all of the Dordogne, the Vézère valley draws more than two million visitors a year. The epicentre of all this activity is **Les Eyzies-de-Tayac**, where the Musée National de la Préhistoire contains an almost overwhelming display of important finds. The choice of sites nearby is bewildering, but at the very least you should visit the **Grotte de Font-de-Gaume** and the **Abri du Cap Blanc**, both located in the Beune valley to the east of Les Eyzies and harbouring the finest cave paintings and bas-relief sculptures still open to the public.

Also within striking distance of Les Eyzies, this time to the north, are the **Grotte de Rouffignac**, one of the area's largest caves, with a breathtaking array of animal engravings accessible only by an underground electric train, and the **Château de l'Herm**, an evocative ruined castle with literary associations.

BUILDING BLOCKS

The hallmarks of the Périgord region are the primitive-looking stone huts called **bories**, and the mottled-grey roofs made of limestone slabs – **lauzes** – used on cottage and château alike. Although they are now protected, the cost of maintaining these roofs – the stones weigh on average 500kg per square metre – means that many have been replaced with terracotta tiles. A floor made out of *lauzes* is called *pisé*, and is commonly found in châteaux and chapels, the stones inserted upright into a bed of clay and lime. While you'll find *lauze* roofs and, to a lesser extent, *pisé* floors in evidence throughout the region, *bories* are less common. The best examples are at the Cabanes du Breuil, near Sarlat.

Back on the River Vézère, the market town of **Le Bugue** gives access to the **Grotte du Sorcier**, with its highly significant human image, and the stunning chasm of the **Gouffre de Proumeyssac**.

North along the river from Les Eyzies is a more diverse collection of sights, ranging from the semi-troglodytic settlements at **La Madeleine** and **La Roque St-Christophe** – where a whole town was built into the cliff face – to prehistoric theme parks and the appealing Renaissance castle, the **Château de Losse**. Finally, there's the pretty town of **Montignac**, just a couple of kilometres from the valley's biggest name, the cave of **Lascaux**. Lascaux itself has been closed to the public since 1963, but its legendary paintings – with all their exceptional detail, colour and realism – have been faithfully reproduced in the brand-new, showstopping **Lascaux IV**.

GETTING AROUND   THE VÉZÈRE VALLEY

As far as transport is concerned, Le Bugue, Les Eyzies and Terrasson, the latter being the northern gateway to the valley, are all accessible by train, while you can get to Montignac by bus from Sarlat and Brive (via Terrasson) if you plan carefully – however many bus services are aimed at schoolchildren and are generally timed for the start and the end of the school day, so aren't very convenient for visitors. Note also that as many of the area's sights are at least a couple of kilometres away from these transport hubs, you'll rely heavily on walking or taxis if you don't have your own vehicle.

Les Eyzies-de-Tayac and around

The principal base for visiting the Vézère valley is **LES EYZIES-DE-TAYAC**, 20km northwest of Sarlat, its one main street dramatically located between the river and a towering cliff into which is built the **Musée National**, home to the largest collection of Paleolithic art in France. While it offers a good choice of hotels and restaurants out of season, Les Eyzies can get extremely crowded with visitors in summer.

Pôle International de la Préhistoire
30 rue du Moulin • Free • http://pole-prehistoire.com

Before tackling the Vézère-valley sites, you might want to pop to the **Pôle International de la Préhistoire** information centre, on the east side of town, for a quick introduction to what's on offer. All the prehistoric sites in the Dordogne region are marked on a 3D model, with interactive displays, and two slide presentations show how the area has evolved over the last 400,000 years. Knowledgeable staff are available to answer questions and can help plan an itinerary; they also organize various events and temporary exhibitions.

Musée National de la Préhistoire
Charge • http://musee-prehistoire-eyzies.fr

Under the jutting limestone cliff that dominates Les Eyzies, Paul Dardé's 1930 statue of Neanderthal man, portrayed as an ape-like hunk, stands staring out over the Vézère. Beside him, the **Musée National de la Préhistoire** occupies the remains of a castle built

> ### VISITING THE VÉZÈRE VALLEY PREHISTORIC CAVES
>
> Visitor numbers to most caves are severely restricted, either for conservation reasons or simply because the site can only hold a certain number of people at a time. At the most popular, including the Grotte de Font-de-Gaume (see page 127) and Grotte des Combarelles (see page 128), you have to buy **tickets** in advance by phoning the ticket office or visiting in person, though in some cases it's now also possible by email. If you can, buy your tickets several weeks in advance, sometimes longer during peak periods. The new Lascaux IV (see page 138) had not opened to the public at the time of writing, but given the scale of the new complex, queues are likely to be less of an issue here than they were at Lascaux II.
>
> In all cases you have to join a **guided tour**, which usually lasts around 45min. Some are offered in English, while others provide a translated text, but they are tiring – and the talks get repetitive. Unless you're a real prehistory buff, limit yourself to just two or three sites, rather than risk losing that sense of magic.
>
> The remote location of the caves makes them hard to access for **travellers with disabilities**. As a reconstruction, Lascaux IV is more accessible, as are the copies at Le Thot. But if you're in doubt, it's best to ask.

into the rock as well as a striking new building constructed around it. This stunning museum is a vital first stop on any tour of the region's prehistoric sites, and contains a vast array of increasingly sophisticated stone tools of the Paleolithic era (two million to ten thousand years ago). There is so much to see that it can get a bit overwhelming; allow at least two hours for a visit.

The **first floor** is devoted to blades found at various archeological sites; the spear- and axe-heads appear as delicate and perfect as the day they were made, and are accompanied by some engaging short films showing how these blades were made and then used. Look out also for a life-sized giant elk. **Upstairs** are some good re-creations (and the odd original) of engravings and sculptures from the era; highlights include a bison head carved into a stone (now the symbol of the museum); and an oil-burning torch used to illuminate the caves when painting took place.

Musée de l'Abri Pataud
Charge • http://mnhn.fr • Closed for renovations at the time of writing

In the late nineteenth century, local farmer Martial Pataud discovered prehistoric remains when he was cutting a new road beside what is now Les Eyzies' Musée National. The rock shelter (*abri*), which had been occupied for over 15,000 years before the roof collapsed around 20,000 years ago, yielded a rich hoard of finds, a selection of which are now on display in the next-door **Musée de l'Abri Pataud**, occupying what was previously the Patauds' wine cellar. Much of the excavation was carried out in the late 1950s and early 1960s, one of the first "modern" digs which enabled unusually precise analysis of the successive human occupations – unless you're an archeology buff this may not seem hugely exciting, but the guide's explanations help sort out all the different eras mentioned at other sites.

The site is still being explored, but the most famous find so far is a female "Venus" figurine discovered in 1958. The small bas-relief you see today, with her pendulous breasts and rounded belly, is a copy. Archeologists also found six skeletons, including a young mother with her newborn baby and a pearl necklace; again, you see a copy here alongside a bronze statue modelled from her bone structure, while the original pearls are in the town's Musée National (see page 123). Look out, too, for the enchanting little ibex (*bouquetin*) carved on the museum's rock ceiling 17,000 years ago.

Fortified church of Tayac

If you're here in summer and feel the need to get a bit of space from the crowds on the Les Eyzies' street, head down to the riverbank, where there's a nice picnic area and riverside path, or 500m past the railway station to the twelfth-century **fortified church of Tayac**. Nobody ever went to much effort to prettify it, but it's a forbidding defensive structure, with no steeples, but two broad parapets to give archers a proper shot at any attackers.

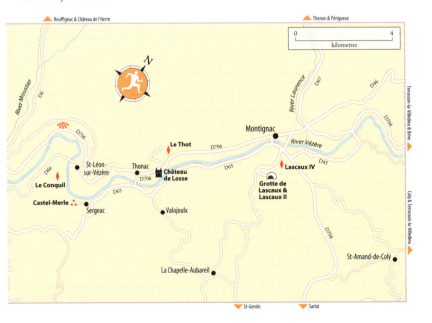

CANOEING THE VÉZÈRE

Les Eyzies is the main base for **canoeing trips** on the Vézère River, which is narrower and quieter than the Dordogne, cutting a thin channel between high cliffs and wooded banks. The scenery is perhaps less dramatic than the château-studded stretch of the Dordogne around Beynac, but you do pass beneath several of the troglodytic forts and dwellings lining the valley. Three **companies** cluster around the bridge just north of the town centre, operating from Easter to late September, depending on the weather; all will drive you upstream so you can canoe back down to Les Eyzies; prices range depending on starting point and rental time.

CANOE RENTAL COMPANIES
Les 3 Drapeaux http://canoes-3drapeaux.fr.

AVCK http://vezere-canoe.com.
Canoës Vallée Vézère http://canoeezere.com.

ARRIVAL AND INFORMATION

LES EYZIES-DE-TAYAC

By train A stop on the Périgueux–Agen train line, Les Eyzies' *gare SNCF* lies about 500m northwest of the centre, just off the main road before you cross the river.
Destinations Agen (2–5 daily; 1hr 50min); Belvès (2–4 daily; 30min); Le Bugue (2–7 daily; 7min); Le Buisson (2–7 daily; 15min); Périgueux (4–7 daily; 30–50min); Siorac-en-Périgord (2–5 daily; 25min).
Tourist office On the main road right in the town centre (Jan–March, Oct–Dec Tues, Wed & Fri 10am–12.30pm & 2–5pm, Tues & Thurs 10am–12.30pm; April–June Mon–Sat 9.30am–12.30pm & 2–6pm, Sun 9.30am–12.30pm; Sept Mon–Sat 9.30am–6pm, Sun 9.30am–12.30pm; July & Aug daily 9.30am–6.30pm; 05 53 06 97 05, http://lascaux-dordogne.com). In addition to plentiful information on local sights and *chambres d'hôtes*, it also offers free wi-fi access and bike rental (reserve in advance in high season), and there's a 24hr ATM outside.
Hiking The tourist office sells hiking maps of the area and gives out a leaflet describing the "Chemins de la Préhistoire", two hikes up the valley to Laugerie-Basse (8km round trip) and beyond to La Madeleine (15km round trip). Along the route you'll find information panels in English.

ACCOMMODATION

While there is some great **accommodation** in Les Eyzies, they can be pricey, especially in high season, when it's better to stay out of the main centre or in one of the villages around. Note that most places close in winter, so it's wise to book ahead if you're visiting between October and April.

IN LES EYZIES

Le Centenaire 2 av Cingle, http://hotelducentenaire.fr. There's a lot to like about this recently renovated hotel, from the bright, blinged-out rooms to the classy restaurant with its traditional Périgord dishes, but the real highlights are the park-like grounds and impressive swimming pool. €€€
Le Cro-Magnon 54 av de la Préhistoire, http://hotelcromagnon.com. The *Cro-Magnon* is a sunny, inviting building with yellow shutters and vine-covered walls built into the cliff on the north side of town. Rooms are bright with writing desks and walls hung with oil paintings of roses. There are good communal areas, with open hearths, armchairs and a small library, as well as a pool. The restaurant serves one daily *menu* with a choice of seasonal dishes. €€€
Des Falaises 35 av de la Préhistoire, 05 53 06 97 35. The best-value rooms in Les Eyzies, located behind a central café-bar run by a friendly owner, are bright, cheerful, clean and well-kept. All are en suite (though there's no TV) and the marginally more expensive ones at the back of the building have their own balconies. €€

★ **La Ferme de Tayac** 14 rue de Tayac, http://fermedetayac.com. Though only 1km from Les Eyzies, this welcoming Dutch/English-run *chambre d'hôte* in twelfth-century buildings beside Tayac church is a real delight. The six beautifully appointed rooms and spacious communal areas are full of artistic touches, as are the flower-filled gardens. There's a pool and bikes available for guests to borrow. Three-night minimum stay required, though it's always worth checking. No children. €€
De France 1 rue du Moulin, 05 53 06 97 23. Right next to the Musée National entrance, this place has the advantage of being away from the main road and has quiet and comfortable rooms that gather a lot of sunlight. Unfortunately, the bathrooms are a bit dated. Breakfast is taken at the terrace-café opposite. €
★ **Les Glycines** 4 av de Laugerie, http://les-glycines-dordogne.com. Les Eyzies' most beguiling hotel stands on the main road just north of the centre. It's a romantic place, with light, airy rooms, full of drapes and frills, and a beautiful garden behind, crisscrossed by shady paths, with a swimming pool in the middle. The nicest rooms open directly onto the garden. There's also a spa centre and a bistro in addition to the main restaurant. Book online in advance for discounts. €€€
Hostellerie du Passeur Place de la Mairie, http://hostellerie-du-passeur.com. The vine-covered *Du Passeur* is

in a prime spot right in the centre beside the tourist office, but set back from the road. The rooms are pleasant enough, many decked out in rich ochre hues, and have three-star comforts. Downstairs is a smart restaurant with a super terrace by the river. €€

★ **Le Moulin de la Beune** Rue du Moulin-Bas, http://moulindelabeune.com. A pretty, converted mill building on the southern edge of Les Eyzies, this old-fashioned hotel has simple, spacious and well-priced rooms, some looking out onto its peaceful garden and the rushing stream. There is also a lovely restaurant, *Au Vieux Moulin* (see below), so it's well worth considering the half-board option. €€

La Rivière 3 rue du Sorcier, http://lariviereleseyzies.com. A good, inexpensive choice about 1km from Les Eyzies on the Périgueux road. There are six unfussy rooms, all en suite, in a Périgord farmhouse with access to a pool, bar, laundry and a simple restaurant. There's also a well-tended, four-star campsite, which shares the same facilities as the hotel. €

AROUND LES EYZIES

La Grange du Mas Le Mas-de-Sireuil, http://grange-du-mas.com. Welcoming *chambre d'hôte* with five cutesy rooms on a working farm just outside the village of Sireuil, 5km east of Les Eyzies. For the full French rural experience, it's a hard one to top. It only offers half-board, but it's good value, comprising produce from the farm and including drinks. There's also a pool and tennis court. €€

Laborderie Tamniès, http://hotel-laborderie.com. Perched 13km up the Beune valley, northeast of Les Eyzies, this geranium-decked hotel on the edge of a pretty hamlet occupies four separate buildings, with a big choice of rooms – the best are in the newer blocks with balconies or terraces overlooking the garden and pool – and a good restaurant (see below). Early booking advisable in summer. €€

EATING

IN LES EYZIES

★ **Au Vieux Moulin** Rue du Moulin-Bas, http://moulindelabeune.com. Attached to the *Moulin de la Beune* hotel, this is one of Les Eyzies' best restaurants. You can enjoy great dishes like green risotto with snails, sitting either in the old-fashioned stone-walled dining room, or outside in the garden where the tiny River Beune rushes past. €€

Les Glycines 4 av de Laugerie, http://les-glycines-dordogne.com. For a gastronomic treat try the restaurant at the *Les Glycines* hotel. There is a strong emphasis on local and seasonal produce, including vegetables and salads from the hotel garden. Reservations highly recommended. €€€

AROUND LES EYZIES-DE-TAYAC

Auberge de Layotte http://aubergelayotte.com. It's worth searching out this rustic *auberge* lost in the middle of nowhere – signed off the D47 north of Les Eyzies, at the end of a dirt track – for a taste of old-style country cooking. Run by an enthusiastic young couple, there's just one five-course *menu* offering such delights as nettle soup, home-cured hams, beef stew and walnut cake. Everything but the wine, bread and cheese is home-made. By reservation only. €€€

Laborderie Le Bourg, http://hotel-laborderie.com. This hotel restaurant is equally popular for its pretty country setting in the village of Tamniès en Périgord as its good-value *menu*, a cut above the standard. Think Aquitaine sturgeon in truffle cream or mushroom-stuffed quail. €€

Grotte de Font-de-Gaume

Charge • http://sites-les-eyzies.fr • The caves are just over 1km east of Les Eyzies along the D47 to Sarlat

Since they were first discovered in 1901, over two hundred Magdalenian-era (18,000–10,000 years old) polychrome paintings and engravings have been found in the narrow tunnel of the **Grotte de Font-de-Gaume**. In order to preserve the artwork, only 78 people are allowed to enter the cave each day (26 allocated to advance bookings, and 52 available on the day), and numbers may be further restricted in the future (see page 124).

The cave mouth is no more than a fissure concealed by rocks and trees above a small, lush valley. Inside is a narrow twisting passage of irregular height over 100m long, where you quickly lose your bearings in the dark. The majority of the **paintings** depict bison, but also horses, mammoths, reindeer and wild cats, and many unexplained signs such as the so-called "**tectiforms**", comprising a very gently inclined, upside down "V" with vertical lines beneath.

The first painting you come to is a frieze of bison at about eye level: reddish-brown in colour, massive, full of movement and an almost palpable force. Further on, a horse stands with one hoof slightly raised, resting; another appears to be galloping or jumping and, in a breathtakingly tender depiction, one reindeer gently licks another's nose. But the most miraculous painting of all is a **frieze of five bison** discovered in 1966. The colour, remarkably sharp and vivid, is preserved by a protective layer of

CAVE ART

Thousands of years ago, early inhabitants of the Dordogne and Lot region created some of the most expressive and moving prehistoric **paintings**, **engravings** and **reliefs** seen anywhere in the world. While these stunning works of art lie scattered throughout the area, hidden deep within limestone caves and on cliff walls, by far the greatest concentration is in the **Vézère valley** in the heart of the Dordogne.

The **Cro-Magnon people** who swept across Europe 40,000 or so years ago are responsible for the earliest cave art in the region. Named after a rock shelter near Les Eyzies, where the first skeletons were discovered, they were a nomadic people, who tracked herds of reindeer across what was then steppe, occasionally settling in riverside rock shelters under overhanging cliffs. They developed increasingly sophisticated tools using bone, ivory and antlers and later crafted ornaments such as necklaces. Some 20,000 years ago, the Cro-Magnon had honed their artistic skills sufficiently to depict supremely realistic animals on the walls of their rock shelters, by means of engraving and sculpting with flints or painting with dyes made from charcoal, manganese dioxide and red ochre.

Approximately 17,000 years ago, during what is now known as the **Magdalenian** period – named after another site in the Vézère valley – there was a real explosion in the quantity and level of sophistication of prehistoric art. It was prompted by the use of the tallow lamp, fuelled with reindeer fat, which allowed artists to penetrate deep within the limestone caves. They covered the walls of passages and cavern ceilings with hundreds of drawings, paintings and engravings. In some places artists used the natural contours of the rock to produce supremely realistic, almost 3-D representations of horses, bison and other animals. Some of the drawings are almost like caricatures, in which mammoths are portrayed by just a couple of lines. Occasional human figures also appear, most spectacularly in the Grotte du Sorcier (see page 133).

The question of why these cave-dwellers dedicated such skill and time to their art evokes endless debate. While it's likely that the significance of the caves was in some way spiritual, the exact nature of the relationship between Cro-Magnon people and their art remains opaque. Some scholars believe that the paintings and engravings were some form of **ritual practice** or **magic** to evoke a successful hunt, while others think they have a **shamanistic role**, with the animals advancing into the caves as into the afterlife.

You'll often hear guides at the sites lament the fact that we know so little, but perhaps the desire for categorical meaning misses the point – that the paintings and engravings reveal a desire to capture elusive, transcendent beauty – or in other words, "art for art's sake". Whatever the truth, not knowing certainly adds to the wonder and magic of these caves.

---

calcite. Shading under the belly and down the thighs is used to add volume, with a sophistication that seems utterly modern. Another panel consists of **superimposed drawings**, a fairly common phenomenon in cave-painting, sometimes the result of work by successive generations, but here an obviously deliberate technique: a reindeer in the foreground shares legs with a large bison to indicate perspective.

Grotte des Combarelles

Charge • Tickets available from Font-de-Gaume booking office (see box) • http://sites-les-eyzies.fr • The caves are 2km southeast of Les Eyzies, just along the D47 from Font-de-Gaume

The myriad engravings of the **Grotte des Combarelles** were discovered in 1901, a few days before those at the Font-de-Gaume. Only five decorated caves had been found prior to this, and with the jury still out on primitive man's artistic abilities, they were an incredibly significant discovery. As with Font-de-Gaume, visitor numbers are restricted: just 42 people are allowed in per day, with seven tickets sold in advance and 35 on the day.

You make your way down a long, claustrophobic tunnel, stopping every now and then while the guide picks out a tiny selection of the six-hundred-plus **engravings** identified so far. It is a veritable Magdalenian menagerie: mostly horses, but also bison, reindeer, mammoths, rhinos, bears, ibex, aurochs and wild cats; stylized human figures and geometric symbols also feature.

A good deal of imagination is required to recognize some of the fainter outlines, often superimposed one upon another, while others are astounding in their simplicity and realistic treatment – among the finest are the heads of a horse and a lioness, where the dips and projections in the rock provide eyes, nostrils and even bone structure.

Roc de Cazelle
Charge • http://rocdecazelle.com • The caves are 2.5km southeast of Les Eyzies, some 2km further along the D47 from the Grotte des Combarelles

Arriving at **Roc de Cazelle**, a theme park that reconstructs life 12,000 years ago, you'll be greeted by mammoths roaring and the sound of people chipping flints. It's great for children, and the imaginative design helps bring the surrounding caves to life. Various scenes – from hunting and gathering to painting and sculpting – are scattered around a wooded valley once occupied by prehistoric man, culminating in a real troglodyte fortress and a troglodyte farm that was inhabited up to the 1960s.

Abri du Cap Blanc
Charge • Tickets available from Font-de-Gaume booking office (see box) • http://sites-les-eyzies.fr • The site is about 7km east of Les Eyzies, signed left off the D47 shortly after the Grotte des Combarelles

Not a cave but a natural rock shelter, the **Abri du Cap Blanc** lies on a steep wooded hillside above the River Beune. The shelter contains a superb **sculpted frieze** of horses and bison dating from the middle Magdalenian period (16,000–13,000 years ago), discovered in 1909 behind thick layers of sediment. Visitor numbers are limited to 105 people a day, with 35 tickets sold in advance and 70 on the day (see page 131).

Unfortunately, the excavation was carried out in such a hurry that the frieze had been badly damaged before anyone realized it was there. Even so, it is quite remarkable, mainly for its scale – the middle horse, which closely resembles the wild Przewalski horse of Central Asia, is virtually life-size – but also the depth of some of the sculptures. The bodies were obviously polished to set them off against the rough background, while traces of ochre and manganese pigments indicate that they were also painted at one time.

Château de Commarque
Charge • http://commarque.com • The château is 10km east of Les Eyzies, and drivers must approach from the south, following signs from the D47 Sarlat road; there's a 600m walk from the car park to the entrance, though anyone with reduced mobility can drive right to the site

Southeast along the Beune valley from Abri du Cap Blanc you come to the elegant sixteenth-century Château de Laussel (closed to the public) and, on the opposite side, the romantic ruins of the **Château de Commarque**. Dating from the twelfth century, Commarque was a **castrum** – a fortified village made up of six separate fortresses, each belonging to a different noble family, of which the best preserved is that built by the powerful Beynac clan in the fourteenth century. The site was abandoned some 200 years later, then left to moulder until the late 1960s when the present owner, Hubert de Commarque, came to the rescue.

The ruins have now been made structurally sound and it's possible once again to climb the Beynac's 30m-high tower for **views** over the surrounding countryside. In summer, the site makes a spectacular setting for concerts, plays and other events, including child-friendly activities such as archery, cave-painting and sculpture.

Grotte du Grand Roc
Charge • www.grotte-grand-roc.fr • The caves are 2km north of Les Eyzies on the D47 to Périgueux

The entrance to the **Grotte du Grand Roc** lies under the cliffs that line much of the Vézère valley. There's a great view from the mouth of the cave, which was discovered in

1924 in the continuing search for prehistoric art. Instead, they found a fantastic array of **rock formations** along some 80m of tunnel. Most unusual are the still-unexplained *excentriques* growing in all directions, and triangles formed by calcite crystallizing in still, shallow pools.

Abri de Laugerie Basse
Charge • http://les-grands-sites-du-perigord.com • The site is 5km northwest of Les Eyzies

Sixty years before the discovery of the Grotte du Grand Roc (see above), Edouard Lartet and Henry Christy had identified a rock shelter further along the same cliff. The **Abri de Laugerie Basse** was inhabited almost constantly over the last 15,000 years – most recently in the form of farmhouses built against the rock – and yielded hundreds of **engravings** and **sculptures**, not on the rock face but on pieces of bone or fashioned out of individual stones. The majority date from the late Magdalenian period (13,000–10,000 years ago) when prehistoric art reached its peak.

They include a mysterious engraving of a heavily pregnant woman lying under a reindeer, and a sculpted female torso, the first so-called "Venus figure" discovered in France – both are obviously symbols of fertility, though it's not known whether they relate to fertility rites; the originals are displayed in the Musée National de la Préhistoire at Les Eyzies. These and other important finds are covered in a short film before visiting the shelter; there's little to see otherwise, though during the visit you learn a lot about the history of the excavations and what conditions were like during the Magdalenian era.

Abri du Poisson
1hr guided visits by advance booking only via the Font-de-Gaume ticket office (see page 131), or by phone • Charge • http://sites-les-eyzies.fr • The site is 4km northwest of Les Eyzies, just before the Grotte du Grand Roc

More interesting than the nearby Abri de Laugerie Basse is the **Abri du Poisson**, a rock shelter – one of many along a side valley – that contains one of the very few **sculpted fish** in prehistoric art. It's a real beauty too, a 1m-long male salmon, complete with gills and beak, probably carved about 25,000 years ago. The deep-cut rectangular outline is not a prehistoric picture-frame, however, but the remains of an abortive attempt by a Berlin museum to acquire the salmon soon after it was discovered in 1912. Since then, the shelter has been kept sealed up and can now be visited by a maximum of twenty people per day.

Grotte de Rouffignac
Charge • http://grotteroufffignac.fr • The site is 20km north of Les Eyzies

North of the Grotte du Grand Roc (see page 129), the D47 turns northwest to follow the Manaurie valley. Seven kilometres beyond the village of **Manaurie**, you'll pass a right turn signed to the **Grotte de Rouffignac**, another seven kilometres uphill among dense woods. One of the best caves in the region for children, the visit here kicks off with a 1km-ride on a little **electric train** along the bed of an underground river that dried up about three million years ago. On the way the guide points out where hibernating bears scratched their nests and human visitors left their mark in the form of graffiti – including a priest, Abbé de la Tour, in 1808. In fact, records show that the cave was known about in the sixteenth century, but it took until 1956 before the 13,000-year-old monochromatic drawings and engravings were recognized. Over 260 **animal figures** have been identified so far, the vast majority of which are mammoths, including a superb patriarch, his great tusks arcing under a piercing eye. Most dramatic is the final chamber, when you descend from the train to wander around beneath a ceiling covered with mammoths, woolly rhinos, horses, bison and ibex. When these drawings were done, the cave here was less than 1m high – proof that the authors were prepared to suffer for their art, and of their mysterious obsession with penetrating as deep into these caves as possible.

> **TICKETS FOR ABRI DU CAP BLANC, ABRI DU POISSON, FONT-DE-GAUME AND DES COMBARELLES**
>
> Because of the limit on visitor numbers allowed to enter Abri du Cap Blanc, Abri du Poisson and the caves of Font-de-Gaume and des Combarelles, it is essential to **book tickets ahead** by phone or online (http://sites-les-eyzies.fr) several weeks or, if you can, months in advance at any time of year, and as early as possible if you plan on visiting in July and August, especially for Font-de-Gaume. Tickets go on sale in January for the coming year. Note that you have to pay for your tickets by credit card at least fifteen days in advance, and there's a booking fee. If you haven't got a ticket, you can try queuing up at the Font-de-Gaume ticket office first thing in the morning for one of the few tickets for all three sites which are sold on the day, but you'll need to get there early. Given the high demand for tickets, it's worth considering a visit to one of the valley's less popular caves instead; note also that none of the above caves are really suitable for children.

Rouffignac

Some 5km north of the Grotte de Rouffignac and 25km from Les Eyzies, **ROUFFIGNAC** was destroyed by German troops in 1944, who drove everyone out before torching the town. Rouffignac was subsequently rebuilt – the only buildings to survive from the original village were the **Église Saint-Germain de Rouffignac**, with its carved portal and unusual twisted columns inside, and three nearby houses.

Château de l'Herm

Charge • http://chateau-lherm.com • The château is 4km north of Rouffignac and 22km from Les Eyzies

The **Château de l'Herm** has an unhappy history, a complicated tale of murders, forced marriages and inheritance disputes. In the end the castle was abandoned and left to crumble away for over three centuries to leave an atmospheric ruin engulfed by trees. Since 2000, however, a massive restoration project has been underway, initially to protect the existing structure from further decay. Two big round towers and some fifteenth- and sixteenth-century decorative touches remain: a late Gothic doorway opens onto a spiral stone staircase, crowned by a beautiful palm-tree vault, while three sculpted fireplaces cling one above the other to the wall of an otherwise empty shell. At the bottom of the keep, you can still distinguish the castle's grim-looking dungeons. It was these evocative ruins, looking out over the thickly wooded country where rural rebels thrived, which inspired Eugène Le Roy for his novel *Jacquou le Croquant*, in which a nineteenth-century rebellion culminates in the Château de l'Herm being burned to the ground.

Le Bugue and around

LE BUGUE lies on the north bank of a meander in the Vézère, 11km downstream from Les Eyzies, and though tourist facilities are thinner on the ground it makes a reasonable alternative base, especially for the family-friendly historical theme park and zoo just outside town and the Proumeyssac and du Sorcier caves, slightly further afield. Le Bugue itself is fairly attractive with a riverfront setting and scattering of old houses along the River Doux, which flows into the Vézère here. On Tuesdays and Saturdays, it comes alive with one of the better **markets** in the area. The heart of Le Bugue is **place de la Mairie**, the town centre and market square, from where there are good views in both directions along the river. From here, **rue de Paris**, the main shopping street, heads north towards Le Bugue's old quarter around the generously named **Grande Rue**.

Village du Bournat

Charge • http://lebournat.fr • The village is just under 1km southeast of Le Bugue

Younger children will have a whale of a time at the **Village du Bournat**. This is a fair re-creation of a Périgord village in the early 1900s complete with *lauze*-roofed cottages, chapel, schoolhouse, baker, flourmill, fairground rides and so forth. The entry price seems expensive, but there's a lot to see, including demonstrations of local crafts, such as clog- and barrel-making, potting and basketry, and you can come and go as you please within a day. There's a restaurant and snack bar on site.

Aquarium du Périgord Noir
Charge • http://aquariumperigordnoir.com • The aquarium is just under 1km southeast of Le Bugue, adjacent to the Village du Bournat

The **Aquarium du Périgord Noir** is home to one of the largest collections of freshwater fish in Europe, as well as numerous reptiles and an impressive alligator park. At set times each day you can watch – and children can assist with – the feeding of the more benign species.

Labyrinthe Préhistorique
Charge • http://labyrinthe-prehistorique.com • Just under 1km southeast of Le Bugue, adjacent to the aquarium

If you've young children in tow, you might want to head to Le Bugue's newest attraction, the **Labyrinthe Préhistorique**, a theme park centred on the history of the region's caves which opened in 2016. Kids will enjoy a trek through the maze of mirrors in pursuit of Cro-Magnon man, the cave inhabited by models of prehistoric beasts, and can try their hand at cave-painting.

ARRIVAL AND DEPARTURE — LE BUGUE

By train Trains on the Périgueux–Agen line pull into Le Bugue's gare SNCF, roughly 2km southeast on the D703; call Taxis Sourbier (05 53 07 41 35) if you need a taxi. Note that the station is unstaffed, so you'll need to buy tickets from the machine.

Destinations Agen (3–6 daily; 1hr 30min); Belvès (3–6 daily; 25min); Le Buisson (3–7 daily; 8min); Les Eyzies (4–7 daily; 7min); Périgueux (4–7 daily; 45min); Siorac-en-Périgord (3–6 daily; 20min).

INFORMATION AND ACTIVITIES

Tourist office Bang in the town centre at 22 place de l'Hôtel de Ville (Jan–March & Oct–Dec Mon–Fri 10am–12.30pm & Tues, Wed & Fri 2–5pm; April–June Mon–Sat 9.30am–12.30pm & 2–6pm & Sun 9.30am–12.30pm; July & Aug daily 9.30am–6pm; Sept Mon–Fri 9.30am–6pm, Sat 9.30am–1pm & 2–6pm, Sun 9.30am–12.30pm; 05 53 07 20 48, http://lascaux-dordogne.com).

Canoe rental Canoëric (http://canoe-perigord.com), beside the Village du Bournat, has rentals.

Horseriding Ferme Équestre de Belle Oreille (http://belleoreille.ffe.com) is a few kilometres to the northwest of Le Bugue in the village of St-Avit de Vialard.

ACCOMMODATION

IN LE BUGUE

Le Cygne 2 rue du Cingle, http://lecygne-perigord.com. Though it's on the main road, this good-value place on the edge of the town centre is the most appealing hotel in Le Bugue. It offers comfortable, if plain, rooms, most of them with double-glazed windows. There's also a very good restaurant (see below). €

Le Royal Vézère Place de l'Hôtel-de-Ville, http://hotel-royal-vezere.com. Once Le Bugue's grandest hotel, this three-star occupies a prime position on the river right in the town centre. Its other main draws are a rooftop swimming pool and good restaurant. Cheaper rooms face onto the road, but it's worth upgrading to one with river views. €

Les Trois Caupain Le Port, 05 53 07 24 60. A welcoming and well-equipped three-star campsite located on the riverbank 1km east of town. Among its facilities, it boasts two pools, one of them heated, and a bar-restaurant in season. Mobile homes available too. €

AROUND LE BUGUE

★ **L'Auberge Médiévale** Audrix, http://auberge-medievale.fr. In the tiny, picturesque hamlet of Audrix, 6km from Le Bugue past the Gouffre de Proumeyssac, is this delightful, bargain-priced traditional country hotel. With its eight simple but pretty rooms, all with en-suite facilities and views either of the Romanesque church or the valley below, it really is one of the most peaceful and idyllic spots in the region. €

Brin d'Amour St-Cirq, http://brindamourcamping.com. Tucked away up in the hills north of St-Cirq, midway between Le Bugue and Les Eyzies, this three-star campsite is an excellent choice if you've got your own transport: small, friendly, well run and lacking the regimented feel of so many sites. Guest facilities include a heated outdoor swimming pool, tennis court, an on-site restaurant, small grocery store for essentials plus a handful of mobile homes for rent. €

EATING

IN LE BUGUE
Le Cygne 2 rue du Cingle, http://lecygne-perigord.com. While this hotel restaurant is lacking in atmosphere, it serves excellent food, with a choice of regional *menus* Alternatively, you can eat from the limited *carte*. €€

Le Pha 25 rue du Jardin-Public, http://lepha.fr. Friendly little place opposite *Le Cygne*; in fine weather, get here early or phone ahead to reserve a table overlooking the river. It serves an unusual mix of Asian and French dishes: everything from the regular *magret* (duck breast) and local salads to king prawns in peanut sauce, beef and ginger soup or banh bao (Vietnamese steamed dumplings). €€

Le Royal Vézère Place de l'Hôtel-de-Ville, http://hotel-royal-vezere.com. The restaurant at the *Royal Vézère* hotel is in a prime position in the town centre, with a terrace jutting out over the river. It offers nicely presented traditional cuisine on a wide choice of *menus*. €€

AROUND LE BUGUE
★ **Auberge Médiévale** http://auberge-medievale.fr. The restaurant of Audrix's charming hotel serves delicious and well-priced regional cuisine from a broad range of four- to five-course *menus*. House specialities include warm scallops with truffles, and langoustine ravioli. In summer you can sit out in the shade of a vine-draped trellis. €€

Du Château Campagne, 05 53 07 23 50. If you're looking for somewhere to eat between Le Bugue and Les Eyzies, try this traditional bistro-restaurant in the attractive village of Campagne. Serving Périgordin cuisine, plus a choice of fish dishes. €€

Gouffre de Proumeyssac

Charge • http://gouffre-proumeyssac.com • In July & Aug reserve well in advance by phone or online to save queuing; to descend in the basket, phone ahead at any time of the year (online reservations not accepted) • The caves are 5km south of Le Bugue on the D31E2

High-tech has hit the Vézère in a big way at the **Gouffre de Proumeyssac**, a vast and spectacular limestone cave. Its 40m-high vault dripping with multicoloured stalactites, ranging from fine needles to massive petrified waterfalls, is dubbed the "crystal cathedral". To heighten the sense of atmosphere you enter in the dark, then the music builds as lights pick out various formations before revealing the whole chamber in a grand finale.

It's cleverly done, though some will find it too commercialized, even down to stacks of calcite-coated pottery souvenirs, and a far cry from when the cave was first opened in 1907. At that time the only way in was via a basket lowered through a hole in the roof under flickering torchlight – you can still make the descent by eleven-person **basket**, which rotates as it makes its way down.

Even before the chasm was fully explored and its size and beauty discovered, it had a gruesome notoriety in local folklore: it gets a mention in Eugène Le Roy's 1899 work *Jacquou le Croquant* as the "*Trou de Pomeissac* near Le Bugue, into which so many people had been thrown after being murdered on the neighbouring highway, that the hole had to be blocked up..."

Grotte du Sorcier

Charge • 05 53 07 14 37 • The cave is 6km east of Le Bugue

South from Le Bugue via the D703, a left turn down a quiet back road just before the road crosses the train line takes you eventually to the village of **ST-CIRQ**, halfway to Les Eyzies. St-Cirq is known above all for the **Grotte du Sorcier**, a shallow cave with some thirty **engravings** dating from between 17,000 and 19,000 years ago.

The majority of the engravings in the cave depict animals (look out for the tremendous image of the horse turning its head back towards the entrance), but the most significant is the "**Sorcerer**" himself, a rare image of a human being in Magdalenian cave art. The enigmatic figure has been interpreted in countless ways: as a fertility symbol, half man and half pregnant woman; as a shaman or spiritual leader, with his musical instrument and dancing legs; or indeed as a man's head with the body of a horse.

However you choose to see him, he makes a fascinating counterpoint to the supremely realistic animals you see elsewhere: the Sorcerer is compelling evidence of ancient cave art's figurative or metaphorical purpose.

After the guided tour of the cave, have a quick look around the site's **museum**, a collection of blades and fossils dating from the different eras in which it was occupied. Then, if you're feeling athletic, climb up to explore the vestiges of a **medieval fortress** and look-out posts in the rock face beyond the museum.

The central Vézère valley

To the northeast of Les Eyzies, the D706 follows the River Vézère all the way to Montignac, taking you past a range of sights appealing to all ages, from the rockshelters of **La Madeleine** and **La Roque St-Christophe** to the Renaissance splendour of the **Château de Losse** and **Le Thot**, a wildlife park with a prehistoric theme. On the way, you'll pass the prettiest village in the whole valley – **St-Léon-sur-Vézère**.

Tursac

The village of **TURSAC** sits astride the main D706 road 5km upstream from Les Eyzies. Though there's nothing remarkable to see here, the village boasts a recommended restaurant and makes a good base for campers exploring this stretch of valley.

ACCOMMODATION AND EATING — TURSAC

La Ferme du Pelou http://lafermedupelou.com. Of the two good campsites near Tursac, this two-star site signed off the D706 to the south of the village is the more basic but is spectacularly located, perched on the hilltop overlooking La Madeleine and its meander from the east. Pitches are spacious, grouped around an old Périgordin farmhouse with chickens running around amid the flowers. There are two pools and lots of walks around, plus mobile homes to rent. €

★ **La Source** Lieu-dit Le Bourg, 09 67 54 89 07. Tursac's central square, just off the main road, is home to this well-regarded restaurant with a pleasant garden and imaginative daily specials, including wild salmon in a shellfish sauce, or beef slow-cooked in beer. It also provides vegetarian options if you phone a day ahead. Reservations recommended. €

Le Vézère Périgord http://levezereperigord.com. Just over 1km north of Tursac, this is a well-run, spacious and good-value campsite set back from the main road among trees. Facilities include a decent-sized pool with water slides, a tennis court and a fitness room. There's also a bar, restaurant and grocery store in season plus mobile homes to rent. €

La Madeleine

Charge • http://la-madeleine-perigord.com • The site is 3km northwest Tursac on the opposite side of the river

The semi-troglodytic medieval settlement of **La Madeleine** lies near the neck of a huge meander in the Vézère, where the river takes a three-kilometre loop to cover less than 100m as the crow flies. The cliffs here have been inhabited on and off for the last 15,000 years. Indeed, the prehistoric rock shelter down by the water's edge yielded such a wealth of late-Paleolithic tools and engravings that archeologists named the period Magdalenian; one of the more intriguing finds was a carving of a man with a bestial head, believed to be a mask, now on display at Les Eyzies' Musée National (see page 123). There's a copy here, too, along with copies of other important finds, such as a bison with its finely engraved head looking back over a powerful shoulder.

Further up the cliff subsequent settlers constructed a whole **village** complete with fortress, drawbridge, square and chapel, all dating back to the tenth century. La Madeleine was inhabited until 1920, and the Resistance used it as a hideout, but now the chapel is the only building completely intact. Nevertheless, enough remains to give a good sense of what such cliff-dwellings were like.

Préhisto-parc

Charge • http://prehistoparc.fr • The park is 2km northwest of Tursac, just beyond the turning to La Madeleine on the D706

Plastic Neanderthals hunting mock mammoths to an accompanying soundtrack won't be everyone's cup of tea, but the **Préhisto-parc** will probably please the kids. A woodland walk takes you past tableaux of encampments as well as costumed staff making flints, painting, sculpting and generally being busy in a prehistoric sort of way.

Maison Forte de Reignac

Charge • http://maison-forte-reignac.com • Maison Forte de Reignac is adjacent to the Préhisto-parc, 2km northwest of Tursac and just beyond the turning to La Madeleine on the D706

A fortified, semi-troglodytic feudal residence whose knights owed allegiance to the superior lord at St-Christophe, the **Maison Forte de Reignac** was occupied throughout the Middle Ages and into the twentieth century. It presents an intriguing combination of primitive cave-dwelling (some of the rooms occupy the old rock shelters) and medieval opulence.

The three storeys of the house are furnished with items from different periods of its occupation and contain interesting **displays** on the feudal system (pick up the English leaflet at the entrance for full translations). The most interesting **rooms** are the grand reception room on the ground floor, with its authentic *pisé* floor, monolithic washbasin and smoking wood fire, and the last room you see, the former bedroom of the countess of Reignac, which is very elegantly furnished. Above the house, you can climb to higher rock shelters to appreciate the defensive nature of the site, and admire the views along the valley. The visit ends with rather a gruesome display of instruments used for torture and punishment.

La Roque St-Christophe

Charge • http://roque-st-christophe.com • The site is 3km upriver from Tursac

The enormous natural refuge of **La Roque St-Christophe** is made up of about one hundred **rock shelters** on five levels, hollowed out of the limestone cliffs. The whole complex is nearly one kilometre long and up to eighty metres above ground level, where the River Vézère once flowed.

The earliest traces of **occupation** go back over 50,000 years, although permanent settlement dates from around the ninth century when the site's natural defences really came into their own. At its peak during the Middle Ages, the settlement had grown into a veritable town clinging to the rock face – with its own marketplace, church, prison, abattoir, baker and artisans' workshops – and was able to shelter over a thousand people in times of trouble. And there was no shortage of those, culminating in the Wars of Religion when Protestant sympathizers took refuge here. After they were kicked out in 1588, Henri III ordered the town and fortress demolished – which means you need a good imagination to re-create the scene from the various nooks and crannies hacked into the rock. In summer, there are frequent **guided visits** (in French only). Although instructive they're long and a bit tedious – better to take one of their English-language leaflets and wander at your own pace. The second half of the **trail** is perhaps the more interesting, with its re-creation of a medieval kitchen, weapons of war and, below that, a Neolithic cave scene complete with unlikely attacking bears.

St-Léon-sur-Vézère and around

With its gurgling river and honeycomb-coloured stone buildings, **ST-LÉON-SUR-VÉZÈRE**, 6km above Tursac, is by far the most attractive village in the whole Vézère valley. It sits off the main road in a quiet bend of the river guarded by two châteaux – one topped by a fairytale array of turrets – and boasts one of the region's most harmonious Romanesque churches, **Église de St-Léon-sur-Vézère**; the tree-shaded riverfront outside makes for a perfect picnic spot. In summer the church serves as one of the principal venues, along with St-Amand-de-Coly (see page 140), for classical music concerts during the **Festival du Périgord Noir** (see page 115). For the best views of the village, walk over the iron-girder bridge and turn left along a footpath on the opposite bank.

Le Conquil

Charge • http://parc-aux-dinosaures.com

Up the hill on the far side of the bridge from St-Léon-sur-Vézère lies **Le Conquil**, an attraction largely aimed at families with its "dinosaur park" and a nicely situated was top obstacle course, with **zipwires** running along the bank of the Vézère. It also includes a series of shallow **troglodytic shelters**, the most interesting of which contains dozens of niches in the rock, used for housing pigeons in the Middle Ages. Otherwise, the caves don't have much to see, but children will enjoy wandering through the woods trying to spot the full-size model dinosaurs and other animals lurking in the trees, before you get up to the clifftop belvedere. Overall, Le Conquil can't really compare to some of the other attractions in the valley, but it's a good (if expensive) bet if you're after something of interest to suit all ages.

INFORMATION AND ACTIVITIES — ST-LÉON-SUR-VÉZÈRE

Tourist office There's a summer-only office opposite the municipal campsite at the entrance to St-Léon (May, June & Sept Tues–Sat 10am–noon & 4–6pm; July & Aug Tues–Sun 10am–1pm & 2–7pm; 05 53 51 08 42, http://slve.fr).
Canoe rental APA (http://canoevezere.com), by the bridge in St-Léon, operates from Easter to mid-Nov (depending on the weather), and offers various route options; the whole stretch from Montignac to St-Léon, and then St-Léon to Les Eyzies, takes two days (total 30km).

ACCOMMODATION AND EATING

Auberge du Pont Le Bourg, 05 53 50 73 07. A lovely wisteria-covered restaurant with a shady summer terrace beside the bridge. It serves a wide choice of dishes in generous portions, including fresh salads, Limousin beef and a selection of vegetarian options, plus wood-fired pizzas and a wicked array of home-made ice creams and sorbets. €€
★ **Le Clos des Songes** Place de l'Église, http://leclosdessonges.com. Opposite the church, this *chambre d'hôte* is set in a beautifully renovated village house of soft-coloured stone with four very different, artfully decorated rooms, such as the "Voyage" with its blissed-out Buddhas and smiling Hindu deities, or the earthy tones of the "Nature". The fab breakfast featuring local produce is a highlight. €€€
Camping Municipal 05 53 51 08 42. St-Léon's small municipal campsite, with just 26 pitches, is right on the river beside the bridge. There are no frills, but it is beautifully quiet and well maintained. €
★ **Déjeuner sur l'Herbe** 05 53 50 69 17. Tucked down beside the church you'll find this tiny shop selling top-notch local produce to eat at picnic tables along the riverbank or to take away. Its selection includes tasting platters of cheese or charcuterie, and *tartines* (open toasted sandwiches). €
Le Paradis http://le-paradis.fr. Excellent five-star campsite, 3km south of St-Léon on the D706, where thick hedges separate the pitches. Facilities include four nicely designed pools set among luxuriant vegetation; a restaurant, bar and shop; wi-fi and a communal herb garden. You can rent bikes and canoes, and it also organizes canoe trips. Not surprisingly, you need to book early for the summer season. It has a whole host of permanent accommodation available to rent by the week in the high season. €

Castel-Merle

Charge • http://castel-merle.com

Southeast across the valley from St-Léon-sur-Vézère, just beyond the village of **SERGEAC**, the rock shelters of **Castel-Merle** have yielded a terrific number of flints, bones and beads over the years, including a necklace of shells from the Atlantic, presumably obtained by trade. In 2007, excavation teams also discovered the earliest evidence so far of mural wall art, a series of animal engravings dating from around 37,000 years ago, during the early Aurignacian period.

Guides take you on a fascinating French-language tour (thorough English-language booklet available) visiting five of the ten shelters. Only one of these still contains any **cave art**, including three rather poorly preserved bison sculptures, but you learn a lot about the history and significance of the site, and the lives of the people who once lived here. You can also try throwing a spear using a prehistoric propelling device – it's not easy, but adds some interest for those with children.

ACCOMMODATION — SERGEAC

Auberge de Castel-Merle Sergeac, http://hotelcastelmerle.com. A handsome country inn perched on the hill above the Castel-Merle rock shelters and still run by the descendants of Marcel Castanet, who first excavated the site. The rooms are cheerful, but its main attribute is its clifftop terrace, where guests can eat dinner overlooking the Vézère on fine evenings. The friendly, English-speaking owners can also provide a wealth of information about the area. €€

Château de Losse

Charge • http://chateaudelosse.com

Of several castles along the Vézère valley, the Renaissance **Château de Losse** stands out as the most striking. It occupies a rocky bluff four kilometres upstream from St-Léon on the main D706, though the best views are from the opposite bank, where the D65 provides a quiet and picturesque back-road from St-Léon to Montignac.

The present castle was constructed in the 1570s by **Jean II de Losse**, royal tutor and the governor of Guyenne, on medieval foundations. It has changed little since then, and is a well-proportioned L-shaped building surrounded by dry moats and watchtowers. Inside, the château's present owners have established an impressive collection of sixteenth- and seventeenth-century **furniture** and **tapestries**. Among the latter, the Florentine *Return of the Courtesan* is particularly successful in its use of perspective, while the colours of this and the Flemish rendition of knights preparing for a tournament remain exceptionally vibrant. There's also a rare, tulip-decorated tapestry dating from around the time of the Dutch tulipomania in 1634, when tulips cost more than gold.

On your way out, note the inscription over the unusually imposing gatehouse which quotes one of Jean II's favourite maxims: "When I thought the end was in sight, I was only beginning." His perhaps jaundiced view is forgivable – of his five sons, four were killed in war and the fifth had no heirs to inherit the family estates. After the tour you are free to wander the beautifully tended **gardens**, including beds of lavender and rosemary and a charming little knot garden.

Le Thot

Charge • http://lascaux-dordogne.com • Le Thot is 1km into the hills to the west of the Château de Losse

A combination of museum and animal park, **Le Thot** focuses on prehistoric art, not only the technical aspects but also some of the **wildlife** that provided inspiration: Przewalski horses with their erect manes, plus ibex, deer and European bison are all resident here. You'll also see **aurochs**, though these primitive wild cattle really died out in the 1600s – the beasts here are a close approximation achieved through selective breeding in the early twentieth century.

The **museum** explains the different techniques and styles of cave art, and allows you to appreciate how skillfully the artists depicted these same animals. But the most interesting aspect is the reproduction of four **friezes** from the Lascaux caves, including a rotund black cow who seems almost to be dancing on her slender legs, and two powerful bison back-to-back. Experts then explore the paintings and speculate on their meaning in three video presentations, unfortunately in French only.

Montignac and around

Some 26km upstream from Les Eyzies, **MONTIGNAC** is an attractive town, with a vibrant annual **arts festival** in July (see page 115). The town serves as the main base for exploring the Vézère valley's northern sights, foremost of which is the spectacular new complex containing reproductions of the renowned **Lascaux** cave paintings, though the Romanesque abbey church of **St-Amand-de-Coly** is also worth a visit.

Montignac straddles the Vézère; to the north of the river lies the **old town**, home to numerous timbered fourteenth- to sixteenth-century houses and centred on pretty **place d'Armes**, a harmonious square of warm, sun-bathed stone, adorned by hanging creepers and smart blue shutters. Nearby is **place Carnot**, where a **market** is held on Wednesday and Saturday mornings, beneath the dominant spire of the square's somewhat unexciting twentieth-century church.

To the west of the two squares, the narrow alleyway of **rue des Jardins** leads uphill to give a view of the town's abandoned feudal castle (not open to the public), which was the abode of the once powerful counts of Périgord.

Home to the tourist office and most hotels, the **Faubourg** area south of the river is less attractive, though it does have some elegant buildings, including the galleried former **hospice** immediately south of the bridge, where the town's municipal offices are now housed, and a number of older timbered structures on **rue de la Pégerie**.

ARRIVAL, INFORMATION AND ACTIVITIES — MONTIGNAC

By bus Buses from Périgueux, Sarlat and Brive via Terrasson stop on place Carnot and place Tourny, at the north end of rue du 4-septembre. Those serving St-Léon only stop on place Tourny. However, as all these services are aimed at schoolchildren, and run once or twice a day during term-time only, they're not really a viable option for visitors.

Tourist office Place Bertran-de-Born (Jan–March, Oct–Dec Tues, Wed & Fri 10am–12.30pm & 2–5pm, Tues & Thurs 10am–12.30pm; April–June Mon–Sat 9.30am–12.30pm & 2–6pm, Sun 9.30am–12.30pm; Sept Mon–Sat 9.30am–6pm, Sun 9.30am–12.30pm; July & Aug daily 9.30am–6.30pm; 05 53 51 82 60, http://lascaux-dordogne.com). It sells a map (€2.50) of 31 walking routes around Montignac.

Canoe and kayak rental Montignac has two outlets: Les 7 Rives (05 53 50 19 26) beside Pont de la Paix; and Kanoak (http://canoe-montignac.com) below the old bridge. Both open roughly June–Sept; possible routes include the 2hr descent from Thonac or the 3hr paddle from St-Léon.

ACCOMMODATION

De Bouilhac 6 av Professeur Faurel, http://hoteldebouilhac.com. In an imposing manor house, hung with chandeliers and rich drapes, this is easily the most luxurious option in town. The sixteen rooms and suites are all unique, and many come with freestanding bathtubs. There's a pool, spa and fine-dining restaurant. €€

★ **Hostellerie la Roseraie** Place d'Armes, http://laroseraie-hotel.com. In a characterful ivy- and wisteria-clad building on a quiet square, this is the nicest place to stay in Montignac. The fourteen rooms are decorated with period furniture and floral touches and there's an unusual mechanical piano in the lounge. The spacious garden has a landscaped springwater pool and an abundance of roses. *La Roseraie* is also home to one of Montignac's best restaurants – if you're staying here, it's well worth considering the *demi-pension* option. €€€

Le Lascaux 109 av Jean-Jaurès, 05 53 51 82 81. About 300m out of Montignac on the Sarlat road, this welcoming three-star offers bright, modern rooms, not huge at the cheaper end but equipped with nice touches such as a tea-maker and music station. There's a sizeable garden and a restaurant in addition to secure parking. €€

★ **La Licorne** Valojoulx, http://licorne-lascaux.com. In the picturesque village of Valojoulx, 7km south of Montignac via a turnoff from the D65 towards St-Léon, you'll find this beautiful and welcoming *chambre d'hôte*. It offers five homely rooms, filled with accents of the countryside, in buildings dating back to the thirteenth century that overlook a garden and heated pool. The best are the huge "Mélilots", complete with a four-poster bed, and "Les Templiers", which opens onto the garden. Breakfasts are generous, and it also offers excellent home-cooked dinners. €€

Le Moulin du Bleufond Av Aristide-Briand, http://bleufond.com. A well-tended three-star campsite on the riverbank 500m downstream from Montignac, where each pitch is sheltered behind a thick hedge. Facilities include a heated pool, tennis court and sauna. €

Le P'tit Monde 54 rue du 4-septembre, http://hotellepetitmonde.com. A short walk from the centre along the Sarlat road, this is the least expensive option in town, offering simple, well-priced rooms with TV and either shared or en-suite facilities. It also has a small garden with plunge pool. €

EATING

For consistent quality and gracious surroundings, you can't beat the hotel-restaurant at *La Roseraie*, but if your priority is the setting, head to the northern riverbank where a number of **restaurants** – with not a lot to choose between them – have outside seating right on the river, beneath medieval timbered supports.

La Chaumière 53 rue 4-septembre, 05 53 50 14 24. If you're looking for something different, head for this cosy little place serving hearty meat and cheese specialities of the Savoie. Try *chiffonnade* (ultra-thin slices of ham), *raclette* (melted cheese served with boiled potatoes and cold meats) or *tartiflette* (potatoes cooked with onions, bacon and lashings of cheese). Portions are generous and everything is home-produced. €€

Hostellerie la Roseraie Place d'Armes, http://laroseraie-hotel.com. The restaurant of this aptly named hotel, with its rose-flanked terrace, serves a seasonal *menu*. Dishes might include local beef or duck or strawberries from Les Eyzies. €€

Lascaux IV

Charge • http://lascaux.fr • The complex is just outside Montignac along the road to Lascaux II and the original cave system

The incredible **Lascaux IV** (also known as the Montignac-Lascaux Parietal Art International Centre or CIAP) replaced Lascaux II as the main monument to the caves' original glory when it opened in 2016. Costing around €60 million to build, the complex has taken prehistory into the digital age: the entire Lascaux complex has been reproduced in perfect form, and there are also museums, 3D visualizations, films and interactive displays.

The reproductions of the **cave paintings** are undeniably impressive, carried out over two years by a dedicated team of 25 specialists in mineral reproduction of prehistoric art, mostly fine-art painters alongside moulders and resin sculptors. Their completed work was deemed to pass muster by independent experts who compared the new paintings with the originals to ensure that the visitor experience is as close to the real thing as possible.

THE GROTTE DE LASCAUX AND LASCAUX II-IV

Arguably the most spectacular cave in the Dordogne, and certainly the most well-known, the **Grotte de Lascaux** was discovered in 1940 by four teenagers in search of their dog, which had fallen into a deep cavern on a hill just south of Montignac. The cave was found to be decorated with marvellously preserved **animal paintings**, executed by Cro-Magnon people some 17,000 years ago, which are among the finest examples of prehistoric art in existence. Lascaux was opened to the public in 1948, and over the next fifteen years the humidity created by more than a million visitors caused algae and then an opaque layer of calcite to form over the paintings. The algae was cured by disinfection, but even though access to the cave was strictly controlled from 1963 onwards, limited only to scientists and others with special permission, **fungal contamination** continues to threaten the paintings today. In 2001, feather-shaped patches of white mould, later identified as *Fusarium solani*, common in agricultural areas, began spreading rapidly throughout the cave. In a controversial emergency measure, the authorities sprayed it with antibiotics and fungicides and, when they failed to halt the spread of the mould, covered the floors with quicklime. This controlled the contamination, but soon created other problems in this incredibly fragile environment. The quicklime was eventually removed in 2004.

Then, while attempts to formulate a global conservation programme were proceeding, new **black stains** were discovered on the ceilings in 2006. By 2007 they had spread to some of the paintings, most notably the Black Cow. The stains appear to be a complex contamination which is not yet fully understood. This time the Scientific Committee authorized localized chemical treatment, after which the cave was sealed off for three months. According to the latest surveys, the contamination seems at least to be stabilized, and a climate-control system installed in 2012 is designed to stop further degradation, and appears to be working.

As to what is causing these contaminations, no one yet knows for sure. Various theories put forward include global warming, rising humidity, badly designed or inadequate climate-control systems and the presence of humans. To complicate matters further, these prehistoric caves are very poorly understood, and every treatment so far has led to unexpected side-effects.

THE REPLICA CAVES

After the Lascaux caves were closed to the public in 1963, the authorities decided to build a **replica** so that visitors could continue to enjoy the remarkable artwork. Opened in 1983, just 200m from the original and 2km south of Montignac, **Lascaux II** was the result of ten years' painstaking work by twenty artists and sculptors, using the same methods and materials as the original cave painters. After thirty-plus years in service, however, the sheer number of visitors and the erosion and vibrations they and their vehicles were causing had started to create problems within the real cave system, and the rather cramped and uninspiring Lascaux II was itself replaced by the lavish state-of-the-art **Lascaux IV** complex, built well away from the real cave system on the outskirts of Montignac. Even though Lascaux IV has now opened, it's still possible to visit Lascaux II, but only by advance reservation; see http://lascaux.fr for more information. And in case you're wondering, there is a **Lascaux III**, though it's a travelling exhibition about the caves rather than a static site.

Visits start by being whizzed 21,000 years back in time to a period when the Dordogne was cold steppe and wolves, reindeer and mammoths roamed the tundra. You then follow in the footsteps of the boys who first discovered Lascaux in the 1940s and enter the "**cave**" itself, where sounds are muffled and the atmosphere damp and dark – while it can't offer the excitement of the real thing, the reproduction is still breathtaking. Highlights of the cave art include the **Hall of Bulls**, where five huge aurochs – one 5.5m long with an astonishingly expressive head and face – dominate the ceiling, while the **Axial (Painted) Gallery** is covered with more cattle surrounded by deer, bison and horses rendered in distinctive Lascaux style, with potbellies and narrow heads. Some are shaded or spotted with different coloured pigments, while others, like the bulls, are drawn in black outline. One particularly dynamic series is of three horses appearing to be in the different phases of breaking into a gallop. You don't have to be an expert to appreciate the incredible skill employed by the prehistoric artists, who would have painted these animals from memory by the light of flickering oil lamps; nor to appreciate their sense of perspective and movement, and the sheer energy they manage to convey.

In high season visits are guideded only, in groups of thirty at a time (in low season you can go it alone with just a torch). Emerging from the cave, you enter the **Interpretation area**, where the history and formation of the cave and paintings is explained. Finally, there's a 3D digital tour of the original cave and various temporary exhibitions.

St-Amand-de-Coly

Nine kilometres east of Montignac, the village of **ST-AMAND-DE-COLY** boasts the superb fortified Romanesque **Abbaye de St-Amand-de-Coly**. Despite its size and bristling military architecture, the twelfth-century abbey church manages to combine great delicacy and spirituality. It is supposedly built over the burial place of the sixth-century St Amand, who gave up soldiering to become a hermit. Despite a promising start, however, the abbey never really prospered and had largely been abandoned by the late 1400s. In 1575 a Protestant garrison withstood a heavy siege here for six days, after which the building continued to crumble until 1868, when it was classified as a historic monument; since then it has been entirely restored.

With its purity of line and simple decoration, the church is at its most evocative in the low sun of late afternoon or early evening. Its **defences**, added in the fourteenth century, left nothing to chance: the church is encircled by ramparts, its walls are 4m thick, and a passage once skirted the eaves, with numerous positions for archers to rain down arrows and blind stairways to mislead attackers. Walk up the hill behind the church to admire its vast *lauze* roof and defensive elements.

In the autumn you might catch a classical music concert in the church during the **Festival du Périgord Noir** (Aug to early Oct; see page 115).

ACCOMMODATION AND EATING	**ST-AMAND-DE-COLY**

Manoir d'Hautegente Coly, http://manoir-hautegente.com. A very grand – but not standoffish – creeper-clad manor house some 3km north of St-Amand, beyond the village of Coly. Set in its own grounds well back from the road, the hotel has a pool, sumptuous rooms overlooking the grounds to the river and one of the region's best restaurants. In fine weather, tables are set up on the terrace, overlooking the water; it's magical at night. Dishes include eggs with truffles, rabbit stuffed with dried tomatoes and basil or inside-out lemon meringue pie. €€€

Table de Jean Coly, http://manoir-hautegente.com. Beside the road in the village of Coly, the same team behind the *Manoir d'Hautegente* have opened a convivial bistro, popular with both locals and tourists for its well-presented but fresh, affordable dishes. There's a daily changing lunch *menu*, and evening *menus* which are a little higher in cost. Old photos and exposed stone walls set the scene. €€€

Terrasson-la-Villedieu

Beyond Montignac the prehistoric sites die out and the Vézère valley becomes busier and more industrialized as it opens out towards **TERRASSON-LA-VILLEDIEU**, 15km upstream, and Brive (see page 74). The old part of Terrasson, a knot of lanes on the river's south bank, merits a quick wander; head up from the arched stone bridge to the ramparts for panoramic views, and to the sixteenth-century **Église St-Sour** beyond. But the main reason for coming here is to visit its resolutely contemporary garden, **Les Jardins de l'Imaginaire** on a terraced hillside to the west of the church.

Les Jardins de l'Imaginaire
Place de Genouillac • Charge • http://jardins-imaginaire.com

Designed by American landscaper Kathryn Gustafson, the **Jardins de l'Imaginaire** explore common themes found in gardens throughout history and among different cultures, from the Romans' sacred groves and the Hanging Gardens of Babylon to moss, water and rose gardens, the last a magnificent display of nearly two thousand varieties. In this respect this is much more than "just" a garden, which is why they insist you go with a guide to explain the complicated symbolism (though this can be rather tedious if you just wanted to relax under a tree in some pretty gardens); English-language texts are available. The gardens are full of imaginative touches: a forest of wind chimes, a stark line of weathervanes and, above all, the use of water to splendid effect.

ARRIVAL AND INFORMATION　　　　　　　　　　　　　TERRASSON-LA-VILLEDIEU

If you're travelling by public transport, you might find yourself passing through Terrasson since it lies on the Brive–Bordeaux train line; buses hereabouts, however, are timed primarily for schoolchildren, so aren't of much use. While the Brive-Vallée de la Dordogne airport is not that far away, there is no direct public transport to Terrasson; you have to travel via Brive.

By train Terrasson's *gare SNCF* lies on the north side of town at the far end of avenue Jean-Jaurès.

Destinations Bordeaux (8 daily; 2hr–2hr 30min); Brive (9 daily; 15–20min); Périgueux (10 daily; 35–50min).

Tourist office Rue Jean-Rouby, immediately west of place de la Libération (April–June & Sept Mon–Sat 9.30am–12.30pm & 2–6pm; July & Aug daily 9.30am–6pm; Oct–Dec Mon–Sat 9am–12.30pm & 2–5.30pm; Jan–March Mon–Sat 9am–12.30pm & 2–5pm; 05 5350 37 56, http://vezere-perigord.fr).

ACCOMMODATION AND EATING

★ **La Mandragore** Place de l'Abbaye, http://restaurant-mandragore.fr. Perched above the river near the abbey church, this restaurant has unbeatable views from its terrace. The chef cooks up unusual takes on local produce, such as Chinese-style duck with bamboo shoots and glass noodles, and early strawberries with basil-flavoured *fromage blanc*, all beautifully presented and often garnished with flowers. In addition to a short *carte* it offers a fixed *menu* which changes every day and a *menu dégustation*. €€

The middle Dordogne

The stretch of river to the south of Sarlat sees the Dordogne at its most appealing, forming great loops between rich fields, wooded hills and craggy outcrops. This is also castle country, where great medieval fortresses eyeball each other across the valley. Most date from the Hundred Years' War, when the river marked a frontier of sorts between French-held land to the north and English territory to the south.

For the visitor today, things start slowly in the west with the service town of **St-Cyprien** and nearby **Belvès**, the latter a sleepy little place where people once lived in troglodyte houses beneath its streets, but châteaux come thick and fast thereafter. The first you reach on the river's north bank is at **Beynac-et-Cazenac**, a stunning village of russet-hued, stone-roofed cottages cascading to the river, and overlooked by one of the most photogenic châteaux in the Dordogne. A short distance further upstream, the **Jardins Suspendus de Marqueyssac** provide respite from the history among Italian-style terraced gardens and woodland promenades, with views of both Beynac and its arch-rival over on the south bank, the craggy **Château de Castelnaud**. Then a brief diversion westwards brings you to the far-from-militaristic château of **Les Milandes**, once owned by the cabaret artist Josephine Baker and now set up as a museum in her honour.

Heading back upstream, the next stop is **La Roque-Gageac**. This lovely village caught between the river and the rock face is up there with Beynac and Castelnaud as one of the Dordogne's most photographed – and visited – sights. Across on the south bank, **Domme**, a fortified *bastide* town perched on the cliff edge, is no pushover on either the tourist stakes or in terms of its views. From up here you can take in a 10km sweep of the river, giving you a foretaste of the **Cingle de Montfort**, a particularly picturesque meander set off by yet another glorious château to the east. Before you cross from the Dordogne *département* into the Lot, the **Château de Fénelon** is an attractive blend of medieval and Renaissance architecture with good collections of furniture and weaponry.

GETTING AROUND — THE MIDDLE DORDOGNE

You can just about forget about public transport in this area. St-Cyprien, Siorac-en-Périgord and Belvès are accessible by train, but the picturesque Sarlat line runs past all the prime sights around Beynac without stopping. The only place accessible by bus is Carsac, a village with a pretty church east of Montfort, which is a stop on the Sarlat–Souillac route.

St-Cyprien and around

Despite its location, just 20km west of Sarlat and 10km south from Les Eyzies, **ST-CYPRIEN** remains a refreshingly workaday place set back from the busy D703. Admittedly, it hasn't got much in the way of sights, but the whole place really comes to life on Sunday mornings for one of the area's best **markets**. The hillside setting is also attractive and, although the town itself has few accommodation options, hotels and *chambres d'hôtes* in neighbouring villages make it a possible base.

The old centre's narrow lanes of medieval houses and labourers' cottages, a good number still unprettified, hold the greatest interest. They zigzag up from the modern, lower town towards the austere **Église St-Cyprien** on rue Bertrand de Got, founded by twelfth-century Augustinian monks. You certainly can't accuse the church of being pretty either, though there's a certain robust grandeur about its Romanesque tower and the echoing nave. The interior is worth a look for some fine eighteenth-century sculpted wooden statues on its retables, and is an evocative setting for classical music concerts in summer.

ARRIVAL AND INFORMATION — ST-CYPRIEN

By train St-Cyprien's train station, on the Bordeaux–Sarlat line, is located about 1km south of the centre. There's no ticket office, so buy your tickets on the train or from the station machines.

Destinations Bergerac (11 daily; 1hr–1hr 30min); Bordeaux (3–6 daily; 2hr 15min); Le Buisson (4–6 daily; 15min); Sarlat (4–6 daily; 25min); Siorac-en-Périgord (1–2 daily; 8min).

Tourist office Place Charles-de-Gaulle, in the centre of the lower town (March–May & Oct Mon–Fri 9.30am–12.30pm & 2–6pm, Sun 9.30am–12.30pm; June–Sept Mon–Sat 9.30am–12.30pm & 2–6pm, Sun 9.30am–1pm; 05 53 30 36 09, http://perigordnoir-valleedordogne.com). The office produces a good (free) walking map of St-Cyprien and coordinates an active programme of concerts, events and activities in summer.

ACCOMMODATION AND EATING

There are no particularly good **accommodation** options in St-Cyprien, but you'll find plenty of potential places to stay scattered in the hills and villages around. There is a cluster of traditional abodes near the typical Périgord village of Meyrals, 5km to the north; the other option is to head 8km downstream to Siorac-en-Périgord – a junction, albeit infrequently served, on the Sarlat–Bordeaux and Agen–Périgueux train lines. Across the river from Siorac, the village of Le Coux-et-Bigaroque also has a good place to stay.

MEYRALS

Le Chèvrefeuille Pechboutier, http://lechevrefeuille.com. English-owned, family-friendly *chambre d'hôte* in a hamlet 2.5km west of Meyrals. It has five pretty en-suite rooms, a pool and spacious garden, plus additional facilities including a well-equipped shared kitchenette, laundry room and bikes. Two nights' minimum stay required. €€

★ **Domaine de la Rhonie** Boyer, http://domainedelarhonie.com. You're assured a warm welcome at this beguiling country inn lost in the middle of nowhere, 3.5km northeast of Meyrals off the C3. A working farm, it offers twelve cheerful, modern rooms set in extensive grounds with a covered and heated pool, and an excellent restaurant, which focuses on traditional Périgord cuisine. Expect dishes using geese fattened on the farm itself and their walnuts, in addition to other local produce. This means meat-heavy *menus* featuring dishes such as foie gras and succulent *magret* (grilled breast of goose) served with *pommes sarladaises* (potatoes in a creamy sauce). €€

La Ferme Lamy Boyer, http://sarlat-dordogne-lamy.com. You'll need to book early to nab one of the twelve stylish rooms at this three-star hotel surrounded by woods and fields. The whole place is immaculate, from the en-suite bathrooms to the big infinity pool and flower-filled garden, not to mention the breakfast-spread of home-made jams and breads. €€

SIORAC-EN-PÉRIGORD

Auberge du Trèfle à Quatre Feuilles 173 rue de la Gare, http://letrefle4feuilles.com. In the centre of Siorac, with seven good-value rooms located in a separate building to the rear of a popular restaurant. They are functional but bright and well kept, all with en-suite bathrooms, TV and double-glazing. It's wise to book ahead to sample the delights of the restaurant. Working with fresh, mostly local produce, it offers well-priced four-course *menus*, which might feature foie gras, tartare of pollock with lemon and beetroot, and a strawberry tart with a green-apple sorbet. €

Camping du Port http://campingduport.net. An inexpensive and relaxed two-star campsite on the riverbank beside the bridge; to reach it, turn down behind the Carrefour supermarket. Mature trees provide plenty of shade, there's an on-site snack bar in July and August, and caravans are available to rent. €

Le Petit Chaperon Rouge La Faval, http://chaperon rouge.fr. On the north side of the river from Siorac, set on a hillside just off the D703, this is an inexpensive, peaceful country inn. In high season you'll need to book early to stay in one of its nine homely rooms: nothing fancy but impeccably maintained. Their restaurant is authentic and good value, with a summer terrace shaded by lime trees. In winter, meals are served in an old-fashioned, floral dining room among gleaming tableware. €

LE COUX-ET-BIGAROQUE

Manoir de la Brunie http://manoirdelabrunie.com. Characterful *chambre d'hôte* in a fifteenth-century manor house 1km northwest of Le Coux-et-Bigaroque, signed off the D703. There are two *gîtes*, sleeping six or 10 people, with high ceilings and period furniture. There's a saltwater pool and extensive parkland with splendid views over the Dordogne valley. Evening meals on request. €€€

Belvès

Accessible by public transport, and a possible base before you reach the most touristy stretch of the Dordogne valley, the picturesque hilltop town of **BELVÈS** is 12km south of St-Cyprien. There's no mistaking the town's strategic importance, encircled by ramparts on a promontory above the Nauze valley and bristling with seven towers – even the central square is called **place d'Armes**. These days, however, the only battles likely to take place here involve haggling over prices at the Saturday-morning **market** under the old *halle*, or a hotly disputed game of *boules*.

Several fine streets, lined with handsome houses from various eras, lead off place d'Armes: **rue Rubigan**, reached under the old stone gateway, is a narrow, winding medieval street, while on **rue des Filhols** you can see the imposing tower of the Maison des Consuls and, further up, a battered ornate Renaissance facade slapped on the twelfth-century Hôtel Bontemps. **Rue Jacques-Manchotte**, on the other side of the square, leads past shops and cafés towards the imposing thirteenth-century **Église Notre-Dame**, an interesting example of early, undecorative Gothic architecture, where recently discovered medieval frescoes are currently being restored.

On the way, if it's open, you could also pop into the **Organistrum**, 14 rue Jacques-Manchotte (no fixed hours; free; 05 53 29 10 93), a combined museum and workshop producing medieval instruments. Music-lovers might also be interested in Belvès' principal annual event, the **Festival Bach**, dedicated to the composer, with at least one concert in the church during the first fortnight of August (see page 115).

Troglodyte houses

Place d'Armes • Charge, tickets sold at the tourist office • 05 53 29 10 20

In 1907 the wheel of a cart crossing place d'Armes broke through the roof of a warren of **troglodyte houses**. Hollowed into the rampart wall, these damp, dark and insalubrious dwellings were inhabited from the twelfth century up to the mid-1700s, after which they were blocked up and forgotten. So far eight "houses" have been opened: single rooms averaging a mere twenty square metres apiece for a family plus animals. It's hard to imagine what they must have been like to live in, even if the more sophisticated dwellings boast chimneys, raised sleeping areas and shelves cut into the soft rock.

Filature de Belvès
Fongauffier • Charge • http://filaturedebelves.com

In the Nauze valley just below Belvès, on the D710, the former woollen mill of **Filature de Belvès** produced top-quality yarn for the Aubusson tapestry workshops until the 1990s. It has now been opened as a museum, where you learn about the history of wool in the area and how the raw fleeces were processed into various grades of yarn.

The machines you see today date from the late 1940s, when electricity replaced water power, and though none of them is working, films of similar machines in action give the general idea. The visit ends with the chance to try felt-making, weaving or using vegetable dyes. It makes for a fun hour or so, particularly if you have children in tow.

ARRIVAL AND INFORMATION **BELVÈS**

By train Belvès lies on the Agen–Périgueux line, with the *gare SNCF* down on the main road below the town.
Destinations Agen (3–5 daily; 1hr–1hr 15min); Le Bugue (3–5 daily; 25min); Le Buisson (3–5 daily; 15min); Les Eyzies (3–5 daily; 30–40min); Périgueux (3–5 daily; 1hr–1hr 15min); Siorac-en-Périgord (3–5 daily; 6min).
Tourist office On the ground floor of the fifteenth-century Maison des Consuls, just off the market square at 1 rue des Filhols (March: Mon–Sat: 10am–12.30pm & 2–6pm; April, May, Oct & Nov daily 10am–12.30pm & 2–6.30pm; June & Sept daily 10am–1pm & 2–7pm; July & Aug daily 10am–7.30pm; Dec–Feb Tues–Fri 10am–12.30pm & 2–5.30pm, Sat 10am–12.30pm; 05 53 29 10 20, http://perigordnoir-valleedordogne.com).

ACCOMMODATION AND EATING

Hôtel Clément V 15 rue Jacques-Manchotte, http://clement5.com. Halfway up the main shopping street, this is an eighteenth-century former grocery turned boutique hotel, with palatial rooms decorated in puffy claret-red furnishings, four-posters beds, stone floors and lots of old black-and-white pictures on the walls. The bathrooms are particularly impressive. It's somewhat expensive compared to similar places in the region, however. €€

Le Home 3 place de la Croix-des-Frères, http://lehomedebelves.fr. This friendly, one-star hotel really has the feel of old-fashioned, small-town France, and you half expect prices to be quoted in francs. There are ten no-frills rooms, singles and doubles, the cheapest with tiny bathrooms. The restaurant is popular at lunchtime for its good-value traditional cuisine, with *à-la-carte* and evening *menus*. €

Manoir de la Moissie Bd de la Moissie, http://lamoissie.fr. On the western edge of Belvès by the municipal tennis courts, signed off the D53 Monpazier road, this sixteenth-century manor house is now a stylish *chambre d'hôte* and artists' residence. Four beautifully decorated and spacious rooms sit under the eaves, while guests also have access to an enormous communal room downstairs, a TV room and washing machine, as well as the surrounding park. Secure parking available. €

Les Nauves Le Bos Rouge, http://lesnauves.com. Belvès' nearest campsite is in a quiet spot 4km southwest off the D53 Monpazier road. It offers good-size plots and a pool, and organizes various kids' activities in July and August. From June to September and at weekends it also opens a grocery store, bar and restaurant, and cabins are available. €

Beynac-et-Cazenac

Clearly visible on an impregnable cliff-edge along the Dordogne's north bank, with its **château** soaring above the valley and standing sentry over a bend in the river, the eye-catching village of **BEYNAC-ET-CAZENAC** was built in the days when the Dordogne was the only route open to traders and invaders. Nowadays the busy main road squeezes between the cliffs and the water, creating a horrible bottleneck in midsummer (arrive first thing in the morning to beat the coach groups), but nonetheless postcard-perfect Beynac is easily a highlight of the region.

Château de Beynac
Charge • http://chateau-beynac.com

It's three kilometres by road from the Beynac-et-Cazenac waterfront to the **Château de Beynac**; alternatively, you can walk up the steep lane among the *lauze*-roofed cottages in fifteen minutes. The lichenous-grey castle is protected on the landward side by double walls and ditches; elsewhere the sheer drop of almost 150m does the job. The redoubtable

Richard the Lionheart nevertheless took and held Beynac for a decade, until a gangrenous wound ended his term of bloodletting in 1189; apparently the heart-shaped keys and keyholes were fashioned in his memory. Though the English regained the castle briefly – thanks to the Treaty of Brétigny rather than any military prowess – in essence Beynac remained loyal to the French Crown during the Hundred Years' War.

The buildings are in surprisingly good condition thanks to a mammoth **restoration project** over the past forty years, which is scheduled to continue until at least 2030. If the French-language guided tour is too much for you, you can go it alone with a rather brief English-language leaflet, available from the ticket office. You enter into a **guardroom**, one of the castle's more atmospheric rooms along with the **great hall**, where the nobles of Beynac, Biron, Mareuil and Bourdeilles – the four baronies of Périgord – met; note the unusual ox-skull motif over the fireplace, also found at the Château de Lanquais. The twelfth-century **kitchens** have a cobbled ramp allowing horses access to the central courtyard, and are kitted out with no-nonsense tables, vats, meat-hooks and great pulleys. If it looks familiar, that's because it featured in Luc Besson's epic, *Jeanne d'Arc*.

For most people, however, it's the **views** that steal the show, notably from the top of the keep, where you get a stupendous – and vertiginous – sweep over the surrounding châteaux: Marqueyssac (see below), Fayrac (see page 149) and Castelnaud (see page 148).

ARRIVAL AND INFORMATION
BEYNAC-ET-CAZENAC

By car You need your own vehicle to travel to Beynac. Parking is available down by the river, in three car parks on the road up to the castle and beside the castle itself. Other than the last of the three on the road to the castle, all charge a fee; once you've bought a ticket, you can move to the other car park if you choose.

Tourist office At the bottom of the road up to the château (Feb, March, Oct, Nov & Christmas hols Fri 2–5pm, Sat 10am–1pm & 2–5pm; April–June & Sept daily 10am–1pm & 2–5pm; July & Aug daily 10am–1pm & 2–6pm 05 53 29 43 08, http://beynac-en-perigord.com).

ACCOMMODATION AND EATING

Le Capeyrou http://campinglecapeyrou.com. A three-star campsite on the riverbank immediately east of Beynac, with unbeatable views up to the château. The best plots are those lined up along the river, though they could do with more hedges around. There's a good-size heated pool and well-equipped children's play area, plus a bar. €

Du Château Le Bourg, http://hotelduchateau.fr. A two-star hotel on a rather busy junction, where the road heads up to the castle. The rooms are a bit of an afterthought to the main business of the restaurant, but they're bright and impeccably clean, equipped with satellite TV; those at the front have double-glazing and a shared terrace with river views, best appreciated in the quiet of the evening. There's a tiny pool and one of Beynac's better restaurants, which has great-value *menus*, including a weekend lunch *menu* and a three-course evening *menu*. House specialities include *tourin* (the local garlic soup), eggs baked with truffles, and sturgeon in a Monbazillac sauce. It also offers large salads, omelettes and a few vegetarian dishes. €€

La Petite Tonnelle Le Bourg, http://la-petite-tonnelle.fr. This well-respected restaurant is surprisingly relaxed, despite its location on the road up to the château, opposite *Pontet*. In addition to daily specials, it offers an array of *formules* and *menus*, plus a fine choice of local wines. Everything is home-made, including home-smoked duck breast and Scottish salmon; try the John Dory in a shellfish sauce. Reservations recommended. €€

Pontet Rue de la Balme, http://hostellerie-maleville.com. With the benefit of being off the main drag, on the road leading up to the château, this little place offers thirteen very comfortable rooms, all a/c, with en-suite bathrooms and TV. The attached *Maleville* restaurant has well-priced lunch *menus*. €

Jardins Suspendus and Château de Marqueyssac

Charge, option of a combined ticket with Château de Castelnaud • Candle-lit evenings July & Aug Thurs 7pm–midnight • http://marqueyssac.com

Three kilometres east of Beynac, the Dordogne loops south round a long and narrow wooded promontory, at the tip of which the **Château de Marqueyssac** presides over its terraced "hanging" gardens, the **Jardins Suspendus de Marqueyssac**. A few rooms of the

THE LIGHTER SIDE OF BEYNAC

Particularly in summer, the tiny village of Beynac-et-Cazenac, cramped between road and cliff-face, can get oppressively crowded. Thankfully, there are a number of ways to escape and enjoy a more peaceful perspective on the countless castles in the area.

RIVER TRIPS

Gabarres de Beynac (Charge; http://gabarre-beynac.com), based on a jetty next to the riverside car park, offers 50min **river cruises** on their replica *gabarres*, the traditional wooden river craft, affording excellent views of castle and village. During holidays and high season, you can expect at least one departure an hour, but at other times and on wet days you might have to wait a while for the boat to fill up.

CANOEING

The stretch of the Dordogne between Vitrac and Beynac, taking you past a breathtaking parade of castles, is the most stunning **canoe trip** in the region. If you hire a canoe in Beynac, the company will drive you upriver before you paddle back down to your vehicle; prices start at €16. In town, you'll find Copeyre Canoë (http://canoe-copeyre.com), while Canoës Roquegeoffre (http://canoe-roquegeoffre.com), based 3km downstream near Saint-Vincent-de-Cosse, offers the best value around and is open all year.

HOT-AIR BALLOONING

The ultimate slow-paced activity, **hot-air ballooning** is also a possibility here: if you phone ahead, Montgolfière et Châteaux (http://montgolfiere-chateaux.fr; from €180 per adult per hour) will collect you from Beynac's riverside car park to take you to the launch site.

WALKING

The cheapest way to escape from the crowds around Beynac's port and castle is to **walk** inland away from the river; the tourist office sells maps which detail five suggested **routes** around Beynac from 4km to 10km, with the longer itineraries taking you to the beautifully unspoilt fifteenth-century church of Cazenac, where some unusual modern stained-glass windows depict scenes from daily life in this area in the nineteenth century. For another pretty walk, head roughly south along the riverbank, starting next to the campsite; there are lots of perfect picnic stops along the way.

---

château, a typically mellow Périgord mansion of the late eighteenth century, are now open to the public, but it is the surrounding gardens and the **views**, encompassing the châteaux of Beynac, Fayrac and Castelnaud, that are the star attractions.

The **gardens** were first laid out in the 1600s by the then owner, Bertrand Vernet de Marqueyssac, under the inspiration of Le Nôtre, the landscaper responsible for Versailles. However, most of the features you see today were added two centuries later when the 500m-long **Grande Allée** was established – thousands of box trees clipped into plump cushions – and 6km of woodland walks opened up along the ridge to the east. In recent years, landscape gardeners have added more modern touches, including sculptures and the "boxwood chaos" resembling angular stone blocks. All paths lead to a 130m-high **belvedere**, from where you can see La Roque-Gageac nestling under its cliff (see page 149). The gardens are also the best in the Sarlat area for children, with a **maze**, **playground** and various kid-friendly activities such as mask-making. The gardens are also home to a **Via Ferrata**, an exhilarating **cliff-walk** suspended 100m up along a narrow path and a series of ropes, beams and brackets attached to the rock face, to which you are secured by a safety line. It's restricted to those over 8 years old and 1.3m in height, and entry is included in the main ticket price; however, hours vary so phone ahead or check the website for the current schedule.

On Thursday evenings in July and August thousands of **candles** and **fairy lights** give the gardens a magical touch. Between Easter and mid-November, the restaurant-*salon de thé* serves meals and light refreshments; note that in high season **picnicking** within the gardens is forbidden – you have to eat in the dedicated area just by the entrance gate, which can be a bit of pain.

Castelnaud-la-Chapelle

Rivals for centuries, the feudal fortresses of Beynac and **CASTELNAUD-LA-CHAPELLE**, on the Dordogne's south bank some 4km upriver of Beynac, now vie over visitor numbers. There's no question that Beynac has the edge, with its more dramatic location and arguably the better views, but the **Château de Castelnaud** provides the more entertaining and informative visit; allow at least a couple of hours.

Château de Castelnaud

Charge • http://castelnaud.com • There's a charge for the upper car park, closest to the château, from where it's still a fair walk down; alternatively, you can park for free in the lower car park on the main road, and then walk up

Like Beynac, the **Château de Castelnaud** was founded in the twelfth century and bitterly fought over on many occasions, starting with the bellicose Simon de Montfort, who seized it as early as 1214 during his Cathar crusades. During the Hundred Years' War the lords of Castelnaud sided with the English, slugging it out for nearly four decades with the French at Beynac until Charles VII besieged Castelnaud in 1442. After holding out for three weeks, a treacherous English captain handed over the keys in return for his life and the princely sum of four hundred crowns.

Heavily restored in the last decades, the château now houses an excellent **museum of medieval warfare**. Its core is an extensive collection of original weaponry, including all sorts of bizarre contraptions, such as an "organ" which sprayed lead balls from its multiple barrels, and a fine assortment of armour.

This is easily the most enjoyable château in the area for families. Throughout the year, but particularly during school holidays, staff give demonstrations of iron forging, weaponry and firing the trebuchet siege engine.

Éco-musée de la Noix du Périgord

Charge • http://ecomuseedelanoix.fr • The park is on the D57 south of Castelnaud, by the turning up to the Château de Castelnaud

The **Éco-musée de la Noix du Périgord** is considerably more interesting than it might sound. This part of the Dordogne is prime walnut-growing country, and as well as detailing oil pressing, the exhibits here reveal all kinds of unexpected nut-related titbits, such as the fact that Louis XI's beard was trimmed using heated walnut shells, and that walnuts were used in the insulation of American spaceships. They also point out the nuts' many health benefits, before you're shepherded through to the well-stocked shop, which makes a good place to pick up some unusual – and completely organic – walnut souvenirs. If you're lucky the mill itself will be working (July & Aug Tues, Wed & Thurs afternoons), but otherwise there's a self-explanatory video. The adjacent orchard, scattered with picnic tables and giant walnuts rendered in cement, might appeal to young children.

ACTIVITIES — CASTELNAUD-LA-CHAPELLE

Bike rental From Castelnaud-la-Chapelle you can follow the quiet Voie Verte cycle route along the lovely Céou valley to Daglan and L'Abbaye-Nouvelle, in the Lot. Hire from Bike Bus (http://bike-bus.com), at the Voie Verte car park.

Canoe rental On the riverfront, beside the bridge, you can rent canoes at the Base Municipale Canoë-Kayak (http://canoescastelnaudlachapelle.fr).

ACCOMMODATION

Lou Castel http://loucastel.com. While there are no hotels in Castelnaud, you'll find this lively and well-equipped four-star campsite set among oak woods on the plateau roughly 3km to the south. It has several pools, water slides, a grocery store, bar and restaurant, as well as children's activities in July and August. There are also fixed tents and chalets to rent. €

★ **La Tour de Cause** Pont-de-Cause, http://latourdecause.com. High-quality *chambre d'hôte* in a lovely Périgordin manor house in the hamlet of Pont-de-Cause, 2km south of Castelnaud on the D57. There's a choice of three rooms downstairs and two up in the eaves, all different (1950s style in one, and tropical bird in another) and all with their own charm. Guests also have access to a communal living room and kitchen area and a saltwater pool. The Belgian owners, who worked as chefs in their homeland, go out of their way to make you comfortable, and prepare copious breakfasts; fabulous evening meals are also available. Four-night minimum stay in July and August. €€

La Treille Le Port, Vitrac, http://latreille-perigord.com. Quaint, if a little dated, hotel with warm service, opening out directly onto the river in Vitrac. The restaurant is great value, with wonderful views. €

Les Milandes

Charge • http://milandes.com

From Castelnaud-la-Chapelle it's a scenic drive 5km west along the river past **Château de Fayrac** (not open to the public) with its slated pepper-pot towers – an English forward position in the Hundred Years' War, built to watch over Beynac – to **Les Milandes**. Built in the late 1400s, the château was the property of the Caumont family (the lords of Castelnaud) until the Revolution, but its most famous owner was the Folies Bergère star, **Josephine Baker** (see box), who fell in love with it while visiting friends in the area in 1937.

It's easy to see why she liked it so much. The Renaissance château, sitting high above the Dordogne, has all the necessary romantic ingredients: towers, machicolations, balustrades, gargoyles, ornate dormer windows and terraced gardens shaded by great, glossy-leafed magnolias. After she bought Les Milandes in 1947, Josephine set about modernizing it, adding creature comforts such as the en-suite **bathrooms**, whose decor was inspired by her favourite perfumes – Arpège-style black tiles with gold taps and ceiling in one, Dioresque pink marble with silver-leaf in another. But it's really the stories surrounding Josephine and Les Milandes that are more intriguing than the château itself. Her rollercoaster life story is enough to fill a book, but you can trace the broad outlines from the collection of **photos** and **posters**. The few **costumes** that escaped the auctioneer's hammer in 1968 are also on display, though these are somewhat moth-eaten after mouldering in the cellar for 25 years.

After visiting the château, you can explore the gardens, daily **falconry demonstrations** are held (check the website for exact times). From the terrace, there are views down on the J-shaped swimming pool belonging to one of the many fun-parks that Josephine established in the area.

La Roque-Gageac

The village of **LA ROQUE-GAGEAC**, on the Dordogne's north bank 5km east of Beynac, is almost too perfect, its ochre-coloured houses overlooking the lazy-flowing river and sheltering beneath dramatically overhanging rust-coloured cliffs. Regular winner of France's prettiest village contest, it inevitably pulls in masses of tourist buses, and since the main road separates the village from the river, the noise and fumes of the traffic can become oppressive.

The best way to escape is to slip away through the lanes and alleyways that wind up through the terraced houses. The other option is to rent a canoe and paddle over to the opposite bank, where you can picnic and enjoy a much better view of La Roque than from among the crowds milling around beneath the village, at its best in the burnt-orange glow of the evening sun.

INFORMATION AND ACTIVITIES **LA ROQUE-GAGEAC**

Tourist office Occupies a hut by the main car park on the Sarlat side of town (daily: April–June & Sept 10am–1pm & 2–5pm; July & Aug 10am–1pm & 2–6pm; Oct Mon–Sat 10am–1pm & 2–5pm; 05 53 29 17 01). On Friday evenings

PÉRIGORD WALNUTS

According to archeological evidence, **walnuts** have formed part of the Périgordin diet for more than 17,000 years. In medieval times, walnut oil was so valuable that it was sometimes used as a form of currency, and in the seventeenth century it was exported by river (via Bordeaux) to Britain, Holland and Germany. Walnuts are still central to the local economy today: rich in polyunsaturated fats, potassium, magnesium and vitamin E, both nuts and oil are marketed for their health-giving properties – they're said to help reduce cholesterol, stimulate the memory and protect against the effects of ageing. The nuts are also incorporated into bread, cakes, tarts and ice cream, or served whole with salads and the local *Cabécou* cheese. Green walnuts are often pickled in vinegar, but can also be made into jam or used to flavour wines and liqueurs. Not even the leaves are wasted: picked young, they give a distinctive tang to walnut apéritif.

In recognition of the walnut's importance to the economy – and indeed culture – of the region, four varieties (Grandjean, Marbot, Corne and Franquette) were granted an **Appellation d'Origine Contrôlée** (AOC) in 2002, to guarantee that you're buying only premium-quality, locally grown produce. Walnuts are grown in the Lot, Corrèze and Charente *départements*, but the heart of the industry is the Dordogne, with more than 40 square kilometres of orchards. To capitalize on the AOC label, the local authorities have put together a **Route de la Noix**, along the Dordogne valley from Argentat to Beynac and north to Hautefort. Free leaflets outlining the suggested itineraries are available from tourist offices, indicating producers and traditional oil mills open for visits as well as specialist patisseries and restaurants serving dishes with a nutty theme.

---

between mid-June and mid-September at 9pm it organizes guided tours of the village (charge).

Boat trips An almost compulsory activity in La Roque-Gageac is to take a boat trip down river in a *gabarre* (traditional flat-bottomed river craft). They're lots of fun and offer good views of the village, passing through a pretty stretch of riverbank forest where birds of prey and waterbirds are common, then pressing on to Castelnaud-la-Chapelle before returning along the same route. The 1hr trips are run by Gabares Norbert (http://gabarres.com) and Gabarres Caminades (http://gabarrecaminade.com), both based beside the main car park on the east side of La Roque and offering live (and often quite amusing) commentary in French or a pre-recorded, rather more dry English version on a headset.

Canoe rental Canoë Dordogne (http://canoesdordogne.fr), which is based just at the eastern end of the car park, and Canoë Vacances (http://canoevacances.com), which is 1km or so further east of La Roque in the direction of Vitrac and Sarlat. Rates at both start at €9/hr.

ACCOMMODATION AND EATING

La Belle Étoile http://belleetoile.fr. The nicest of the town's hotels is the family-run *La Belle Étoile*, on the main road below the fort, with fifteen airy and perfectly adequate rooms. It's worth paying extra for one at the front with river views. The hotel also boasts La Roque's best restaurant which, with its shady terrace and river views, makes a great place for a splurge, though you'll need to book ahead. It offers a varied selection of regional specialities, with three-course *menus*, all beautifully presented, and attentive service. €€

La Ferme Fleurie Le Colombier, http://fermefleurieperigord.com. For a peaceful place to stay, head 5km northwest of La Roque (just off the D703), to this *auberge* surrounded by flower-filled gardens. The floral theme is continued in the eight simple en-suite bedrooms. It also offers more basic accommodation in shared dorms (breakfast included) in its *gîte d'étape*, and there's a good-value guests-only restaurant serving evening meals at communal tables. €

Manoir de la Malartrie Vézacn, http://chambresdhotes-lamalartrie.com. This *belle époque* château offers luxurious *chambre d'hôte* accommodation on the D703 just west of La Roque. Even if the faux-medieval exterior isn't quite your cup of tea, the stately interiors are sumptuous and it's in a perfect setting, with a heated pool, beautiful formal gardens and terraces overlooking the river. The only slight hiccup is the proximity of the road. Three-night minimum stay in high season. €€€

Domme and around

High on the scarp on the south bank of the Dordogne, 5km southeast from La Roque-Gageac and 10km due south of Sarlat, **DOMME** is an exceptionally well-preserved, terribly pretty *bastide*, now wholly given over to tourism; fortunately, though, most of the village is pedestrianized so crowds never seem quite as heavy as in La Roque-Gageac. Architecturally beautiful it might be, but Domme's foremost attraction, however, is its position.

From the chestnut-shaded **Esplanade du Belvédère** at the town's northern edge, you look out over a wide sweep of river country encompassing everything from Beynac to the Cingle de Montfort. The drop here is so precipitous that fortifications were deemed unnecessary when the *bastide* was founded in 1281. They lived to regret it: in 1588 a small band of Protestants scaled the cliffs at dawn to take the town completely by surprise. The intruders stayed four years, during which time they destroyed the church amongst other buildings, before they were forced to abandon the town again to Catholic control.

Thursday morning is **market** day, when stalls spill out of the central square south down the main commercial street, the **Grande-Rue**, itself lined with souvenir shops.

Porte des Tours
http://sarlat-tourisme.com

Much of Domme's thirteenth-century walls and three of the gateways they skirted remain. Of the latter, the best-preserved and most interesting is easterly **Porte des Tours**, flanked by two round bastions. In 1307 a group of Templar knights was imprisoned here for eleven years.

Guided tours of the gateway reveal traces of the graffiti they carved on the walls depicting Crucifixion scenes, the Virgin Mary, angels and various secret signs. Alternatively, you can see photos of the carvings in the town's Musée des Arts et Traditions Populaires.

Musée des Arts et Traditions Populaires
Place de la Halle • Charge • http://tourisme-domme.com • Closed for renovation works at the time of writing

Located on Domme's central square, the **Musée des Arts et Traditions Populaires** focuses on local life in the nineteenth and twentieth centuries. The displays are nicely done, if not wildly interesting, but are worth a quick glance.

Grotte de Domme
Place de la Halle • Charge • Tickets cover entry to the Musée des Arts et Traditions Populaires, and are available at Domme's tourist office

Extending for hundreds of metres under the village from beneath the timbered market hall, the **caves** of Domme definitely can't compete with most Dordogne caverns, but you're likely to have them to yourself and the way out from the caves is enjoyable in itself: a lift takes you up the cliff-face from the exit, affording panoramic views, then there's a pleasant stroll back to town along the promenade de la Falaise.

Jardin Public
Rue du Vieux Moulin • Free

For perhaps the most calm and tranquil viewpoint in Domme, follow the lanes westward from the tourist office to the small but perfectly formed **Jardin Public**. The gardens also hold a very heavily restored twelfth-century **mill**, used to grind the wheat for the town's bread.

Cénac

On the way to or from Domme, it's worth making a brief stop in **CÉNAC**, down by the river some 1km from town, to admire its Romanesque church, the **Chapelle St-Julien**, located a short distance along the D50 to St-Cybranet.

Apart from a lovely *lauze* roof, its main calling card is the remarkably distinct carving on the capitals, featuring various animals and demons, including Daniel taming the lions.

JOSEPHINE BAKER AND THE RAINBOW TRIBE

Born on June 3, 1906, in the Black ghetto of East St Louis, Illinois, **Josephine Baker** was one of the most remarkable women of the twentieth century. Her mother washed clothes for a living and her father was a drummer who soon deserted his family, but despite such humble beginnings Baker was the most celebrated cabaret star in France by the late 1920s, primarily due to her role in the legendary **Folies Bergère** show in Paris. On her first night, de Gaulle, Hemingway, Piaf and Stravinsky were among the audience, and her notoriety was further enhanced by her long line of illustrious **husbands and lovers**, which included the crown prince of Sweden and the crime novelist Georges Simenon. She also mixed with the likes of Le Corbusier and Adolf Loos, and kept a pet cheetah, with whom she used to walk around Paris. During the war, she was active in the **Resistance**, for which she was awarded the Croix de Guerre. Later on, she became involved in the Civil Rights movement in North America, where she insisted on playing to non-segregated audiences, a stance that got her arrested in Canada and tailed by the FBI in the US.

By far her most bizarre and expensive project was the château of **Les Milandes**, which she rented from 1938 and then bought in 1947, along with three square kilometres of land, after her marriage to the French orchestra leader Jo Bouillon. Having equipped the place with two hotels, three restaurants, a mini-golf course, tennis court and an autobiographical wax museum, Baker opened the château to the general public as a model multicultural community, popularly dubbed the "village du monde".

Unable to have children of her own, in the course of the 1950s she adopted babies (mostly orphans) of different ethnic and religious backgrounds from around the world. By the end of the decade, she had brought twelve children to Les Milandes, including a Black Catholic Colombian and a Buddhist Korean, along with her own mother, brother and sister from East St Louis.

Over 300,000 people a year visited the château in the 1950s, but her more conservative neighbours were never very happy about Les Milandes and the so-called **Rainbow Tribe**. In the 1960s, Baker's financial problems, divorce and two heart attacks spelt the end of the project, and despite a sit-in protest by Baker herself (by then in her sixties), the château and its contents were auctioned off in 1968. Still performing and as glamorous as ever, Josephine died of a stroke in 1975 and was given a grand state funeral at La Madeleine in Paris, mourned by thousands of her adopted countryfolk.

INFORMATION AND ACTIVITIES — DOMME

Tourist office Domme's tourist information centre is located in the town centre at place de la Halle (mid-Feb to April & Sept daily 10am–noon & 2–6pm; May & June daily 10am–12.30pm & 1.30–6pm; July & Aug daily 10am–7pm; Oct to mid-Nov & Christmas hols daily 10am–noon & 2–5pm; mid-Nov to mid-Feb Mon–Fri 10am–noon & 2–4.30pm; 05 53 31 71 00, http://tourisme-domme.com).

Canoe and kayak rental Beside the bridge below Domme, Canoë Raid Cénac Périgord Loisirs (http://canoecenac-perigord-dordogne.com) offers a 2hr, 10km descent from Cénac to Beynac.

ACCOMMODATION AND EATING

Cabanoix et Châtaigne 3 rue Geoffroy-de-Vivans, http://restaurantcabanoix.com. Cosy little restaurant located just off the Grande-Rue with a well-deserved reputation for its creative takes on traditional local cuisine. Foie gras features strongly, though there are always a couple of fish and vegetarian dishes. There's a broad range of *formules* and *menus* to choose from, with three-course options and vegan and vegetarian *menus* available with advance booking. No views, but a quiet courtyard or tables by the fire in winter. Reservations recommended. €€

L'Esplanade 2 rue Pontcarral, http://esplanade-perigord.com. The smartest place to stay in Domme, *L'Esplanade* can be found perched right on the cliff edge. The clutch of spacious and elegant guest rooms are prettily decked out in soft pastels, and it has an excellent restaurant, where the chef dishes up delights such as scallops with green asparagus. In winter, there's a sublime *menu de truffes* and in summer, cheaper midday meals are available on the terrace. Note that opening days can vary, especially in winter – phone ahead to be sure. €€

Le Sawadee Le Couderc, http://restaurant-thai-dordogne.com. An excellent Thai restaurant comes as somewhat of a surprise in the midst of the Dordogne, but this place has it all: woks, curries, soups and hot and cold salads. There's an extensive cocktail menu, and drinks can also be ordered by the pitcher. €

Upstream towards Souillac

If you're taking the prettier north bank of the Dordogne from Domme, the spectacular, white-walled **Château de Montfort** (not open to the public) soon swings into view atop its well-defended promontory. The distinctive, Disneyesque turrets (which are a nineteenth-century reconstruction) make the whole thing look like a Snow White fantasy. To complete the picture it overlooks the almost perfect curve of the **Cingle de Montfort**, not the biggest but certainly the tightest of the Dordogne's many meanders.

Carsac-Aillac

Two kilometres east of the Château de Montfort, the inviting little Romanesque **Église de Saint-Caprais** below the village of **CARSAC-AILLAC** makes a good place to pause. Though the meadow setting is delightful, the church's **carvings** are the main point of interest: in this case Arabic-influenced capitals around the choir and some later keystones. Note, too, the Stations of the Cross made by Russian abstract artist Léon Zack, who was a refugee here during World War II. Carsac also has some decent **accommodation** options, which could be used as a base for Sarlat, only 10km to the northwest.

ARRIVAL AND DEPARTURE **CARSAC-AILLAC**

By bus Buses on the Sarlat–Souillac route stop outside the post office in Carsac-Aillac.

Destinations Sarlat (15–20min); Souillac (45min).

ACCOMMODATION AND EATING

Delpeyrat http://hotel-delpeyrat.fr. In the centre of Carsac, the likeable family-run *Delpeyrat*, with old-fashioned rooms, most of them set back from the road overlooking a small garden, is one of those classic roadside hotels that must have been running for years with nothing much changing. Downstairs is a restaurant serving equally homely cooking. €

Le Relais du Touron Le Touron, http://lerelaisdutouron.com. Set in extensive grounds 500m along the Sarlat road from Carsac, the *Relais* makes a peaceful place to stay. The rooms are fairly functional but spacious and well-kept, occupying a modern block beside an outdoor pool and a lily-filled pond. Restaurant meals also available. Regularly booked out for private events. €€

Château de Fénelon

Ste-Mondane • Charge • http://chateau-fenelon.fr • The château is on the south bank of the Dordogne, along the D50 some 5km from Carsac-Aillac

Clamped to its own rocky outcrop, with triple walls and great round towers topped with *lauzes*, the **Château de Fénelon** exudes all the might of the original medieval fortress. As you get closer, however, the Renaissance-era additions and other, later embellishments become more apparent – the large mullion windows and the gallery closing the interior courtyard, for example.

The castle's most illustrious occupant was **François de Salignac de la Mothe-Fénelon**, who was born here in 1651. Private tutor to the heir to the throne and later archbishop of Cambrai, he fell from grace when King Louis XIV interpreted his work *Télémaque* – which recounts the adventures of Ulysses' son – as a thinly veiled attack on the Crown.

His intention had been to teach the young prince the finer points of kinghood, but for his pains Fénelon was banished to Cambrai, where he died in 1715. He is remembered with much pride at Fénelon today. There's a mock-up of his study and numerous portraits, but the present owners have also amassed a worthwhile collection of period furniture, tapestries and medieval weaponry. The ornate walnut chimneypieces are also eye-catching.

The Upper Dordogne valley and Rocamadour

- **159** Souillac and around
- **163** Rocamadour and around
- **168** Martel and around
- **171** Carennac and around
- **172** Bretenoux and around
- **174** Beaulieu-sur-Dordogne and around
- **175** St-Céré and around

CARENNAC

The Upper Dordogne valley and Rocamadour

In its upper reaches the Dordogne river cuts a green swathe through the rocky limestone plateau of Haut-Quercy, as the northern sector of the Lot *département* is traditionally known. This is a land of walnut orchards and strawberry fields and although the cliffs rise to considerable heights in places, the valley here lacks the drama of the perched castles and towns immediately downstream. Instead, away from the main towns, it offers a slow, lazy river and a pace of life to match: quieter lanes, more modest castles and a succession of unspoiled riverside villages that proudly proclaim their status as among the most beautiful in France.

The main gateway to the Upper Dordogne valley is **Souillac**, a busy little town whose major attraction is its domed abbey church. A short distance upstream, an attractive back road strikes off along the River Ouysse, a minor tributary of the Dordogne, heading southeast to the spectacular pilgrimage town of **Rocamadour**, whose seven religious sanctuaries are built almost vertically into a rocky backdrop.

THE UPPER DORDOGNE VALLEY

HIGHLIGHTS
1. Église Ste-Marie
2. Rocamadour
3. Carennac
4. Gouffre de Padirac
5. Château de Castelnau
6. Beaulieu-sur-Dordogne
7. Château de Montal
8. Autoire

GOUFFRE DE PADIRAC

Highlights

❶ **Église Ste-Marie** The image of the prophet Isaiah in Souillac's abbey church is a masterpiece of Romanesque art. See page 159

❷ **Rocamadour** One of France's top pilgrimage sites defies gravity in its spectacular cliff-edge location. See page 163

❸ **Carennac** Wander the lanes of this typical Quercy village and then peek inside its serene cloister. See page 171

❹ **Gouffre de Padirac** Take a boat trip on an underground river, accessed via an immense cavern. See page 172

❺ **Château de Castelnau** Fans of military architecture shouldn't miss this brooding fortress. See page 173

❻ **Beaulieu-sur-Dordogne** Laidback market town on the banks of the Dordogne that sees fewer tourists than it deserves. See page 174

❼ **Château de Montal** Admire some of the region's finest Renaissance carvings on the facade and staircase of this magnificent stately home. See page 177

❽ **Autoire** A picture-perfect village, encircled by limestone cliffs and serving up some impressive views. See page 178

HIGHLIGHTS ARE MARKED ON THE MAP ON PAGE 156

FESTIVALS, EVENTS AND MARKETS

The Upper Dordogne hosts a wide range of **festivals** and **events** throughout the summer season, and many of the villages host special markets and small fêtes to celebrate the autumn harvest. The main festivals are detailed below, but for the full schedule, pick up the free *Calendrier des Fêtes des Villes et Villages* booklet from tourist offices. Where we haven't given a specific information number or website, contact the relevant tourist office.

Second Sunday in May Beaulieu-sur-Dordogne: Fête de la Fraise. France's strawberry capital gets down to some serious baking with an 800-kilo strawberry tart. There's a great strawberry market, too.

Late May or early June Rocamadour: Fête des Fromages Fermiers (http://fromages.rocamadour.free.fr). At Pentecôte (Whit Sunday) artisan cheese producers gather above the town at L'Hospitalet to show off their wares, while folk concerts are staged around town.

June–Sept Rocamadour: Spectacles Équestres de Durandal (http://rocamadour-horseshow.com). Medieval jousting, horseback stunts and vaulting displays on the hilltop behind the château. Performances are held regularly between June and September.

Mid-July to mid-August St-Céré and around: Festival de St-Céré et du Haut-Quercy (http://festival-saint-cere.com). Three weeks of opera, recitals, orchestral works and chamber music in St-Céré (including the châteaux of Montal and Castelnau), Beaulieu, Martel, Cahors and Souillac. Tickets required.

August Rocamadour: Cantica Sacra (http://rocamadourfestival.com). Ten days of sacred singing performances and workshops in an exceptional setting.

Third weekend in July Souillac: Souillac en Jazz (http://souillacenjazz.fr). International jazz acts let rip in the streets of Souillac for six days of concerts, films, exhibitions and a feast on the final night. The big-name, ticket-only events take place outdoors next to the abbey church.

Early September Rocamadour: Semaine Mariale. The week dedicated to the Virgin Mary is celebrated with pilgrimages, prayers and Masses, including torchlight processions to the Chapelle Notre-Dame.

Third weekend in September Rocamadour: Rassemblement Européen de Montgolfières. Hot-air balloons take off from the valley below Rocamadour; for the best views, take up position early on the Belvédère in L'Hospitalet.

MARKETS

The main **markets** in this region are at Beaulieu-sur-Dordogne (Wed & Sat); Bretenoux (Tues & Sat); Martel (Wed & Sat); St-Céré (Sat & first and third Wed of the month); and Souillac (Fri). In addition to the weekly market, an annual truffle market takes place in Martel (Wed & Sat mornings) between mid-December and the end of January.

Back on the Dordogne, near the little village of **Lacave**, the river meanders in a northeasterly direction through walnut forests and dozing villages to the dramatic crags around **Gluges**, where it has carved the **Cirque de Montvalent** out of the plateau. North of here, the market town of **Martel** sees surprisingly few tourists despite its medieval centre full of turreted mansions, while to the east, **Carennac** merits a stop for its picturesque lanes and the twelfth-century carved portal adorning its church. Carennac also lies within striking distance of the **Gouffre de Padirac**, where a collapsed cavern has left a gaping hole in the limestone plateau. Upstream of Carennac the Dordogne valley begins to open out to form a broad plain around its confluence with the Cère. **Bretenoux**, the main town guarding the Cère valley, isn't itself a particularly engaging place, but it's more than compensated for by the nearby **Château de Castelnau**, which still dominates the country for miles around. North of Bretenoux is the pleasing town of **Beaulieu-sur-Dordogne**, while south is **St-Céré**, which provides a good base for exploring the region. Beneath the brooding towers of its ruined château, a scattering of stone and half-timbered townhouses attests to the St-Céré's fifteenth- and sixteenth-century heyday, while there's more Renaissance architecture on show at the **Château de Montal**, a few kilometres to the west. The nearby villages of **Autoire** and **Loubressac**, meanwhile, are rooted firmly in the Quercy soil, their houses sporting little pigeon-lofts and the red-tiled roofs splayed gently above the eaves, which are typical of the region.

GETTING AROUND — THE UPPER DORDOGNE VALLEY

By train Souillac, Rocamadour, St-Denis-près-Martel (for Martel) and Bretenoux can be reached by train. Gignac (Cressensac-Gignac station) is also on the train line, and is just 5km from the Brive-Vallée de la Dordogne airport.

By bus Most small towns have no public bus service and can only be reached by car, but daily bus services run between Souillac, St-Denis-près-Martel (for Martel), St-Céré and Bretenoux. However, they are aimed at schoolchildren and run at school drop-off and pick-up times during term-time only, so are an inconvenient option for travellers. Nonetheless, a comprehensive timetable, *Les Bus du Lot*, is published annually and available at tourist offices; you can also get bus information by contacting the transport information desk of the Conseil Général du Lot (05 65 53 43 91, http://lot.fr).

Souillac and around

Traffic-ridden **Souillac** suffers from being the major gateway to both Sarlat and the Périgord Noir to the west and the upper reaches of the Dordogne valley to the east, and though the nearby A20 *autoroute* brings some relief, it will never be a particularly pretty place. Souillac's main attraction is the **Église Ste-Marie**, with its exquisite carvings, but the town also has a small enclave of old streets, which are worth a quick wander. A handy landmark to aim for is the semi-ruined **belfry** of the disused **Église St-Martin**, partially destroyed in the Wars of Religion, on the southeast corner of the old centre; you can get a good view down into the nave from of a window inside the tourist office (see page 160).

Immediately upstream from Souillac, the valley is dominated by the A20 road-bridge, but a few meanders of the river later and you're back among quiet lanes and unspoilt scenery. One place to head for is **Lacave**, a village on the south bank with some passably interesting limestone caves. From Lacave you can take an attractive detour south along a tributary river, the Ouysse, as it cuts its way through a mini-gorge in the limestone plateau, to visit a 600-year-old working flour mill, the **Moulin de Cougnaguet**. Continue on this route and you will eventually find yourself in Rocamadour (see page 163).

Église Ste-Marie

Place de l'Abbaye • http://sanctuairerocamadour.com

One block west of the belfry of St-Martin lies a wide, open space dominated by the beautiful Romanesque **Église Ste-Marie**. The Byzantine domes of this abbey church are reminiscent of the cathedrals of Périgueux and Cahors, though on a smaller scale, while its largely unadorned interior conveys a far greater sense of antiquity. The first church on this site belonged to a priory founded in the tenth century, which became an abbey five hundred years later. Badly damaged during both the Hundred Years' War and Wars of Religion, the church was restored in the seventeenth century before being abandoned during the Revolution. Sadly, only fragments of the **Romanesque sculptures** that once graced the main (west) portal have survived, but those that do remain – now reassembled inside the west door – are superb. Those on the tympanum tell the story of a local monk, Théophile, who was dismissed from the treasury for corruption. Desperate to regain his position, he is said to have made a pact with the Devil, but then fell seriously ill and, full of remorse, besought the Virgin Mary for forgiveness. His luck was in: the final scene depicts Théophile's dream of the Virgin accompanied by St Michael driving the Devil away. The greatest piece of craftsmanship is the **bas-**

relief of the prophet Isaiah to the right of the door. Fluid and supple, it appears that the elongated, bearded figure clutching his parchment and with one leg extended is dancing for joy as he proclaims news of the coming of the Messiah.

Musée de l'Automate

Place de l'Abbaye • Charge • http://musee-automate.fr

Behind the Église Ste-Marie, to the west, the **Musée de l'Automate** contains an impressive collection of nineteenth- and twentieth-century mechanical dolls and animals that dance, juggle and perform magical tricks. Most come from the once-famous Roullet-Decamps workshops in Paris and include such pieces as a life-size 1920s jazz band, Charlie Chaplin and a woman doing the twist.

ARRIVAL AND INFORMATION — SOUILLAC

By air Brive-Vallée de la Dordogne airport (http://aeroport-brive-vallee-dordogne.com) is a 25min drive north of Souillac; the nearest train station is Cressensac-Gignac. For taxis call Bernard Mauvais (06 08 61 38 65, http://taxi-souillac.fr).

By train Getting to Souillac by train is not a problem since it lies on the main Paris–Toulouse line. The *gare SNCF* is just over 1km northwest of town; take av Jean-Jaurès and then av Martin-Malvy, which will bring you out at the west end of av Gambetta, the old quarter's main east–west artery.

Destinations Brive (10 daily; 25min); Cahors (6–9 daily; 40min–1hr); Cressensac/Gignac (1–2 daily; 15min); Gourdon (4 daily; 15min); Montauban (2–4 daily; 1hr 30min); Paris (4–6 daily; 4hr 30min); Toulouse (9daily; 1hr 55min).

By car Place du Foirail provides the most convenient car parking for the centre.

By bus Buses to and from Souillac are aimed at schoolchildren, and hence aren't a viable option for visitors.

Tourist office Bd Louis-Jean Malvy, across the road from place du Foirail (July & Aug Mon–Sat 9.30am–1pm & 2–6.30pm; mid-July to mid-Aug Sun 10am–1pm; April–June, Sept & Oct Mon–Sat 10am–12.30pm & 2–6pm; 05 65 33 22 00, http://tourisme-vallee-dordogne.com).

GETTING AROUND

Bike and canoe rental Copeyre Canoë (http://copeyre.com), next to *Les Ondines* campsite (see below), has electric bikes, canoes, kayaks and stand-up paddleboards.

ACCOMMODATION

Chastrusse Nadaillac-de-Rouge, 05 65 37 60 08. Delightfully unpretentious place some 10km southwest of Souillac, with homely rooms looking out over a flower-lined terrace and a well-sized pool. There's a restaurant serving specialities like garlic-stuffed snails and walnut tart. Half- and full-board options are available. €̄

Domaine de la Paille Basse http://lapaillebasse.com. Some 9km northwest of Souillac, signed off the D15 to Salvignac, this swish five-star campsite offers cosy bungalows, chalets and "glamping" tents, along with ample grassy camping spots. A great choice for families, there are also two swimming pools with water slides, children's playgrounds, tennis courts and a discotheque. Minimum one-week stay for chalets/bungalows. €

Grand Hôtel 1 allée de Verninac, http://legrandhotel.net. Exceedingly friendly staff, comfortable modern rooms and a handy location next door to the tourist office make this well-priced hotel a top choice. The downstairs restaurant is always packed, with ample seating on the shady terrace. €

Les Ondines Rue des Ondines, http://camping-lesondines.com. Huge three-star campsite in a tranquil riverside location. The heated pool, splash pools and multiple playgrounds make it a good option for young families. €

★ **Le Pavillon Saint-Martin** 5 place St-Martin, http://hotel-saint-martin-souillac.com. Housed in a sixteenth-century stone-and-brick mansion, *Le Pavillon Saint-Martin* has bags of character and it's easily Souillac's most stylish hotel. The eleven rooms each have their own unique flair, with the decor ranging from nostalgic florals to modern colour-blocking and colour schemes from pastel pink to eye-popping tangerine. Breakfast is served in the atmospheric vaulted cellar and free private parking is available. €€

La Vieille Auberge 1 rue de la Recège, http://la-vieille-auberge.com. An upmarket option located in Souillac's old quarter at the west end of avenue Gambetta. Rooms are spotless and modern, there's private parking available (charge) and a swimming pool out back. Stick around to dine at the hotel restaurant. €€

EATING

Along with the places listed below, don't forget Souillac's hotel **restaurants**, which are all worth trying. There are also several delightful **cafés** offering more basic food. Head west into the old quarter, well away from the traffic-ridden centre, where the streets are cobbled and the town pump still works; you may see Souillac in a new light.

Le Beffroi 6 place St-Martin, 05 65 37 80 33. With a prime location right on place St-Martin, *Le Beffroi* makes a lively spot for people-watching: grab a seat on the terrace beneath the lamp-lit wisteria. €€

Lycée d'Hôtellerie Av Roger-Couderc, http://quercy-perigord.mon-ent-occitanie.fr. Sample the skills of Souillac's future generation at the *Lycée* (college), situated on a hill to the west of the old quarter, where you can act as a guineapig for trainee chefs and waiting staff. Don't be put off, though – with the *menus* set in advance and the trainees trying hard to impress, the food is typically excellent. €€

Mon Petit Resto – L'Entracte 32 rue de la Halle, 05 65 37 63 98. The best spot in town to grab lunch on a budget – set *menus* change daily according to what's in season. Be sure to sample the home-made ice cream or passionfruit sorbet. €

Lacave

Following the Dordogne upstream along the D43 you soon leave the *autoroute* behind as you crest the hill and drop down to **LACAVE**, on the river's south bank and 14km southeast of Souillac. It's a tranquil basecamp for those visiting nearby Rocamadour and boasts some excellent Michelin-star restaurants to splash out on, but there's no public transport so you'll need your own vehicle.

Grottes de Lacave
Charge • http://grottes-de-lacave.com

A cavernous hole in the limestone cliffs overshadowing Lacave village marks the entrance to a series of underground lakes, together making up the **Grottes de Lacave**, which can be visited on guided tours. You travel the first few hundred metres by electric train, after which there's a lift up to the kilometre-long gallery, resplendent with all manner of stalactites and stalagmites, from petrified "waterfalls" to great organ pipes. But the highlight here is the magical reflections in the lakes' mirrored surfaces – at one point they also use ultraviolet light to reveal the glittering fluorescence of the "living" water-filled formations, while the older, dry deposits remain lost in the darkness.

ACCOMMODATION AND EATING — **LACAVE**

★ **Château de la Treyne** http://chateaudelatreyne.com. Set high above the Dordogne valley, 6km west of Lacave on the Souillac road, this idyllic château strikes the perfect balance between timeless luxury and modern creativity. The foundations are traditional – inlaid wood ceilings, regal tapestries and twinkling chandeliers – but there are plenty of surprises: an opulent gold and marble bathroom, an eye-popping red boudoir or whimsical print-on-print decor, while each of the seventeen rooms is infused with its own character. There's also a Michelin-starred restaurant, where chef Stéphane Andrieux whips up dishes like beef and foie gras millefeuille, followed by coconut and strawberry mousse. All that, plus a pool, tennis courts and some 300 acres of parks and gardens. €€€€

Le Pont de l'Ouysse http://lepontdelouysse.fr. A stylish country hotel, 1km west of Lacave on the Souillac road,

---

HIKING THE GR6 FROM LACAVE TO ROCAMADOUR

The **GR6 long-distance hiking route**, one of France's *Grandes Randonnées* (http://gr-infos.com), runs all the way from Sainte Foy-la-Grande, near Bordeaux on the west coast, to Foulllouse in the Hautes-Alpes, crossing the entire width of France. The 1100km route also passes through the heart of the Lot valley, offering ample opportunities for day-hikes or longer walks, with marked trails connecting towns like Souillac, Lacave, Rocamadour and Gramat.

The most scenic stretch for a day hike is the route **from Lacave to Rocamadour** (some 14km), stopping along the way at the Moulin de Cougnaguet. From Cougnaguet, the route runs alongside the River Ouysse past another mill – this was once big wheat country and even in high summer the Ouysse, part of which flows underground, never dries up – before turning eastwards along the River Alzou. Gradually the valley closes in until you round a bend and see the pilgrimage town of Rocamadour clinging to the cliff like a lost city. From Rocamadour, it's possible to continue along the GR6 or veer south along the GR46.

with a Michelin-starred restaurant offering delights such as lobster or caramelized pigeon, and a terrace overlooking the river. The twelve immaculate rooms each have hardwood floors, chic furnishings and individual touches, and the pastoral views from the windows are nothing short of magnificent. €€€

Calès

From where the River Ouysse empties into the Dordogne just west of Lacave, a minor road heads south along the tributary, winding its way up the valley side to the plateau near the village of **CALÈS**, 5km later. The village is a neat and tidy place with little more than a couple of decent hotels in its centre, but it's a quiet alternative to Rocamadour and the nearby **Moulin de Cougnaguet** makes a worthy detour. There are no buses, so you'll need your own transport to get here.

ACCOMMODATION AND EATING   CALÈS

Le Petit Relais Le Bourg, http://hotel-petitrelais.fr. Well-kept, family-run hotel with a pleasingly rustic atmosphere, spick-and-span rooms and a pretty, flowery terrace where you can enjoy above-average cuisine. €€

Moulin de Cougnaguet

Charge • http://cougnaguet.com

At Calès the road from Lacave joins the D673 and turns east before dropping back down to the river, which has here carved out a mini-gorge. For an interesting diversion, turn left just after crossing the river and wind along the gorge for approximately a kilometre until you reach the **Moulin de Cougnaguet**. The fourteenth-century fortified mill only ceased working commercially in 1959 and is now open to visitors for **guided tours**. During the tour, the enthusiastic owner points out its many defensive features – including arrow slits and sluice gates which, when opened from inside the mill, unleashed a torrent of water to sweep away anyone attempting to ford the millrace – and also puts the mill through its paces. Standing close to 1.5 tonnes of stone spinning at eighty revolutions per minute, you get a real feel for the pent-up power of the water waiting calmly upstream.

Rocamadour and around

Halfway up the northern cliff face of the deep and abrupt canyon of the River Alzou, the spectacular setting of **ROCAMADOUR** is hard to beat, with the turrets and spires of the **Cité Religieuse** at its heart, sandwiched between the jumbled roofs of the medieval town and the château's crenellated walls above. However, as you draw closer the spell is broken by the constant stream of pilgrims and more secular-minded visitors, particularly in summer, who fill lanes lined with shops peddling incongruous souvenirs.

The main reason for Rocamadour's popularity – going back centuries – is the supposed miraculous properties of the statue of the **Black Madonna**, enshrined in the Cité's smoke-blackened **Chapelle Notre-Dame**. Modern tourists are also courted with a number of secondary attractions, including two wildlife parks, scattered on the plateau to the north and east of town.

Even if those don't appeal, it's worth venturing up to the lofty hamlet of **L'Hospitalet**, poised on the cliff (1.5km by road) to the east of Rocamadour, for the finest views of the town.

Brief history

The first mention of Rocamadour's **Chapelle Notre-Dame** dates from 1105, although evidence suggests pilgrims started coming here as early as the ninth century. However, things really got going when a perfectly preserved body was discovered in a rock-hewn tomb beside the chapel in 1166. It was promptly declared to be that of Zacchaeus, later **St Amadour**; according to one legend, Zacchaeus – a tax-collector in Jericho at the time of Christ – was advised by the Virgin Mary to come to France and lived out his years in Rocamadour as a hermit. As tales of the saint and associated miracles spread, the faithful began to arrive in droves from all over Europe. St Bernard, numerous kings – including Henry II of England and Louis IX of France (St Louis) – and thousands of ordinary mortals crawled up the **Grand Escalier** (the pilgrims' staircase) on their knees to pay their respects and to seek forgiveness or cures. Others came simply to plunder the shrine – among them the Young King Henry (see page 169) – but they were easily outclassed by the Huguenots, who, in 1562, tried in vain to burn St Amadour's corpse and finally resigned themselves to hacking it to bits instead. In the meantime, centuries of warfare and plague led to a decline in the number of pilgrims. The buildings gradually fell into ruin until the bishops of Cahors, hoping to revive the flagging pilgrimage, financed a massive reconstruction in the early nineteenth century and so gave us the Rocamadour we see today.

Old town

Rocamadour's **old town** is easy enough to find your way around since there's just one street, pedestrianized **rue de la Couronnerie**, which runs west from **Porte du Figuier** – one of Rocamadour's four medieval gateways – to the wide stone staircase leading up to the sanctuaries, roughly 300m later.

La Cité Religieuse

The steep hillside above rue de la Couronnerie supports no fewer than seven chapels, known collectively as "Les Sanctuaires", or the **Cité Religieuse**. There's a lift dug into the rock-face (see page 166), but it's far better to climb the 216 worn and pitted steps of the **Grand Escalier**, up which the devout once dragged themselves on their knees to the doors of the Cité. Inside lies a small square, le **Parvis**, completely hemmed in by the various chapels.

Basilique St-Sauveur

The largest chapel in the Cité Religieuse is the **Basilique St-Sauveur**, a vaulted Romanesque-Gothic hall which, up until 1900, provided lodgings for pilgrims who couldn't afford anything better. An unusual and rather rickety-looking twentieth-century wooden gallery covers the rock-face wall and there are several paintings of notable visitors on the other walls. The slightly sparse altar has a fine bronze frontal of the Ascension, surmounted by a rather gruesome sixteenth-century Christ on the Cross.

Chapelle Notre-Dame

The little **Chapelle Notre-Dame** is nestled against the rock and the wall of the Basilique St-Sauveur, and is where the miracle-working twelfth-century **Black Madonna** resides. The crudely carved statue, less than 70cm tall, still wears a faint smile despite her mutilated state, though the adult-featured Jesus balanced on her knee looks decidedly out of sorts. The rest of the chapel is unremarkable, but note the empty recess in the rock outside, where St Amadour's body was found, and a rusty sword protruding from the cliff above. According to local tradition this is **Durandal**, the trusty blade of the legendary Roland whose heroic exploits are recorded in the twelfth-century *Chanson de Roland* (*The Song of Roland*), though it's not revealed exactly how it got here from northern Spain, where Roland supposedly died in battle against the Moors in 778.

Beside the chapel's ornately carved door there are also some faded fifteenth-century **frescoes** depicting a macabre fight between the Living and the Dead.

Chapelle St-Michel
Accessible only by guided tours of the Cité

Opposite the Chapelle Notre-Dame, tucked tightly into a corner of the place Parvis with one long wall of overhanging rock, the twelfth-century **Chapelle St-Michel** is home to two incredibly well-preserved twelfth-century polychrome paintings of the Annunciation and the Visitation.

Château de Rocamadour
Charge

East of the Cité Religieuse there's a sandy esplanade and the funicular (see page 166) that will take you to the top of the cliff. Alternatively, you can walk up the shady zigzag path, *Le chemin de croix (Calvary)*, past tableaux depicting the Stations of the Cross, or take a more direct and steeper path to come out near the **Château de Rocamadour**, a full 150m above the river below. While the château itself, a mostly nineteenth-century reconstruction, is private, you can walk round the **ramparts** and soak up dramatic views over the valley.

Rocher des Aigles
Charge

The road leading west from Rocamadour's château brings you almost immediately to the **Rocher des Aigles**, a wildlife park and breeding centre for birds of prey. The cages seem uncomfortably small, but with a production rate of nearly a hundred chicks a year the birds can't be overly stressed about it. There's a film explaining the breeding programme, which aims to reintroduce a number of rare species to the wild, and you can also see the hatching room where scrawny chicks warm themselves under sun lamps. Best, though, are the thirty-minute **flying demonstrations**, in which a dozen or so condors, fish eagles and other such majestic birds are allowed to soar free over the valley.

L'Hospitalet

It's worth coming up to **L'Hospitalet** for the tremendous views of the medieval Cité from the cliff-edge belvedere. It's stunning at any time, but particularly magical at night when the buildings are illuminated (March–Nov & Christmas hols). To get to the area, head east from the top of the funicular and follow the cliff-edge road for around 700m until you join the D673 from Calès. After another 150m you'll reach the modern, plate-glass **tourist office** (see page 166), which marks the western extent of L'Hospitalet. From the bottom of the valley, follow the main road east from Porte du Figuier which winds up the valley side to L'Hospitalet; pedestrians can use the quieter Voie Sainte, a narrow lane which branches off left after a couple of hundred metres.

L'Hospitalet's name refers to a pilgrims' hospital founded on the clifftop here in the thirteenth century, of which only a few ruined walls and the **Chapelle Notre-Dame**, containing a copy of the Black Madonna, remain. A crossroads lying immediately to the northeast of the chapel represents the centre of modern L'Hospitalet, which consists of a scattering of hotels, cafés and shops.

Forêt des Singes
Charge • http://la-foret-des-singes.com

About 300m east of L'Hospitalet, the **Forêt des Singes** wildlife park is one of the better such parks, with some 150 Barbary apes roaming twenty hectares of oak and scrubland in relative freedom. The aim is conservation – so far around six hundred young

> **WALK WITH THE ANIMALS**
>
> If you're a keen walker and happen to be in the area in the last week of April, you might like to join in the **Transhumance**, a five-day, 70km walk spearheaded by a flock of sheep. Open to the public, the route starts off in Rocamadour and heads to Luzech, via narrow country lanes and rolling fields. Unlike in mountainous regions in France, transhumance is not yet a tradition in the Lot, but local associations, as well as the Conseil Général (http://lot.fr), are actively promoting it in the hope that it will become so. There's a practical side to the idea, too: as the sheep traverse fields lent by local landowners, they will eat down the grass, in a demonstration of ecological land maintenance.

monkeys have been reintroduced to North Africa. The best time to visit is during the cool of the early morning or evening and in early summer when the youngsters are frolicking about.

La Borie d'Imbert

Charge • http://laboriedimbert.com

An attraction worth visiting, particularly for those with children, **La Borie d'Imbert** is a small country farm situated on the D247 in the direction of Souillac. The old farmhouse, La Maison de Justine, has countrified rooms complete with traditional cookware and furniture, while the baby farm animals are a sure winner for the very young. The goats are milked every day from 5 to 6pm, and in the farm shop you can taste and buy the Rocamadour goat's cheese (see page 167) and home-produced charcuterie. There's also a busy schedule of special events throughout the summer, including wine tasting, cheesemaking workshops or hands-on animal workshops for kids.

ARRIVAL AND INFORMATION ROCAMADOUR

By car Rocamadour is pedestrianized, so unless you have access to hotel parking you'll have to park in L'Hospitalet at the top of the hill. There is a large, free car park at the top of the funicular or else paid parking outside the tourist office in L'Hospitalet. Otherwise, you can park in the valley several hundred metres below, and rather than walking into town from the valley car park, you could take Le Petit Train.

By train Travelling to Rocamadour by public transport is awkward. There are no buses, and the rather confusingly named Rocamadour-Padirac *gare SNCF*, on the Brive–Figeac line, lies 3km away to the northeast of Rocamadour (and some way from the town of Padirac itself). If you don't want to trek into Rocamadour alongside the main road, you can call Taxi Herbert (05 65 50 14 82 or 06 81 60 14 60). Note that the station is rarely staffed, and there's no ticket machine, so check the times of return trains carefully on arrival and buy a return ticket beforehand.

Tourist office Rocamadour has two tourist offices, both with the same hours and contact details (Sept–June daily 10am–12.30pm & 2–6pm; July & Aug daily 9.30am–7pm; 05 65 33 22 00, http://tourisme-vallee-dordogne.com); the main one is located on the western outskirts of L'Hospitalet, while a second information point is located on rue de la Couronnerie next to the *Hôtel de Ville*. Both offer guided tours of the Cité and sell tickets to regional attractions.

GETTING AROUND

By lift In the village centre, a lift (charge) links the town's main street, rue de la Couronnerie, with the Cité Religieuse above.

By funicular A funicular (charge) departs from just east of the Cité to emerge on the clifftop near the château and the upper car parks.

Le Petit Train As well as running a circular route from the Porte du Figuier (charge; http://lepetittrainderocamadour.com), Le Petit Train also offers two 30min evening tours around the Cité with a commentary.

ACCOMMODATION SEE MAP PAGE 162

One of the benefits of staying over in Rocamadour is that you can enjoy the town at its quietest in the early morning and late evening, and the **hotels** here are not too expensive. The downside is that everywhere is completely booked up in summer for miles around, and most places close during the winter months. Outside these periods, there are some good options, with a choice between central Rocamadour, the modern places in L'Hospitalet or somewhere in the surrounding countryside.

OLD TOWN
★ **Grand Hôtel Beau Site** Rue de la Couronnerie, http://beausite-rocamadour.com. Chic, modern rooms with wood floors, spacious bathrooms and tasteful splashes of colour make this the top choice in town. Best of all is the setting: a lovely old mansion with its original beams, plus an annexe across the street overlooking the valley. There's also an excellent restaurant, *Jehan de Valon*, a bistro and free parking right outside. €€

Lion d'Or Porte du Figuier, http://liondor-rocamadour.com. Just inside the old city gate at the east end of rue de la Couronnerie, this old-fashioned, family-run hotel is one of the cheaper options in the old quarter. Expect to get what you pay for though – the en-suite rooms are small but adequate, and wi-fi is only available in public areas. There's also a decent on-site restaurant. Closed Feb. €

Le Terminus des Pèlerins Place de la Carreta, http://terminus-des-pelerins.fr. Friendly, good-value hotel in a great location at the bottom of the Grand Escalier. The brightly painted rooms are well-furnished and comfortable, and the best ones have terraces overlooking the valley. Its restaurant is also a safe bet, popular for its traditional and regional cuisine. €

L'HOSPITALET AND AROUND
Amadour Place de l'Europe, L'Hospitalet, http://amadour-hotel.com. Sleek modern rooms with tasteful decor and a pop of colour make this a stylish choice. The best rooms have a private terrace, while the family rooms (sleeping 4–5) are spacious and great value. Closed mid-Oct to March. €€

Le Belvédère L'Hospitalet, http://hotel-le-belvedere.fr. This busy, well-located hotel looks out across the valley and it's worth paying extra for a room with a view. Doubles are roomy and comfortable, with parquet floors and floor-to-ceiling windows, plus there's a pool and an excellent restaurant with *menus*. €€

Camping Les Cigales http://camping-cigales.com. This well-equipped three-star campsite east of the *Amadour* hotel has plenty of shady plots, plus two swimming pools, sports fields, mini golf and a restaurant. Closed Sept–May. €

Domaine de la Rhue http://domainedelarhue.com. This family-run *chambre d'hôte* has bags of character, with its ivy-covered facade, wood-beamed interiors and rustic furnishings. There are five rooms available, housed in a converted stable block, plus a studio flat, a swimming pool and beautiful gardens. It's 6km northeast of Rocamadour, off the D840; hikers can head to town on foot (60min); otherwise, it's 10min by car. €€€

Le Paradis du Campeur http://leparadisducampeur.com. This fairly basic two-star campsite offers ample space for campers, a heated pool and children's playground. Situated next to the *Amadour* hotel. Closed Sept–April. €

Le Ryokan Mages, http://leryokan.com. Inspired by a Japanese country inn, this chic *chambre d'hôte* occupies a converted stone barn decked out in a Japanese theme. Rooms have a homely vibe, dotted with mementos of the hosts' travels in Asia, and you'll be assured a warm welcome. It's just south of Rocamadour and signed off the D32. Closed Nov–March. Weekly rates only. €€€€

Le Troubadour Belveyre, http://hotel-troubadour.com. A kilometre north of L'Hospitalet on the D673, this is a pocket of tranquillity away from the crowds of Rocamadour, offering ten rooms with comfy beds and country-style decor. The real highlight is the garden setting, complete with pool, bikes and a guests-only restaurant (*menus*), where you can tuck into regional delights like *cassoulet périgourdin* flavoured with herbs from the hotel garden. €€

Les Vieilles Tours Lafage, http://vtrocamadour.com. Luxe furnishings and polished wood floors bring this beautifully restored country home bang up to date, while original beams and pigeon towers retain a touch of authenticity. There's also a pool and an excellent restaurant, with some intriguing dishes such as walnut-stuffed snails, crayfish risotto and chocolate figs. Half-board obligatory July and Aug. It's located 3km west of L'Hospitalet just off the D673. €€

EATING   SEE MAP PAGE 162

Eating in Rocamadour is a mixed bag and there are a good few greasy fast-food joints and tourist traps. In general, the best **restaurants** are those attached to the hotels, along with a few everyday recommendations; note that most places are closed in winter. The local speciality, which you'll find on most menus, is **Rocamadour**, a round disc of goat's cheese, often served on toast or with a walnut salad, or occasionally flambéed in brandy or drizzled with honey. Elsewhere in the region it is known as *Cabécou*, but cheeses produced around Rocamadour warrant their own special *appellation* – and even their own festival (see page 158). You can buy it at shops selling the inevitable foie gras and other regional produce.

Au Panorama L'Hospitalet, 05 65 40 67 36. The simple but tasty food at this bright, modern restaurant is a hit with both locals and in-the-know tourists. Opt for a seat on the terrace and tuck into perfectly cooked *galettes*, a hearty portion of steak and fries or a generous salad. €

Les Goûts et les Couleurs Pech de Bardy, http://goutsetcouleurs.fr. A short drive out of town, 1.5km from Rocamadour toward Pauillac, and worth seeking out on a sunny summer afternoon to cool off with a delicious ice cream or sorbet in the relaxing garden. Home-made with milk (goat and cow) from the owners' farm, there are almost forty flavours to choose from, including passionfruit, pistachio, blueberry and *spéculoos* (gingerbread biscuits) plus home-made cream and caramel sauce to top it off. €

★ **Jehan de Valon** Rue de la Couronnerie, http://beausite-rocamadour.com. In a spectacular setting overlooking the Alzou valley, this elegant terrace restaurant is the most romantic spot in town. Impeccable service, beautifully presented dishes and a scrumptious lemon meringue *tarte* add to the effect. Splash out on the seasonal *menu* and sample delicacies like langoustines, quails' eggs and Rocamadour cheese. There's also a vegetarian *menu*. €€€

Le Roc du Berger Bois de Belvyre, http://rocduberger.fr. A wooden country inn, 1.5km from Rocamadour in the direction of Payrac and situated in the middle of a truffle orchard. Traditional dishes such as *confit de canard* and lamb steaks are given extra flavour by being cooked over an open fire. Reservation strongly advised in high season. €€

Martel and around

Fifteen kilometres east of Souillac, **MARTEL**'s medieval centre is built in a pale, almost white, stone, offset by warm reddish-brown roofs. A Turenne-administered town, its heyday was during the thirteenth and fourteenth centuries when the viscounts granted certain freedoms, including the right to mint money, and established a royal court of appeal here. The good times ceased, however, when the wars showed up: Martel was occupied briefly by English forces during the Hundred Years' War and suffered again at the hands of the Huguenots in the sixteenth century.

Despite the town's rather turbulent past, on the whole the compact old centre has survived remarkably intact, with the exception of the ramparts, which have been dismantled to make way for the wide boulevard that now rings Martel's pedestrianized centre. Take any of the lanes leading inwards and you will soon find yourself in the cobbled main square, **place des Consuls**. It is mostly taken up by the eighteenth-century *halle*, scene of a busy market on Wednesday and Saturday mornings, but on every side there are reminders of the town's illustrious past: most notable is the grand Gothic **Palais de la Raymondie** on the square's east side, now occupied by the *mairie*. Begun in 1280, it served as both the Turenne law courts and fortress, hence the large square tower – one of seven that gave the town its epithet, *la ville aux sept tours*. On the square's south side is another one of the towers – a circular five-storey turret belonging to the **Maison Fabri**. According to tradition, this striking building is where Young King Henry, son of Henry II, died in 1183 (see box).

One block south of here, rue Droite leads east to the town's main church, **St-Maur**, built in a fiercely defensive, mostly Gothic style, with a finely carved Romanesque tympanum depicting the Last Judgement above the west door.

ARRIVAL AND INFORMATION MARTEL

By train The *gare SNCF* is at St-Denis-près-Martel, 7km to the east of Martel, on the Brive La Gaillarde and Rodez lines. For taxis into town, call Mme Daubet (05 65 37 34 87).
Destinations Figeac (5–6 daily; 1hr); Gramat (5–6 daily; 20–30min); Rocamadour-Padirac (4–5 daily; 15–20min); Souillac (3 daily; 25min); Vayrac (2 daily; 5min).
By tourist train In season, a tourist train runs along a splendid stretch of decommissioned line from Martel towards St-Denis and back – but not as far as St-Denis station – along cliffs 80m above the Dordogne (http://trainduhautquercy.info). It departs from the otherwise disused station 200m south of town; reservations are recommended.

Tourist office Palais de la Raymondie, on place des Consuls (April–June, Sept & Oct Mon–Sat 9am–noon & 2–6pm; July & Aug daily 9.30am–1pm & 2–6.30pm; mid-July to mid-Aug Sun 9.30am–1pm; 05 65 37 43 44, http://martel.fr); staff can provide further information about the tourist train and Martel's events.

ACCOMMODATION

Auberge des 7 Tours Av de Turenne, http://auberge7tours.com. The rooms at this *auberge* are small, but the size is compensated for by tasteful decor, modern bathrooms and a leafy terrace restaurant with great views over the town. The food is simple but tasty, with mains including veal and tuna steak, and menus. €€

★ **Château de Termes** http://chateau-de-termes.com. An idyllic 7.5-acre plot high in the hills, 3km north of St-Denis-prés-Martel, allowing you to get back to nature without losing the comforts of home. There are cosy wooden cabins and ten self-contained *gîtes*, all with a kitchen and lounge, plus three *chambre d'hôte* rooms with spectacular

THE TALE OF YOUNG KING HENRY

At the end of the twelfth century, Martel provided the stage for one of the tragic events in the internecine conflicts of the **Plantagenet** family. When Henry Plantagenet (King Henry II of England) imprisoned his estranged wife Eleanor of Aquitaine, his sons took up arms against their father. The eldest son, also **Henry** (nicknamed the Young King since he was crowned while his father was still on the throne), even went so far as to plunder the viscountcy of Turenne and Quercy. Furious, Henry II immediately stopped his allowance and handed over his lands to the third son, Richard the Lionheart. Financially insecure, and with a considerable army to maintain, Young King Henry began **looting** the treasures of every abbey and shrine in the region. Finally, he decided to sack the shrine at Rocamadour. This last act was to mark his downfall, for shortly afterwards he fled to Martel and fell ill with a fever. Guilt-ridden and fearing for his life, he confessed his crimes and asked his father for forgiveness. Henry II was busy besieging Limoges, but sent a messenger to convey his pardon. On the messenger's arrival in Martel, Young Henry died, leaving **Richard the Lionheart** heir to the English throne.

views over the valley. Kids and adventurous adults will be in their element with tennis courts, go-karts, a trampoline, zipline swing and fishing lessons, but best of all is the communal atmosphere – bring-your-own barbecues and shared lounges mean you can mingle with other travellers, plus the hosts are exceedingly friendly and you can even help yourself to fresh eggs from the chicken pen. Breakfast and daily bread delivery available on request. €

★ **Relais Ste-Anne** Rue du Pourtanel, http://relais-sainte-anne.com. This gorgeous maison d'hôte occupies a former girls' boarding school and is set in immaculate gardens with its own chapel, pool and beautifully appointed rooms. €€€

EATING AND DRINKING

Au Hazard Balthazar Rue Tournemire, http://lesbouriettes.com. Tuck into wholesome home-made dishes like lamb stew or *magret de canard* in rustic surroundings, then pick up local products like truffle oil and fruit chutney in the shop downstairs. €€

Ferme Auberge Moulin à Huile de Noix 05 65 37 40 69. Some 3km east of Martel, off the D703 to St-Denis and Bretenoux, this family-run restaurant oozes character. It's attached to a working walnut-oil mill (demonstrations on Mon and Thurs afternoons in July and Aug), and you can expect authentic home-cooked cuisine made with fresh seasonal ingredients. €€

★ **Le Petit Moulin** Rue Droite, http://moulincastagne.com. This chic little restaurant in the heart of Martel is beloved by locals and tourists alike, and for good reason. Expect fresh, seasonal dishes with a personal touch and highlights including local speciality Quercy lamb and indulgent millefeuille. There's also a great kids' *menu*, vegetarian options and an excellent regional wine list. €€

Plein Sud Place des Consuls, 05 65 37 37 77. This humble locals' haunt is well situated in the centre of town and offers a surprisingly wide menu, including a good selection of pizzas, some regional dishes and a choice of salads. €

★ **Le Pourquoi Pas?** Le Barry, http://lepourquoipas.fr. Tucked away in the pretty village of Floirac, 4km south of St-Denis-près-Martel, *Le Pourquoi Pas?* might have only one thing on the menu – crêpes – but the choice is remarkable. Opt for a savoury crêpe with cheese, smoked salmon or ratatouille; indulge your sweet tooth with fillings like Nutella, caramel or coconut; or go all-out with a Cointreau-doused crêpe *flambée*. There's a sunny garden terrace open in summer, plus a range of Belgian beers on tap. €

Meyronne

Roughly 10km south of Martel as the crow flies, the sleepy hilltop village of **MEYRONNE** is certainly worth a lunchtime stop. In the eleventh century the bishops of Tulle, northeast of Brive, built a château here to defend what was then an important bridging point over the River Dordogne. The château has since been transformed into a hotel-restaurant, but its brooding facade still presides over the town, affording spectacular views along the valley from its terrace.

ACCOMMODATION AND EATING   MEYRONNE

★ **La Terrasse** Place de l'Église, http://hotel-la-terrasse.com. Housed in the town's château, *La Terrasse* is charmingly eclectic, with its sloping ceilings, oak beams and spiral stairwell jazzed up with colourful bed linen and mismatched furniture. The creative flair extends to the restaurant, which has *menus* and great views from the terrace. €€

★ **Le Virage** Rue de la Poutine, Montvalent, 09 53 98 34 46. This aptly named restaurant, 6km east of Meyronne, offers magnificent views over the valley from its breezy terrace. Head here in the evening when you can watch the sunset while listening to live music and dining on delicious, well-priced cuisine. Expect classic French dishes like *confit de canard* or chocolate fondant cake, prepared to perfection. €

Creysse

CREYSSE, some 3km northeast of Meyronne, is an idyllic hamlet – with a dinky market hall and fast-running stream – that sits in the lee of a knuckle of rock, where a fortified gate and scraps of wall are all that remain of a château once owned by the viscounts of Turenne. Their twelfth-century **chapel**, standing immediately above the village, has fared rather better (ask for the key at the *mairie*), and is worth a look for its *pisé* floor and unique arrangement of two apsidal chapels.

ACTIVITIES   CREYSSE

Bike and canoe rental On the riverside by the bridge, Port Loisirs (http://portloisirs.com) offers canoe rental as well as caving and climbing tours in the area.

ACCOMMODATION AND EATING

Auberge de L'Île http://auberge-de-lile.com. With its stone-and-brick facade, gabled windows and leafy riverside plot on the main street, just east of the canal, it's hard to resist this charming country hotel. Inside, rooms are simple but surprisingly modern with wood floors and sparkling bathrooms. There's also a decent restaurant which serves tasty traditional dishes such as Quercy casserole and *tartiflette de Rocamadour*, and plenty of seating on the tree-shaded terrace. €€€

Camping du Port http://campingduport.com. Excellent three-star campsite by the Dordogne river, 100m east of Creysse. A good spot for kids, with a riverside beach, pool, small restaurant and a range of five-person cabins for rent by the week. €

Gluges

The cliffs lining the Dordogne valley are more dramatic upstream from Creysse. For the most impressive scenery, follow the D23 northeast for 2km and then branch right along the D43. The road narrows to a single track – with passing spaces – cut into the rock.

> ### LA MÔME PIAF AND THE ÉGLISE DE GLUGES
>
> **Édith Giovanna Gassion** was one of the most enigmatic figures of twentieth-century France. Born in 1916 in the backstreets of Paris, she rose to fame and became a cultural icon. She was nicknamed "La Môme Piaf", a colloquialism meaning "the little sparrow" in reference to her diminutive size – she was 142cm tall – by nightclub owner Louis Leplée, who first discovered her in the Pigalle area of Paris in 1935. Despite her subsequent success, Piaf led a troubled and turbulent life, gradually becoming more and more reclusive. She liked to escape whenever possible to the peaceful atmosphere of the Dordogne valley, and the tiny troglodyte village of Gluges became one of her favourite spots; she would come here to wander the lanes and pray in the little **Église de Gluges**. One evening as the *curé*, Monsieur Delbos, was locking the doors he turned to find Piaf standing behind him. He told her that he would soon have to close the church permanently, as the repair bills were more than the congregation could afford – the two stained-glass windows particularly were badly damaged and no longer safe. Piaf offered to fund the replacement windows on condition that the donation would remain anonymous until after her death. The windows were duly replaced and the *curé* kept his promise. In 1963, after Piaf's untimely death at the age of 47, he finally revealed her secret to his congregation. A special Mass was held for her, and the tiny square in front of the church was renamed **place Édith Piaf** in her honour.

You emerge 2km later at another huddle of houses, **GLUGES**, whose prime attraction is its location under the cliffs and its views south to the **Cirque de Montvalent**. Here, the meandering river has carved a great semicircle out of the cliffs; for a sweeping panorama, climb up to the hilltop **Belvédère de Copeyre**, signed off the main road 1km above Gluges to the east. In the lee of the great cliff, you can still see the ruined troglodyte chapel of **Saint-Pierre-ès-Liens**, founded by Gaillard Mirandol on his return from the First Crusade in 1095. It was eventually superseded by the little village **church**, which is worth a quick peek, as there's a fascinating tale attached to it (see box).

ACTIVITIES   GLUGES

Bike and canoe rental Copeyre Canoë (http://copeyre. com), down by the *Les Falaises* campsite.

ACCOMMODATION

Les Falaises http://camping-lesfalaises.com. This two-star campsite is simple but well kept, with a leafy riverside location opposite the village and canoe rental. €

Carennac and around

CARENNAC is without doubt one of the most beautiful villages along this part of the Dordogne valley. It sits on a terrace above the river's south bank 16km or so east of Martel; backtrack to Gluges and then head upstream on the D43 for the prettiest route in – as you approach from the west, you'll get one of the best views of Carennac's towers and higgledy-piggledy russet-tiled roofs. Carennac is best known for its typical Quercy architecture and the richly carved tympanum of its Romanesque priory church, the **Église St-Pierre**. Founded in the eleventh century by Benedictine monks, the priory grew rich from pilgrims en route to Santiago de Compostela. Sacked during the Hundred Years' War, it then enjoyed a second renaissance in the late fifteenth and sixteenth centuries, when the church was restored and the **Chateâu des Doyens** was built alongside it. But by the 1700s, the rot had set in as the monks became lazy and corrupt, and the priory was finally closed after the Revolution.

Église St-Pierre

Tucked in behind the **Château des Doyens**, the **Église St-Pierre** is set in a small cobbled courtyard, with houses clustered so tightly round the priory buildings that it's hard to tell them apart: follow the road along the riverbank and you'll soon find the gateway. Straight ahead of you, the church's twelfth-century tympanum – in the style of Moissac and Cahors – dominates its recessed west door, with its carvings in exceptionally good condition.

South of the church, still inside the courtyard, you can gain access to the **cloister and chapter house**. The cloister's Romanesque and flamboyant Gothic galleries were somewhat mutilated during the Revolution, but they are in any case overshadowed by the late-fifteenth-century, life-size *Mise au Tombeau* ("*Entombment of Christ*") on display in the chapterhouse. So supremely detailed is the sculpture that you can even see the veins in Christ's hands and legs. Joseph of Arimathea and Nicodemus, holding either end of the shroud, are richly attired as a fifteenth-century nobleman and pilgrim respectively, while behind them Mary Magdalene, her hair a mass of ringlets, ostentatiously wipes away a tear.

Château des Doyens and the Espace Patrimoine

Free • http:// vallee-dordogne.com

In the sixteenth century the *doyens* (deans) in charge of Carennac's priory and its dependent churches built themselves a grand residence abutting the church's north wall, referred to nowadays as the **Château des Doyens**. A few stone chimneypieces and the great hall's painted ceiling remain from this era, but little else, since the building has been partially modernized to serve as an **Espace Patrimoine**. Displays cover the geography, history, architecture and economy of the Dordogne valley from Bretenoux downstream to Souillac, and provide a good overview of what the region has to offer. Staff here also organize a broad range of guided visits (to Carennac, Martel and Souillac, for example, some in English) and workshops based on the art and history of the Dordogne valley; call or visit the website for further information.

ARRIVAL AND INFORMATION   CARENNAC

By train Carennac's nearest *gare SNCF* is at Vayrac, 8km northwest on the other side of the river, on the Brive–Aurillac line; note that there are no ticket sales at this station, but you can buy tickets from the conductor on board the train. Services are more frequent to St-Denis-près-Martel, 10km to the west, on the Brive–Figeac line.

Tourist office In the priory courtyard (April–June, Sept & Oct Mon–Sat 10am–12.30pm & 2–6pm, Sun 2–6pm; July & Aug daily 9.30am–1pm & 2–7pm; 05 65 10 97 01, http://vallee-dordogne.com).

Canoe rental You can rent canoes from Saga Team (http://dordogne-soleil.com) at the *L'Eau Vive* campsite.

ACCOMMODATION AND EATING

L'Eau Vive http://camping-lot-eauvive.com. Kid-friendly campsite 1km east of Carennac with shady plots, a swimming pool, mini golf and a snack bar. Wi-fi available at reception. €

Hostellerie Fénelon Le Bourg, http://hotel-fenelon.com. Carennac's only hotel is efficiently run, with clean, comfortable standard rooms (plus cheaper ones with bath only for those on a budget) as well as a pool. There's also a decent restaurant serving up regional cuisine. €

Relais de Gintrac Gintrac, 05 65 38 49 41. A very popular, if isolated, place – about 3km from Carennac southeast along the D30 – offering wholesome country cooking washed down with well-priced wines. €€

Gouffre de Padirac

Charge • http://gouffre-de-padirac.com • The nearest *gare SNCF* is Rocamadour-Padirac, more than 10km to the west, from where you could take a taxi

Local legend holds the Devil responsible for opening the gaping mouth of the **Gouffre de Padirac** in the middle of the limestone plateau 10km south of Carennac. The hole is over 30m wide and 75m deep, its sides festooned with dripping ferns and creepers, though the sense of mystery is somewhat diminished these days by the presence of a lift-cage built against the side. Rather than the Devil, the chasm was probably formed by a cave roof collapsing centuries ago; locals took refuge here during the Hundred Years' War and probably long before.

The cave system was not properly explored, however, until 1889 when spectacular **stalactites** – the biggest a staggering 75m tall – and lakes were discovered. Even today teams are still exploring the caves and passages.

The visit starts with a **boat trip** along an underground river, after which you walk on past barrages and massive cascades formed by calcite deposits over the millennia. The lakes are pretty, but the most notable feature here is the sheer scale of the formations and the height of the passages carved out of the rock, reaching nearly 100m at their highest. Be warned, though: it is very, very touristy and it's best to pre-book your tickets if you plan to visit in peak periods – otherwise, expect a long wait. In wet weather you'll need a waterproof jacket.

Bretenoux and around

Some 10km east of Carennac, the *bastide* town of **BRETENOUX**, founded in 1277 by the barons of Castelnau, sits on the south bank of the River Cère just upstream from where it joins the Dordogne. It was obviously a pretty little place at one time – the cobbled and arcaded **place des Consuls** behind the tourist office is a delight, especially on **market** days (Tues and Sat mornings) – but these days the town suffers from a busy main road and modern development. With its good transport connections, however, Bretenoux is a useful staging post for the nearby towns of St-Céré and Beaulieu-sur-Dordogne (see pages 175 and 174). East of here, the journey to Aurillac takes you through a very picturesque and otherwise inaccessible landscape, popular with walkers and cyclists.

ARRIVAL AND INFORMATION BRETENOUX

By train Bretenoux's *gare SNCF*, on the Brive–Aurillac line, is officially known as Bretenoux-Biars since it is located some 2km north of the River Cère in the town of Biars. Taxis wait outside the station, or call ahead (05 65 10 90 90).
Destinations Aurillac (6 daily; 45min–1hr); Brive (5 daily; 45min–1hr); St-Denis-près-Martel (3–4 daily; 20min).

Tourist office Avenue de la Libération, just south of the bridge (July & Aug Mon–Sat 9.30am–7pm, Sun 10am–1pm; April–June, Sept & Oct Mon–Sat 10am–noon & 2–6pm; 05 65 38 59 53, http://vallee-dordogne.com).
Canoe rental Available through Copeyre Canoe (http://copeyre.com).

ACCOMMODATION AND EATING

There are no **hotels** in Bretenoux itself, but there are a few options in the countryside around the village, as well as in Port-de-Gagnac, 6km northeast on the D14 on the north bank of the Cère.

BRETENOUX

Chez Ju Place des Consuls, 05 65 39 72 39. There are very few restaurants in Bretenoux, and *Chez Ju* is far and away the best of the small selection. Plenty of vegetarian options, generous portion sizes and local produce. Dogs welcome, even inside. €€

★ **Domaine de Granval** http://domainedegranval.com. A charming *chambre d'hôte*, 2km south of Bretenoux on the D803, with five lovely rooms all at ground level. There's a pool, and breakfast is served on the terrace; but it's the typical French hospitality and quiet country atmosphere that makes it a winner. €€

PORT-DE-GAGNAC

Auberge du Vieux Port http://auberge-vieuxport-lot.com. Cosy *auberge* right on the waterfront with spotless rooms, modern bathrooms and welcoming, English-speaking staff. The restaurant serves great-value regional cuisine like pan-fried lamb sweetbreads and Quercy-style *flambée*. €€

★ **Hostellerie Belle Rive** 05 65 38 50 04. The twelve individually decorated rooms at riverside *Hostellerie Belle Rive* are bright, sunny and full of personal touches. Stick around for dinner – the chef is a local celebrity, and the focus is on fresh local ingredients. €

Château de Castelnau

Charge (guided tour included in entry price) • http://castelnau-bretenoux.monuments-nationaux.fr

Bretenoux lies within striking distance of the **Château de Castelnau**, 2.5km to the southwest – one of this region's most outstanding examples of medieval military architecture. The great fortress dominates an abrupt knoll to the east of the village, its sturdy towers and machicolated red-brown walls visible for miles around. It dates from the mid-tenth century, but took on its present form – a triangular fort with a massive square keep and three round towers, the whole lot surrounded by ramparts and dry moats – during the Hundred Years' War under the ownership of the powerful barons of Castelnau. By the early eighteenth century, however, the Castelnau family had died out. Their abandoned château was sacked during the Revolution, sustained even greater damage in a fire in 1851 and was left to rot until it was salvaged, somewhat bizarrely, in 1896 by a celebrated tenor of the Parisian Comic Opera, **Jean Mouliérat**. He threw his fortune into its restoration and into amassing the valuable but rather dry collection of religious art and furniture from the fifteenth to eighteenth centuries, which populates the handful of rooms you see on the guided tour. The **views** from the ramparts, though, are extremely impressive; on a clear day you can just make out the towers of Turenne, nearly 30km to the north.

As you exit the castle's inner enclosure, turn left along the walls to take a quick look in the **Collégiale St-Louis**. Built of the same red stone and with powerful buttresses, this little Gothic church contains a fine fifteenth-century polychrome statue of the Baptism of Christ – note the startled expression of the angel holding his clothes – and a macabre treasure in the form of a bone from the arm of St Louis (alias King Louis IX of France). In 1970 the relic was taken to St Louis in America to commemorate the founding of the city.

Beaulieu-sur-Dordogne and around

At Bretenoux the River Dordogne turns northwards to Biars; the valley here is wide and industrial, with factories such as Andros churning out sufficient quantities to make this the "jam capital" of Europe. Aspects improve 8km north of Biars at **BEAULIEU-SUR-DORDOGNE**, beautifully situated on a wide bend in the river. It's a perfectly proportioned town, with an **abbey church** that boasts another of the great masterpieces of Romanesque sculpture, and yet is refreshingly untouristy.

Arriving from Bretenoux, the main road skirts south of Beaulieu's compact and semi-pedestrianized core of old streets. On its way it passes through a large square, **place Marbot**, which represents the town's modern centre, off which rue de la République leads north to **place du Marché** and the **Église St-Pierre**. It won't take long to cover the rest of Beaulieu, but it's worth devoting half an hour or so to wandering its maze of lanes. In particular, there are a number of half-timbered houses along **rue Ste-Catherine**, running east from place du Marché, while if you head northwest along rue de la République and rue de la Chapelle you'll pass some handsome sculpted facades before emerging beside the **Chapelle des Pénitents** in an attractive spot on the riverbank. This twelfth-century chapel now makes a splendid venue for the occasional art exhibition or concert; if it's open, it's worth popping in to see the collection of religious art.

Église St-Pierre
Place du Marché

Place du Marché boasts some nicely faded stone and half-timbered buildings, along with the twelfth-century **Église St-Pierre**, a surprisingly large abbey church whose architecture reflects its position on the border between Limousin and Languedoc. The pairs of rounded arches piercing the belfry, for example, are typical Limousin styling, while the subject matter and style of carving on the magnificent **south portal** belongs firmly to the south. The **tympanum** is presided over by an oriental-looking Christ with one arm extended to welcome the chosen on the Judgement Day. Around him a mass of angels and apostles, even the dead rising from their graves below, seem ready to burst with vitality.

ARRIVAL AND INFORMATION BEAULIEU-SUR-DORDOGNE

By train It's just over 6km from Beaulieu-sur-Dordogne to the Bretenoux-Biars *gare SNCF*. Unfortunately, there are no connecting buses, but you could call a taxi to travel into Beaulieu (05 55 91 02 83).
Tourist office The tourist information centre is on the south side of place Marbot (April–June, Sept & Oct Mon–Sat 10am–12.30pm & 2–6pm; July & Aug daily 9.30am–1pm & 2pm–6.30pm; mid-July to mid-Aug Sun 10am–1pm; 05 55 91 09 94, http://vallee-dordogne.com).
Boat trips From May to October traditional wooden *gabares* depart from the riverbank near the Chapelle des Pénitents for a 1hr jaunt upstream; contact the tourist office to book.

ACCOMMODATION

★ **Auberge de Jeunesse** Rue de la Chapelle, http://hifrance.org. Welcoming hostel set in a striking half-timbered and turreted building, with surprisingly modern dorms inside and a well-equipped kitchen. Meals are available on request for groups of ten or more. €
Huttopia http://europe.huttopia.com. Leafy riverside campsite, on the island to the north of the town's main road-bridge, with plenty to keep the kids entertained, including a pool, splash-pool, playground, ping-pong and kayaks for hire. €
Les Flots Bleus Place du Monturu, http://hotel-flotsbleus.com. This friendly riverside hotel offers generously sized

rooms in a tranquil location, but the real highlight is the waterfront restaurant (see below). Opt for a room with a view over the Dordogne. €
Relais de Vellinus Place du Champ-de-Mars, http://vellinus.fr. Let down by its rather uninspiring facade, this friendly hotel is nonetheless comfortable, well-furnished and spotless, and it's the top pick for those on a budget. The in-house restaurant is excellent, serving elegantly presented dishes and mouth-watering desserts. €
★ **Le Turenne** 1 bd St-Rodolphe-de-Turenne, http://leturenne.com. With its bold colour palette and innovative decor, Le Turenne is the kind of hotel that puts a smile on your face. The smart and stylish rooms are jazzed up with giant Buddhas, faux-fur bed runners and embossed wallpaper, while the staff go out of their way to make you welcome. There's also a restaurant serving delicious gourmet cuisine. €

EATING AND DRINKING

Chez Colette 27 rue du Général-de-Gaulle, 05 55 28 22 71. Red-and-white checked tablecloths, cutesy knick-knacks and smiley staff ensure a warm welcome at this homely café. There's a small and often-changing menu, with excellent salads, and everything is home-made. €€
L'Abbatiale 5 rue de la République, 05 55 19 00 31. Pizzeria serving delicious Napolitan pizzas and ice creams. Friendly, efficient service and good prices. Try the burrata and mortadella pizzas. €
Les Flots Bleus Place du Monturu, http://hotel-flotsbleus.com. The most romantic restaurant in town, with a perfect riverside setting and a summer terrace that faces Beaulieu's Chapelle des Pénitents. The cuisine is just as impressive, with creative use of seasonal ingredients and beautifully presented dishes that will have you reaching for your camera. €€

Argentat

Upstream from Beaulieu, the Dordogne valley becomes wilder as you enter the first forest-covered foothills of the Massif Central. It makes for a lovely drive along the D12 as far as **Argentat**, the last town of any size on the river, where it's easy to while away an hour or so sitting at one of the waterside cafés. Beyond Argentat, however, the Dordogne changes character entirely, due to a series of hydroelectric dams that turns the river into a succession of huge reservoirs.

St-Céré and around

About 9km south of Bretenoux on the River Bave, a minor tributary of the Dordogne, you come to the medieval town of **St-Céré**, dominated by the brooding ruins of the **Château de St-Laurent-les-Tours**, whose powerful twin keeps are the first things you see when arriving in the town from the north. Once part of a fortress belonging to the viscounts of Turenne, the château is now home to an engaging museum dedicated to local tapestry designer Jean Lurçat, who revitalized contemporary French tapestry. However, St-Céré's prime attraction is its old centre, peppered with picturesque half-timbered houses. The town sits in the valley to the southwest where the old houses cluster round place du Mercadial and place de l'Église. These two squares lie north and south respectively of rue de la République, the main shopping street cutting through the old centre which, at its southeast end, comes out into **place de la République**, a big, open square where you'll find car parks, cafés and the town's main tourist facilities, as well as its Sunday-morning **market**; a much larger market spreads throughout the old town on the first and third Wednesdays of the month.

St-Céré makes a useful base for exploring the surrounding area. The town lies on the border between the empty but glorious wooded hills of the Ségala to the east and south, and the dry limestone *causse* to the west. However, the region's most impressive sight, and one not to be missed, is the Renaissance **Château de Montal**, 2km west of St-Céré, with its sculpted facade and grand staircase. From here you can loop south via the **Grottes de Presque** – a limestone cave with a tremendous variety of unusually colourful concretions – to arrive at the lip of the Cirque d'Autoire for dramatic views over the russet-red roofs of **Autoire** village, which provide a splash of colour in the valley far below. On the way back to St-Céré the route passes through another captivating little village, **Loubressac**, which can hardly have changed for centuries.

Brief history

St-Céré owes its existence to the martyrdom of **Ste Spérie** in 780. Born the daughter of the then lord of St-Laurent, Sérenus, Spérie pledged her life to God at an early age, and when later she refused to marry a local nobleman, she was beheaded by her brother and buried on the riverbank. Later a chapel was erected on the spot around which the town began to develop in the tenth century. It lay initially under the jurisdiction of the counts of Auvergne, but was transferred to the Turenne viscounts in 1178. They beefed up the fortress and, as usual, granted the town a certain degree of autonomy. Its heyday didn't arrive, however, until after the fifteenth century when St-Céré's wealthy **merchants** began investing in the noble houses that can still be seen around the town today.

Place du Mercadial and around

The best of St-Céré's fifteenth-century townhouses lie in the streets to the north of rue de la République, notably around **place du Mercadial**, which is particularly appealing; to find it, walk one block north from rue de la République and turn left along rue du Mazel. You come out opposite the town's most eye-catching building, the **Maison des Consuls**, where the administrative council used to meet – it now hosts various fine art exhibitions in summer. Beneath the pitched tile roof, the building's most striking feature is the slightly overhanging upper storey of neatly layered brick in a timber frame. The same design is echoed in the **Maison Arnoud**, on the north side of the square, whose ground floor is a mere 3m wide. **Rue St-Cyr**, the lane to the right of this house, takes you east and then south past several elegant Renaissance buildings and into a recently renovated area of courtyards and alleys.

Église Sainte-Spérie

12 rue Paramelle

There's not much of interest on the south side of rue de la République, though the **Église Sainte-Spérie**, largely rebuilt after the Wars of Religion, is worth a quick peek for its eighteenth-century altarpiece with a statue of Ste Spérie standing on the left. It was carved by a local monk who received 240 *livres* and, for some reason, four handkerchiefs for his pains.

Atelier-Musée Jean Lurçat

Charge • http://musees.lot.fr • 1km or so above St-Céré – take avenue du Docteur Roux heading northeast past the hospital and then follow the signs winding uphill

Only the ramparts and two square towers of the **Château de St-Laurent-les-Tours** remain, the smaller one dating from the late twelfth century and the taller, eastern tower from the 1300s. The rest of the castle was destroyed during the Wars of Religion, but around 1895 the then-owner built himself a neo-Gothic mansion between the two towers. It is this building in which Jean Lurçat (1892–1966) set up his studio in 1945 and which is now the **Atelier-Musée Jean Lurçat**. Locally born Lurçat is best known for his big, bold tapestries, of which the most famous is the eighty-metre-long *Chant du Monde* ("*Song of the World*"), now on display in Angers, but you can get an idea of his distinctive style – typically incorporating animals and birds, both real and fantastic, against dark blue or black backgrounds – in the Atelier. Alongside his sketches and illustrations, a slideshow of the *Chant du Monde* and a short biographical film, the museum's highlight is the artist's unmistakable paintings, which cover the ceilings and doors.

ARRIVAL AND INFORMATION — ST-CÉRÉ

By train The nearest *gare SNCF* to St-Céré is Bretenoux-Biars, a good 10km to the north, from where there are buses on two days a week (Wed & Sat; Delbos 05 65 38 24 19) on to St-Céré.
Tourist office On the north side of place de la République (daily: July & Aug 9.30am–1pm & 2–6.30pm; mid-July to mid-Aug Sun 10am–1pm; April–June, Sept & Oct Mon–Sat 10am–12.30pm & 2–6pm; 05 65 38 11 85, http://vallee-dordogne.com).
Bike rental Cycles St-Chamant, 45 rue Faidherbe (05 65 38 03 23), to the west of place de la République.

ACCOMMODATION

Le Soulhol Quai Salesses, http://camping-le-soulhol.fr. Three-star campsite, beside the river and a short walk east of the *Victor Hugo*, offering a heated pool, BBQ area, bike rental and free wi-fi throughout the site. €
Les Trois Soleils de Montal Les Prés de Montal, http://3soleils.fr. The Michelin-starred restaurant (see below) is the undisputed star here, but *Les Trois Soleils* is also St-Céré's most elegant hotel. Expect timeless luxury with well-furnished rooms, garden views and a wonderfully romantic terrace. €€€
★ **Victor Hugo** 7 av des Maquis, http://hotel-victor-hugo.fr. Behind the quintessentially French facade, with its traditional wooden shutters and flowery terrace overlooking the river, *Victor Hugo* is all modern, with sunny, spacious rooms. Add to that an excellent restaurant (which serves a perfect steak), welcoming staff and a convenient location, just minutes from place de la République, and it's the best deal in town. €

EATING

In addition to the *Trois Soleils* (see below), the best places to eat in St-Céré are the **restaurants** at the *De France* (see above) and *Victor Hugo* hotels (see above). Otherwise, try the cafés and brasseries around place de la République and place du Mercadial.
Pizzeria du Mercadial 4 place du Mercadial, 05 65 38 35 77. Tasty food and generous portions are the order of the day at this rustic pizzeria, and the terrace seating is ideal for people-watching. Pizza is the obvious choice, but there's also a wide selection of pasta dishes and grills. €
Le Puymule 1 place de l'Église, 05 65 34 27 40. In a gorgeous old building with exposed beams, bare stone walls and raffia mirrors on the walls, this restaurant serves hearty classics, like burger and chips, and more refined plates that verge on fine dining. €€
★ **Les Trois Soleils de Montal** Les Prés de Montal, http://3soleils.fr. A Michelin-starred treat with candle-lit tables set amid beautiful gardens and creative dishes whipped up from local ingredients; specialities include roasted pigeon and miso-marinated foie gras. The lunchtime weekday *menu* is a bargain. €€€

Château de Montal

Charge • http://chateau-montal.fr

Two kilometres west of St-Céré, the **Château de Montal** is a superb example of French Renaissance architecture, and has recently reopened after extensive renovations. Its fascinating history began in 1523 when **Jeanne Balzac d'Entraygues**, the widow of Amaury de Montal, started transforming the medieval fortress into a Renaissance palace, as was all the rage. But then came news that her eldest son, Robert, had been killed in Italy and poor Jeanne lost the heart to continue.

Nevertheless, the de Montal family continued to own the château up to the Revolution, after which it was bought by a certain Monsieur Macaire who gradually sold off the chimneypieces, sculptures and even the carved window surrounds. Rescue was at hand, however, in the form of **Maurice Fenaille**, a rich industrialist and patron of the arts, who bought the château in 1908 and began to slowly restore it to its former glory.

In just five years he managed to track down nearly everything that had been sold, including some of the original wallcoverings, and also filled the rooms with a fine collection of Renaissance and Louis XIII furnishings, before giving the whole caboodle to the state in 1913. Later, during World War II, Montal was chosen as a hiding place for thousands of paintings from the Louvre, including the *Mona Lisa*, which were moved from Paris for safekeeping.

The inner courtyard
The rear of the château, which you see first on approach, still exudes a thoroughly medieval air with its small windows, steep *lauze* roof and pepper-pot towers, but turn the corner into the **inner courtyard** and you're immediately transported to sunny Italy. The lovely pale stone of the two facades is worked into delicate carvings, including a frieze of mermaid-like sibyls and, above, busts representing three generations of the de Montal family: Jeanne is flanked by her husband and son Robert on the west wing, while her parents take pride of place over the front door.

The interior
The craftspeople went to work inside as well as on the outside, particularly on a magnificent **staircase** made from the same local limestone. As you climb up, notice the carving on the panels above, each bearing a different design, which gets finer and more elaborate towards the top. The rest of the interior can't quite compare, but there are some massive old oak tables, a good, homely kitchen and an excellent collection of tapestries, including a rare example featuring a pastoral scene with descriptive boxes of text, like an early cartoon.

Grottes de Presque
Charge • http://grottesdepresque.com

About 3km southwest from the Château de Montal, the D673 cuts through a hillside as it climbs up onto the *causse*. When this road was dug in 1825, engineers discovered the entrance to the **Grottes de Presque**. The cave system is not only unusually accessible, with just a few stairs, but it also contains a marvellous variety of **stalactites** and **stalagmites**, some up to 10m high, as well as columns, semi-translucent curtains and glistening crystalline cascades. The other notable feature is the sheer amount of **colour**, from pure white to grey, yellow and deep orange. This is the result of rainwater picking up iron, manganese and other minerals as it percolates through the 90m of rock above, minerals that are then deposited along with the calcite, drip by drip, inside the cave.

Autoire
Eight kilometres by road west of the Grottes de Presque (follow the D673 southwest for another 4km and then turn right on the D38), the River Autoire has carved an impressive canyon and waterfall, the **Cirque d'Autoire**, into the limestone plateau. The D38 brings you in above the *cirque* – for the best views, walk west from the car park (€2/day) for about five minutes, following the footpath across a bridge and up onto the opposite hillside.

In the valley bottom, some 2km below you, lies the extremely pretty little village of **AUTOIRE** where the ochre-hued houses, including several rather grand piles built by nobles from St-Céré in the fifteenth and sixteenth centuries, snuggle round a very plain, solid Romanesque church.

ACCOMMODATION AND EATING — AUTOIRE

Auberge de la Fontaine http://auberge-de-la-fontaine.com. This lovely hotel is on Autoire's main street opposite the church. It's a simple country inn offering basic but well-kept rooms and a restaurant with good regional country cooking washed down with Côteaux de Glanes wines. €€

La Cascade 06 07 85 90 62. Autoire's longest-running crêperie has been serving up delicious home-made crêpes and *galettes* since 1976. Take a seat on the pretty terrace looking out over the valley, or cosy up inside. Service leaves much to be desired. €

Loubressac

It's 8km back to St-Céré from Autoire, but it's worth taking a short diversion 6km northwest along the D135, little more than a country lane, to **LOUBRESSAC**. The narrow lanes of this fortified hilltop village are full of flowers and typical Quercy houses. You can't visit the château standing on the cliff edge, but there are grand **views** from the lookout point immediately to the east of the village, taking in the whole sweep of the Dordogne, Bave and Cère valleys across to St-Céré and the châteaux of Castelnau and Montal.

INFORMATION   LOUBRESSAC

Tourist office In season a tourist office opens up just outside Loubressac's southern gateway (mid-June to Sept Mon–Fri 10am–12.30pm & 2–6pm; 05 65 33 22 00, http://vallee-dordogne.com).

ACCOMMODATION AND EATING

Le Cantou La Place, 5 place du Foirail, http://hotel-lecantou354.com. Simple but comfortable rooms in a tranquil location, offering beautiful views over the valley from the communal terrace. There's also a restaurant that serves regional specialities like Quercy lamb and walnut salad, and foie gras. €€

La Garrigue http://camping-lagarrigue.com. Small but pleasant three-star campsite with a swimming pool, 200m south of the village. €

Relais de Castelnau Rue de Padirac, http://relaisdecastelnau.com. Looking out over the Dordogne valley, the modern *Relais de Castelnau* boasts dramatic views as well as an outdoor swimming pool and a good-quality restaurant. €€

The Lot valley and around

184 Cahors
194 East along the Lot
200 The Célé valley
202 Figeac
207 The Causse de Gramat
209 Gourdon
211 The Bouriane
212 West along the Lot from Cahors
219 Villeneuve-sur-Lot and around
222 The bastide country

CHÂTEAU DE BONAGUIL

The Lot valley and around

Like the Dordogne, the River Lot rises in the foothills of the Massif Central and is dammed in its upper reaches to form huge reservoirs. It begins to get more interesting, however, where it enters the Lot *département*, the boundaries of which roughly coincide with the old province of Quercy. Here the serpentine river carves its way through the immense limestone plateau – encompassed by the Parc naturel régional des Causses du Quercy – that characterizes the region.

The largest town in the Lot valley, and capital of the *département*, is **Cahors**. It may lack the higgledy-piggledy charm of Sarlat or Bergerac, but compensates with a pleasingly workaday atmosphere and a wonderful riverside location. It also boasts the best example of a fortified medieval bridge left in France, the **Pont Valentré**, while the country round about produces an extremely distinctive dark, almost peppery red **wine**.

The Lot valley is at its most picturesque upstream from Cahors. The scenery may not be as dramatic as the middle reaches of the Dordogne, but the sheer cliffs here host their fair share of perched fortresses and feudal villages. Foremost among these is spectacular **St-Cirq Lapopie**, while the nearby **Grotte de Pech-Merle**, with its glittering rock formations and prehistoric cave art, draws almost as many visitors. Pech-Merle lies in the hills above the wild and pretty **Célé valley**, which leads northeast to lovely, medieval **Figeac**, the Lot's second largest town.

North and west of Figeac stretches the **Causse de Gramat**, the biggest and wildest of the region's limestone *causses*. With its huge vistas, it makes a welcome change from the confining valleys and a great place for walking or cycling, though it has few notable sights beyond the village of **Assier**, in the far southeast, with its extraordinary church. On its western edge the Causse de Gramat suddenly gives way to a lovely area of gentle wooded hills known as the **Bouriane**. Again, there are no must-see sights, though its capital, **Gourdon**, a once-prosperous town built of butter-coloured stone, is worth a stop-off, and the nearby **Grottes de Cougnac**, with a smattering of prehistoric cave paintings and some exceptionally delicate limestone concretions, repay a visit.

Returning to the Lot valley, the river south of Cahors wriggles its way westwards through vineyards and past ancient towns and villages. By far the most striking of these is **Puy-l'Évêque**. An outpost of the bishops of Cahors, the town's medieval and Renaissance houses jostle for space on a steep incline, reaching upwards like trees for light, though none is equal to the bishop's thirteenth-century keep towering above. An even more dramatic sight lies in store in the country northwest of Puy-l'Évêque, where the **Château de Bonaguil** is an outstanding example of late-fifteenth-century military architecture, its great bulk silhouetted against the wooded hillside.

Further downstream things begin to quieten down again as the valley flattens out towards **Villeneuve-sur-Lot**. Despite unattractive modern suburbs, the town has a decent supply of hotels and restaurants, and with the river sliding through an old centre built of stone and warm red brick, it's a pleasant and convenient place to stay. Villeneuve – as its name indicates – was also one of the many "new towns", or *bastides*, founded in this area in the thirteenth and fourteenth centuries. You'll find the best examples of *bastide* architecture in the hills to the north, where the villages of **Monflanquin** and **Monpazier** seem hardly to have changed since the Middle Ages. The same can't be said for the **Château de Biron**, lying between the two, which was altered and expanded extensively during the Renaissance, but its superb hilltop location makes it hard to resist.

GETTING AROUND — THE LOT VALLEY AND AROUND

By car Given the paucity of public transport, you'll need your own vehicle for exploring much of the Lot valley, and

PONT VALENTRÉ

Highlights

❶ Pont Valentré This iconic medieval bridge guarding the town's western approaches is at its most atmospheric at sunset. See page 190

❷ Wine tasting in Cahors Sample the distinctive, full-bodied wines of Cahors, dark enough to merit the nickname of "black wines". See page 193

❸ St-Cirq Lapopie High above the River Lot, this former feudal stronghold boasts stunning views and labyrinthine alleys. See page 195

❹ Quercy saffron The Lot's signature spice is more than just a cooking ingredient – it's the focal point of the harvest festival at Cajarc, one of the region's largest. See page 198

❺ Grotte de Pech-Merle Dazzling limestone formations and over 500 prehistoric drawings make this cave unmissable. See page 200

❻ Figeac A laidback riverside town with plenty of medieval architecture and a fascinating museum of writing. See page 202

❼ Château de Bonaguil One of the last medieval fortresses built in France, and now a magnificent ruin. See page 217

❽ Bastides Monpazier provides an almost perfect example of the region's myriad fortified towns. See page 223

HIGHLIGHTS ARE MARKED ON THE MAP ON PAGE 184

a car is essential for the Célé valley, the Bouriane and other places off the beaten track.

By train SNCF trains between Brive-la-Gaillarde and Toulouse, via Gourdon and Cahors and to Rodez, stop at Gramat, Assier, Figeac and Capdenac, while the Figeac–Cahors line passes Cajarc. Funel is also connected to Cahors, Agen and Penne-d'Agenais.

By bus The only regular SNCF bus services in the region run east from Cahors to Figeac and west to Fumel – timetables are available at tourist offices. Many smaller towns have no public bus service, and though there are buses from Cahors and Figeac to Gramat and Gourdon, these are aimed at school drop-offs and pick-ups, and are not a viable option for visitors. Nonetheless, a comprehensive bus timetable, *Les Bus du Lot*, is published annually and available at tourist offices; otherwise contact the transport information desk of the Conseil Général du Lot (05 65 53 43 91, http://lot.fr).

Cahors

A sunny southern backwater built in a tight meander of the River Lot, **CAHORS** was the chief town of the old province of Quercy and is now the modern capital of the Lot *département*. Its somewhat troubled history has left a warren of dark medieval lanes, a rather knocked-about cathedral and impressive fortifications, among them Cahors' famous landmark, the turreted **Pont Valentré**. Another reason to come here is to sample the local **wines**, heady and black but dry to the taste (see page 193).

Compact and easily walkable, Cahors is bordered on three sides by the River Lot and protected to the north by a series of fourteenth-century fortifications. Most sights of interest lie within the cramped confines of the medieval streets on the peninsula's eastern edge, focused around the twin domes of the **Cathédrale St-Étienne**. From here, **rue Nationale** leads south past the former homes of wealthy merchants to the flood-prone artisans' quarter, while north of the cathedral the land continues to slope gently upwards along **rue du Château-du-Roi**, where bankers and aristocrats once lived,

THE LOT VALLEY AND AROUND

HIGHLIGHTS
1. Pont Valentré
2. Wine tasting in Cahors
3. St-Cirq Lapopie
4. Quercy saffron
5. Grotte de Pech-Merle
6. Figeac
7. Château de Bonaguil
8. Bastides

CAHORS THE LOT VALLEY AND AROUND

towards the old town gate with its guardhouse and tower. Of medieval Cahors' three fortified bridges, only westerly **Pont Valentré** remains – one of the finest surviving bridges of its time. More recent history is commemorated in a couple of passably interesting **museums** and, on a fine day, there are good views from the summit of **Mont St-Cyr**, which overlooks the town from the southeast.

Brief history

Both the names Quercy and Cahors derive from the area's first-known inhabitants, the local Gaulish tribe known as the **Cadurci**. At some time between the seventh and fifth centuries BC they founded their settlement near a sacred spring, immediately across the river to the southwest of modern Cahors, which the Romans, who arrived in overwhelming force in 51BC, later called **Divona Cadurcorum**. Following successive Vandal and Frankish invasions after the fifth century, only a few fragments of Roman stonework remain, as well as the spring, which continues to supply Cahors' drinking water.

It wasn't until the seventh century that the then Bishop (later Saint) Didier finally erected a wall to protect the nascent town and his rapidly growing cathedral. The **bishops of Cahors** gradually spread their net until they not only ruled over a vast area extending down the Lot as far as Puy-l'Évêque but also controlled the all-important river trade. By the early thirteenth century Cahors was entering its **golden age**, as powerful local merchants known as Caorsins, together with Lombard bankers fleeing the Cathar crusades, turned the town into Europe's chief banking centre – a wealth that was reflected in the gentrification of various townhouses, bridges and cathedral. When the local bishop, Jacques Duèze, was named **Pope John XXII** in 1316, Cahors had reached its apogee. His greatest legacy was a university, which remained one of the most important in France for the next four centuries.

FESTIVALS, EVENTS AND MARKETS

Festivals and **events** are held throughout the Lot valley during the summer season, and many of the villages host special markets and small fêtes to celebrate the harvest season. The principal festivals are detailed below, but for the full schedule, pick up the free *Calendrier des Fêtes des Villes et Villages* booklet from tourist offices. Where we haven't given a specific information number or website, contact the relevant tourist office.

May Albas: La Fête du Vin (http://albas.fr). The area's largest wine festival is held biennially, kicking off with a barrel of wine being paraded through the village and including various wine-tasting and dinner events starting from around €15 a head.

Mid-July Monpazier: Fête Médiévale (Dates vary, check http://fetes-medievales.com). In addition to its many small summer events, Monpazier steps back in time for five days, with banquets, concerts and equestrian displays.

Mid-July Cahors: Blues Festival (http://cahorsbluesfestival.com). A week of blues, jazz and rock, where French and international artists bare their souls in the streets: head to Les Docks, Théâtre de Verdure, rue Wilson and boulevard Gambetta. The early performances are free, later ones are ticketed. The tourist office has a leaflet with all details.

Mid-July to mid-August Cahors: Festival de St-Céré et du Haut-Quercy (http://festival-saint-cere.com). Three-week festival of opera, orchestral works and chamber music, with ticketed concerts in Cahors' cathedral and Musée Henri-Martin.

Late July Cajarc: Africajarc (http://africajarc.com). Cajarc moves to an African beat during three days of concerts, exhibitions, craft displays, markets and food stalls. Tickets required for the main concerts.

First weekend in August Gourdon: Grande Fête Médiévale (http://medievalesdegourdon.jimdo.com). Gourdon lets rip with two days of junketing complete with jugglers, fire-eaters, musicians and the works.

Early August Puy-l'Évêque: Fête Votive. One of the area's most important local fêtes, lasting five days with a free dance every night, a funfair and a fireworks spectacular with music on the Sunday.

Early to mid-August Château de Bonaguil: Festival du Bonaguil Fumel (http://festivaldebonaguil-fumel.fr). Bonaguil's inner court and moats make a spectacular venue for this festival of French theatre, held over eight or nine days. There's a play or musical event every night (tickets required), as well as workshops, street theatre and lectures.

Mid-August Monflanquin: Journées Médiévales (05 53 36 40 19). Two days of mead, minstrels and merry japes as Monflanquin goes medieval. Jousting, banquets, siege engines – you name it. You can even rent costumes.

First weekend in September Peyrusse-le-Roc: Spectacle Pyrosymphonique. The ruined towers of Peyrusse make a spectacular setting for a son-et-lumière-cum-fireworks display.

Late October Cajarc: Fête du Safran (http://safran-du-quercy.com). Cajarc hosts the region's biggest saffron fair, featuring an array of saffron-infused products, cooking demonstrations and a growers' competition.

MARKETS

The region's main **markets** take place at Aiguillon (Tues & Fri); Cahors (Wed & Sat); Cajarc (Sat); Duravel (Sat); Figeac (Sat); Fumel (Sun); Gourdon (Tues & Sat, also Thurs in July & Aug); Gramat (Tues & Fri); Luzech (Wed); Monflanquin (Thurs); Monpazier (Thurs); Monsempron-Libos (Sun); Prayssac (Fri) and Villeneuve-sur-Lot (Tues & Sat).

By now, however, the English and French armies were at loggerheads. Cahors was never attacked during the Hundred Years' War, but the end result was the same: under the Treaty of Brétigny (1360) it succumbed reluctantly to **English occupation**. When French rule was eventually restored around 1440, the Caduriciens set about rebuilding their ravaged town, adding a few Italianate flourishes and developing a distinctive decorative style comprising carved or moulded rose blossoms, flaming suns and the so-called "*bâtons écotés*" ("pruned branches"), which is still in evidence today.

Unlike several of its neighbours, Cahors remained staunchly Catholic during the **Wars of Religion**. As a consequence, it was sacked by the Protestant Henry of Navarre, the future King Henry IV of France, when he seized it after a brief battle in 1580. Later the same year, however, one of many peace treaties saw the town returned to the Catholic fold. By way of recompense, Henry later donated six thousand *livres*, half of which went towards restoring the cathedral.

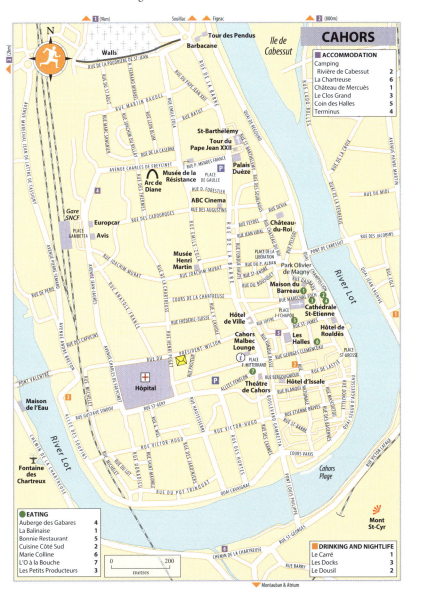

Over the years Cahors gradually expanded to fill the entire peninsula, though it was not until the nineteenth century that Bishop Didier's ramparts were finally razed. They were replaced by a tree-lined boulevard that was later named after Cahors' most famous son, the politician **Léon Gambetta** (see box). The heart of present-day Cahors is **place François-Mitterrand**, named after yet another politician, a recently renovated wide open square. During the renovation process, and excavation of the car park housed underneath, a staggering amount of ancient ruins were uncovered. Work was stopped, archeologists called in and part of a **Roman amphitheatre** emerged. The much-needed car park was still built, but it contains a semicircle of the amphitheatre (the rest is under the old college), carefully lit for public display – a parking facility and a day out in one.

Cathédrale St-Étienne
Place Jean-Jacques Chapou • Free

The oldest and simplest of the region's Périgord-style Romanesque churches, the **Cathédrale St-Étienne** dates largely from the early twelfth century, when Bishop Didier's original cathedral was rebuilt in part to house the relic of the Holy Coif, said to have covered Christ's head in the tomb. According to local legend, it was brought back from the Holy Land around this time by Bishop Géraud de Cardaillac.

Numerous reconstructions of the building have been carried out over the centuries, meaning St-Étienne's exterior is rather unexciting, with the notable exception of the elaborately decorated portal above the **north door**. Carved in around 1140, it depicts Christ's Ascension. Side panels show scenes from the life of St Stephen (St Étienne), the first Christian martyr, who was stoned to death around 35 AD, while the outer arch portrays people being stabbed and sliced with axes.

Inside, the cathedral is much like Périgueux's St-Étienne (see page 55), with a nave lacking aisles and transepts, roofed with two monumental domes. High in the west dome, original fourteenth-century frescoes again depict the stoning of St Stephen, encircled by eight giant prophets. In 1988 further paintings from the same era were discovered behind layers of plaster just inside and above the west door. They consist of faded but beautiful Creation scenes, including Adam and Eve in the Garden of Eden and many finely observed birds and animals.

To the right of the choir, the aptly named **Chapelle Profonde** ("Deep Chapel") bears scars from the Wars of Religion, when Protestant armies hacked away at its carvings. They also caused irreparable damage to the **cloister**, accessed by a door next to the Deep Chapel, though the flamboyant Gothic colonnades still retain some intricate craftsmanship. The door surrounds are also beautifully carved, if rather battered; that on the northeast wall leads into the **Chapelle St Gausbert** (only accessible as part of the guided tours run by the tourist office; see page 192), which holds the **Holy Coif** – a decidedly unimpressive, rather grubby looking piece of padded cloth – among chalices, gilded statues and other treasures.

> ### JACQUES DUÈZE AND CHÂTEAUNEUF-DU-PAPE
> Cahors' home-grown cleric, **Jacques Duèze**, was immensely fond of his native town, and no less fond of its powerful black wines. So much so that when elected to the papacy, as John XXII, and forced to move his episcopal seat from Cahors to the Holy See in Avignon, he devised a wheeze for continuing to imbibe his favourite tipple. Rather than having the wine transported 400 kilometres from the Cahors vineyards to the papal palace, he built a new summer palace on the banks of the Rhône and planted his beloved Malbec vine-stock around it. Thus a new wine was born, which the locals christened **Châteauneuf-du-Pape** – in essence a Cahors wine in all but name.

Place Jean-Jacques Chapou

The square on which Cathédrale St-Étienne stands, **place Jean-Jacques Chapou**, commemorates a local Resistance leader killed in a German ambush in July 1944. On its west side, look for a sign above what is now a bank announcing *Bazar Gênois: Gambetta Jeune et Cie*. This is where **Léon Gambetta** (see box), the son of an Italian grocer, spent his childhood. At its southern end the square extends into place Galdemar, popularly known as place de la Halle. The covered **Les Halles** at its centre, built as a corn exchange in 1865, provides the focus for Cahors' lively markets. There's a fresh food **market** in here (Tues–Sat 7.30am–12.30pm & 3–7pm, Sun 9am–noon), and a more extensive market on Wednesday and Saturday mornings spreading north into the cathedral square; in winter (Nov to mid-March), the *halle* plays host to a Saturday morning *marché au gras*, selling all manner of duck and goose products. Nearby place François-Mitterrand also hosts an antiques fair-cum-flea market on the first and third Saturdays of the month.

Medieval Cahors

A warren of narrow lanes and alleys fills the area between boulevard Gambetta and the eastern riverbank, where the majority of houses, turreted and built with flat, thin southern brick, have been handsomely restored during recent decades. From the market square, **rue Nationale** cuts almost due south through the heart of medieval Cahors to where the old Roman bridge once stood – the foundations are still just visible when the water level is low. Other roads worth exploring in the area are canyon-like **rue Bergougnioux** and its easterly extension **rue Lastié**, which comes out among a pretty group of brick and timber buildings around **place St-Urcisse**.

One of Cahors' most attractive corners lies just north of the cathedral along **rue Daurade**, where a lovely row of buildings overlooks a little park named after the sixteenth-century poet Olivier de Magny, who lived at no.12. His house is overshadowed, though, by the thirteenth-century **Maison du Bourreau** (no public access), the "executioner's house", with its big arched openings and line of double windows above. The name dates from the Revolution, when the public executioner lived here; naturally, the building is said to be haunted.

Continuing north along rue Daurade you reach the southern end of **rue Château-du-Roi** and its extension, **rue des Soubirous**. This is the "upper town", where the houses become distinctly grander. One of the most imposing is the fourteenth-century **Château du Roi** itself, built by cousins of Pope John XXII but later taken over by the king's emissary when the bishops lost their stranglehold on Cahors in the fifteenth century. Its massive, featureless walls can be easily seen from the eastern riverbank, though there's no public access to the interior.

Wealthy Caduriens were very fond of adding turrets to their homes and there are a number of examples scattered through the Soubirous quarter. To see them properly it's best to head down to the river – rue du Four-Ste-Catherine provides the most interesting route – to a vantage point across **Pont de Cabessut**. Cahors' skyline stretches in front of you from the cathedral domes in the south via Collège Pélegry, with its crenellated hexagonal turret, and the square, solid tower of the Château du Roi. In the far distance the **Tour du Pape Jean XXII** and the **Tour des Pendus** pinpoint Cahors' northern ramparts, which still stretch partway across the peninsula.

Musée de la Résistance

Place Charles-de-Gaulle • Free • 05 65 22 14 25 • Closed at the time of writing, due to reopen in 2025

In a small building on the north side of place Charles-de-Gaulle, the **Musée de la Résistance** documents the history of the local Resistance movement against the broader context of German occupation, deportations and, finally, Liberation in 1945. The most

> ## LÉON GAMBETTA
>
> Heralded as the "father of the Republic", **Léon Gambetta** was born in Cahors in 1838. After graduating as a lawyer, he specialized in defending republican sympathizers accused of political crimes against Emperor Napoléon III. The republicans soon rallied around Gambetta – a charismatic man and a great orator – and, when Napoléon was forced to surrender to an invading Prussian army in 1870, he was among those who quickly proclaimed the **Third Republic**, the regime which continued to govern France until 1940. It had a rocky start, however. With the Prussians besieging Paris, Gambetta fled the capital by balloon to organize the war effort in the provinces. While he opposed the armistice signed in 1871, Gambetta and his band of moderate republicans, or "Opportunists", were able to keep the Republic afloat despite constant attacks from both the monarchist majority and the radical Left. He served as president of the National Assembly from 1879 to 1882, but later that year his career was cut short when he accidentally shot himself with a revolver, and died soon after.

interesting section, on the ground floor, deals with local history, where you can read about Jean-Jacques Chapou, after whom the cathedral square is named, and about the *Mona Lisa*'s sojourn in the area.

Musée Henri Martin

792 rue Émile-Zola • http://museehenrimartin.fr

Housed in a seventeenth-century former episcopal palace, the **Musée Henri Martin** was closed for extensive renovations at the time of writing – check the website or ask at the tourist office for an update. Its permanent collection ranges from Gallo-Roman pots to works by nineteenth- and twentieth-century artists such as Dufy, Vlaminck and Utrillo, and comprises over two thousand documents, photographs, sculptures and paintings. Highlights include seventeen oil paintings by local artist **Henri Martin** (1860–1943), whose mix of Impressionism and Pointillism perfectly evokes the lazy sun-filled landscapes of this part of France; and an important collection dedicated to **Léon Gambetta**.

Pont Valentré

The main reason most people venture to Cahors is to see the dramatic **Pont Valentré**, which guards the western river crossing. Its three powerful towers, originally closed by portcullises and gates, made it an independent fortress, which was so imposing, in fact, that the bridge was never attacked. Building it was a problem, however: work started in 1308, but the bridge was not completed for another seventy years. According to legend, the Devil was to blame – at least in part. The story goes that the architect, exasperated at the slow progress, sold his soul in exchange for the Devil's assistance. As the bridge was nearing completion, he tried to wriggle out of the deal by giving the Devil a sieve with which to carry water for the masons. The Devil took revenge by creeping up the central tower every night to remove the last stone, thus ensuring that the bridge would never be finished. If you look carefully at the top of the tower's east face, you'll see a little devil, which was added when Pont Valentré was renovated in 1879.

Maison de l'Eau

Chemin de la Chartreuse • Charge • 05 65 24 09 15

At the west end of the Pont Valentré, the old **Maison de l'Eau** pumping station is now home to a small museum detailing the bridge's history. Most of the information is in

> **LES JARDINS SECRETS**
>
> A quirky way to unearth Cahors' history is to find the **Jardins Secrets**, a series of around thirty gardens making use of otherwise vacant patches of land dotted around the old town and the river. Medicinal herbs, vines and fruit orchards all feature, laid out as they would have been by monks or local gardeners. Pick up a map of the garden locations from the tourist office (see page 192) or at the boat-tour ticket booths near Pont Valentré; all the descriptions are in English.

French, but you can pick up a leaflet that has the basics in English. Glass floors show off the pumping mechanism below, while the café makes for a pleasant, if rather pricey, riverside spot.

Mont St-Cyr

All around Cahors rise the dry, scrubby uplands of the *causse*. These valley-sides were carpeted with vines from Roman times until the nineteenth century when phylloxera set in, after which the land was used for grazing sheep; now, however, only the lines of tumbled-down stone walls and abandoned farmhouses remain. One of the few landmarks around is the red-and-white TV mast on the summit of **Mont St-Cyr**, overlooking Cahors to the southeast. At 264m, this is the place to head for bird's-eye views of the town: the division between medieval and seventeenth-century Cahors becomes very apparent from the summit, particularly in summer when tree-lined boulevard Gambetta picks out the former course of the ramparts.

It's a stiff but straightforward **climb to the summit** of Mont St-Cyr. From the southern end of boulevard Gambetta, cross Pont Louis-Philippe, then take the steps behind the Virgin's statue and keep going up for about twenty to thirty minutes. Though you can drive, it takes almost as long, as the road winds for about 5km among stunted oaks and pines across the plateau. Apart from the views, there are picnic tables at the top and a summer-only café-bar.

Cahors Plage

Place des Acacias • First week of July to second week of Aug daily 1pm–7pm • Free

Landlocked Cahors might be miles from the coast, but in high season you can still cool off at the free riverside **Cahors Plage** beside Pont Louis-Philippe. The lively beach comes complete with imported sand, straw parasols and picnic tables, while beach bars and a bouncy castle make it the perfect spot for families on a sunny afternoon.

ARRIVAL AND DEPARTURE — CAHORS

By train The *gare SNCF* sits 500m northwest of the centre of town, on place Jouinot-Gambetta.
Destinations Brive (7–12 daily; 1hr 10min); Gourdon (6–10 daily; 30min); Montauban (up to 16 daily; 45min–1hr); Paris-Austerlitz (5 daily; 5–6hr); Souillac (6–10 daily; 45min); Toulouse (7–14 daily; 1hr 25min).

By bus The *gare SNCF* is the terminus for many buses, while others stop on place de Charles-de-Gaulle at the north end of rue de la Barre. The tourist office (see page 192) stocks bus timetables.
Destinations Albas (30min); Bouziès (30min); Cajarc (1hr); Figeac (1hr 45min); Fumel (1hr–1hr 15min); Luzech (20min); Monsempron-Libos (1hr 15min–1hr 30min); Puy-l'Évêque (45min); Tour-de-Faure (40min); Vers (15–20min).

By car The most convenient places to park are in the Parking de l'Amphithéâtre under the allées Fénelon or on place Charles-de-Gaulle.

GETTING AROUND

Car rental Avis, opposite the train station on av Jean-Jaurès (http://avis.fr).

Taxis There are taxi stands outside the train station and on bd Gambetta, or call Allô Taxi (05 65 22 19 42). Uber (http://uber.com) is also in operation in Cahors.

Bike, kayak and boat rental V-lot, just south of the

Pont Valentré on Quai Valentré (http://v-lot.fr) rents bikes and electric bikes plus saddle-bags, trailers and emergency phones. Alternatively, Base Nautique (July & Aug only; http://antinea-lot.fr) in Douelle, about 10km west of Cahors, rents bikes for €19 per day, plus kayaks, pedalos and motorboats.

INFORMATION AND TOURS

Tourist office Cahors' tourist office (Nov–March Mon–Sat 9.30am–12.30pm & 2–6pm; April, May & Oct Mon–Sat 9am–12.30 & 1.30–6.30pm; June–Sept Mon–Sat 9am–7pm, Sun 10am–6pm; 05 65 53 20 65, http://tourisme-lot.com) occupies a handsome building on the north side of place François-Mitterrand. It provides detailed walking maps of the town, and can help booking tours and wine tasting sessions.

Boat rental and tours Babou Marine (http://babou-marine.fr) rents motor-boats for up to twelve people. Croisières Fénelon (http://bateau-cahors.com) puts on a varied programme of excursions such as a day-trip to St-Cirq Lapopie which includes a meal. There are ticket booths for both companies beside the Pont Valentré jetty.

Canoe tours Departing from the jetty below Pont Valentré, Safaraid (http://canoe-kayak-dordogne.com) offers half- and full-day tours around the Cahors meander of the Lot, with English commentary.

ACCOMMODATION   SEE MAP PAGE 187

Cahors has a broad range of **hotels** and some good options for those on a budget, although the choice, particularly in the middle price categories, is not particularly inspiring. Instead, there's better value for money in the surrounding region, though you'll need your own transport to get there.

CAHORS

La Chartreuse Chemin de la Chartreuse, http://hotel-la-chartreuse.com. Modern, minimalist rooms and a prime riverside location just a 5min walk from the city centre make *La Chartreuse* a good choice. There's also a pool, terrace and a well-appointed restaurant serving evening *menus*. €€

Coin des Halles 30 place St-Maurice, http://lecoindeshalles-hotel.com. Right in the heart of the old town in the corner of the market square, this hotel offers clean, bright rooms, though some are a little on the small side. The bar-restaurant teems with life all day long. €

Terminus 5 av Charles-de-Freycinet, http://balandre.com. Housed in a nineteenth-century bourgeois residence and once one of Cahors' grandest hotels, *Terminus* is looking a little scuffed around the edges these days. Nonetheless, the rooms are spotless and spacious, staff are exceedingly friendly and quirky touches like a piano on the landing help make it nostalgic rather than shabby. The excellent in-house restaurant *Le Balandre* is reason alone to stay. €

AROUND CAHORS

Camping Rivière de Cabessut Rue de la Rivière, http://cabessut.com. Three-star campsite in a quiet spot beside the river just over 1km from Cahors across Pont de Cabessut; facilities include a shop, snack bar, small swimming pool and canoe rental. €

Château de Mercuès Mercuès, http://chateaudemercues.com. High on its promontory 6km to the northwest of Cahors, this thirteenth-century castle was once the residence of the bishops of Cahors. It is now a glamorous four-star hotel with pool, tennis courts, excellent wine cellars (free tastings for guests in July & Aug) and a good restaurant with evening *menus*. €€€€

Le Clos Grand 12 rue des Claux Grands, Labéraudie, http://leclosgrand.fr. Cahors' best budget option is located in Pradines, a suburb 5km northwest of the city. It's a welcoming spot, with a pool, a pleasant shady garden and en-suite rooms equipped with balconies or small terraces. The restaurant is also a popular haunt of locals, serving good-value *menus* at lunch. €

EATING   SEE MAP PAGE 187

Cahors has no shortage of good places to **eat**, many of which make full use of the excellent local produce. Most are concentrated in the streets of the medieval town, though you'll also find **brasseries**, **pizzerias** and **cafés** along boulevard Gambetta. There are also plenty of boulangeries and pâtisseries, and the *halles* has a splendid *fromagerie*.

★ **Auberge des Gabares** 24 place Champollion, 05 65 53 91 47. A rare find in the city, this authentic family-run *auberge* serves up rustic country cuisine on a wisteria-covered terrace overlooking the Lot. There's a single *menu* that changes daily, with the emphasis on hearty, no-fuss cuisine – think tasty soups, casseroles and meat dishes, with generous servings. Weekday *menus* are great value. €

La Balinaise 29 rue Maréchal Foch, http://labalinaise.fr. Beautifully presented Indonesian cuisine with plenty of vegetarian options. The menu changes regularly, but includes specialities like peanut-coated tofu skewers, slow-cooked peppery pork and black rice pudding. €

Bonnie Restaurant 27 place Jean Jacques Chapou, http://bonnierestaurant.fr. A pint-sized restaurant with fixed *menus* (choice of two dishes) served in three to five services. On the last Sunday of the month, it hosts an epic brunch. €

Cuisine Côté Sud 24 place Champollion, http://cuisine-cotesud.com. A small but chic restaurant by the riverside serving above-par cuisine, this is the ideal spot for a stylish

THE WINES OF CAHORS

So dark that they're often referred to as "black wines", the **red wines of Cahors** are by far the most distinctive of the southwestern wines, full-bodied with lots of tannin, and they generally need long ageing to bring out their best: the accepted period is about ten years; longer than that and many are past their peak. The dominant **grape variety** is Malbec (also known as Auxerrois or Cot), which gives the wine its rich tannin content, its colour and its ability to age. Up to thirty percent of another grape variety is permitted for AOC Cahors, usually Merlot and Tanat – Merlot for roundness and aroma, Tanat to help the ageing process. However, most of the very best wines are 100 percent Malbec. The distinctive bite of a young Cahors wine goes well with charcuterie and stews, while the more aromatic older wines usually accompany red meats, game and the local goat's cheese, *Cabécou*.

VINEYARDS

There are approximately 43 square kilometres under vines in the *appellation*, which stretches from Cahors west along the Lot for 30km to Soturac, producing on average 240,000 hectolitres (roughly 32 million bottles) per annum. Before **visiting the vineyards**, pick up a copy of the free *Cahors and La Vallée du Lot et du Vignoble*, which details the two hundred or so producers in the *appellation*; it's available from the tourist office and from wine merchants in Cahors (see below).

BUYING AND SAMPLING WINE

In general, you can expect to pay between €10 and €25 for a decent Cahors, although some of the region's prestige wines fetch €70 or more. For an introduction to what's on offer, head for the imposing **Château Lagrézette** (http://chateau-lagrezette.com), 10km northwest of Cahors on the D12 midway between Douelle and Mercuès. In addition to sampling its award-winning wines, you can visit the magnificent, state-of-the-art *chais* dug into the hillside, though it's best to call in advance to arrange this. South of the city, on the N20, the **Atrium** (http://g-vigouroux.fr) outlet sells wines from the Châteaux de Mercuès and arranges vineyard visits. Also worth a visit for its reliably good wines – if not for its ambience – is the **Côtes d'Olt** co-operative (http://vinovalie.com) on the river's south bank about 17km west of Cahors on the D8 in the commune of Parnac. In the city itself, the **Cahors Malbec Lounge** (05 65 23 82 35) on place François-Mitterrand by the tourist office, offers wine-tasting sessions (no reservation necessary).

---

lunch date. Opt for the lamb moussaka. €€

Marie Colline 173 rue Georges-Clemenceau, 05 65 35 59 96. Vegetarian restaurants are in short supply in Cahors, and this one is unsurprisingly popular, so it's best to reserve a table in advance. Choices are limited: two entrées and two main dishes which change daily – but it's all freshly made, using locally grown vegetables. €€

★ **L'O à la Bouche** 56 allées Fénelon, http://loalabouche-restaurant.com. Cahors' favourite fine-dining restaurant occupies a chic open-plan space in the centre of town, with tables billowing out onto place François-Mitterrand in summer. Here you can watch chef Dive conjure up such delectable treats as smoked duck with marinated courgettes and ratatouille terrine. €€€

Les Petits Producteurs 4 place Champollion, http://lespetitsproducteurs.fr. A communal space shared by farmers, winemakers and artisans, there's no better place to sample high-quality produce. Truffles, terrines, tapenades – they're all here, and you can even pick up a gift hamper to go, filled with regional specialities. €

DRINKING AND NIGHTLIFE   SEE MAP PAGE 187

Cahors is not exactly a hub for **nightlife**, but there's more here than meets the eye, especially in season. For events, ask at the tourist office, which publishes lists of the many festivals (see page 186), exhibitions, concerts and plays taking place in the city. Classical concerts are also held in the cathedral.

Le Carré Quai Jean-Lagrive, 90 80 44 48 72. This little nightclub on the east bank of the river plays a mix of French and international pop music, with a crowd mostly of under 30s.

Les Docks 430 allées des Soupirs, http://lesdocks-cahors.fr. Down on the waterfront, *Les Docks* serves as a youth venue, skate park and events space, with live bands playing each Friday.

Le Dousil 124 rue Nationale, http://ledousil.free.fr. This wine bar is a great place to sample local reds before setting off on the wine trail. It dishes up good food, too, including cheese or charcuterie platters, tapas and *tartines*. Wine is sold by the glass or bottle.

ENTERTAINMENT

Grand Palais Cahors Place Bessières, http://cinelegrand palais.fr. Shows a range of international movies and new releases. VF means dubbed in French; VOST is the original version with subtitles.

Théâtre de Cahors Place François-Mitterrand, http://mairie-cahors.fr. For plays, the principal venue is this very plush Neoclassical theatre, which puts on a varied programme of theatre, dance, concerts and opera.

DIRECTORY

Hospital Centre Hospitalier Jean Rougier, 449–335 rue du Président Wilson (05 65 20 50 50). Emergencies should head round the back of the building.

Police Commissariat de Police, 1 rue de l'Ancienne Gendarmerie (05 65 23 17 17).

East along the Lot

Upstream from Cahors, the Lot valley becomes narrower and the cliffs higher. The river is confined to ever-tighter turns and castles sprout from inaccessible knuckles of rock, often with red-tiled villages clinging to their flanks. Delightful **St-Cirq Lapopie**, 30km or so east of Cahors, perched precariously on the edge of a 100m drop, is the most dramatic sight in the whole valley. Further along the river's south bank on the D8, the Renaissance **Château de Cénevières** boasts an interesting history, as well as some unusual frescoes and a good collection of period furniture. The only major settlement along this stretch of river is **Cajarc**, an important market town with an incongruous modern art gallery; the town is also a stop on the pilgrims' road to Santiago de Compostela. Continuing upstream, the scenery takes over once again as the Lot winds its way past more medieval villages and castles, and beneath a 300m-high belvedere, the **Saut de la Mounine**, on the valley's southern lip. There's nothing particular to stop for along the last stretch of river heading northeast to **Capdenac**, near **Figeac**. Instead, you could take a diversion south across the *causse* to where the **Grotte de Foissac** harbours some prehistoric remains alongside a varied and colourful array of stalactites and stalagmites, and then press on across country to the atmospheric ruins of **Peyrusse-le-Roc**.

GETTING AROUND   EAST ALONG THE LOT

The Lot valley is unusually well served by **public transport**, with an SNCF running along the river's north bank from Cahors to Figeac. It stops at almost every village en route, though you'll have to walk across the river to villages on the south side, and will need your own transport to explore the high country on either side.

Vers

Immediately east of Cahors, the Lot valley is taken up with a busy main road, train tracks and scattered modern developments, above which soars the bridge for the A20 *autoroute*. However, things improve dramatically after the village of **VERS**, some 15km upstream, where the main D653 to Figeac strikes off northeastwards. Vers itself doesn't merit a stop, unless you are in search of overnight **accommodation**.

ARRIVAL AND DEPARTURE   VERS

By bus Buses stop near *La Truite Dorée* hotel.

ACCOMMODATION AND EATING

La Truite Dorée Rue de la Barre, http://latruitedoree.fr. At the entrance to the village overlooking the River Vers where it flows into the Lot from the north, *La Truite Dorée* is the most attractive accommodation option in Vers. Rooms in the modern annexe have balconies over the river and there's an excellent restaurant, much patronized by locals. €€

Bouziès

East of Vers, the D662 hugs the north bank of the River Lot as it meanders back and forth beneath cliffs that loom ever higher as you near **BOUZIÈS**, located on the south bank across a narrow suspension bridge. The main reason for coming here is to walk along the **chemin de halage**, a towpath cut into the cliff just above water level on the river's south bank. In pre-railway days it was used by men hauling produce-laden *gabares* boats upstream; it now forms part of the GR36 long-distance footpath, indicated by red-and-white markers, which you can join at the car park on the east side of Bouziès. The rock-hewn section starts after about 500m and extends for some 300m; if you're feeling energetic, you can then continue on to St-Cirq Lapopie (see page 195).

Another way of exploring the riverbank is to take to the water. Bouziès is a **boating** and **canoeing** centre, with several companies setting up shop on the south side of the bridge in the summer.

ARRIVAL AND ACTIVITIES — BOUZIÈS

By bus SNCF buses stop on the main road near the bridge. Destinations Cahors (45–50min); Cajarc (40min); St-Cirq Lapopie (10min).

Boat rental You can hire canoes from various outlets along the river during the summer months (check http://tourisme-lot.com).

ACCOMMODATION AND EATING

Les Falaises Le Bourg, http://hotel-falaises-bouzies46.fr. The sole choice if you want to stay in Bouziès, *Les Falaises* offers clean albeit outdated rooms, a swimming pool and a decent restaurant right in the village centre. €

St-Cirq Lapopie

The gravity-defying village of **ST-CIRQ LAPOPIE** sits 5km east of Bouziès, clinging to the cliffside above the south bank of the Lot. Blessed with quaint cobbled lanes, half-timbered houses and gardens virtually unspoilt by modern intrusions, it's easy to see how it earned itself the title of *Village préféré des Français* ("France's favourite village") back in 2012, though the honour has since been passed on to Cordes-sur-Ciel. Today, St-Cirq remains an irresistible draw for visitors and tour-bus crowds overwhelm its narrow streets during the summer months, but it's still worth the trouble, especially if you visit early or late in the day.

With a warren of alleyways snaking off from a single main street, St-Cirq is easy to navigate: simply follow the steep **rue de la Peyrolerie** downhill between the medieval gates of Porte de la Peyrolerie and Porte de Pélissaria, in between which it's variously known as **rue Droite** and **rue de la Pélissaria**. Along the way, stop off to stroll the central square, **place du Sombral**, where a small market is held on Wednesday mornings throughout summer, and admire the jumble of stone and half-timbered houses with their steeply pitched and gabled Quercy roofs.

Brief history

There has been a **castle** on this rocky protuberance, known as **La Popie**, since Gallo-Roman times, if not before. It was such a strategically important site that in the Middle Ages it was owned by not only the viscount of St-Cirq but also the other three viscounts of Quercy (Gourdon, Cardaillac and Castelnau). A feudal town soon grew up within the protection of its walls, although it wasn't a particularly safe haven: St-Cirq took a battering from the English during the Hundred Years' War, while in the Wars of Religion it was seized by the Protestant Henry of Navarre, who ordered the castle to be destroyed in 1580 to keep it from the Catholics. Undaunted by these events, local craftspeople built up a reputation for their skill in **wood turning**, specifically of boxwood, which they fashioned into goblets, furniture and taps for casks. They continued to ply their craft into the nineteenth century, but following industrialization

St-Cirq went into steep decline until it was rediscovered in the early twentieth century by the artistic fraternity, most famously **Henri Martin** (see page 190), **Man Ray** and the surrealist poet **André Breton**, who came to live here in the 1950s. The fame of St-Cirq has been spreading ever since.

Château and Église St-Cirq

The first place to seek out in St-Cirq Lapopie is the ruined **château** to the north of place du Sombral. Precious little remains of the castle, but the site is fantastic, plunging down to the river 100m below. Further east along the cliff edge, the fortified **Église St-Cirq** is now the village's dominant building. It's in a pretty sorry state itself, though you can still make out faint traces of thirteenth-century murals where the original Romanesque chapel was incorporated into a larger church three hundred years later.

Musée Rignault
Le Bourg • Charge • http://musees.lot.fr

Below the Église St-Cirq, to the east, the **Musée Rignault** occupies a lovely fortified mansion with a romantic little rock garden and various other embellishments added by an art dealer who came to live here in 1922. A few pieces of his wide-ranging art collection are on display, while the rest of the space is given over to temporary exhibitions.

Maison Daura
Le Bourg • Free • 05 65 40 78 19

Maison Daura, near the entrance to St-Cirq Lapopie, was once the home of Catalan painter **Pierre Daura**. It's an exceptionally beautiful example of Gothic architecture, with archetypal windows and perfectly preserved doors, a fit setting for the purpose it now serves – a residence for international artists. It hosts frequent **modern art exhibitions**, which are open to the public and well worth a look; the tourist office will have all details of what's on.

ARRIVAL AND INFORMATION ST-CIRQ LAPOPIE

By bus Buses on the Cahors–Figeac route drop you across the river from St-Cirq in the hamlet of Tour-de-Faure; from here you can call a taxi (Philippe Merle; 06 03 15 41 67) or leg it up the steep hill for the last 2km.

By car There are three car parks for St-Cirq: the lowest, 800m below the village, is free; the one closest to the village centre charges; as does the third, which sits 300m above the village.

Tourist office Place du Sombral (April, May & Oct Mon–Sat 10am–1pm & 2–6pm, Sun 11am–1pm & 2–5pm; June & Sept daily 10am–6pm; July & Aug Mon–Sat 9.30am–7pm, Sun 10am–6pm; Nov–March Mon–Sat 9.30am–12.30pm & 2–5.30pm; 05 65 31 31 31, http://tourisme-lot.com); staff can furnish you with a handy English-language walking guide to St-Cirq.

Activities Kalapca Loisirs (http://kalapca.com) at the *Camping de la Plage* (see below) offers a host of different activities, including canoeing, guided walks, rock climbing and canyoning.

ACCOMMODATION

There are various **accommodation** options in the village itself, all of which get booked up weeks ahead in summer. The best bet if you don't have a pre-booked room is to look in **Tour-de-Faure**, on the other side of the river.

Auberge du Sombral Place du Sombral, http://lesombral.com. Spotless, albeit sparsely furnished, rooms in the heart of the village, plus a decent restaurant. €

Camping de la Plage http://campingplage.com. Well-run three-star campsite down by the bridge, offering a restaurant/snack bar and canoe and bike rental. €

Les Gabarres Le Roucayral, http://hotellesgabarres.com. The functional rooms at this hotel in Tour-de-Faure are more than compensated for by friendly, welcoming staff and a wonderful setting including a pool, flower-filled terrace and garden. For a nominal extra charge, you can upgrade to a room with a kitchenette. €

Maison Redon La Combe, http://maisonredon.com. A quiet and peaceful *chambre d'hôte* in an ivy-covered house, with five spacious, well-appointed rooms and a lovely garden. €

Le Mas de Laval http://masdelaval.fr. Some 3km southeast of St-Cirq, this charming *chambre d'hôte* is full of rustic charm, plus there's a large pool, delicious all-organic cuisine (reservations required) and horseriding tours available. Rates by the week only. €€€

★ **St-Cirq** Tour-de-Faure, http://hotel-lesaintcirq.com. St-Cirq's most lavish hotel is perched at the top of the valley, offering spectacular views over the town. There are a range of well-furnished rooms and romantic suites to choose from, plus an indoor pool, hamam and spa. Free shuttles to the village are also available. €€

La Truffière http://camping-truffiere.com. A spacious, well-managed campsite on the plateau 3km southeast of St-Cirq via the D42. There's a restaurant (July & Aug only), plus a heated pool and children's play area. €

EATING

The nearest food shop is a small grocer down in Tour-de-Faure. If you're self-catering you might like to head 12km south to the charming little town of Limogne where you'll find everything you need, including a Sunday morning **market**.

★ **Le Cantou** Rue de la Pélissaria, 05 65 35 59 03. St-Cirq's top restaurant offers limited options but executes each dish to perfection, blending some unusual ingredients into tasty creations. Tuck into green asparagus and pesto panna cotta, savour monkfish in a coconut-milk sauce, then indulge in gingerbread and walnut tiramisu. €€

Le Gourmet Quercynois Rue de la Peyrolerie, http://legourmetquercynois.com. Take a table on the leafy terrace or cosy up by the open fire at this traditional restaurant and enjoy dishes such as pork with honey and herbs, or duck with truffles. €€

Lou Bolat Just inside Porte de la Peyrolerie, http://loubolat.fr. Reliably good food with a terrace overlooking the valley and a choice of crêpes, omelettes and salads on offer, as well as home-made ice creams in the summer months. €

Château de Cénevières

Charge • http://chateau-cenevieres.com • The nearest bus stop is in St-Martin-Labouval, a good 1km downstream and across on the north bank

Seven kilometres out of St-Cirq Lapopie, along the quiet D8 road (avoid the main D662), is the **Château de Cénevières**, perched on a rocky spur just beyond Cénevières village. The château, which largely dates from the sixteenth century in its present form, belonged to the **de Gourdon** family for nine hundred years until the line petered out in 1616. The last in line, Antoine de Gourdon, was a fervent supporter of the Reformation, so much so that the Protestant leader Henry of Navarre stayed here before attacking Cahors in 1580. Antoine brought back a rich haul that included the cathedral's principal altar – the boat carrying it, however, capsized and the altar is now somewhere at the bottom of the Lot. The château was saved from being torched during the Revolution by a quick-thinking overseer who opened the wine cellars to the mob, though he couldn't save the library, nor the coat of arms and other carvings on the facade. Cénevières was sold only once during its long history, to the ancestors of the present owners in 1793. Over the years they have uncovered several unusual Renaissance-era **frescoes**: notably, a frieze of the Istanbul skyline in the grand salon, and scenes from Greek mythology alongside what is believed to be a representation of an alchemist's fire and the philosopher's stone adorning a little vaulted chamber.

Cajarc

CAJARC, which lies on the river's north bank 9km upstream from Calvignac, is the biggest town on the Lot between Cahors and Capdenac. It consists of a small core of old lanes encircled by the **boulevard du Tour-de-Ville**, where you'll find a cluster of cafés, brasseries and small shops. A lively **market** takes place each Saturday afternoon on place du Foirail, off Tour-de-Ville opposite the tourist office (see page 198), while the town is also the focus of the region's **saffron** production (see page 198), hosting the annual Fête du Safran each October.

Maison des Arts Georges-Pompidou

134 av Germain-Canet • Free • 05 65 40 78 19

Cajarc's only sight as such is the **Maison des Arts Georges-Pompidou**, on the northeastern outskirts on the D19 Figeac road. The gallery is named in honour of the former French president, who bought a holiday home near here in 1963, and hosts three or four major contemporary art exhibitions a year.

THE LOT VALLEY AND AROUND EAST ALONG THE LOT

QUERCY SAFFRON

Saffron was originally introduced to the Quercy region by returning crusaders in the twelfth century, and quickly became a major source of income. However, production of the spice declined drastically in the eighteenth century, largely due to the significant manpower requirements. Obtained from the dried stigmas of the saffron crocus, the spice can only be picked by hand early on autumn mornings. It takes 200,000 flowers and over forty hours' labour to obtain a kilogram of dried saffron, and pound for pound it's more expensive than gold. Historically, the spice has been used in sweet and savoury dishes, particularly in central Asia, as well as for dyeing cloths, as a hangover remedy and to cure tuberculosis and measles. It's also supposed to have cancer-suppressing properties.

Around seventy farms in the Lot valley area now produce saffron commercially, and many of them can be visited, particularly around harvest time in **October**. Their organization's website, http://safran-du-quercy.com, details recipes using saffron, and they host a major **saffron fair** at Cajarc (see page 197) at the end of October to celebrate the harvest, with plenty of opportunities for tasting and buying.

ARRIVAL AND INFORMATION   CAJARC

By bus SNCF buses stop on the north side of town on place du Foirail.
By train The train station is on avenue de la Gare, just north of the riverfront.
Destinations Bouziès (3–6 daily; 40min).

Tourist office Housed in a converted chapel on boulevard du Tour-de-Ville (April Tues–Sat 2.30–6pm; May, June & Sept Mon–Sat 9.30am–12.30pm & 2.30–6pm; July & Aug daily 9.30am–12.30pm & 2.30–6.30pm; 05 65 40 72 89, http://tourisme-lot.com).

ACCOMMODATION

Gîte d'Étape Place du Foirail, 06 14 66 54 89. A great-value *gîte d'étape* with comfortable rooms and individual shower and kitchen facilities on each floor. No wi-fi, and no meals served, but there are restaurants within walking distance. March–Oct by reservation only. €

Maison du Safran 32 bd du Tour-de-Ville, http://alleedesvignes.com. Part bistro (lunchtimes Mon–Sat), part gastronomic restaurant (evenings and Sun lunch), *Maison du Safran* is a swish, modern affair, hung with the works of local artists. Tempt your taste buds with delicacies like wild truffles. €€€

Mas de Garrigue La Garrigue, Calvignac, http://masdegarrigue.com. A few kilometres back from Carjac towards Cahors lies this delightful *chambre d'hôte*, set in a restored fifteenth-century hunting lodge. It offers five beautifully appointed bedrooms, plus evening meals available on Mon and Thurs by reservation only. €€

La Peyrade Rue de Cahors, http://hotel-gite-lapeyrade.fr. This simple, sparsely furnished hotel is nonetheless a welcoming option for budget travellers. As well as rooms there are small apartments sleeping up to four, plus a restaurant. €

La Segalière 380 av François-Mitterrand, 05 65 40 65 35, http://cajarcbluehotel.fr. The smartest hotel in town, around 400m east on the D662 to Capdenac. Expect bright, well-furnished rooms, some with balconies, plus a swimming pool and ample grassy gardens. There's also a decent restaurant. €€

Le Terriol http://campingleterriol.com. A basic two-star municipal campsite, beside the river roughly 200m southwest of the centre. It offers laundry facilities and a communal freezer; the municipal swimming pool is next door. €

Upstream to Capdenac

Upstream from Cajarc, the Lot twists through one more giant meander and then straightens out until you reach the next big loop at Capdenac. Buses follow the northerly route past a succession of picturesque villages and castles, but if you've got your own transport, the less-travelled roads along the river's south bank make for a more interesting journey through walnut orchards and past weathered farm buildings, then up on to the flat, empty *causse* with little sign of habitation, save for the occasional dolmen or *cabane*, the traditional, stone-built shepherds' huts.

A few kilometres further on you drop back down to the river along tiny lanes that wend their way northeastwards for about 15km before hitting the main D922. Turn left here and you'll be in Figeac (see page 202) in about ten minutes. Alternatively, if you cross over and follow the D86 along the river, another 7km will bring you to **CAPDENAC**, a major railway town on the south bank of the River Lot. Capdenac itself is of little interest, but the hilltop enclave of Capdenac-le-Haut is a charming spot full of cobbled lanes and artisan shops, that has been honoured with the title of one of France's *'Plus Beaux Villages'*. The highlight is its hilltop medieval castle, where you can walk the ramparts for a great view, looking out over the town and river to the north.

Grotte de Foissac
Charge • http://grotte-foissac.fr

One of the area's less-frequented caves, the **Grotte de Foissac** lies about 3km west across the *causse* from Foissac village. The cave was discovered in 1959 by a local potholing club, who found not only a huge cavern of colourful and varied concretions – including delicate needles, some bulging out into onion shapes – but also evidence of human activity going back at least four thousand years. From the number of **skeletons** and their positions, it seems that, unusually, the cave was used as a cemetery. It was also a source of clay – you can still see where people dug it out with their hands, and they also left large and beautifully fashioned pots, probably for storing grain. But the most moving evidence is the lone footprint left by a child deep inside the cave.

Peyrusse-le-Roc

Twenty kilometres east of Foissac village, via beautiful back lanes through Naussac and along a scenic brook, the ruined towers of **PEYRUSSE-LE-ROC** are well worth a look. The "modern" village, a tiny weatherworn huddle of half-timbered houses gathered round a seventeenth-century church, sits above a narrow valley. On the valley sides, hidden in the steep woods, lie the scattered remains of a fortified medieval town which once sheltered some 4500 people – a sizeable population in those days – who were seeking their fortunes in the local silver mines. But their luck ran out in the early sixteenth century, when silver from the recently discovered Americas began to flood the market, and the town was eventually abandoned around 1700. The site is gradually being tidied up and some of the buildings restored, but it still remains an atmospheric place.

A path leads from the northwest corner of the church square to a pinnacle of rock crowned by **twin towers**, all that's left of the medieval fortress that protected the town. If you've got a head for heights, you can scramble up the iron ladders for a vertiginous view of the gorge. From here a cobbled mule trail leads steeply down through the woods, where the stones of a Gothic church, synagogue and hospital stand roofless, to the river and a little thirteenth-century chapel, complete but not open to the public. To return to the modern village, follow the river downstream and pick up another path,

> ### THE LEGEND OF MONKEY'S LEAP
>
> Around 7km east of Cajarc, where the D127 first climbs up from the Lot river, the road skirts along the edge of a 300m-high cliff formed by the meander. The spot is known as the **Saut de la Mounine** ("Monkey's Leap"), after a legend concerning a local lord who ordered his daughter to be thrown off the cliff when she fell in love with a boy he disapproved of. A hermit took pity on the girl and secretly dressed a monkey in her clothes instead. When the poor beast was chucked over the edge, the lord of course repented, and was only too relieved to discover he'd been outwitted. He apparently forgave his daughter, but history doesn't relay whom she married. Whatever the outcome, it's a marvellous **view** from up here, taking in the meander filled with patchwork fields and the ruined Château de Montbrun on the far hillside – where the lord and his fortunate daughter once lived.

which takes you past the old market hall to the village gate. It's possible to do shorter circuits simply by following the signs, or you can buy a guidebook and map from the **tourist office** beside the church (Mon–Sat 10am–noon; 05 65 80 49 33).

The Célé valley

Instead of following the River Lot east from Cahors, you can take an alternative route to Figeac along the wilder and narrower **Célé valley**, which joins the Lot 1km or so upstream from Bouziès (see page 195). A single road winds through the luxuriant canyon-like valley, frequented mainly by canoeists and walkers on the GR65 footpath, which runs sometimes close to the river, sometimes on the edge of the *causse* on the north bank. The major settlement along here is **Cabrerets**, a village not far upstream from the Célé's confluence with the Lot, which serves as a base for the nearby cave system of **Grotte de Pech-Merle**. Continuing northeast, the valley is punctuated by a succession of villages and hamlets built against the cliff face. Of these, two in particular stand out: **Marcilhac-sur-Célé**, about halfway along the valley, for the atmospheric ruins of its abbey; and the tiny hamlet of **Espagnac-Ste-Eulalie** in the north, where another, more substantial church sports a delightfully whimsical belfry.

GETTING AROUND   THE CÉLÉ VALLEY

By canoe There's no public transport along the Célé but it's possible to traverse the valley by canoe; rental outlets in St-Cirq and Marcilhac can organize pick-up and drop-off along the river.

Cabrerets

CABRERETS lies 4km up the Célé from its confluence with the Lot, the approach guarded by the sturdy **Château de Gontaut-Biron** (closed to the public), on a small flood plain where the River Sagne joins the Célé. It's a pretty enough spot, but the only real reason to linger in Cabrerets is to take advantage of its tourist amenities.

INFORMATION   CABRERETS

Tourist office There's a small seasonal tourist office in the village centre (May Sat & Sun 10am–1pm & 2–6pm; July & Aug Tues–Sat same hours; June & Sept Thurs–Sat same hours; 05 65 31 27 12) that sells handy guides detailing walks in the area.

ACCOMMODATION AND EATING

Auberge de la Sagne http://aubergedelasagne.com. The small, smart and absolutely spotless *Auberge de la Sagne*, 1km west of Cabrerets on the road to the Grotte de Pech-Merle, is perhaps the best of the accommodation options hereabouts. There's a pool, a well-tended garden and a restaurant offering good-quality home cooking. €
Le Cantal Cabrerets, 05 65 31 26 61. Petite and very basic two-star campsite immediately north of Cabrerets on the other side of the Célé. Closed mid-Oct to mid-April. €
Des Grottes Le Bourg, http://hoteldesgrottes.com. Modern, well-furnished rooms with either a bath or shower at this central hotel overlooking the Célé. There's also a pool, a pretty terrace and a good restaurant. €

Grotte de Pech-Merle

Charge • http://pechmerle.com

Up in the hills 3km west of Cabrerets by road, or 1km via the footpath from beside the *mairie*, the **Grotte de Pech-Merle** takes some beating. Discovered in 1922 by two local boys, the galleries are not only full of the most spectacular limestone formations – structures tiered like wedding cakes, hanging like curtains, and shaped like discs or "cave pearls" – but also contain an equally dazzling display of more than five hundred **prehistoric drawings**. To protect the drawings, tickets are restricted to seven hundred per day (it's advisable to book four or five days ahead in July and August, and at least one day ahead at other times; online bookings must be made at least a week in advance), and the guides make sure you're processed through in the allotted time. If possible, it's worth allowing yourself time to visit the **museum**, located beside the ticket office (same hours and ticket as the cave), before your scheduled tour. A twenty-minute film, subtitled in English, provides an excellent overview of Pech-Merle and its prehistoric art.

Chapelle des Mammouths
The Grotte de Pech-Merle's drawings date mostly from the early Magdalenian era (10,000–17,000 years ago), contemporaneous with much of the cave art in the Vézère valley (see page 128), with which they share many similarities. The first drawings you come to are in the so-called **Chapelle des Mammouths**, executed on a white calcite panel that looks as if it's been specially prepared for the purpose; note how the artists used the contour and relief of the rock to do the work, producing utterly convincing mammoths with just two lines. In addition to the mammoths, there are horses, oxen and bison charging head down with tiny rumps and arched tails; the guide will point out where St-Cirq's André Breton added his own mammoth – he was fined but the damage was done.

The horse frieze
After the Chapelle des Mammouths comes a vast chamber containing the glorious **horse frieze**, the oldest of the drawings (at around 25,000 years). Two large horses stand back to back, the head of one formed by a natural protuberance of rock, and their hindquarters superimposed to provide perspective. The surface is spattered with black dots of some unknown symbolic significance and silhouettes of hands, while the ceiling is covered with finger marks preserved in the soft clay. On the way you pass the skeletons of cave-hyena and bears that have been lying there for thousands of years, and, finally, the footprints of an adolescent preserved in a muddy pool some eight thousand years ago.

Musée de l'Insolite
Charge • http://museedelinsolite.com
Don't miss the gloriously eccentric **Musée de l'Insolite** (Museum of the Quirky), situated on the D41 heading up the Célé some 9km from Cabrerets. After about 3km you emerge from a tunnel and are suddenly confronted by old bikes, mannequins and even the shells of cars hanging from the rock face. They belong to a sculptor with an engaging sense of humour, and are mostly based on wordplay and puns in French. There's an outdoor garden and an indoor gallery, both full of bizarre montages fashioned out of tree stumps, old machines and other bits of scrap.

Marcilhac
MARCILHAC, 16km upstream from Cabrerets, is home to the partly ruined **L'Abbaye de Marcilhac** (guided tours by advance booking only; charge). Founded some time prior to the ninth century, this Benedictine abbey had the good fortune to be in charge of the modest sanctuary at Rocamadour (see page 163), in which St Amadour's body was discovered in 1166. The subsequent revenue from pilgrims and benefactors led to a brief golden age, which came to an end when English troops laid waste to the building in the Hundred Years' War. It never really recovered and was abandoned after the Reformation. Entering the abbey from the south, a rather primitive and badly damaged ninth-century Christ in Majesty decorates the tympanum over the ruined door. In the damp interior of the **church** itself are late-fifteenth-century frescoes of the Apostles and another Christ in Majesty, with the local nobility's coats of arms below. The few

religious treasures that survived – such as a seventeenth-century polychrome pietà and a nicely rendered statue of a pilgrim – are now on display in the small **Musée d'Art Sacré** (free) in a handsome half-timbered house immediately west of the abbey church.

INFORMATION AND ACTIVITIES — MARCILHAC

Tourist office The Musée d'Art Sacré (see above) doubles as a seasonal tourist office (mid-June to mid-Sept 10.30am–12.30pm & 2.30–5.30pm; 05 65 40 68 44, http://marcilhac.fr).

Bike and boat rental Passion Aventure (http://location-canoe-cele.com), along the river by the bridge, offers canoe and kayak tours through the Célé valley from €15 per person for a 3hr tour.

Espagnac-Ste-Eulalie

The tiny and beautiful hamlet of **ESPAGNAC-STE-EULALIE** lies about 12km upriver from Marcilhac and is reached via an old stone bridge. Immediately across the bridge, an eye-catching octagonal lantern crowns the belfry of the **Prieuré Notre-Dame-du-Val-Paradis**; visits can be organized via the Mairie on Chemin des Dames (05 65 40 09 17). The building itself is strangely ill-proportioned, a result of the nave being truncated in the Hundred Years' War, which somehow adds to its charm. Inside, apart from a typically over-the-top altarpiece from the Counter-Reformation, the most interesting features are the ornate **tombs** of the church's thirteenth-century benefactor, Aymeric d'Hébrard de St-Sulpice, a local man who became bishop of Coimbra in Portugal, and those of the duke of Cardaillac and his wife, who financed the rebuilding of the choir in the fourteenth century.

ACCOMMODATION AND EATING — ESPAGNAC-STE-EULALIE

Gîte d'Étape http://espagnac-ste-eulalie.fr. An ancient fortified gateway south of the church now houses a *gîte d'étape* offering very good-value accommodation, including dormitories for four or eight people. Kitchen and dining facilities are also available to guests. €

Le Moulin Vieux http://camping-lemoulinvieux.com. A good three-star campsite in Brengues, 3km back downstream from Espagnac. Facilities include a restaurant (July & Aug), pool, mini-golf and canoe hire. €

Figeac

Situated on the River Célé some 70km east of Cahors, **FIGEAC** is a very appealing town with an unspoilt medieval centre that, surprisingly, is not encumbered by tourism. Its principal church, the **Église St-Sauveur**, contains a sumptuous rendition of the Passion of Christ in a side chapel, and there's an excellent **museum** devoted to famed locally born Egyptologist Jean-François Champollion. Apart from these two sights, it's a pleasure just to wander the narrow lanes, lined with a delightful array of houses, both stone and half-timbered, adorned with carvings, ornate colonnaded windows and elaborate ironwork.

Figeac's old quarter sits on the north bank of the Célé, its ramparts and ditches now replaced with a ring of boulevards. From the southern boulevard, the town's main artery and principal shopping street, pedestrianized **rue Gambetta**, leads north from the old stone bridge, **Pont Gambetta**, through place aux Herbes, to **place Carnot**, where a food market is held each Saturday, and to neighbouring **place Champollion**.

Brief history

Like many other provincial towns hereabouts, Figeac owes its beginnings to the foundation of an **abbey** in the early days of Christianity, one which quickly became wealthy thanks to its position on the pilgrim roads to both Rocamadour (see page 163) and Santiago de Compostela. In the Middle Ages the town flourished as a trading centre, exporting wine and woollen fabrics throughout Europe, so much so that the wealthy merchants began to challenge the abbey's authority. In 1302 King Philip IV (the Fair) resolved the issue by sending his representative, the **Viguier**, to bring Figeac directly under royal control. At the same time, he granted the town the all-important right to mint money. Figeac's fortunes declined during the Hundred Years' War, then revived at the time of the Renaissance, but it was the Wars of Religion that pushed it into eclipse. The town threw in its lot with the Protestants in 1576, providing them with an important safe-haven, until it was brought forcefully back into line in 1622. Figeac later became an important centre for tanning hides, and received a further boost with the arrival of the railway in 1862.

During **World War II** the Germans converted Figeac's Ratier metal workshop into a factory churning out propellers for Luftwaffe bombers. When the Resistance destroyed the plant in 1944, more than five hundred local men were carted off to concentration and labour camps, from which at least 120 failed to return at the end of the war. By the 1960s Figeac's old quarter had declined to such an extent that the majority of buildings were

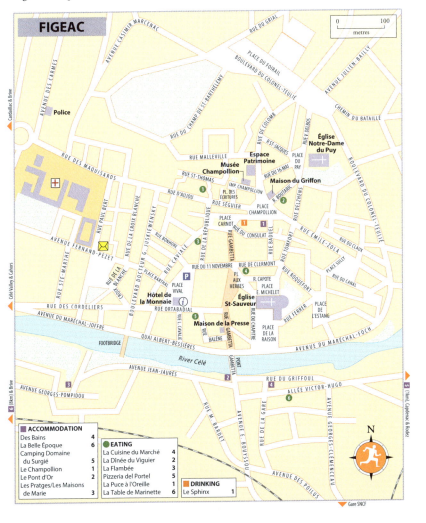

Place Vival and the old quarter

The best place to start exploring Figeac is on **place Vival** to the west of rue Gambetta, where the tourist office occupies the eye-catching **Hôtel de la Monnaie**. The building's origins go back to the thirteenth century when the city's mint was located in this district, and it's typical of Figeac's medieval merchants' houses, starting off with arcaded openings on the ground floor, while the colonnaded and sculpted windows above indicate the living quarters.

Église St-Sauveur

6 rue Ferrer • Free • http://paroissedefigeac.fr

On the eastern side of rue Gambetta, the much-altered **Église St-Sauveur** stands on a big, gravelled square overlooking the river. Its lofty yet restrained nave provides a striking contrast to the intimate **Notre-Dame-de-la-Pitié** chapel, to the south of the choir. The real highlight lies in the chapel itself, which is decorated with heavily gilded but dramatically realistic seventeenth-century carved wood panels depicting the Passion of Christ.

Place Carnot

Cafés spread their tables under the nineteenth-century *halle* in the middle of **place Carnot**, at the top of rue Gambetta, surrounded by a delightful range of stone and half-timbered houses. Some sport open wooden galleries at the top; another typical feature of this region, these *solelhos* were used for drying and storing foodstuffs. On the eastern side lies *Le Sphinx* café, where the father of Jean-François Champollion (see box) had his bookshop, while the *halle* springs to life each Saturday morning, when it hosts a sizeable food **market**.

> ### CHAMPOLLION AND THE ROSETTA STONE
>
> **Jean-François Champollion** was born in Figeac in 1790, the son of a bookseller who opened a shop on place Carnot, in what is now *Le Sphinx* café. His interest in Egypt was first sparked by news coming back from Napoleon Bonaparte's 1798 Egyptian adventures, and when an acquaintance showed him the ancient Egyptians' so-far indecipherable script two years later, he became hooked. Declaring that he would solve the puzzle, Champollion set about studying ancient and Middle Eastern languages – he eventually mastered a mind-boggling total of twenty – and poring over hieroglyphs. One of the most important resources available was the **Rosetta Stone**. A slab of black basalt measuring around 120cm in height and 80cm wide, the stone was discovered in 1799 by French soldiers building fortifications around the town of Rosetta in the Nile delta; three years later it fell into British hands when they seized Egypt from the French, and it now resides in London's British Museum.
>
> The crucial significance of the Rosetta Stone is that the same text – a decree issued in 196 BC recording the honours to be accorded to the young Pharaoh Ptolemy – is repeated in three different scripts: **hieroglyphics**, **demotic** (an abbreviated, cursive form of hieroglyphics used for everyday affairs) and **Greek**. By being able to translate the Greek, scholars then had fresh clues, but it took until 1822 before Champollion made the final breakthrough when he realized that hieroglyphs were, broadly, not pictograms but phonetic characters. Within two years he had identified the majority of symbols, and all this without having set foot in Egypt. He made his one and only voyage to the country in 1828, but died of a stroke four years later at the age of 41.

Place Champollion

Place Carnot opens into the grander but equally alluring **place Champollion**, named after **Jean-François Champollion**, who finally cracked Egyptian hieroglyphics by deciphering the Rosetta Stone (see box). The square's south side is dominated by a stunning, white-stone Gothic mansion with a row of handsome ornamental windows, filled with lacy trefoil stonework. Opposite, on the corner with rue de Colomb, the **Maison du Griffon** is far less ostentatious, but this is Figeac's oldest house, built in the twelfth century and named after a barely visible griffin carved on the left-hand window arch (now blocked up) on the third floor.

Musée Champollion
Place Champollion • Charge • http://musee-champollion.fr

Jean-François Champollion was born in a house off place Champollion, to the northwest of the square, which now contains the fascinating **Musée Champollion**, dedicated not only to Champollion's life and work but also to the history of writing, with displays on Egyptian, Chinese, Mayan and Hebraic systems. In addition to many beautiful examples of hieroglyphic script, the museum houses an excellent collection of Egyptian funerary objects from the sixth and seventh centuries BC: sarcophagi, amulets and statues of the gods and goddesses, such as Bastet, a superb bronze cat, and an exquisitely crafted head of the god-king Osiris.

Place des Écritures

At the west end of impasse Champollion, a gigantic reproduction of the Rosetta Stone – the work of American artist Joseph Kossuth – forms the floor of the tiny **place des Écritures**, above which is a little garden with medicinal herbs and tufts of papyrus in pots. If it's open, you can cut through the **Espace Patrimoine** (free), a one-room exhibition illustrating Figeac's history and architecture, to rue de Colomb.

Église Notre-Dame-du-Puy
1 rue Victor-Delbos • Free • 05 65 50 31 08

The large square tower looming over rue Delzhens is the last vestige of the fourteenth-century residence of the Viguier, royal representative of King Philip IV (the Fair). You'll get a better view of it if you continue on up the hill to the **Église Notre-Dame-du-Puy**. Transformed into a veritable fortress by the Protestants in the late 1500s, then partially destroyed by Catholic reprisals, it now contains little of interest, but its cedar-shaded terrace is a peaceful spot from which to look down on the roofs of Figeac. When you're done, take cobbled rue St-Jacques, twisting and turning down the hillside back to rue de Colomb and place Champollion.

ARRIVAL AND DEPARTURE — FIGEAC

By train Figeac's *gare SNCF* – on the Toulouse–Clermont-Ferrand and Toulouse–Figeac–Brive lines – lies about 600m south of the town centre.
Destinations Assier (4–7 daily; 25min); Brive (5–7 daily; 1hr 20min); Clermont-Ferrand (3 daily; 4 hr); Cordes (4–5 daily; 1hr 20min); Gramat (4–5 daily; 30min); Laguépie (3–5 daily; 1hr); Najac (3–5 daily; 50min); Paris-Austerlitz (1–7 daily; 7hr); Rocamadour (4–5 daily; 40min); St-Denis-lès-Martel (3–5 daily; 55min); Toulouse (9 daily; 2hr 20min); Villefranche-de-Rouergue (3–6 daily; 45min).

By bus SNCF buses stop at the train station. For details of all bus routes, call the central information desk (05 65 53 43 91).
Destinations Bouziès (1hr 10min); Cahors (1hr 45min); Cajarc (30–35min).

By car If you're arriving by car, note that the old quarter is largely pedestrianized. The most convenient parking is along the riverbank, where it's free, or on place Vival.

GETTING AROUND AND INFORMATION

Bike rental Office Intercommunal du Sport du Pays de Figeac/Cajarc, 2 av du Général-de-Gaulle (http://

oisgrandfigeac.com).
Car rental ADA, on the road west to Cahors (http://ada.fr); Avis, 1 av Georges-Pompidou (05 65 30 13 10). Both offer station pick-ups on request.
Taxis Bernard Taxis (05 65 50 00 20, http://bernard-taxi.fr).
Tourist office Place Vival, in the *Hôtel de la Monnaie* (April & Sept Mon–Sat 9am–12.30pm & 2–6pm, Sept only Sun 10am–1pm; May, June & Oct Mon–Sat 9am–12.30pm & 2–6pm, Sun 10am–6.30pm; July & Aug daily 9am–7pm; Nov–March Mon–Fri 10am–12.30pm & 2–6pm, Sat 10am–12.30pm & 2–5pm; 05 65 34 06 25, http://tourisme-lot.com). It sells a do-it-yourself *Keys to Figeac* guide which follows "keys" marked around the city.

ACCOMMODATION   SEE MAP PAGE 203

Des Bains 1 rue du Griffoul, http://hoteldesbains.fr. Far nicer than its two stars would lead you to believe, *Des Bains* is one of the best choices in town for well-priced, central accommodation. Rooms are spotless and the more expensive ones have a/c and balconies. What makes the hotel special, though, is the friendly and energetic hosts, who are a mine of information about the local area. €

★ **La Belle Époque** Le Coustal, Camboulit, 05 65 40 04 42. Buried deep in the heart of the countryside, off the D19 7km southwest of Figeac, this fabulous *chambre d'hôte* is a home away from home, set on a restored seventeenth-century farm. The five individually decorated rooms are full of artful touches, with doors opening out onto the tranquil garden, where camping spots are available. There's also a pool and an acclaimed restaurant where highlights include succulent *filet mignon de porc* and the sublime profiteroles. €

Camping Domaine du Surgié Le Terrier, http://domainedusurgie.com. Well-equipped four-star campsite 2km east of Figeac on the riverside that has a restaurant, a good shop, several pools and a leisure programme in high season. €

Le Champollion 3 place Champollion, 05 65 34 04 37. This welcoming place offers ten surprisingly modern en-suite rooms above a popular café right in the centre. Try and snag one of the two rooms overlooking the square. €

Le Pont d'Or 2 av Jean-Jaurès, http://hotelpontdor.com. Traditionally decorated with spick-and-span rooms and spacious bathrooms, this well-situated hotel offers a restaurant bar, rooftop pool and gym. For the best views, opt for a room with a balcony overlooking the riverfront. €€

Les Pratges/Les Maisons de Marie 6 av Jean-Jaurès, http://maisonsdemarie.com. These five charming *chambre d'hôte* rooms and six well-equipped *gîtes* set in tranquil grounds make an excellent alternative to the city centre. There's also a pool, and a small park on the doorstep. €€

EATING   SEE MAP PAGE 203

Figeac's old centre offers plenty of choice, with **restaurants** serving everything from pizza to haute cuisine. For picnic food, there's a handy supermarket on the corner of rue Gambetta and rue de Clermont, and the charcuterie at 20 quai Bessières sells a wide range of salads as well as meats.

La Cuisine du Marché 15 rue de Clermont, http://lacuisinedumarchefigeac.com. A family-run fine-dining establishment, serving fresh local produce, as the name suggests. Menus change with the seasons and feature regional specialities like Quercy lamb and smoked wild salmon. €€€

★ **La Dînée du Viguier** 52 Rue Emile Zola, http://mercure-viguierfigeac.com. A luxurious setting, impeccable service and a menu of timeless French gastronomy add up to make this one of Figeac's top restaurants. Reservations are essential. €€€€

La Flambeé 28 rue Caviale, 05 65 34 72 12. Tuck into delicious chargrilled meats and pastas, or sample more adventurous dishes like *escargots* or shrimp flambéed in whisky at this popular local haunt. The *menus* are great value, but beware: it gets busy, so it's best to book ahead. €€

Pizzeria del Portel 9 rue Ortabadial, http://restaurant-delportel.net. Pizza isn't the only option at this lively central restaurant, although they are an excellent choice – there are also generously portioned salads and no fewer than seven varieties of *moules-frites* including pesto and Roquefort. The outside terrace is an added bonus. €

★ **La Puce à l'Oreille** 5 rue St-Thomas, 05 65 34 33 08. Located north of place Carnot in a handsome fifteenth-century residence with an interior court for fine weather, and walls adorned with work by local artists, this place serves rich Quercy fare, including succulent pan-fried lamb. Make sure you leave room for one of its indulgent desserts – the lemon tiramisu is a hit. There's an extensive regional wine list. €€€

La Table de Marinette 51 allée Victor-Hugo, http://restaurant-table-marinette.fr. It's worth venturing both across the river to this stylish Art Deco restaurant. *Menus* include some tasty meat and fish dishes – the veal is particularly good. Plenty of vegetarian options are on offer too. €€€

DRINKING   SEE MAP PAGE 203

Le Sphinx 7 place Carnot, 05 65 40 25 54. An elegant cocktail bar situated right on the market square, *Le Sphinx* makes the ideal spot for a post-sightseeing *apéro*. There's also a decent selection of traditional food with *menus*.

DIRECTORY

Hospital Centre Hospitalier, 33 rue des Maquisards (05 65 50 65 50).

Police Commissariat de Police, Cité Administrative, place des Carmes (05 65 50 73 73).

The Causse de Gramat

After the intimate beauty of the Lot and Célé valleys, the wide horizons of the **Causse de Gramat** to the north make a refreshing change. It's an empty land with few people or villages, filled only with the sound of sheep bells and the cicadas' persistent clamour during the tinderbox-dry summers. Across the gently undulating landscape of scrubby pines and oaks, and close-cropped grass spattered with orchids and aromatic plants, you'll come across dolmens, shepherds' dry-stone huts and strange *lacs de St-Namphaise* – water holes hacked out of the rock – but little else to make you want to stop. The exceptions are mostly along the *causse*'s southern boundary, starting off in the far southeast with **Assier**, a small village put on the map by a vainglorious military man who built a château and church here. From Assier the route tracks westwards through a series of picturesque villages to the even more diminutive **Caniac-du-Causse**, last resting place of the hermit St Namphaise. At Caniac the route turns northwards into the wildest part of the *causse* towards the busy market town of **Gramat**, home to an above-average wildlife park.

GETTING AROUND · CAUSSE DE GRAMAT

Assier and Gramat both lie on main train lines, but to do the *causse* justice you really do need your own means of getting about. With few roads and only a sprinkling of villages, this is a great area for walking or mountain biking; most tourist offices have maps of recommended routes.

Assier

If it weren't for the immoderate – and immodest – nature of Galiot de Genouillac, **ASSIER**, some 17km northwest of Figeac, would probably have remained an insignificant village. Chief of artillery under François I and an inspired tactician, de Genouillac earned his stripes during the decisive French victory at Marignano in 1515 during the Italian wars, after which he returned to his native village bathed in glory to erect a **château** befitting his status.

You can get a better idea of de Genouillac's decorative tastes from the **Église Saint-Pierre**, which he also had built in the village square. It's an extraordinary edifice, not just because of its size and the feeling that it was built to the glory of de Genouillac rather than God, but mainly due to a frieze running round the exterior depicting Roman centurions, guns being hauled across the Alps, flame-spewing cannon and cities under siege – all beautifully realized but hardly normal church ornamentation. Less surprisingly, the most interesting feature inside is the great man's tomb in an intricately vaulted chapel near the west door. He appears twice: as a bearded man lying with his feet on powder sacks, and as a soldier leaning nonchalantly against a cannon.

Château d'Assier

Charge · http://assier.monuments-nationaux.fr

Built in the latest Renaissance style, the **Château d'Assier** was said to rival the châteaux of the Loire, with its vast interior courtyard flanked by four round towers, its galleries, loggias and carved friezes – and liberal repetition of de Genouillac's motto: *J'aime fortune* ("In love with chance/success"). After 1768, however, the château and its contents were sold off lock, stock and barrel to raise money, leaving only part of the west wing – and even that is in a pretty poor state. It's still worth taking a peek inside, where there are some wonderful frescoes to admire.

ARRIVAL AND INFORMATION ASSIER

By train Assier is a stop on the main Figeac–Brive train line. The *gare SNCF* lies nearly 1km west of the village. Destinations Brive (9–10 daily; 1hr); Figeac (4–7 daily; 25min); Gramat (3–8 daily; 10–15min).

Tourist office On the northeast corner of place de l'Église (mid-June to mid-Sept Mon–Sat 10am–12.30pm & 3–6pm; 05 65 40 50 60).

EATING

L'Assiérois http://lassierois.com. This humble country restaurant offers evening and lunchtime *menus*. Dishes focus on local seasonal ingredients but there are also a few surprises such as shrimp with a Thai-style ginger sauce, and a mojito sorbet. €€

The southern causse

With your own transport, you can take a circuitous route from Assier through **the southern causse** before cutting northeast to Gramat. There are a few scattered sights to aim for, but on the whole it's the scenery that takes precedence in this high, open country with its grand vistas.

Five kilometres southwest of Assier on the D653, **LIVERNON** is the first of a string of attractive villages, in this case distinguished by a particularly appealing Romanesque belfry, with its rhythmically spaced arches. The route then meanders further south via **ESPÉDAILLAC** – a cluster of crumbling towers and pigeon-lofts – to **QUISSAC**, roughly 10km from Livernon. The main claim to fame of this tiny village is that the ninth-century soldier-turned-hermit **St Namphaise** lived in a nearby grotto. He's a very important person on the *causse*, since it was he who, according to legend, dug the shallow ponds in the rock that are characteristic of this region, thus providing water for flocks of sheep; ironically, he is said to have been killed by an irate bull. There's a statue of Namphaise dressed as a soldier in Quissac church, and you can see one of his famous *lacs* about 1km south of the village beside the Coursac road.

The dying Namphaise supposedly threw away his hammer – with which he presumably created the ponds – and declared that he would be buried wherever it came to rest; it landed 8km away in what is now the village of **CANIAC-DU-CAUSSE**. It's a sleepy, flowery place, undisturbed by the trickle of visitors coming to view Namphaise's small, unadorned sarcophagus lying in a diminutive twelfth-century crypt beneath the village church.

From Caniac cut north across country on the D42, keeping a lookout on the right for signs down a dirt track to the **Site de Planagrèze**, a couple of kilometres later. At the end of the track various footpaths and biking trails strike out across the *causse*, while one of the more accessible dolmens stands a short walk south. On the way you pass a fenced-off area, in the middle of which is another typical feature of the *causse*, a limestone sinkhole, the **Igue de Planagrèze**; in this particular case potholers have so far explored 800m of tunnels.

From here the D42 continues north to Fontanes-du-Causse, where there's a choice of routes to Gramat: you can either stick to the back lanes, or cut west to the faster D677.

Gramat

The biggest town on the *causse*, and its capital, **GRAMAT** developed at the junction of two major Roman roads. Its fortunes increased further when pilgrims started passing through en route to Rocamadour (see page 163), and it received another boost when the railway came here in 1863. Even today it's an important market town, with two weekly **markets** (Tues and Fri morning) and bigger *foires* on the second and fourth Thursdays of each month. Though a few vestiges of the medieval town remain, Gramat is mostly of interest as somewhere to base yourself for a day or so; as well as being an ideal starting point for exploring the *causse*, it's within easy striking distance of

Rocamadour, only 9km away to the northwest, and fairly convenient for sights in the upper Dordogne valley (see page 156).

Gramat would be more appealing if it weren't for the busy N140 and D677 funnelling through **place de la République**, a big square on the east side of town. If you walk west from here along the **Grande Rue**, though, you'll suddenly find yourself among the narrow lanes of the old quarter. There's not a lot to see here, but both the place de l'Hôtel de Ville, at the top of the Grande Rue, and the market square, south of the Grande Rue down rue Notre-Dame, are attractive corners.

Jardins du Grand Couvent
33 av Louis-Mazet • Charge • http://grandcouventgramat.fr

South out of Gramat, head to the flourishing **Jardins du Grand Couvent**, laid out behind a convent complex. Spread over thirty-odd acres, it's an idyllic spot for a picnic, with ample grassy lawns hemmed in by colourful flowerbeds. As you stroll around the gardens, you can also see the lovely old wash house and bread ovens used by the nuns until fairly recently. It also runs a small shop, a tearoom and offer accommodation.

Parc Animalier de Gramat
Charge • http://gramat-parc-animalier.com

The main reason for most people's visit to Gramat is the **Parc Animalier de Gramat**, a couple of kilometres south of the Jardins du Grand Couvent, on the D14. Encompassing half a square kilometre of the *causse*, the park is home to an unusually varied selection of animals: the 150 mostly European species include wolves, otters, bears, ibex – with their magnificent curved horns – and *mouflon*, a type of goat crowned with four horns. Allow at least two hours if you want to cover the whole park.

ARRIVAL AND INFORMATION — GRAMAT

By train The *gare SNCF* is 1km south of the centre; if no taxis are waiting, call Adgié (05 65 38 75 07 or 06 71 92 67 00).
Destinations Assier (3–8 daily; 10–15min); Brive (6 daily; 50min); Figeac (4–5 daily; 30min); Paris-Austerlitz (1 overnight/6 daily; 6–7 hr); Rocamadour (4–8 daily; 8min); St-Denis-lès-Martel (4–8 daily; 25min).
Tourist office Place de la République (April–June, Sept & Oct Mon–Sat 10am–12.30pm & 2–6pm; July & Aug Mon–Sat 9.30am–1pm & 2–6.30pm; mid-July to mid-Aug Sun 10am–1pm; 05 65 33 22 00, http://tourisme-lot.com).

ACCOMMODATION AND EATING

Le Centre Place de la République, http://lecentre.fr. Bold artworks and pops of colour lend a cheerful vibe to the otherwise rather basic rooms at *Le Centre*. It's nonetheless comfortable, friendly and good value, plus there's a decent on-site restaurant, with evening *menus*. €€

La Cuisine d'Alain 2 rue de la Liberté, http://lacuisine dalain.com. Decked out like an American diner with chequerboard floors, a vintage jukebox and Route 66 memorabilia, *La Cuisine d'Alain* offers the perfect setting to dig into a hearty home-made burger and fries. €

Le Grand Couvent 33 av Louis-Mazet, http://grand couventgramat.fr. The historic convent welcomes guests throughout the year with a choice of private rooms or dorms with breakfast included and options for half- and full-board available. Reservations are essential. €

★ **Relais des Gourmands** 2 av de la Gare, http://relais-des-gourmands.com. The most appealing place to stay in Gramat and surprisingly quiet, despite its close proximity to the train station. Rooms are simple but elegant, with wood floors, tasteful colour schemes and modern bathrooms. There's also a well-kept pool, a flowery terrace and an excellent restaurant serving a mix of traditional fare and more creative dishes. €€

Gourdon

Thirty-five kilometres west of Gramat, **GOURDON** is an attractive town, its medieval centre of butter-coloured stone houses attached to a prominent hilltop, neatly ringed by shady modern boulevards, known collectively as the Tour-de-Ville. While it has no outstanding sights, Gourdon makes a quiet, pleasant base, not only for the nearby **Grottes de Cougnac**, with their prehistoric paintings, but also for the **Bouriane** (see page 211) to the south. Gourdon also has good produce **markets** on Tuesdays beside the church in place St-Pierre, and on Saturdays beside the post office.

In July and August, a large farmers' market takes place on Thursday mornings in place St-Pierre, while the Tour-de-Ville is closed off on the first and third Tuesdays of each month for a traditional **country fair**.

The Tour-de-Ville

Where the ramparts once stood, Gourdon's medieval centre is now entirely surrounded by the **Tour-de-Ville**. The best-preserved gateway into the centre is southwesterly Porte du Majou, which stands guard over the old town's main street, **rue du Majou**, lined with mellow stone-built houses, some, like the **Maison d'Anglars** at no.17, with its ogive arches and mullion windows, dating back as far as the thirteenth century; look out on the right, as you go up, for the delightfully – and accurately – named rue Zig-Zag.

At its upper end, rue du Majou opens onto a lovely cobbled square beneath the twin towers of the massive fourteenth-century **Église St-Pierre**. Note the traces of fortifications, in the form of machicolations, over the west door, but you'll find nothing of particular interest inside, beyond some seventeenth-century gilded bas-reliefs by a local sculptor depicting the life of the Virgin Mary. The **Hôtel de Ville** – a handsome if unpretentious building whose arcaded ground floor once served as the market hall – stands on the west side of the square, while east of the church in place des Marronniers an ornately carved door marks the home of the Cavaignac family, who supplied the nation with numerous prominent public figures in the eighteenth and nineteenth centuries.

From the north side of the church, a path leads to the top of the hill where Gourdon's castle stood until it was razed in the early seventeenth century in the wake of the Wars of Religion. At 264m in height, it affords superb **views** over the wooded country stretching north to the Dordogne valley.

ARRIVAL AND INFORMATION GOURDON

By train The *gare SNCF* is located roughly 1km northeast of the old centre. From the station, walk south on avenue de la Gare, then turn right onto avenue Gambetta to come out on the south side of the Tour-de-Ville. If you want a taxi, call Taxi Brice (05 65 32 17 25).

Destinations Brive (4–7 daily; 45min); Cahors (6–10 daily; 30min); Montauban (8 daily; 1hr 10min); Paris-Austerlitz (9 daily; 5hr); Souillac (7 daily; 15min); Toulouse (8 daily; 1hr 45min).

GETTING AROUND AND INFORMATION

Car rental ADA 101 av Gambetta (http://ada.fr).
Tourist office 20 bld des Martyrs (Nov–March & Oct Mon–Sat 10am–noon & 2–6pm; April–June Mon–Sat 9.30am–noon & 2–6pm, Sun 9.30am–noon; July & Aug Mon–Sat 9.30am–7pm, Sun 9.30am–12.30pm; Sept & Oct Mon–Sat 9.30am–noon & 2–6pm; 05 65 27 52 50, http://tourisme-lot.com).

ACCOMMODATION AND EATING

Domaine le Quercy http://domainequercy.com. Well-equipped three-star campsite, 1.5km north of Gourdon on the D704 Périgueux road, set beside a leisure lake with a pool and summer-only restaurant. €

Hostellerie de la Bouriane Place du Foirail, http://hotellabouriane.fr. An elegant choice with spacious rooms and chic decor, this country inn is the best bet in town. There's also private parking and a restaurant serving traditional fare. €

La Promenade 48 bd Galiot-de-Genouillac, http://lapromenade-gourdon.fr. The ten cheerful rooms at this small hotel are immaculate and each follow a different theme. There's also a bar/pub with Guinness on tap, cocktails and tapas, and a well-priced restaurant. €

The Grottes de Cougnac

Charge • http://grottesdecougnac.com

Signed off the Sarlat road a couple of kilometres north of Gourdon, the **Grottes de Cougnac** were discovered in 1949 by a local water-diviner. To begin with, all the subsequent explorers found only rock formations – notably ceilings festooned with ice-white needles like some glitzy ballroom decoration – but three years later they hit gold when they came across **prehistoric paintings**. These date from between 25,000 and 19,000 years ago, when Cro-Magnon people ventured deep inside the caves to paint panels of ibex, reindeer and mammoths in elegant outline, using the rock's undulating surface to provide a sense of form and movement. They also left hundreds of mysterious signs – mostly dots and pairs of short lines – in addition to two human figures seemingly pierced by spears, a motif also found in Pech-Merle (see page 200). The temperature inside is 13°C, so take a coat.

The Bouriane

The tranquil **Bouriane** region lies south of Gourdon, a large and very pretty area of luxuriant woods and valleys merging into neighbouring Périgord, and a striking contrast to the sparse upland *causses* to the east. It's primarily a place to wander, with no particular destination in mind, but anyone interested in twentieth-century art should visit **Les Arques**, in the south of the region, where a number of powerful, sometimes disturbing, sculptures by Russian exile Ossip Zadkine are on display.

Salviac

Some 14km south of Gourdon, the first place of any size along the D673 is the fortified village of **SALVIAC**, whose Gothic church (known as the **Abbaye Nouvelle**) was built in the late thirteenth century by Jacques Duèze of Cahors, the future Pope John XXII, and still contains fine stained-glass windows from that era. It's worth a brief stop for the location as much as anything, but is sadly rarely open to the public; call 05 65 41 25 24 to arrange a visit.

Cazals

Seven kilometres southeast of Salviac, the *bastide* town of **CAZALS** has seen better days: its feudal château and ramparts were largely destroyed during the Hundred Years' War, though its big central square remains, giving the town character and hosting a splendid Sunday **market**. On the southern outskirts there is a small multi-sport leisure lake which doubles as a pleasant spot for a picnic.

Rampoux

From Cazals, you can work your way 9km eastwards through enticing back lanes to **RAMPOUX**. This unusually scattered hamlet is home to a Romanesque priory **church** in which one of the original frescoes can still be seen – a very faded Christ in Majesty in the apse. Better preserved are those from the fifteenth century in the south chapel, portraying the life of Jesus.

Les Arques

LES ARQUES sits buried in the countryside 10km southwest of Rampoux and 6km south of Cazals. It's a higgledy-piggledy village on a hillock above the River Masse, but its main draw is the **Musée Zadkine** (charge, children under 13 free; 05 65 22

83 37). A Russian émigré and well-known sculptor, **Ossip Zadkine** set up a studio in Les Arques in 1934 and worked on and off in the village until his death in 1967, producing big, powerful statues full of restless energy. Many are on a mythological or musical theme, such as those of Orpheus and Diana, the latter metamorphosing from tree to woman, and there's a strong Cubist influence, although Zadkine's work grew more abstract towards the end of his life. Some of his most compelling pieces are displayed inside the Romanesque **Église St-Laurent des Arques** opposite the museum, whose cool stone interior provides the perfect foil for a passionate rendering of Christ on the Cross and, in the crypt, the *Pietà*. During his time in Les Arques, Zadkine also discovered some twelfth-century frescoes in the nearby **Église St-André** – you can get a key from the museum.

EATING — LES ARQUES

★ **La Récréation** http://la-recreation-restaurant.com. In season, it's worth timing your visit to the Zadkine museum in order to have lunch in the old schoolhouse at the entrance to the village, now home to an attractive restaurant. Expect some intriguing flavours, like roasted duck breast with lychee or wild seabass with a pink grapefruit sauce. On Thursday evening in season it knocks up delicious tapas dishes, while cooking classes are also available. Reservations essential. €€€

Goujounac

A good place for an overnight stay or tasty meal, charming little **Goujounac**, with its butter-hued stone houses, lies 5km southwest of Les Arques. Its **Église Saint-Pierre** has rather worn Romanesque carvings of Christ in Majesty and the four Evangelists over the south door.

ACCOMMODATION AND EATING — GOUJOUNAC

Camping 46 Rainettes http://camping46rainettes.com. Good-value three-star campsite immediately west of Goujounac on the D660 Villefranche road. Facilities include a large pool with water slides, tennis, and children's play area, making it an ideal spot for families with young children. There are also cabins for rent. €

Hostellerie de Goujounac http://goujounac.com. Opposite the church, this Dutch-owned hotel with five simple rooms offers honest country cooking, plus a pool and tennis courts available at an extra cost. Reservations advised. €

St-Médard

About 7km southeast of Goujounac, the picturesque medieval hamlet of **St-Médard** sits pillowed against a forested hill. Apart from a renowned restaurant and the twelfth-century church, with its particularly decorative stone stoup, there is little to see, unless you should bump into Leon the peacock – the village pet, and a lordly bird that struts the narrow streets in a regal fashion.

EATING — ST-MÉDARD

★ **Le Gindreau** http://legindreau.com. With a deservedly stellar reputation, this Michelin-starred restaurant is a rare treat for foodies. Sample delights like seafood bisque with a shellfish gratin, or local lamb with Rocamadour cheese, potatoes and pickled pork rind; the desserts in particular are real works of art and include cherries soaked in Cahors wine. Splash out on the reliably brilliant seven-course *menu découverte*. Reservations essential in high season. €€€€

West along the Lot from Cahors

The Bouriane's southern boundary is marked by the River Lot, which follows a particularly convoluted course downstream of Cahors as it doubles back on itself again and again between cliffs that gradually diminish towards the west. Standing guard over one of the larger meanders is **Luzech**, whose main claim to fame is the scant remains of a Roman encampment on the hill above the town. Continuing downstream, the route winds through a series of villages perched above the river, culminating in one of the most beautiful along the entire Lot valley, **Puy-l'Évêque**. A castle-town built on a terraced cliff, it dominates the last of the river's meanders, and its wandering lanes, tunnels, staircases and fountains together compensate for the lack of any first-rate sights. The area around **Duravel**, further west again, with its fine selection of hotels and restaurants, provides a good base for visiting the impressive **Château de Bonaguil** in the hills to the north of the Lot. The last of the medieval castles to be constructed in France, and now partially in ruins, it still bristles with sophisticated defensive devices. Back on the Lot, **Fumel** is a major transport hub and service centre, though otherwise contains nothing to make you dally – better to hurry on downriver to where **Penne-d'Agenais**, with its striking basilica, lords it over the valley.

GETTING AROUND — WEST ALONG THE LOT

Public transport along this stretch of the river consists of an SNCF bus that threads along the valley from Cahors via Luzech, Prayssac, Puy-l'Évêque and Fumel to terminate at Monsempron-Libos, on the Agen–Périgueux train line. On the way it also passes through or close by most of the smaller villages cited below, but you'll need your own transport to reach the Château de Bonaguil and Grézels.

Luzech

Twenty kilometres downriver from Cahors, **LUZECH** is situated on the narrow neck of a particularly large meander in the River Lot, overlooked by a twelfth-century **keep**. Little remains of the fortress beyond a few foundation stones, but it's worth trekking up for a splendid view over the Luzech meander. It's 1.5km by road, or you can walk up in about ten minutes from the north end of rue de la Ville; follow signs for the GR36 footpath past the castle keep and then just keep climbing. For a less strenuous jaunt, head south for about 2km to visit a tiny chapel, **Notre-Dame-de-l'Isle**, surrounded by vines and walnut trees on the very tip of the meander.

The town itself has a small area of picturesque alleys to the north of **place du Canal**, the central square spanning the isthmus.

Maison des Consuls

Grande Rue de la Ville • Charge; joint ticket for Ammonite Collection, Ichnospace and Musée Armand Viré available • 05 65 30 58 47

In the centre of town, you'll find the **Maison des Consuls**, built in 1270. The building is home to the tourist office, as well as two of Luzech's three museums. The first houses a fascinating collection of **ammonites**, dating back millions of years and separated into displays that chronicle their evolution.

The **Musée Armand Viré** displays archeological finds from around Luzech. The majority come from the fortress above the town, which has been occupied since the early Iron Age; the Romans reinforced it and erected a temple on the site, which is now known as the Oppidum d'Impernal.

Though there are some delicate Gaulish safety-pins and needles which, alongside other exhibits, demonstrate the huge leap in craftsmanship ushered in by the Romans in the first century BC: look out for the unusual folding spoon and the coins chopped in half for small change.

Ichnospace

Grande Rue de la Ville • Charge; joint ticket with the Musée Armand Viré and Ammonite Collection available • 05 65 20 17 27

You can continue in the prehistoric vein with a trip to the **Ichnospace** in the *médiathèque*, just north of the tourist office. A must for anyone with an interest in palaeontology, highlights include 140-million-year-old dinosaur footprints from nearby Crayssac and various fossils unearthed in the region, displayed over an area of around sixty square metres.

ARRIVAL AND INFORMATION — LUZECH

By bus Buses from Cahors pull in beside a roundabout at the east end of place du Canal.
Destinations Albas (10min); Cahors (25min); Monsempron-Libos (1hr); Prayssac (25min); Puy-l'Évêque (30min).
Tourist office Maison des Consuls (April–June, Sept & Oct Mon–Fri 9.30am–12.30pm & 2–5.30pm; July & Aug Mon–Sat 9.30am–1pm & 3pm–6.30pm; Nov–Mar Wed–Fri 9.30am–12.30pm & 2–5pm; 05 65 20 17 27, http://tourisme-lot.com).

ACCOMMODATION AND EATING

Gîte d'Étape Luzech, 05 65 30 72 32. A good bet for a stopover if you're walking, this *gîte d'étape* is located just before the bridge to the west of town. As well as basic but comfortable rooms, guests can make use of the kitchen, living area and washing facilities. €

★ **Le Vinois** Caillac, http://levinois.com. Some 10km east of Luzech, in the small village of Caillac, this is a sophisticated hotel with trendy Japanese-inspired decor, a well-tended garden and a pool. The on-site restaurant is also excellent, with the chef whipping up delectable dishes concocted from the best local ingredients. Service, in the restaurant and hotel, is exceptional. The restaurant is also open to non-guests. €

Albas

The prettiest route downstream from Luzech – which is followed by the bus – is the D8 along the River Lot's south bank. It's especially beguiling in summer when the intense green of the vines and walnut trees in the valley bottom is offset against the dark-grey cliffs. The river loops back and forth across the flood plain, with a village at the bottom of each meander. The first you come to, and the most attractive, is **ALBAS**, 5km from Luzech, instantly recognizable by its tall church spire. The church is nineteenth century and otherwise uninteresting, but the steep lanes below retain a few noble fourteenth- and fifteenth-century facades, a reminder of when the bishops of Cahors maintained a residence here. The arched double doors of the houses lining the streets conceal deep cellars, reminders of the days when the Lot was fully navigable and Albas was the main port for Cahors wine; hundreds of barrels were stored here to be shipped downstream to Bordeaux and onwards to the world. At the riverside esplanade you can see the spot where the boats were loaded, and it's here that the biennial **fête du vin** (see page 186) kicks off, with a barrel brought downstream, unloaded and paraded through the village. Cross the river by the narrow bridge and look back up at the village for a view that graces a million postcards.

EATING AND DRINKING — ALBAS

La Rose et Le Réséda 43 rue du fond du pal, 06 99 27 93 95. Friendly little restaurant serving good-value fixed *menus*, and an extensive selection of local wines. It regularly hosts exhibitions featuring the work of local artists. €

Castelfranc

Three kilometres west of Albas, at the little hamlet Le Mayne, the bus turns north to cross the river at engaging little **CASTELFRANC**, a riverside *bastide* village built on a grid pattern around a pretty central *place* by the indefatigable bishops of Cahors. On the northern side of the square lies Castelfranc's main attraction, the thirteenth-century **Église Notre-Dame-de-l'Assomption** with its four-bell *clocher mur*, whilst on the southern side there's a good little restaurant (see below).

Wander a couple of hundred metres further south and you'll find yourself back at the river, where Castelfranc has another surprise attraction, a river beach complete with picnic tables.

EATING AND DRINKING — CASTELFRANC

La Vigne Haute 1 av des Tonneliers, http://lavignehaute.net. A comfortable, traditionally furnished restaurant known for its soufflés and grills, which are executed over a charcoal fire in the dining room itself. €€

Prayssac

Heading west from Castelfranc the road hugs the cliff, affording ravishing glimpses of the fertile Lot valley. After a scant couple of kilometres you roll into the bustling little town of **PRAYSSAC**. It isn't the prettiest town in the valley, nor the most historically interesting, but in summer there's a real buzz about it, with a string of great cafés along the plane-tree-lined place d'Istrie, spilling out over shady pavements. Outside the tourist office is a stern statue of **Maréchal Bessières**, Prayssac's most famous son, born here in August 1768. Bessières was a brilliant commander and a great friend of Napoleon Bonaparte. He died in 1813 after a direct hit from a cannonball, which turned out to be a lucky stroke for Wellington and the allies; Napoleon reputedly asserted that had Bessières been with him he would have prevailed at Waterloo.

The real reason for visiting Prayssac is its main **market**, the best in the area, filling the centre around the place de l'Église and spreading into neighbouring streets every Friday morning. In high summer it's best to leave your car at the side of the road, then walk in and soak up the atmosphere. There's also a lovely **riverside walk** between Prayssac and Castelfranc (around 40min), also useful if you're on foot and want to visit the Castelfranc restaurants from Prayssac, as you can't easily walk along the main road.

ARRIVAL AND INFORMATION   PRAYSSAC

By bus SNCF buses from Cahors stop in the rue du Colonel Pardes in front of the place d'Istrie. From Monsempron-Libos they stop in front of the post office.
Destinations Albas (15min); Cahors (55min); Fumel (25min); Luzech (25min); Monsempron-Libos (35min); Puy-L'Évêque (10min).

Tourist office 3 bd de la Paix (April–June, Sept & Oct Mon 2–5.30pm; Tues–Fri 9.30am–12.30pm & 2–5.30pm; July & Aug Mon–Sat 9.30am–1pm & 3pm–6.30pm; Nov–March Wed–Fri 9.30am–12.30pm & 2–5pm; 05 65 21 37 63, http://tourisme-lot.com).

ACCOMMODATION AND EATING

Prayssac has several options for eating. For picnic food there are two good supermarkets, one on the western outskirts towards Puy-L'Évêque, the other on the southern side opposite the *pompiers*. Boulangeries abound, but the best of the bunch is Lasjournias, on the place d'Istrie. There is also a very good *fromagerie* and delicatessen, next door.

Les Catounes 14 place d'Istrie, 05 65 22 43 43. Possibly the best of the cafés around the *place*, with its courtyard decorated in mellow terracotta and lavished with Mediterranean plants, and a stylish interior that doubles as a boutique. Tables burst out through the gates on market days, so get there early or be prepared for a wait. The food is simple but well executed, with some tasty omelettes and *galettes*. €€

Clau del Loup Métairie haute, Juillac, http://claudelloup.com. A beautifully renovated hotel set among walnut orchards in the hamlet of Juillac, 2km south of Prayssac on the D8. As well as four tastefully decorated rooms, it has a charming garden, a covered pool and a stylish restaurant serving excellent regional dishes. €€

La Vénus Place de la Vénus, http://lavenus-restaurant.com. A reliably good little restaurant with an Italian flavour and some excellent fish and seafood options, situated on the eastern side of town. The chef is French and the waitress English, and *La Vénus* is extremely popular with both French locals and British visitors. €€

Bélaye and Grézels

Around 5km south of Prayssac, just off the D8, lies the precipitous medieval hamlet of **BÉLAYE**, worth a trip for the stunning views of the Lot valley alone. Some 4km further west you arrive at the little village of **GRÉZELS**, another episcopal seat, though in this case its château – a very sober affair – has survived thanks to a seventeenth-century rebuild.

Puy-l'Évêque

On the north bank of the River Lot, and 5km from Prayssac, **PUY-L'ÉVÊQUE** contends with St-Cirq Lapopie (see page 195) as the valley's prettiest village. After 1227 it marked the western extremity of the Cahors bishops' domains and it's the remains of their thirteenth-century **château**, a big square keep like that at Luzech, which provide the town's focal point. Puy-l'Évêque changed hands any number of times during the Hundred Years' War, but then withstood a prolonged Protestant siege in 1580 during the Wars of Religion. Ardent anti-clerics tried to change the name to Puy-Libre during the Revolution, then to Puy-sur-Lot, but the locals weren't convinced, and it soon reverted to Puy-l'Évêque (which loosely translates as "bishop").

There are no great sights to speak of, just lanes of medieval and Renaissance houses built in honey-coloured stone. Beside the castle keep at the top of the town, the **place de la Truffière** is the venue for the main weekly **market** (Tues morning); in summer there's also a small Saturday farmers' market in the lower town on place Georges Henry, at the west end of rue des Platanes. From place de la Truffière, **rue du Fort** leads steeply down then flattens out beneath an imposing fourteenth-century building distinguished by its Gothic windows, which served as the bishops' audience chamber. As it curves round the hill, rue du Fort becomes rue Bovila and then peters out beside a staircase descending to rue des Capucins. This road heads back east along the hillside to **place Guillaume-de-Cardaillac** and then **place de la Halle**, the town's two most picturesque corners. Downhill from place de la Halle again, you come to rue de la Cale, with the dark alleys of the artisans' quarter off to the left, and the old **port** just beyond. For the best **view** of the whole ensemble walk out onto the modern bridge which crosses the Lot here. Alternatively, head for the belvedere in front of the **Église St-Sauveur** that guards Puy-l'Évêque's northeast quarter – literally, since it once formed an integral part of the fortifications; look carefully and you can still see where cannonballs found their target during the siege of 1580.

ARRIVAL AND INFORMATION   PUY-L'ÉVÊQUE

By bus SNCF buses from Cahors stop in front of the church on place du Rampeau and down on rue des Platanes to the southeast of the old centre.
Destinations Albas (15min); Cahors (1hr); Fumel (15–20min); Luzech (25–30min); Monsempron-Libos (20–25min); Prayssac (10min).

Tourist office 12 Grande Rue (July & Aug Mon–Sat 9.30am–6.30pm, Sun 9.30am–1pm & 3–6.30pm; April–June, Sept & Oct Mon–Fri 9.30am–12.30pm & 2–5.30pm, Sat 9.30am–-12.30pm; Nov–March 9.30am–12.30pm & 2–5pm; 05 65 21 37 63, http://tourisme-lot.com).

ACCOMMODATION AND EATING

Belle Vue 10 place de la Truffière, 05 65 36 06 60. Perched on the cliffside with views extending over the valley, this hotel certainly lives up to its name. Room standards vary: older ones look a little faded, while others have been given a contemporary makeover. It's worth dining in the restaurant just for the view. €

★ **Camping Les Vignes**. Some 3km south of Puy-l'Évêque, along the river via the D28 (and signed off the road to the bridge from town), you'll find this superb three-star campsite, with exceptionally friendly owners. There's also a small shop, activities for children such as sports and games, plus canoe rental at the supervised river beach in summer. €

Franck Tonel 49 rue Ernest-Marcouly, 05 65 21 32 56. If you want to try a true local speciality, *Franck Tonel* is the place to go. The eponymous owner, an artisan *boulanger* and *pâtissier*, is renowned for his delicious *tarte aux noix*. €

Henry 23 rue du Docteur Rouma, http://hotel-henry.com. Pleasant rooms at a budget price, though you should try and get one at the back to avoid road noise. The restaurant serves reliable regional cuisine with generous portions and *menus*. €

Le Pigeonnier 1 promenade du Héron, 05 65 21 37 77. A lively café-cum-bistro on the south bank of the river offering huge salads, grills and *galettes*, with an unbeatable view of the village thrown in. €€

Martignac

One of the best excursions from Puy-l'Évêque is to the hamlet of **MARTIGNAC**, 2.5km north, where the much-altered Romanesque **Église St-Pierre-ès-Liens** contains some remarkable late-fifteenth- and early-sixteenth-century **frescoes**; hidden under plaster until 1938, they are reasonably well preserved. Characters on the north wall represent the Seven Deadly Sins being escorted to the mouth of Hell, each mounted on a different animal: Lust on a billy goat, Gluttony scoffing ham and wine and riding a pig, and scruffy Sloth on a donkey bringing up the tail. The Seven Virtues surround the apse, their grey robes tumbling about them, with Courage and Temperance being the easiest to recognize – the former holds a serpent, while Temperance carefully waters down her wine.

Duravel

Downstream of Puy-l'Évêque, the Lot valley begins to open out as the hills along the southern bank fade away. Those to the north continue a while longer, providing a green backdrop for the pretty eleventh-century **Église Saint-Hilarion** at **DURAVEL**, 6km from Puy-l'Évêque. Its crypt contains the remains of no fewer than three saints – Poémon, Agathon and Hilarion, their bodies having been brought back from the Holy Land in the eleventh century. The village is unfortunately spoilt by its busy main road, but it's a lively spot on a Saturday morning when a market is held on the **place de la Mairie**.

ACCOMMODATION AND EATING   DURAVEL

Le Clos Bouyssac http://leclosbouyssac.eu. A quiet, shady and very friendly two-star campsite, located just south of Duravel along the riverbank. Facilities include a small shop and snack bar (July & Aug only), pool, riverside beach, canoe hire and volleyball. €

Montcabrier

With your own transport, you can cut northwest across country from Duravel to visit the magnificent ruined castle of Bonaguil. On the way it's worth taking a short detour to **MONTCABRIER**, just over 5km north of Duravel, if for no other reason than this tiny *bastide* seems to have been forgotten by the renovators and tourist authorities. There's a clutch of once-noble residences around the chestnut-shaded main square, but the village is best known for a diminutive statue lodged in the north nave of its quietly crumbling **Église St-Louis**. It is one of the first stone representations of the saint, formerly King Louis IX, showing him as a bearded figure wearing a painted crown. It's also slightly macabre: when Louis died on a crusade in 1270, his body was immediately chopped into pieces and dispatched around Europe to meet the demand for relics. Apparently, one unspecified piece of the king now resides inside this little statue.

Château de Bonaguil

Charge • http://chateau-bonaguil.com • From Montcabrier take the D673 from below the village heading southwest, then turn west through the delightful hamlet of St-Martin-le-Redon and start climbing

As the D673 from Montcabrier crests the ridge above St-Martin-le-Redon you get a stunning view of the **Château de Bonaguil**, perched at the end of a wooded spur some 7km from Montcabrier. The castle dates largely from the fifteenth and sixteenth centuries when Bérenger de Roquefeuil, from a powerful Languedoc family and by all accounts a nasty piece of work, inherited the partially ruined castle. Fearing revolts from his vassals, he decided to transform it into an impregnable fortress, just as his contemporaries were abandoning such elaborate **fortifications**. It took him around forty years to do so, constructing a double ring of walls, six huge towers, a highly unusual, narrow boat-shaped keep and sophisticated loopholes with overlapping lines of fire. Perhaps because of such elaborate precautions, Bonaguil was never attacked, and although some demolition occurred during the Revolution, the castle still stands, bloodied but unbowed.

The site attracts up to two thousand tourists per day in July and August. It's best to arrive first thing in the morning to avoid the worst of the crush, and rather than joining the **guided tours**, which get tedious when it's very busy, it's preferable to buy a guidebook from the ticket gate and do it yourself. The château provides the backdrop for a **firework** extravaganza on the Friday following July 14, and then in early August makes a stunning venue for a **festival** of theatre (see page 186).

EATING AND DRINKING   CHATEAU DE BONAGUIL

Auberge les Bons Enfants http://lesbonsenfants-bonaguil.net. There are a couple of eating places below the castle, including this English-run restaurant, which serves drinks and snacks all day in high season, as well as a more substantial regional *menu*. **€€**

Fumel

Eight kilometres southwest of Bonaguil and 12km west of Duravel, **FUMEL** – an important stronghold in medieval times – is now a busy industrial town, which holds little of interest beyond its transport facilities and a decent hotel. It lies on the north bank of the Lot, spilling along the main road from its old centre – focused around **place du Postel** – in the east, past a huge factory making car parts, and then merges 4km later with the western suburb of **MONSEMPRON-LIBOS**. There is little to say about Monsempron either, except that it happens to be a terminal for both trains and buses. Perhaps for that reason it also hosts a huge, rambling – and often inexpensive – **market**, on the place du Marché, every Sunday.

ARRIVAL AND DEPARTURE   FUMEL

By train You'll find the *gare SNCF* in Monsempron-Libos, set back from the river near the road-bridge at the end of avenue de la Gare.
Destinations Agen (1–3 daily; 40–55min); Le Bugue (3–4 daily; 50min–1hr); Les Eyzies (3–4 daily; 55min–1hr 10min); Penne-d'Agenais (3–5 daily; 15–20min); Périgueux (4–6 daily; 1hr 30min).

By bus SNCF buses from Cahors terminate at the *gare SNCF*, having first called in Fumel at place du Postel.
Destinations (from Monsempron-Libos) Cahors (1hr 15min); Fumel (6–10min); Luzech (50min–1hr); Prayssac (35min); Puy-l'Évêque (30min).

GETTING AROUND AND INFORMATION

Bike rental AJF Cycles, 2 av de l'Usine (05 53 71 14 57) offers bike rental.
Taxis Call Fumélois (05 53 71 39 50).
Tourist office Place Georges-Escandes (July & Aug daily 9.30am–noon & 1.30–7.30pm; Sept–June Mon 1.30–5.30pm & Tues–Fri 9.30am–noon & 1.30–7.30pm; 05 53 71 13 70, http://tourisme-fumel.com).

ACCOMMODATION AND EATING

Le 72 Watt 72 av de l'Usine, http://le72watt.fr. The building is rather bizarre and squat, but rooms are clean and comfortable. The owners have taken the factory theme and run with it, and many of the rooms are decorated with wallpaper patterned with cog wheels. **€**

Camping les Catalpas http://les-catalpas.com. A friendly little place located 3.5km east of Fumel, just past the village of Condat. Facilities include a restaurant/bar (May–Sept only), pool, river beach and *pétanque*. SNCF buses stop 1.5km up the road in Condat itself. **€**

Penne-d'Agenais

The last place worth a stop along the valley before Villeneuve-sur-Lot is the beautiful but touristy old fortress-town of **PENNE-D'AGENAIS**, 15km downstream from Fumel on the river's south bank, where the silver-domed **Notre-Dame-de-Peyragude** teeters on the cliff edge. The church dates back to 1000, but had the misfortune to be built on a particularly strategic pinnacle of rock. After Richard the Lionheart erected a castle right next door in 1182, the church found itself in the crossfire on any number of occasions; in 1412 Penne changed hands no fewer than four times.

The most recent construction was only completed in 1949; there's nothing particular to see inside, and the neighbouring castle was razed during the Wars of Religion, but the climb is rewarded with panoramic views.

From **place Gambetta**, the main square immediately south of the old town, **rue du 14-juillet** ducks under a medieval gate. From here just follow your fancy uphill along narrow lanes lined with an alluring mix of brick-and-stone houses – all incredibly spick and span. A few twists and turns later you emerge beside the basilica.

ARRIVAL AND INFORMATION

By train Penne's *gare SNCF* is located a couple of kilometres southeast of the city centre, along the D103 to Agen. For taxis call Andrée Garcia (06 15 27 05 91).
Destinations Agen (10–12 daily; 20min).

PENNE-D'AGENAIS

Tourist office Rue du 14-juillet, just inside the medieval gate (Mon–Sat 9am–12.30pm & 2–6pm, Sun 2–6pm; 05 53 41 37 80, http://penne-tourisme.com). Staff can supply comprehensive lists of *chambres d'hôtes* and *gîtes* in the area.

ACCOMMODATION AND EATING

Le Bombecul Place Paul-Fromet, http://lebombecul.com Above-average restaurant serving up delicacies like stuffed quails, suckling pig and salmon gravadlax, with some unique flavours. €€

Camping Municipal Les Berges du Lot 05 53 41 22 23. A small, two-star riverside campsite near the bridge over the Lot in St-Sylvestre; facilities include a pool and a children's play area. €

Camping Municipal Lac Férrié 06 80 95 92 89. A three-star campsite beside a lake just north of Penne's *gare SNCF*, with a pool, children's play area and *pétanque*. €

La Maison sur la Place 10 place Gambetta, http://lamaisonsurlaplace.com. Recently transformed from a restaurant to a *chambre d'hôte*, this welcoming townhouse is a model of chic. There are just two rooms, but it's a delightful haven with white-painted brick, neutral furnishings and an upmarket bohemian vibe. €€

Villeneuve-sur-Lot and around

Straddling the river 10km west of Penne-d'Agenais, **VILLENEUVE-SUR-LOT** is a pleasant, workaday sort of town. It has no terribly compelling sights, but the handful of attractive timbered houses in the old centre goes some way to compensate. Founded in 1251 by Alphonse de Poitiers, Villeneuve was one of the region's earliest *bastide* towns (see page 223), and in no time it developed into an important commercial centre, which it remains to this day. As elsewhere, its ramparts have given way to encircling boulevards, but the distinctive chequerboard street-plan survives, along with two medieval gates and the old, arched bridge.

As for excursions further afield, the nearby hilltop village of **Pujols** makes for an enjoyable trip, while further down the Garonne, **Aiguillon** provides a clutch of picturesque medieval lanes perfect for a wander.

Porte de Paris and place Lafayette

The principal entrance to Villeneuve-sur-Lot's *bastide* was northerly **Porte de Paris**, also the prison – one of whose occupants was an unfortunate – and incompetent – baker incarcerated for the heinous crime of turning out substandard bread. From here the semi-pedestrianized rue de Paris leads south to Villeneuve's main square, **place Lafayette**; surrounded by arcaded townhouses in brick and stone, it bursts into life on **market** days (Tues & Sat mornings).

Église Ste-Catherine

Rue Ste-Catherine

Villeneuve-sur-Lot's most striking landmark is the 55m-high, octagonal red-brick tower of the **Église Ste-Catherine**, east of rue de Paris. The church was founded at the same time as the *bastide*, but then rebuilt in the late nineteenth century when it was in danger of collapse. In addition to an unusual north–south axis, the new architects chose a dramatic neo-Byzantine style, with a line of three domes above the nave, mosaic portraits of the six St Catherines – including St Catherine of Alexandria, to whom the church is dedicated, third from the left – and a multitude of saints on a frieze inspired by early Christian art.

A few relics of the old church remain, notably some attractive stained-glass windows, the oldest dating from the fourteenth century.

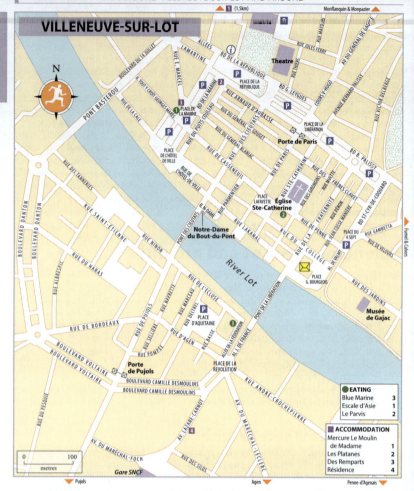

Pont des Cieutats and Notre-Dame-du-Bout-du-Pont

The road running parallel to rue de Paris to the west, **rue des Cieutats**, leads to the thirteenth-century **Pont des Cieutats**, originally topped with three towers reminiscent of Cahors' Pont Valentré (see page 190), and, just beside it on the north bank, a tiny chapel full of candles and votive plaques. The sixteenth-century **Notre-Dame-du-Bout-du-Pont** enshrines a small wooden statue of the Virgin holding Jesus gingerly in her arms. It was found in the river here by a sixteenth-century boatman when his craft mysteriously stopped midstream – or so the legend goes.

Musée de Gajac

2 rue des Jardins • Charge • http://ville-villeneuve-sur-lot.fr

It's worth checking what's on at the **Musée de Gajac**, which has interesting temporary exhibitions that change seasonally, ranging from fine art to photography and archeology. Guided tours are possible if booked in advance – ask at the tourist office (see below) for details.

ARRIVAL AND INFORMATION

By bus SNCF runs regular bus services from Agen calling at Villeneuve's former *gare SNCF* (where there's an SNCF ticket office), a 5min walk south of the centre, and terminating at the *Hôtel de Ville*.
Destinations Agen (8–10 daily; 45–50min).
By car Villeneuve-sur-Lot is easily accessible by car, although most of the centre operates on a one-way system.

VILLENEUVE-SUR-LOT

There is ample open-air and covered parking all around the city, with the most convenient car parks located at place de la Marine, place de la Libération and along bd de la République.
Tourist office 3 place de la Libération (July & Aug Mon–Sat 9.30am–1pm & 2–6pm & Sun 10am–1pm; Sept–June Mon–Sat 9.30am–noon & 2–5pm; 05 53 36 17 30, http://tourisme-villeneuvois.com).

ACCOMMODATION SEE MAP PAGE 220

★ **Mercure Le Moulin de Madame** Rue de Cassencuil, http://all.accor.com. A stunning hotel in an eighteenth-century mill overlooking the Lot, with luxury spa, hot tub and gym. The sumptuous rooms feature plush furnishings and gleaming bathrooms, some with river views. The riverfront restaurant is worth a visit for the views alone. €€
Les Platanes 40 bd de la Marine, http://contact-hotel.com. In the northwest corner of the old quarter, this great-value hotel has been spruced up with bright paintwork and modern furniture. Rooms follow suit all spotlessly clean. €
Des Remparts 1 rue Étienne-Marcel, http://hotel-des-remparts.eu. For a budget option in the heart of the city, this old-fashioned hotel is a welcoming choice. The cheerfully decorated rooms are small but comfortable. €
Résidence 17 av Lazare-Carnot, http://hotellaresidence47.com. A quiet spot not far from the train station with well-kept rooms, friendly staff and a generous continental breakfast (charge). Private parking for an extra charge. €

EATING SEE MAP PAGE 220

Blue Marine 6 allée de la Fédération, http://bluemarine47.fr. The focus is on seafood at this maritime-themed restaurant and there's everything from salmon to lobster. If you're stuck for choice, opt for one of the seafood platters which come laden with oysters, shrimps, langoustines, lobster and shellfish. €€€
★ **Escale d'Asie** 8 rue Tout y Croît Georges Marès, http://restaurant-asiatique-villeneuve-sur-lot.fr. Tasty and beautifully presented Asian cuisine with a wide choice of dishes and excellent-value lunch and evening *menus*. Try the spicy grilled prawns or beef satay, with a side plate of nems (spring rolls), then finish with the banana *flambée* with sake. Takeaway is also available. €€
Le Parvis 41 rue de Penne, http://leparvis.restaurant. Working entirely with local producers, *Le Parvis* specializes in small plates and tapas with hearty salads, burgers and beef tartare for the mains. The light wood interior feels airy and fresh. €€

Pujols

Three kilometres south of Villeneuve, the two-street village of **PUJOLS** stands high above the plain behind its thirteenth-century ramparts. The town is a popular excursion destination, partly because it's a beguiling little place, with its flowery nooks and crannies, and partly for **views** over the surrounding country – for locals, though, the main reason to come to Pujols is gastronomic.

Immediately inside Pujols' main north gate, it's hard to tell where the fortifications end and the Gothic **Église St-Nicolas** begins. It contains nothing of particular note, whereas the **Église Ste-Foy** (open for temporary exhibitions, which take place most of the time between April and October; free), on the far side of the market square, is decorated with fifteenth- and sixteenth-century frescoes. Though faded, many are still visible: around the apse, you can pick out St George poised over the dragon and St Catherine with her wheel of torture. Look out, too, for a painting in the baptismal chapel (first on the left as you enter), depicting the old bridge at Villeneuve-sur-Lot sporting its three towers.

EATING PUJOLS

L'Atelier 7 place Saint-Nicolas, http://latelier-pujols.eatbu.com. A chic, blue-shuttered stone building with a vast courtyard for diners, the restaurant is just as exquisite-looking as the dishes are. A great spot for grabbing a light lunch of *tartines*, salads or sharing platters. Local cheese and charcuterie is everywhere. €
L'Entrepote's 1 rue Bir-Hakeim, http://lentrepotes-pujols.com. No-frills-attached dining (soups, pasta dishes, meat and fish) and generous portion sizes. It's a lively place which hosts regular karaoke nights, and is very popular with locals. €€

Aiguillon

Around thirty kilometres west of Pujols, the hilltop town of **AIGUILLON** has stood guard over the confluence of the Lot and Garonne rivers since Roman times. Nowadays Aiguillon's most imposing building is the eighteenth-century, Neoclassical **Château des Ducs** – now a school – which dominates the western approach to the town. It was built by the duc d'Aiguillon who, having served as an army chief and governor of Brittany under Louis XV, returned to transform his medieval château into a mini-Versailles, though the grand balls and other festivities were soon cut short by the Revolution. The small area of medieval lanes with their half-timbered houses to the north of the château is worth a wander, and the church next to the château boasts a lovely, delicate organ. The town's lively food **markets** are held each Tuesday and Friday on place du 14-juillet.

ARRIVAL AND INFORMATION   AIGUILLON

By train Aiguillon's gare SNCF, on the Agen–Bordeaux train line, lies a 2min walk below the château along av de la Gare. Destinations Agen (12–14 daily; 18min); Toulouse (12–14 daily; 1hr 45min).

Tourist office Beside the château on the central place du 14-juillet (June–Aug Tues–Fri 9am–noon & 2–6pm, Sat 10am–noon; Sept–May Tues–Fri 9am–noon & 2–6pm; 05 53 64 65 31, http://ville-aiguillon.eu).

The bastide country

Although *bastides*, or medieval new towns (see page 223), are by no means unique to this stretch of country north of the Lot, it's here that you'll find the two finest examples. The more southerly of the pair is **Monflanquin**, which makes a good place to start thanks to its museum outlining the history, architecture and daily life of the *bastides*. Northeast, skirting round the flanks of the imposing **Château de Biron**, lies **Monpazier**. This is the most typical of the *bastides*, with virtually no modern development around. There's a small museum here, too, but Monpazier's prime attraction is its atmosphere, "like a drowsy yellow cat, slumbering in the sun" as Freda White so aptly describes it in her classic book *Three Rivers of France*. Neither the Château de Biron nor Monpazier are accessible by **public transport**, so you'll need your own car.

Monflanquin

Some 17km north of Villeneuve-sur-Lot, pretty **MONFLANQUIN**, founded in 1252 by Alphonse de Poitiers, is nearly as perfectly preserved as Monpazier, though less touristy and impressively positioned on top of a steep hill. Despite being built on a slope, it conforms to the regular pattern of right-angled streets leading from a central square to the four town gates. The ramparts were demolished on Richelieu's orders in 1630, but otherwise Monflanquin has experienced few changes since the thirteenth century.

The main square, tree-shaded **place des Arcades** – where the **market** still takes place on Thursdays as decreed in the *bastide*'s founding charter – derives a special charm from being on a slope. Its grandest building is the Gothic **Maison du Prince Noir**, where the Black Prince is said to have stayed, as well as the **Musée des Bastides**. After a wander through Monflanquin's old centre, head north past the **Paroisse de Monflanquin** church, which took on its pseudo-medieval look in the early twentieth century, to end up on a terrace with vast views northeast to the Château de Biron.

Musée des Bastides
Place des Arcades • Charge • http://monflanquin-museedesbastides.com

On the north side of the place des Arcades, above the tourist office, the high-tech **Musée des Bastides** is a treasure trove of information about the life and history of *bastides*. Most of the text is translated into English, but the video and multimedia displays are mostly in French only. Nonetheless, there's plenty of interest, with displays

BASTIDES

From the Occitan *bastida*, meaning a group of buildings, **bastides** were the new towns of the thirteenth and fourteenth centuries. Although they are found all over southwest France, from the Dordogne to the foothills of the Pyrenees, there is a particularly high concentration in the area between the Dordogne and Lot rivers, which at that time formed the disputed "frontier" region between English-held Aquitaine and Capetian France.

That said, the earliest *bastides* were founded largely for **economic and political** reasons. They were a means of bringing new land into production – this was a period of rapid population growth and technological innovation – and thus extending the power of the local lord. But as tensions between the French and English forces intensified during the late thirteenth century, so the motive became increasingly **military**. The *bastides* now provided a handy way of securing the land along the frontier, and it was generally at this point that they were fortified.

As an incentive, anyone who was prepared to build, inhabit and defend the *bastide* was granted various perks and concessions in a founding **charter**. All new residents were allocated a building plot, garden and cultivable land outside the town. The charter might also offer asylum to certain types of criminal or grant exemption from military service, and would allow the election of **consuls** charged with day-to-day administration – a measure of self-government remarkable in feudal times. Taxes and judicial affairs, meanwhile, remained the preserve of the representative of the king or local lord under whose ultimate authority the *bastide* lay.

The other defining feature of a *bastide* is its **layout**. They are nearly always square or rectangular in shape, depending on the nature of the terrain, and are divided by streets at right angles to each other to produce a chequerboard pattern. The focal point is the market square, often missing its covered *halle* nowadays, but generally still surrounded by arcades, while the church is relegated to one side, or may even form part of the town walls.

The busiest *bastide* founders were **Alphonse de Poitiers** (1249–71), on behalf of the French Crown, after he became count of Toulouse in 1249, and **King Edward I of England**, Edward Plantagenet (1272–1307), who wished to consolidate his hold on the northern borders of his duchy of Aquitaine. The former chalked up a total of 57 *bastides*, including Villeneuve-sur-Lot (1251), Monflanquin (1252), Ste-Foy-la-Grande (1255) and Eymet (1270), while Edward was responsible for Beaumont (1272), Monpazier and Molières (both 1284), among others.

spread over two floors, and the collection serves as a comprehensive introduction to the region's medieval past.

INFORMATION

Tourist office Place des Arcades (April–June & Sept Mon–Sat 9.30am–12.30pm & 2–5.30pm; July & Aug daily 9.30am–6.30pm; Oct–March Mon & Wed–Sat 9.30am–12.30pm & 2–5pm, Tues 9.30am–12.30pm; 05 53 36 40 19, http://coeurdebastides.com). They can furnish you with details of the many events taking place here in summer (see page 186).

MONFLANQUIN

ACCOMMODATION AND EATING

La Bastide Place des Arcades, 05 53 36 77 05. In a prime location right on the main square, this popular British-run crêperie serves salads, *galettes* and crêpes on its lovely terrace, which offers splendid views down the length of rue Ste-Marie. €

La Bastide des Oliviers 1 bd Georges-Clemenceau, http://labastidedesoliviers.fr. The best spot to stay in Monflanquin with light, modern rooms equipped with king-size beds, tea- and coffee-making facilities and English TV channels. There's also a restaurant and brasserie on-site, with very reasonable lunchtime *menus*. €

Le Bistrot du Prince Noir Place des Arcades, http://lebistrotduprincenoir.fr. A welcoming bistro in the southwest corner of the main square, where you'll find a varied menu of European foods, complimented by a great wine list. Vegetarians might opt for the aubergine, pesto and mozzarella lasagne, while the fish and chips are (almost) as good as back home. €

Le Café de Gavaudun Gavaudun, 05 47 99 01 60. Some 10km east of Monflanquin, this humble little restaurant is a popular haunt for locals, with delicious cuisine whipped up from fresh market produce. The menu changes depending on what's in season. €

★ **La Table des Sens** 63 rue de Villeneuve-sur-Lot Lougratte, 05 47 66 52 10. Fifteen minutes away in Lougratte, *La Table des Sens* is an elegant choice for fine dining, where you'll find French favourites like snails and foie gras, and mains featuring yellowfin tuna, lobster and rabbit. Expect tip-top service, perfectly cooked dishes and some truly showstopping desserts – for a treat, try the Grand Marnier soufflé. €

Château de Biron

Charge • http://chateau-biron.fr

Twenty-two kilometres northeast of Monflanquin, via a picturesque route along the River Lède, the vast **Château de Biron** dominates the countryside for miles around. It was begun in the eleventh century and added to piecemeal over the years by the Gontaut-Biron family, who occupied the castle right up to the early twentieth century. The biggest alterations were made in the fifteenth and early sixteenth centuries, when Pons de Gontaut-Biron started reconstructing the eastern wing. The result is an architectural primer, from the medieval keep through flamboyant Gothic and Renaissance to an eighteenth-century loggia in the style of Versailles.

Rather than the guided tour (in French only), at busy times it's better to borrow the English-language text from the ticket desk and wander at will. The most striking building in the grassy **lower court** is the Renaissance chapel, where lie the sarcophagi of Pons and his brother Armand, bishop of Sarlat. Though their statues were hacked about during the Revolution, the Italianate biblical scenes and three Virtues carved on the sides still show fine craftsmanship. On entering the cobbled and confined **inner courtyard** around its twelfth-century keep, the route takes you to a dungeon and through the lord's apartments, with their Renaissance chimney and wood-panelled hall, to a vast reception room and an equally capacious stone-vaulted refectory. If the rooms decked out as a tannery, torture chamber and weavers' workshop make you feel as though you're walking through a film set, you are – Biron is a favourite for period dramas.

ACCOMMODATION AND EATING   CHÂTEAU DE BIRON

Auberge du Château Château de Biron, 05 53 63 13 33. The pretty terrace is overflowing with flowers at this tranquil restaurant, perched on the path up to the castle. There's not much choice, but it's all expertly executed and good value. €€

Le Moulinal Lacapelle-Biron, http://lemoulinal.com. Around 6km south of Château de Biron off the D255, Lacapelle-Biron boasts one of the region's best campsites, with indoor and outdoor pools, a range of water slides and toboggans, plus mini-golf, tennis courts and a splash pool for toddlers. There's also a restaurant, bar and bikes for rent, and chalets. €

Le Palissy Place du Monument aux Morts, Lacapelle-Biron, http://lepalissycheznorbert.fr. Head 5km southeast of Château de Biron – by road or on the GR36 footpath – to Lacapelle-Biron and you'll find this friendly bistro-style restaurant on the main road. It has a Dutch chef and consequently rather a polyglot atmosphere, plus some great regional dishes. €€

Monpazier

From the Château de Biron it's 8km north to **MONPAZIER**, the finest and most complete of the surviving *bastides*, made up of a lovely warm-coloured stone on a hill above the River Dropt. Founded in 1284 by King Edward I of England on land granted by Pierre de Gontaut-Biron, and picturesque and placid though it is today, Monpazier has a hard and bitter history, being twice – in 1594 and 1637 – the centre of **peasant rebellions** provoked by the misery that followed the Wars of Religion. Both uprisings were brutally suppressed: the 1637 peasants' leader was broken on the wheel in the square and his head paraded around the countryside. In an earlier episode, Sully, the Protestant general, describes a rare moment of light relief in the terrible **Wars of Religion**, when the men of Catholic Villefranche-de-Périgord planned to capture Monpazier on the same night as the men of Monpazier were headed for Villefranche. By chance, the two sides took different routes, met no resistance, looted to their hearts' content and returned congratulating themselves on their luck and skill, only to find that things were rather different at home. The peace terms were that everything should be returned to its proper place.

During the summer, Monpazier puts on all sorts of **events** to draw the tourists, from book fairs to medieval jamborees (see page 186). Outside these occasions, however, there's not much else to do here beyond soak up the sun at a café on the market square.

Place des Cornières

Given Monpazier's turbulent past, it comes as something of a surprise to find that it has survived so well. Three of its six **medieval gates** are still intact and its central square, **place des Cornières**, couldn't be more perfect, with an oak-pillared *halle* and time-worn, stone-built houses, no two the same. Deep, shady arcades pass beneath all the houses, which are separated from each other by a small gap to reduce fire risk; at the corners the buttresses are cut away to allow the passage of laden pack animals. On Thursday mornings the square comes to life for the weekly **market**, which expands on the third Thursday of each month into a fair. In mushroom season (roughly Aug and Sept depending on the weather) people also come here in the afternoons to sell their pickings, while in December there's a truffle market.

Monpazier's main north–south axis is **rue Notre-Dame**, which brings you into the northeast corner of place des Cornières, past the much-altered **church**. The thirteenth-century building opposite is a bit battered, but this is Monpazier's oldest house, where the tax collector received his share of the harvest.

Ateliers des Bastides

Rue Jean-Galmot • Free • 05 53 22 60 38

The **Ateliers des Bastides** museum sits west of place des Cornières, and boasts a few prehistoric remains and other historical bits and pieces. However, it is largely devoted to local adventurer Jean Galmot, who was born in Monpazier in 1879 and was assassinated in 1928 in French Guiana, then a penal colony, where he was aiding its fledgling independence movement.

There is, however, no information in English. During the summer months the museum also hosts a number of temporary **art exhibitions**.

INFORMATION — MONPAZIER

Tourist office Place des Cornières (Feb–May & Oct–Dec Tues–Sat 10am–12.30pm & 2.30–6pm, Sun 10am–12.30pm; June & Sept daily 10am–12.30pm & 2.30–6.30pm; July & Aug daily 10am–12.30pm & 2–7pm; 05 53 22 68 59). Among all sorts of useful information, it produces a free booklet outlining a DIY tour of the town, with information in English and games for children, as well as a book of eleven waymarked walks in the area.

ACCOMMODATION

Camping de Véronne 05 53 22 65 50. Pleasantly located next to a lake, 3km northwest of Monpazier in Marsalès, this small campsite has two sailboats for children (free) and a restaurant/bar. €

Edward 1er 5 rue Saint-Pierre, http://hoteledward1er.com. Luxurious rooms, some more modern than others, in an authentic nineteenth-century château in the heart of the city. There's also a restaurant (dinner by reservation only) and a bistro (see below) to choose from, and half-board available. €€

Le Moulin de David http://moulindedavid.com. Deluxe four-star campsite in the Dropt valley that's a favourite with tourists, so reserve well in advance. The eco-friendly facilities include a huge pool, a restaurant, snack bar and shop plus children's play areas. Weekly bookings only in July and Aug. €

EATING AND DRINKING

You'll eat very well in the two hotel **restaurants**. Alternatively, the **cafés** and **bars** around place des Cornières are perfect for a sunny lunch or cool afternoon drink; you could also turn north and wander along rue Notre-Dame, where there are more options.

Bistrot 2 Foirail Nord, http://bistrot2.fr. Just outside the town walls, this little bistro is owned by the same people as the *Edward 1er* (see above); you can sit out on the terrace watching the world go by as you sample tasty local dishes. €€

Le Privilège du Périgord 58 rue Notre-Dame, http://privilegeperigord.com. Dine on delicacies like duck with roasted pineapple and sweet potato, or truffle and prosciutto bruschetta at this good-value restaurant, and grab a table in the sunny courtyard. €€€

South of the River Lot

228 Agen and around
238 Moissac and around
242 Quercy Blanc
246 Montauban
250 The Gorges de l'Aveyron and around

ST-ANTONIN-NOBLE-VAL

South of the River Lot

South of the River Lot, the River Garonne in the west and the rivers Tarn and Aveyron in the east define the southern border of the Dordogne and Lot region. On the whole, this area offers less dramatic scenery than further north, but by the same token it sees fewer tourists. It is a fertile land, full of sunflowers and fruit orchards, particularly along the Garonne and spreading over the hills to the north: plums, pears, peaches, cherries, apples, apricots and nectarines all grow here, as well as melons, strawberries and the succulent *chasselas* grapes.

The first of the region's two gateways is **Agen**, the only major town on the Garonne between Bordeaux and Toulouse and more pleasant than it first appears, with an old centre built of pink-mottled brick and a fine local museum. Southwest of Agen, what's left of **Nérac**'s castle and its riverside pleasure gardens – where King Henry IV misspent his youth – still exude a slightly decadent air. The river here is the Baïse, which flows north to join the Garonne near **Buzet-sur-Baïse**, in the centre of a small wine region.

Upstream from Agen, the region's unmissable sight is the abbey church at **Moissac**, with its wonderful carvings. The Garonne valley here is at its flattest and most featureless, but north of Moissac things improve as you climb up onto the low, rolling plateau of the **Quercy Blanc**, which stretches north almost to Cahors. It's a region of white-stone farmhouses, sun-drenched hilltop villages, windmills and *pigeonniers* – pigeon houses, often raised on stilts – by the hundred. Of these, the prettiest village is **Lauzerte**, but **Montpezat-de-Quercy** also merits a visit for its display of religious art, including a series of superb tapestries.

Near Montpezat the N20 and the A20 *autoroute* mark the eastern extent of the Quercy Blanc and funnel traffic south to **Montauban**. This brick-red city, not far north of Toulouse and on the Paris railway line, is the region's second gateway, and justifies a few hours' exploration thanks to its art museum and central square surrounded by elegant townhouses. It sits on the banks of the Tarn in the midst of an alluvial plain which, in the east, gives way abruptly to hills. Running through them, the stunning **Gorges de l'Aveyron** are punctuated with ancient villages perched high above the river, while **St-Antonin-Noble-Val**, with its core of medieval lanes, lies in the valley bottom caught between soaring limestone crags. Beyond St-Antonin, it's worth making a short detour south across the plateau to the aptly named **Cordes-sur-Ciel**, where noble facades line the steeply cobbled lanes, before rejoining the Aveyron beneath **Najac**'s much-contested fortress. The gorge opens out to the north of Najac, but it's worth travelling the last few kilometres to **Villefranche-de-Rouergue**, in the centre of which, in the monstrous shadow of its church tower, lies a perfectly preserved arcaded market square.

GETTING AROUND SOUTH OF THE RIVER LOT

By train Three major train lines fan out across this region from Toulouse: along the Garonne valley to Montauban, Moissac and Agen; north to Cahors; and northeast through Cordes, Najac and Villefranche en route to Figeac.

By bus Bus services in the region are limited and patchy, often running only at school times, and many small villages have no buses at all. There is one regular SNCF service between Agen and Nérac, while private buses (aimed at schoolchildren) link Montcuq and Villefranche-de-Rouergue with Cahors, though they're not much use to visitors.

Agen and around

Agen, capital of the Lot-et-Garonne *département*, lies on the broad, powerful River Garonne halfway between Bordeaux and Toulouse. Close to the A62 *autoroute* and

MOISSAC'S ABBEY CHURCH

Highlights

❶ **Moissac** The carvings decorating the south porch and cloister of Moissac's abbey church are masterpieces of Romanesque art. See page 238

❷ **Quercy Blanc** Take time to savour the bucolic countryside between the Garonne and Lot valleys, dotted with vines, sunflowers and sleepy hilltop villages. See page 242

❸ **Lauzerte** Set on a hilltop amid the fruitful fields of the Quercy Blanc, this perfectly preserved *bastide* village offers outstanding views. See page 243

❹ **St-Antonin-Noble-Val** A compact and charming medieval town set against the limestone cliffs of the Gorges de l'Aveyron. See page 252

❺ **Cordes-sur-Ciel** Perched on its knuckle of rock, this fortified town is the jewel of the Tarn and a favourite haunt of artists and artisans. See page 254

❻ **Château de Najac** Climb the tower of Alphonse de Poitier's erstwhile stronghold for vertiginous views over the Aveyron valley. See page 257

❼ **Villefranche-de-Rouergue** The arcaded and sloping central square makes a superb setting for the weekly market. See page 258

HIGHLIGHTS ARE MARKED ON THE MAP ON PAGE 230

connected to both cities by fast and frequent train services, and to Paris by train and plane, it provides a useful gateway to the southern reaches of the Dordogne and Lot region. However, Agen is more than just a transport hub. Inside the ring of hypermarkets and industrial estates lies a core of old lanes lined with handsome brick houses, several churches worth a look and a surprisingly good fine arts museum, topped off with a number of excellent restaurants and a good choice of hotels. Make sure you try some prunes while you're there – **pruneaux d'Agen** (see page 234) are world famous and the basis for many local desserts.

Agen makes for a pleasant half-day's exploration, or a base from which to cover the surrounding country. The most interesting jaunts take you southwest to **Nérac**, where kings and queens disported themselves on the Baïse's wooded banks, and west to the wine town of **Buzet-sur-Baïse**.

Agen

The old centre of **AGEN** lies on the east bank of the Garonne. It is quartered by two nineteenth-century boulevards – **boulevard de la République**, running east–west, and north–south **boulevard du Président-Carnot** – which intersect at place Goya and make for easy navigation. To the northeast stands **Cathédrale St-Caprais**, somewhat misshapen but worth a look for its finely proportioned Romanesque apse and radiating chapels.

Musée des Beaux-Arts

Place du Dr-Esquirol • Charge • http://musee-agen.fr

Beside the exuberant, Italianate municipal theatre, the **Musée des Beaux-Arts** is magnificently housed in four adjacent sixteenth- and seventeenth-century mansions

HIGHLIGHTS
1. Moissac
2. Quercy Blanc
3. Lauzerte
4. St-Antonin-Noble-Val
5. Cordes-sur-Ciel
6. Château de Najac
7. Villefranche-de-Rouergue

BOAT TRIPS ALONG THE CANAL DE GARONNE

The Canal de Garonne (formerly known as the Canal latéral à la Garonne) was once part of a heaving artery of commerce, forming part of the great Canal de Deux Mers, which links the Canal du Midi at Toulouse with the Garonne River. This in turn finally connected the Mediterranean to the Atlantic. Today the peaceful waterways are given over to pleasure, the canal is clean and overhung with trees, and flotillas of ducks replace the commercial barges. **Locaboat Plaisance** (http://locaboat.com) offers cruises along the canal from March to October; prices vary from €852 to €3600 per week for a three- to five-person boat, depending on the season and the level of comfort.

adorned with stair turrets and Renaissance window details. Inside you'll find a rich variety of archeological exhibits, furniture and paintings – among the latter, a number of Goyas and a Tintoretto rediscovered during an inventory in 1997. Best, though, are the basement's Roman finds, which include intricate jewellery and a superb white-marble Venus.

Église des Jacobins and around

To the west of place du Dr-Esquirol, a clutch of brick and timber houses – the bricks forming neat zigzags within the timber frame – represents Agen's most attractive corner. From here a short and narrow alley, **rue Beauville**, cuts through to rue Richard-Coeur-de-Lion, with more eye-catching facades and the **Église des Jacobins**. This big, brick Dominican church was founded by Dominican monks in the thirteenth century, then served as the Protestants' headquarters before being used as a prison during the Revolution. It now forms an annexe of the Musée des Beaux-Arts and hosts temporary

232 | **SOUTH OF THE RIVER LOT** AGEN AND AROUND

AGEN

ACCOMMODATION
Camping Le	1
Moulin de Mellet	2
Des Jacobins	3
Sera Boutique Hotel	

EATING
Côté Sud	5
Le Margoton	4
Monsieur Jeanne	3
La Part des Anges	2
Quarts Coffee Kitchen	1

DRINKING
La Belle Pinte	2
Le Takeoff	1

FESTIVALS, EVENTS AND MARKETS

The list below comprises some of the biggest and most interesting of the **festivals** and **events** in this region. Where we haven't given a specific information number or website, contact the relevant tourist office.

Late May or early June Moissac: Fêtes de Pentecôte (05 63 04 63 63). A traditional fair on the banks of the Tarn over the Whitsun weekend, with fireworks on the Monday night.

July and August Moissac: Les Soirs de Moissac (05 63 04 06 81). Varied programme of concerts, choral works and recitals, including world music, held in the cloister or the church of St-Pierre (tickets required).

Mid-July Cordes-sur-Ciel: Fête du Grand Fauconnier (http://grandfauconnier.com). This two-day medieval festival converts the town into a costumed extravaganza, complete with exhibitions on medieval crafts and falconry. Daily admission to the old town is €9, and you can hire medieval costumes for the occasion.

Late July Cordes-sur-Ciel: Musique sur Ciel (http://festivalmusiquesurciel.com). Ten days of classical concerts, some by featured contemporary composers, in the church of St-Michel.

Late July to mid-August Lauzerte and around: Festival du Quercy Blanc (http://festivalduquercyblanc.com). Concerts of classical and chamber music held mostly in churches around the region, including Lauzerte, Montcuq, Montpezat-de-Quercy and Castelnau-Montratier. Tickets available from local tourist offices.

End of July or start of August Lauzerte: Les Nuits de Lauzerte (http://nuitsdelauzerte.free.fr). Over the space of a weekend, Lauzerte becomes an art installation and performance space, through which you walk at night, taking your time and wandering at your own pace past street theatre, contemporary dance, music and projections. Tickets from the tourist office.

Early August Villefranche-de-Rouergue and around: Festival en Bastides (http://espaces-culturels.fr). Five days of contemporary theatre and performance art animate the streets of Villefranche and Najac, among other places. Some ticketed events, information from any participating tourist office.

Third weekend in September Moissac: Fête du Chasselas and Fête des Fruits et des Légumes (05 63 04 63 63). Every year the Fête du Chasselas celebrates the local grape, with tastings on offer and a competition to find the pick of the bunch; the event takes place in the market hall. Every two years (in the odd years) the whole range of local fruits plus vegetables are also on display and there is all manner of related events throughout the town.

Second weekend in October Auvillar: Marché Potier (05 63 39 57 33). Some forty exhibitors take part in this important pottery fair held on the place de la Halle.

MARKETS

The main **markets** in the region are at Agen (Wed & Sat); Cordes (Sat), Laguépie (Wed & Sun); Lauzerte (Wed & Sat); Moissac (Sat & Sun); Montauban (Wed & Sat); Montcuq (Sun); Nérac (Sat); St-Antonin-Noble-Val (Sun); St-Nicolas-de-la-Grave (Mon); and Villefranche-de-Rouergue (Thurs).

---

art exhibitions (charge). Inside, you can see unusual Gothic frescoes of leaves and geometric patterns in trompe l'oeil on the walls and ceiling.

West of the church is the river and the public gardens of **Esplanade du Gravier**, where a footbridge crosses the Garonne – from it you can see a 550m **canal bridge** dating from 1843 further downstream.

ARRIVAL AND DEPARTURE   AGEN

By train The *gare SNCF* is located on the north side of town, on boulevard Sylvain-Dumon. From in front of the station, boulevard du Président-Carnot leads south to place Goya, where it crosses the town's other main thoroughfare, the east–west boulevard de la République.

Destinations Bordeaux (up to 20 daily; 1hr–1hr 20min); Moissac (5–9 daily; 25–45min); Monsempron-Libos (4–9 daily; 35–45min); Montauban (up to 16 daily; 40–50min);

PRUNEAUX D'AGEN

Agen grew rich during the seventeenth century thanks to the trade of manufactured goods, such as cloth and leather, flowing through its river port, but the industrial revolution put paid to all that. Since then, the town's prosperity has been based on agriculture – in particular, its famous **prunes**. Plums (*prunes* in French) were introduced to France by crusaders returning from Syria in the eleventh century. It is believed that Benedictine monks at Clairac, near the confluence of the Lot and Garonne, were the first to cultivate the fruit, a variety known as *prune d'Ente*, which thrives on sun, high humidity and chalky soils and is also excellent for drying thanks to its size and high sugar content. Though plums now grow throughout the region, the dried fruit (*pruneaux*) were originally exported via the port at Agen – and are thus known as **pruneaux d'Agen**.

Nowadays these prunes are one of the region's principal money-spinners and in late August the orchards are a hive of activity as the ripe fruit are shaken from the trees. They are dried slowly in hot-air ovens to retain the flavour – during which process they lose three-quarters of their weight. Even so, the biggest prunes weigh in at 20g.

You can learn more facts and figures about prune production in the specialist *confiseries* of Agen and also at an enjoyable farm-museum, **Au Pruneau Gourmand** (charge; http://musee-du-pruneau.com), in the village of Granges-sur-Lot, 10km northeast of Aiguillon. In mid-September, the village of St-Aubin, near Monflanquin hosts a fair devoted to the prune, lasting several days; call Monflanquin tourist office (05 53 49 55 80) for information.

Paris (16 daily; 4 hr); Périgueux (3–5 daily; 2hr–2hr 20min); La Réole (7–10 daily; 50min); Toulouse (12–17 daily; 1hr–1hr 15min).
By bus The *gare routière* is next to the *gare SNCF*. For up-to-date bus schedules ask at the tourist office or phone the transport desk of the Conseil Général on 05 53 69 42 03. Destinations Nérac (40min); Villeneuve-sur-Lot (45min).
By car Free car parking can be found along the riverbank and on place du 14-juillet.

GETTING AROUND AND INFORMATION

Bike rental Comptoir du Deux-Roues, 18–20 av du Général-de-Gaulle (http://comptoir-du-deux-roues.fr; closed Sun).
Car rental Avis, 12 bd Sylvain-Dumon, near the train station and at the airport (http://avis.com); Europcar, 120 bd du Président-Carnot and near the train station (http://europcar.com).
Taxis There is a taxi stand at the train station, or call Agen Taxis (06 09 37 07 74).
Tourist office 38 rue Garonne (July & Aug Mon–Sat 9am–7pm, Sun 9.30am–12.30pm; Sept–June Mon–Sat 9am–12.30pm & 2–6.30pm 05 53 47 36 09, http://destination-agen.com).

ACCOMMODATION
SEE MAP PAGE 232

Camping Le Moulin de Mellet http://camping-moulin-mellet.com. Eight kilometres west of Agen in St-Hilaire-de-Lusignanlies, this friendly campsite boasts two swimming pools, a restaurant, a small petting zoo and plenty of games and activities for kids. €
Des Jacobins 1 place des Jacobins, http://chateau-des-jacobins.com. A fancy hotel with lavishly decorated rooms full of antique furniture and historic knick-knacks. The elegant nineteenth-century townhouse and beautiful gardens are a treat, but don't expect the standard of service that you'd get at a hotel. €€
Serra Boutique Hotel 2–4 av du Général de Gaulle, http://serra-hotel-agen.fr. Fifty Art Deco rooms somehow fit in *Mary Poppins* style into this seventeenth-century building, which is easily the most characterful hotel in town. There's a large wine cellar, a gym and a spa too. €€€

EATING
SEE MAP PAGE 232

The best place to look for somewhere to **eat** in Agen is within the rough semicircle between boulevard de la République, rue des Cornières and rue Émile-Sentini, plus along rue La Fayette and its extension rue Camille-Desmoulins running east from boulevard Carnot. **Ethnic restaurants** and **fast-food** outlets sit on rue Voltaire and rue Garonne further west, while there are a couple of decent **cafés** on boulevard de la République and at its western junction with avenue du Général-de-Gaulle.
Côté Sud 36 cours Gambetta, http://restaurant-cotesud.fr. A modern take on a traditional family restaurant, stylishly decorated in subdued mauves, with comfortable seating

and down-lighting. Expect typical French cuisine with a few surprises along the way. €€

Le Margoton 52 rue Richard-Cœur-de-Lion, http://lemargoton.com. The emphasis is on quality cuisine and fresh local ingredients at this stylish restaurant. The salmon smoked in-house is delicious, while the unique mojito soufflé offers a flavoursome finish. €€€

★ **Monsieur Jeannot** 18 rue des Cornières, 05 40 40 12 24. Rustic French cuisine is the name of the game here, with dishes like *fricassée de lapin* (rabbit stew) or *moules* with red-pesto sauce, served on traditional wooden platters. Lunchtime *menus*, a bargain, are understandably popular with locals, while the tasting *menu* is ideal for hungry gourmands. €€

La Part des Anges 14 rue Émile-Sentini, http://lapartdesanges.eu. This refined little restaurant is the place to go for well-prepared and presented local dishes, such as black Gascon pork, beef from Duras and cheeses aged on the premises. In summer a few tables are set up outside on the pedestrianized street. €€

Quarts Coffee Kitchen 63 rue Molinier, 05 53 96 63 74. One of few places serving food and drinks non-stop throughout the day, *Quarts Coffee Kitchen* welcomes a steady stream of locals and it's easy to see why. There's good coffee, a range of smoothies and a selection of burgers, paninis, salads and cakes to tempt you. The free wi-fi for customers is handy, too and you won't feel out of place getting your laptop out. €

DRINKING

SEE MAP PAGE 232

La Belle Pinte 33 av Michel Serres, 07 86 82 89 35. Bar and beer shop in a reclaimed warehouse, with cheese and charcuterie platters served to soak up the excesses. There's a large selection of local craft beers on tap.

Le Takeoff 26 rue Voltaire, http://thetakeoffbar.fr. Funky lounge bar with a space-age vibe and a great cocktail menu that features all the usual favourites. Drinks are cheapest before 10pm, so get there early.

ENTERTAINMENT

Agen has a reputation for its thespian activities; there are several **theatre groups** that perform in the open air, both in Agen and nearby towns; ask at the tourist office. There's also a **cinema** screening all the latest Hollywood movies alongside French-language films.

Nouveau Théâtre du Jour 21 rue Paulin-Régnier, http://theatredujour.com. Saved from closure in 2023, a local actors' group took over the old theatre, which now hosts artist residences, as well as showing contemporary and classic theatre.

Théâtre Municipal Ducourneau Place du Dr-Esquirol, http://agen.fr. Puts on a varied programme of theatre, dance, concerts and opera by local, national and international artists.

CGR cinéma d'Agen 9 rue de la Prune, http://cgrcinemas.fr. A huge multiscreen cinema in the centre of town.

SHOPPING

Agen's main **shopping streets** are boulevard de la République and boulevard du Président-Carnot, while pedestrianized rue Molinier, south of the cathedral, has a few smarter boutiques. The thing to buy in Agen is prunes (see page 234); you'll find them in the markets and at a number of specialist shops.

DIRECTORY

Hospital Centre Hospitalier, rte de Villeneuve (http://ch-agen-nerac.fr), located 1.5km northeast of central Agen on the N21 to Villeneuve-sur-Lot.

Police Commissariat de Police, 4 rue Palissy (05 53 68 17 00), situated to the south of the old quarter.

Post office 72 bd du Président-Carnot.

AGEN'S MARKETS AND FAIRS

A **fresh-produce market** takes place in the covered market on place Jean-Baptiste Durand. There is also a large **farmers' market** held on Wednesday and Sunday mornings in the Halle du Pin, beside place du 14-juillet, as well as a smaller one on Saturday mornings on the Esplanade du Gravier, and an **organic market**, also on Saturdays, on place des Laitiers, off boulevard de la République. The most interesting of several **agricultural fairs** are the *foire de la prune* (first or second Mon after Sept 15), devoted to plums and prunes, and the *foire aux oies et canards gras* (second Sun in Dec) for foie gras and all manner of products made from duck and goose. The fairs take place in varying locations around the town centre; contact the tourist office (see page 234) for further information.

Nérac

Thirty kilometres across high, rolling hills to the southwest of Agen, you come to the château town of **NÉRAC** on the banks of the River Baïse. It's hard to believe that this drowsy backwater, seat of the **d'Albret** family, once matched the Parisian court in its splendour and extravagance, or that the bitter rivalries between Protestant and Catholic were played out here. Nowadays, it's an attractive and prosperous little place, where you can happily spend a few hours wandering the riverbanks and what's left of the d'Albrets' **castle**.

The d'Albrets first came to Nérac around 1150 and over the next three centuries grew to become one of Aquitaine's most powerful dynasties – largely through a talent for marrying well. First, they gained the Pyrenean kingdom of Navarre when John d'Albret married Catherine of Foix, and then in 1527, their son Henry II d'Albret wed **Marguerite d'Angoulême**, sister to King François I of France. Intelligent and cultured, Marguerite filled her Nérac court with scholars and proponents of the new Protestant faith, including Jean Chauvin (John Calvin), who stayed here briefly in 1534. Neither Henry nor Marguerite converted, but their determined and ambitious daughter, **Jeanne d'Albret**, did so in 1560, thus making Nérac an important Protestant stronghold. Jeanne's son, also Henry, for his part married the young and beautiful **Marguerite de Valois**, sister of the king of France and Catherine de Medici, in 1572 and so ushered in Nérac's golden era. Their court glittered with eminent writers, diplomats and nobles, poets and musicians, while Henry indulged in the innumerable amorous conquests that earned him the nickname *Le Vert Galant*; Queen Margot, as she was called, was no retiring violet either, and the marriage was eventually annulled in 1599, by which time Henry had become **Henry IV** of France and removed his court to Paris.

Château de Nérac
Charge, under-12s free • 05 53 65 21 11

Throughout their glory days, the d'Albrets added to their **château** on the river's west bank, at the far end of the bridge coming into Nérac from Agen. By the sixteenth century they had made it into a comfortable palace, of which only the north wing with its Renaissance gallery still exists, the other three having been partially destroyed in 1621 and finished off during the Revolution. It now houses the **Musée Henri IV**, of which the most interesting displays relate to Henry, Queen Margot and their larger-than-life relatives.

Église St-Nicolas and around

North of the château stands the Neoclassical **Église St-Nicolas**, which was built in the mid-eighteenth century and contains some attractive nineteenth-century stained-glass windows, depicting scenes from the Old and New Testaments. From the terrace here you get good views of the triple-arched **Pont-Vieux** and the ancient roofs of the area known as **Petit-Nérac** on the opposite side of the river. It's worth wandering over the bridge and turning right along rue Séderie, where the wooden balconies of old tanneries overhang the river, to come out beside the **Pont-Neuf** by Nérac's former port, now a marina bustling with cruise boats in summer.

La Garenne

South from Nérac's port across the main road, avenue Georges-Clemenceau, a shady woodland path, leads 1.5km along the riverbank. **La Garenne**, as the area here is known, was laid out as a royal pleasure park in the sixteenth century. The aviaries of exotic birds, the arbours and minstrels have long gone, but it's still a pleasant place to stroll or picnic. Not far from the entrance, look out for the **Fontaine de Fleurette**, marked by a statue of a prostrate and scantily clad young woman. According to legend, Fleurette was a gardener's daughter who had the misfortune to be seduced by *Le Vert*

Galant and, when his attentions drifted elsewhere, drowned herself in the river. The inscription reads: "She gave him all her life. He gave her but one day."

Cap Cauderoue
Charge • http://cap-cauderoue.com

Cap Cauderoue, 5km west of Nérac, is a treetop adventure playground, where visitors make their way, via ropes and swings, around an obstacle course high above the ground. It's popular with older children and teens, and a little muscle is required. The site also offers **activities** such as mini golf, mountain biking, horseback rides, ATV rides, canoeing and archery.

ARRIVAL AND INFORMATION — NÉRAC

By bus Buses from Agen (40min) stop on the central place de la Libération, next to the château.
Tourist office Avenue Mondenard (Sept–June Tues–Sat 9am–noon & 2–6pm, July & Aug Mon–Sat 9am–1pm & 2–6pm, Sun 10am–1pm & 3–5pm; Oct–April Tues–Fri 9am–noon & 2–6pm, Sat 9am–noon & 2–5pm; 05 53 65 27 75, http://albret-tourisme.com).
Boat rental Les Croisières du Prince Henry (http://croisieresduprincehenry.com) offers cruises with French-language commentary on a traditional *gabare*.

ACCOMMODATION AND EATING

Chocolaterie Artisanale la Cigale 2 rue Calvin, http://chocolaterie-la-cigale.fr. Just a couple of minutes' walk south of the *gare SNCF*, this *chocolaterie* is heaven for chocolate lovers, crammed with delicious handmade goodies. €
L'Escadron Volant 7 rue Henri-IV, 05 53 97 19 04. Conveniently situated opposite the château entrance, this popular brasserie has a far-reaching menu of traditional French fare, salads and crêpes. €€
★ **Hôtel Henri IV** 4 place du Général Leclerc, http://hotelhenriiv.fr. Easily Nérac's best hotel, the eleven rooms at *Henri IV* are the epitome of chic, with wood floors, modern bathrooms and tasteful decor. There's also a small pool, a bar, bikes for hire and a well-stocked breakfast buffet. Opt for a deluxe room if your budget allows – the standards are a little on the small side. €€
Moulin des Tours Chemin de Maison Blanche Barbaste, http://chambredhotesmoulindestours.fr. In the tiny village of Barbaste, 6km north of Nérac, this *chambre d'hôte* has five modern rooms with garden views, one with its own Jacuzzi. Great-value meals are also offered. €
Le Vert Galant 11 rue Séderie, 05 53 65 31 99. This canalside restaurant is the perfect spot for lunch, with a great selection of *tartines*; the house speciality is one with duck *confit*, pear and bacon. Also on the menu are over fifty flavours of ice cream, including some wacky options like pumpkin, or tomato and basil sorbet. €€

Buzet-sur-Baïse

BUZET-SUR-BAÏSE lies roughly 30km west of Agen, in the shadow of the Château de Buzet (not open to the public), which stands high on the green hillside, now separated from its village by the *autoroute*. Buzet itself is rather dull, but as the vines on this south bank of the Garonne indicate, you're in wine country and you shouldn't miss the chance to visit the local **wine co-operative**.

Les Vignerons de Buzet
Tasting chargeable, or free with purchase • http://vignerons-buzet.fr • The co-op is around 1.5km east of Buzet-sur-Baïse on the D642

Founded in 1953, **Les Vignerons de Buzet** is France's largest wine cooperative, with around three hundred growers producing an average of fourteen million bottles per year. The majority are strong red wines, which benefit from ageing – Grande Réserve, Baron d'Ardeuil and Château de Gueyze stand out among the many award-winning wines produced by the co-operative, which also offers free tastings. It's also well worth arranging for one of their exceptionally informative **guided tours** of the vinification plant and **chais**.

ACTIVITIES — BUZET-SUR-BAÏSE

Boat trips Aside from wine, the other reason to visit Buzet is to rent a boat for a trip along the Canal de Garonne, or the Baïse or Lot rivers. Nicols (http://nicols.com), based at the *halte nautique* on the canal below Buzet village, has small pleasure boats for rent hourly and by the half-day or day, as well as houseboats for longer excursions.

EATING

★ **Le Vigneron** 20 bd de la République, 05 53 84 73 46. The nicest eating option in Buzet is on the broad main street and offers a four-course *menu du jour* for a mere €15.90. There's also a special Sunday lunch *menu*, including an hors-d'oeuvre buffet and a trolley stacked with delectable home-made desserts. The house speciality is a confection of crêpes layered with *crème pâtissière*, coated in meringue and baked. €€

Moissac and around

There is little of historical interest left in the modern town of **Moissac**, some 40km southeast of Agen, largely because of the terrible damage wreaked by the flood of 1930, when the Tarn, swollen by a sudden thaw in the Massif Central, burst its banks, destroying 617 houses and killing more than a hundred people. Masterpieces of Romanesque sculpture and the model for dozens of churches throughout the region, the cloister and porch of the Benedictine **Église Abbatiale St-Pierre** have made Moissac a household name in the history of art; more prosaically, the town also offers plenty of choice in terms of accommodation and eating.

The flat plains to the south and west of Moissac are less exciting, not least because of the looming presence of a nuclear power plant, but there are, nevertheless, a couple of places worth visiting along the banks of the Garonne: **St-Nicolas-de-la-Grave**, for its nature reserve and little museum devoted to the founder of Detroit, after whom Cadillac cars were named; and **Auvillar**, for its exquisite market square.

Moissac

MOISSAC sits with its back to the old river cliffs on the north bank of the Tarn just before its confluence with the Garonne. The town's compact centre is bordered to the south by the Canal de Garonne, to the east by boulevard Camille Delthil and to the west by boulevard Lakanal, at the south end of which Pont-Napoléon carries road traffic over the Tarn. Moissac's main east–west thoroughfare, named rue Gambetta in the west, rue Ste-Catherine and then rue Malaveille, brings you into the central market square, **place des Récollets**, home to the town's covered *halle*, where a fresh-produce **market** is held (Tues–Sat), spilling over into the square on the weekends.

Église Abbatiale St-Pierre

6 place Durand de Bredon • Charge • Tickets are sold at the tourist office (see page 240) and cover entry to the Musée d'Arts et Traditions Populaires (see page 240)

From Moissac's central place des Récollets, rue de la République leads north towards the red-brick belfry of the **Église Abbatiale St-Pierre**. Legend has it that Clovis first founded a church here in 506, though it seems more probable that its origins belong to the seventh century, which saw the foundation of so many monasteries throughout Aquitaine. The first Romanesque church on the site was consecrated in 1063 and enlarged the following century when Moissac became a stop on the Santiago de Compostela pilgrim route. Since then, the church has survived countless wars, including siege and sack by Simon de Montfort in 1212, during the crusade against the Cathars. Indeed, the fact that it is still standing at all is something of a miracle. During the Revolution the cloister was used as a gunpowder factory and billet for soldiers, who damaged many of the carvings, while in the 1850s it only escaped demolition to make way for the Bordeaux–Toulouse train line by a whisker.

The south porch

Apart from the dumpy, red-brick belfry, the first thing you see approaching the church from the town centre is the great stone arc of the **south porch**, with its magnificent **tympanum**, completed in 1130. It depicts Christ in Majesty, right hand raised in benediction, the Scriptures resting on his knee, surrounded by the Evangelists and the 24 elders of the Apocalypse – every one different – as described by St John in the Book of Revelation. Below, the central pillar bears the figures of St Paul and St Jeremiah, the latter with the most beautifully doleful face imaginable, in the same elongated style as at Souillac.

The interior

There is fine carving on the capitals inside the porch, and the **interior** of the church, which was remodelled in the fifteenth century, is painted with intricate patterns and filled with interesting wood and stone **statuary**. The most outstanding are those in the second chapel on the right as you enter: a lovely stone *Pietà* in which Mary, enveloped in pastel blue, holds her son gently in her arms, and an equally compelling statue of Mary Magdalene with one arm outstretched and a thick tress of hair falling round her knees.

The cloister

The **cloister** is accessed through the tourist office, behind the church to the west, where you can see a ten-minute video (in English on request) describing its main features. The cloister surrounds a garden shaded by a majestic cedar, and its pantile roof is supported by 76 alternating single and double marble columns. Each column supports a single inverted wedge-shaped block of stone, on which each are carved, with extraordinary delicacy, all manner of animals and plant motifs, as well as 46 scenes from the Bible and the lives of the saints, among them Daniel in the lions' den, the Evangelists, fishermen on Lake Galilee, St Peter being crucified upside down and the decapitation of John the Baptist. Despite the damage done during the Revolution, they are in amazingly good shape. An inscription on the middle pillar on the west side explains that the cloister was constructed in the time of the Abbot Ansquitil in the year of Our Lord 1100.

Musée d'Arts et Traditions Populaires

Rue de l'Abbaye • Charge, better rates with a combined ticket with Église Abbatiale St-Pierre; tickets are sold at the tourist office • 05 63 04 03 08

Immediately northeast of Église Abbatiale St-Pierre, and rather less interesting, the **Musée Marguerite Vidal d'Arts et Traditions Populaires** is housed in the former abbots' palace. Apart from a good collection of local ceramics, including faïence from Auvillar (see page 242), it contains a hotchpotch of furniture, ecclesiastical robes and religious treasures, portraits of old Moissac residents and a mock-up of a Quercy farmhouse interior.

ARRIVAL AND INFORMATION — MOISSAC

By train Moissac's *gare SNCF* lies about 500m west of the centre along avenue Pierre-Chabrié; from the station follow this road east and, where it curves northwards, you'll see steps leading down to the church square.
Destinations Agen (6–7 daily; 30min); Montauban (5–7 daily; 20min); Toulouse (4–7 daily; 45min).
By bus Run by Bus Gerla (05 63 04 55 50), the bus to Lauzerte (30min) stops outside the Tribunal but services are limited – you need to book in advance.

Tourist office Opposite the Église Abbatiale St-Pierre, 1 boulevard de Brienne (April–June & Oct Mon–Sat 9am–noon & 2–6pm, Sun 10am–1pm & 3–6pm; July & Aug daily 9am–7pm; Sept daily 9am–6pm; Nov–March Mon–Sat 10am–noon & 2–5pm; 05 63 04 01 85, http://moissac.fr). Staff have details of Moissac's festivals (see page 233) and of concerts taking place in the church and cloister in the summer months.

ACCOMMODATION — SEE MAP PAGE 239

★ **L'Armateur** 22 rue du Pont, http://hotelarmateur.fr. An excellent choice, offering chic and spacious rooms with big comfy beds, plus friendly staff and a quiet location in an elegant eighteenth-century mansion just a short stroll from town. There's also a swimming pool, private parking and a fine restaurant. €€

Le Chapon Fin 3 place des Récollets, http://hotelchaponfin.com. This clean and comfortable two-star hotel is now run by the Inter-Hotel chain. Rooms are simply furnished with no frills, but the staff are welcoming, and the location, right on the market square, is ideal. €€

Crêtes de Pignols 1167 chemin de Lacapalette, http://cretesdepignols.com. Twelve smart, well-appointed rooms are available at this friendly, family-run inn, some 4km northeast of Moissac off the D927. There's also a pool and a pleasant sun terrace, and a restaurant serving tasty regional cuisine. €

Île du Bidounet http://camping-moissac.com. A good-value, shady three-star campsite on a little island 2km from central Moissac across the Pont-Napoléon. Facilities include a pool, bar and children's play area. €

Manoir Saint-Jean Saint-Paul d'Espis, http://manoirsaintjean.com. A stunning country manor located 9km north of Moissac, *Saint-Jean* offers beautiful gardens, a pool and nine suites, all individually decorated with plush furnishings, paintings and chandeliers. There's also a first-rate restaurant serving delicious seasonal produce – organic wines, meat and wild-caught fish with fresh herbs from the garden. €€€

★ **Le Moulin de Moissac** Esplanade du Moulin, http://lemoulindemoissac.com. Occupying a former watermill just east of the Pont-Napoléon, this is the sleekest hotel in town. It's a large, imposing building, but the inside has been beautifully refurbished, and the rooms have very comfortable beds and pristine bathrooms. It also boasts a spa, a terrace overlooking the river and a gorgeous restaurant (see below). €€

Le Pont Napoléon 2 allée Montebello, http://le-pont-napoleon.com. A few very classy rooms above a fine restaurant (see below). The hotel overlooks a busy road beside the bridge, but inside it is a haven of tranquillity and the prices are extremely reasonable. Opt for a room with a view of the river. €

EATING AND DRINKING

SEE MAP PAGE 239

★ **Le Florentin** 6 place Roger-Delthil, http://leflorentin-bistrotgourmand.fr. An elegant but unpretentious restaurant that will appeal to adventurous foodies. Surprise your taste buds with specialities like smoked salmon and grapefruit salad, accompanied by a carefully selected wine list. Prices are reasonable. €€

Kiosque de l'Uvarium 20 av de l'Uvarium, 06 28 93 24 76. A casual place with a large terrace, serving grills, salads and pastas. The adjoining outdoor entertainment space hosts a variety of events on summer evenings, such as theatre, Latin dance displays and even hip-hop gigs. €€

★ **Le Moulin de Moissac** Esplanade du Moulin, http://lemoulindemoissac.com. This sumptuous hotel restaurant is one of the best in the area, tempting the palate with dishes such as locally reared guineafowl simmered in ginger and teamed with mushroom risotto. €€

Le Pont Napoléon 2 allée Montebello, http://le-pont-napoleon.com. This excellent restaurant is attached to *Le Pont Napoléon* hotel (see above), and it's worth eating here at least once, just for a treat. Grab a seat on the riverside terrace and tuck into a hearty plate of roast lamb with artichoke, followed by mandarin soufflé. €€

La Terrasse du Cloître 5 place Durand-de-Bredon, 07 82 82 83 63. The magnolia-shaded terrace at *Auberge du Cloître* makes an idyllic spot to spend a sunny lunch hour and it's in a prime location right by the tourist office. The focus is on fresh local produce, as well as a number of fish and seafood dishes. €

St-Nicolas-de-la-Grave

Eight kilometres southwest of Moissac, the small *bastide* of **ST-NICOLAS-DE-LA-GRAVE** is dominated by a four-square château atop a low rise on the south bank of the Garonne. The château's oldest tower – the fattest of the four, on the northeast corner – is attributed to Richard the Lionheart, who passed through here on his return from the Third Crusade in the late 1100s. Nowadays, however, it houses the *mairie*, and there's nothing to see inside.

Musée Lamothe-Cadillac

Place du Château • Free • 05 63 95 92 55

St-Nicolas is proud of its claim to fame as the hometown of **Antoine Laumet**, founder of Detroit in America, who was born here in 1658. His birthplace, just southwest of the central square, now contains the **Musée Lamothe-Cadillac**, worth a quick browse as much for the story of Laumet's life as for any of the exhibits, which comprise mock-ups of a period bedroom and kitchen, and masses of documentation, some of it in English.

Laumet was an adventurer who, on leaving for Canada in 1683, adopted the upper-crust name of de Lamothe-Cadillac. He later turned up in America in the service of King Louis XIV, where he founded a number of forts, among them a cavalry outpost called *le détroit* between lakes Erie and Huron in 1701. Two hundred years later, a Detroit car company was looking for a name at the same time as the city was celebrating its anniversary. They decided to honour Detroit's founding father, and thus were Cadillacs born.

ARRIVAL AND INFORMATION

ST-NICOLAS-DE-LA-GRAVE

By car There's no public transport to St-Nicolas, so you'll need a car to get here.

Tourist office Place du Château (July & Aug daily 9.30am–12.30pm & 2–6pm; Sept–June Mon 9.30am–12.30pm, Tues–Thurs 2–5pm, Fri 9.30am–12.30pm & 2–5pm; 05 63 94 82 81, http://ville-stnicolas82.fr). When the office is closed, the *mairie* on rue du Champs-de-l'Église will provide local information.

ACCOMMODATION

Au Château 1 bd des fossés-de-Raoul, 05 81 11 94 63. A lovely *chambre d'hôte* set inside an old *maison de maître* surrounded by silver-leaved olive trees and lush flower-filled gardens. There are six beautifully decorated guest rooms and suites to choose from, plus a private swimming pool. €€

Camping Plan d'Eau 05 63 95 50 00. Decent two-star campsite 2km north of the village, where the Garonne and Tarn rivers form a large lake; the campsite is part of a leisure complex with snack bar and canoe and bike rental among other facilities, and you can also go birdwatching in the adjacent nature reserve. €

Auvillar

AUVILLAR, 14km west of St-Nicolas, is perched on a cliff on the Garonne's south bank. Its feudal château and ramparts were demolished in the eighteenth and nineteenth centuries, but thankfully the wonderful old village centre remains. From the main road skirting south of the village, you duck under the seventeenth-century **Tour de l'Horloge** to find yourself in the gently sloping triangular-shaped **place de la Halle** surrounded by a harmonious ensemble of brick and timber buildings with arcades running all around.

At the square's cobbled centre stands a pleasing circular stone-pillared market hall, built in the early nineteenth century.

Musée du Vieil Auvillar
Place de la Halle • Charge • 07 82 86 66 15

It's worth poking your nose into the **Musée du Vieil Auvillar**, on the place de la Halle's north side, for its collection of local pottery. Auvillar was already known for its pottery production in the sixteenth century, but in the following century they began making faïence of sufficiently high quality to rival that imported from Holland and Italy. Local potters still have a good reputation, as witnessed by the big pottery fair held every October (see page 233).

ARRIVAL AND INFORMATION   AUVILLAR

By car There's no public transport to Auvillar, so you'll need your own vehicle.

Tourist office 4–6 rue du Couvent (April–June & Sept to mid-Oct daily 10am–12.30pm & 2–6pm; July & Aug daily 10am–12.30pm & 2–7pm; mid-Oct to March Tues–Sun 2–5.30pm; 05 63 39 89 82, http://auvillar.fr).

ACCOMMODATION AND EATING

De l'Horloge 2 place de l'Horloge, http://hoteldelhorlogeauvillar.com. A convenient spot to sleep or eat in Auvillar, *De l'Horloge* is located right beside the gate tower. Rooms are spacious but simple and sparsely furnished, but the hotel restaurant offers a shady terrace looking out over the main street. €€

Quercy Blanc

North of Moissac, the land gradually rises to gently undulating, green and woody country, cut through by parallel valleys running down to meet the Garonne and planted with vines, sunflowers and maize, as well as apple and cherry orchards. It's a very soft landscape, the villages are small and widely scattered, and the pace of life seems about equal with that of a turning sunflower. This is the **Quercy Blanc**, named after the area's grey-white soils and building stone, a region with few sights, but one which lives up to the image of deepest rural France.

The single most interesting place to head for is **Lauzerte**, atop a river bluff 25km north of Moissac. Further north again, **Montcuq** distinguishes itself with its solid square keep, the remnants of a twelfth-century fortress, standing guard over the medieval village, while way over to the southeast, **Montpezat-de-Quercy** is home to a Gothic church with a surprising collection of art treasures, including a beautiful and complete set of Flemish tapestries.

Further east still, **Lalbenque** is the truffle centre of the south and a name that reverberates around the high temples of gastronomy.

GETTING AROUND   QUERCY BLANC

Public transport Options are very limited in the Quercy Blanc: there's no train line, and though there are bus services between Lauzerte from Moissac, and Montcuq and Lalbenque from Cahors, you have to book in advance for them all, as they run by reservation only.

By car Given the paucity of public transport in the Quercy Blanc, you'll really need your own vehicle to travel around the region.

Lauzerte

The sleepy hilltop village of **LAUZERTE** stands on a promontory between two rivers, a press of white-walled houses contained within its medieval ramparts, with the "new" town spilling down the south and eastern slopes. The site's strategic importance was not lost on the counts of Toulouse, who took control of Lauzerte in the late twelfth century and granted it the status of a *bastide* in 1241, with all the rights and privileges that entailed. The other notable event in Lauzerte's history took place fifty years later, when the townspeople threw out the English occupiers. By way of reward the French king, Philip IV, elevated Lauzerte to capital of the Bas Quercy (Lower Quercy) region and seat of the royal seneschal (the king's representative). However, its heyday came to an end in the late sixteenth century when Lauzerte was demoted to a mere district capital in the aftermath of the Wars of Religion.

Nevertheless, a few vestiges of these glory days remain in the old town, which lies clustered around the pretty, arcaded central square, **place des Cornières**, where Lauzerte's **market** is held each Wednesday and Saturday, and the **Église St-Barthélémy**. The church's origins go back to the thirteenth century, but it was largely rebuilt after the Protestants wreaked their havoc, and its main point of interest nowadays is the gilded Baroque altarpiece, dedicated to the Virgin Mary and depicting scenes from her life, which fills the north chapel. Behind the church, there are good views of the patchwork landscape all around from the **place du Château**, where the castle once stood on the promontory's northern tip. From here **rue de la Garrigue**, and its extension **rue de la Gendarmerie**, double back south of the church, running along the ridge past a number of thirteenth- and fourteenth-century merchants' houses with their big ground-floor arches and colonnaded windows above.

ARRIVAL AND INFORMATION — LAUZERTE

By bus There is a bus service run by Bus Gerla (05 63 04 55 50) to Lauzerte from Moissac, but it only operates on Wednesdays and Saturdays, returning to Moissac at 2pm; a reservation is necessary. Buses leave from outside the Crédit Agricole bank.

By car There is car parking in the lower section of the town, from where you can walk up to the medieval town via a series of steps, or you can drive to the top and park just outside the ramparts, where there is a large car park.

Tourist office 3 place des Cornières (July & Aug daily 9am–7pm; Sept–June Mon–Sat 9am–noon & 2–6pm; 05 63 94 61 94, http://lauzerte-tourisme.fr).

ACCOMMODATION AND EATING

Aube Nouvelle Durfort-Lacapellete, 05 63 04 50 33. Located 9km south of Lauzerte on the D2, this Belgian-run hotel is set in a lovely manor house with beautiful gardens. There's also a good restaurant serving delicacies like rabbit in brown ale and *cassoulet d'escargots*. €

★ **Le Belvédère** Montagudet, http://lebelvedere.biz. For a touch of luxury, head to *Le Belvédère*, where highlights include a spa and an infinity pool looking out over the valley towards Lauzerte. Rooms are sunny and spacious, with huge comfy beds and private balconies, while the excellent restaurant offers "slow food" cuisine and an impressive wine list. €€

Le Quercy Faubourg d'Auriac, http://hotel-du-quercy.fr. *Le Quercy* offers a handful of old-fashioned but perfectly comfortable rooms, but the real draw is the restaurant. In addition to traditional local dishes, such as *cassoulet* or farm-raised chicken cooked in Cahors wine, it serves a good range of fish and seafood dishes, and game in season. Reserve a table in advance. €

La Table des Trois Chevaliers Place des Cornières, 05 63 95 32 69. Situated in the beautiful central square, this is a popular spot for relaxed weekend dining, serving dishes like goat's cheese lasagne and gourmet fish and chips. €€

Musée du Corbillard et de l'Attelage

Charge • 05 63 95 84 02 • The museum is 8km southeast of Lauzerte, at the end of a long lane signed off the D16 Molières road 2km east of Cazes-Mondenard

Just outside the village of **Cazes-Mondenard**, with its pretty Gothic church, the quirky **Musée du Corbillard et de l'Attelage** is centred on its collection of **hearses**, kick-started in 1970 when Monsieur Quercy was given an old hearse. Once he'd acquired a second one, word spread, and nearby parishes rushed to offer him theirs. By the time of his death, he had amassed nearly a hundred different models, some horse-drawn, others pulled by hand, from the seventeenth century up to the first motorized model manufactured by Peugeot in 1949. His family now continue his work. The collection also includes a large number of regular carriages, all in excellent condition, and some early farm machinery. After the tour, you are offered tastings of wine, pâtés and other local produce, and in season they also serve regional meals if you book in advance.

Montcuq

Thirteen kilometres northeast of Lauzerte along the Petite-Barguelonne valley, **MONTCUQ** – pronounce the "q" if you don't want to be saying "my arse" – is built around the flanks of a conical hill, on top of which stands a huge square keep. Like Lauzerte, Montcuq guarded the ancient road to Cahors and lies on the Santiago de Compostela pilgrim route, but it seems to have had the knack of picking the wrong cause: it sided with the Cathars, was condemned for collaborating with the English and later became a Protestant stronghold. As a result, there's not much in the way of sights, though it's an attractive little place and has a very good Sunday morning **market** on place de la République.

Torre de Montcuq
Charge • 05 65 31 80 05

To get the lie of the land in Montcuq, the best thing to do is climb up the **Torre de Montcuq**. Any of the lanes leading uphill from rue de la Promenade, the wide boulevard to the south of the old town, will take you there. It was built at the turn of the eleventh century as part of a larger fortress, and although Louis IX ordered the ramparts destroyed, the ditches filled in and the tower's top knocked off in the aftermath of the Cathar crusades, at 24m, it's still a fair climb. The effort is rewarded with all-round views – and even when the tower is closed, the pinnacle of rock it stands on is high enough to give a good panorama, looking down over the maze of stone and half-timbered houses, and the **Église St-Hilaire**.

ARRIVAL AND INFORMATION

By bus Raynal Voyages (05 65 23 28 28) runs buses to Cahors, though you need to book in advance. They stop on rue de la Promenade near the tourist office.
Tourist office 8 rue de la Promenade (April–June, Sept & Oct Mon–Sat 9am–12.30pm & 3–6pm, Sun 10am–12.30pm; July & Aug Mon–Sat 9am–12.30pm & 3–6pm, Sun 10.30am–1pm; Nov–March Tues–Sat 9am–noon; 05 65 22 94 04, http://ccquercyblanc.fr).

ACCOMMODATION

Du Parc http://auberge-du-parc.wixsite.com. A comfortable, albeit somewhat old-fashioned hotel with a large garden and a guests-only restaurant, located on the Belmont road, 500m west of Montcuq. $\overline{€}$

> ### MONTCUQ MONOPOLY
> In 2007, Hasbro, makers of **Monopoly**, opened an internet voting site to decide which towns would feature on a new French version of the game. As a joke, web users started a campaign to feature Montcuq, reasoning that most foreigners would rudely mispronounce the name. It took off, and Montcuq won – but Hasbro decided to overrule the popular vote and use Dunkerque instead. The outcry was, predictably, huge. To make up for the lack of democratic compliance, Hasbro agreed to issue a special Montcuq version of Monopoly. The town was allowed to choose which streets would be used, and a local artist provided images. Look out for this unusual souvenir in shops around town.

Castelnau-Montratier

The D4 southeast of Montcuq takes you on a rollercoaster ride across the valleys and intervening hills, on one of which stands **CASTELNAU-MONTRATIER**, 20km from Montcuq, with its incongruous neo-Byzantine church and spacious market square.

Lalbenque

If you happen to be in the Quercy Blanc on a Tuesday between December and March, head to the village of **LALBENQUE**, some 22km east along the D19 from Castelnau-Montratier. Its eleventh-century **Église Saint-Quirin** deserves more than a passing glance for its gilded wooden altarpiece, said to have been purchased in the late eighteenth century by a local carter from revolutionaries in Cahors for the paltry sum of 50 francs. Knowing he'd purchased a looted sacred treasure at a bargain price, he began to suffer twinges of conscience and confessed to his local priest, who immediately absolved the penitent and claimed the prize for his church, where it's been ever since.

At any other time of year, once you've inspected the church, that's just about it – Lalbenque is a sleepy little white-stone town, barely distinguishable from all the others in the Quercy Blanc. However, pull in at around 2pm on a Tuesday afternoon between December and March, and you'll witness a market like no other, the **Marché aux Truffes**, when trestle tables laden with **black truffles** line the main street, and a long rope stretches the length of them, holding back a seething mass of buyers, locals and tourists. At 2.30pm sharp, a bell rings and the rope is hauled away as buyers from all over France surge forward to begin negotiations. A price per kilo is announced for the day, but that's just a guide, with some pretty sharp bargaining being necessary before all parties are satisfied. Truffles are rare and capricious, resisting every effort at widespread cultivation – the majority are still found in the wild. It's therefore the intrepid hunters who have the advantage; and before long only a few small specimens remain for the tourists to savour in a sumptuous truffle omelette that night.

ARRIVAL AND INFORMATION — LALBENQUE

By bus Raynal Voyages (http://raynal-voyages.fr) runs buses to Cahors, though you need to book in advance. They stop on place de la Bascule, just north of the tourist office, and Ateliers municipaux.

Tourist office Place de la Bascule (March–June Mon–Wed & Sat 9am–1pm, Wed–Fri 2–5pm; July & Aug Mon–Fri 9am–1pm & 2–6.30pm, Sat 9.30am–1pm, Sun 9.30am–12.30pm; Sept Mon & Sat 9am–1pm, Tues–Fri 9am–1pm & 2–5pm; Oct & Nov Tues & Sat 9am–1pm, Wed 9am–1pm & 2–5pm, Fri 2–5pm; Dec–Feb Tues & Wed 9am–1pm & 2–5pm, Fri 2–5pm, Sat 9am–1pm; 05 65 31 50 08, http://lalbenque.net).

ACCOMMODATION AND EATING

Au Gout Dujour 26 rue du Marché aux Truffes, http://au-gout-dujour.fr. A chic navy and exposed-stone interior with a glass-fronted kitchen so that you can see your meal being prepared. Classic French cuisine served in style, with plenty of vegetables. Dessert is the showstopper. €€

Le Logis de Reyjade Place de République, Montdumerc, 05 65 22 89 56. A few kilometres southwest of Lalbenque just off the D10, this *chambre d'hôte* is dotted with beautiful eighteenth-century antiques and boasts a pretty garden, but the decor leans on the side of old-fashioned rather than timeless. €€

Montpezat-de-Quercy

Ten kilometres southwest of Lalbenque through twisty country lanes lies the interesting hilltop village of **MONTPEZAT-DE-QUERCY**. Traces of its medieval heyday remain in the arcaded central square and lanes of half-timbered houses, but the main reason to stop here is the **Collégiale St-Martin**, with its unusually rich hoard of treasures, standing at the southeast end of the promontory on which the village is built.

Collégiale St-Martin

Free

The **Collégiale St-Martin** was founded in the early fourteenth century by Cardinal Pierre des Prés (1281–1361), a local who grew wealthy in the service of the Avignon popes. With its high and severe single nave, the interior of the church is unexciting, at least in comparison with the fourteenth- to sixteenth-century **artworks** arrayed in the side chapels. Best are the battered but still lovely *Vierge aux Colombes*, her face framed by golden ringlets, in the second chapel on the left; a polychrome *Pietà* in the first on the right; and, next door, an English alabaster triptych depicting the Birth, Resurrection and Ascension of Christ – in the last only his feet are visible as he's whisked heavenwards. The Collégiale St-Martin's finest treasures, though, are the five Flemish **tapestries** grouped around the choir. They were made especially for the church in the early sixteenth century, a gift from Jean IV des Prés, bishop of Montauban, and portray events from the life of St Martin de Tours, to whom the church is consecrated. The most famous scene is that in the first panel, where the future saint – at the time in the service of the Roman army – shares his cloak with a crippled beggar. The workmanship throughout is of superb quality, while the colours remain amazingly vibrant. Also in remarkably good condition is the white-marble sarcophagus and statue of Pierre des Prés, to the right of the choir, with his feet resting on a lion while his well-fed face is bathed in a contented grin.

ARRIVAL AND INFORMATION — MONTPEZAT-DE-QUERCY

By car There's no public transport to Montpezat, so you'll need your own vehicle. The best place to park is on place de la Résistance, but there is also ample street parking outside the tourist office.

Tourist office 24 bd des Fossés (Sept–June Mon 2–5.30pm, Tues–Sat 9.30–12.30pm, Tues, Thurs & Fri 2–5.30pm; July & Aug Tues–Sat 9.30am–12.30pm & 2–6pm, Sun 9.30am–12.30pm & 2–5pm; 05 63 02 05 55, http://montpezat-de-quercy.com). The office doubles as a Maison des Vins where you can buy the local Côteaux du Quercy wines and pick up a brochure listing vineyards to visit, though it doesn't offer tastings.

ACCOMMODATION AND EATING

Camping Révéa le Faillal http://revea-vacances.fr. A well-tended two-star municipal campsite in a leisure park on Montpezat's northern outskirts. Facilities include a pool, tennis, mini-golf, and basketball and volleyball courts. €

Ferme-Auberge de Coutié 05 63 67 73 51. You'll eat very well at this atmospheric *ferme-auberge* on a Quercy farm surrounded by ducks and orchards; it's on the D20, 9km southwest of Montpezat and signed to the east of Espanel hamlet. €€

Montauban

Lying 20km east of Moissac and 50km north of Toulouse, **MONTAUBAN** is a prosperous, middle-sized provincial city and the capital of the largely agricultural *département* of Tarn-et-Garonne. The most interesting area is the small kernel of streets based on the original *bastide*, a harmonious ensemble of warm, pink brick which looks its best at sunset, or at night when the steeples, massive old bridge and riverside facades are illuminated.

Enclosed within an inner ring of boulevards between **allée de l'Empereur** to the east and the river to the west, the old centre follows the typical *bastide* pattern, with a grid of streets around an arcaded market square, the glorious **place Nationale**, where a daily fresh food market takes place. Between the main shopping streets of pedestrianized **rue de la Résistance** and **rue de la République**, which intersect in the *bastide*'s southern corner, lie a labyrinth of enticing alleys, covered passages and interior courtyards. The greatest delight is simply to wander – the centre is only a ten-minute stroll from end to end – taking in the scattered sights as you go, of which the highlight is the **Musée Ingres Bourdelle**, dedicated to Montauban's most famous son.

MONTAUBAN **SOUTH OF THE RIVER LOT** | 247

Just south of the cathedral, allée du Consul Dupuy hosts a busy farmers' **market** on Saturday mornings, while on Wednesday mornings, another market is held in place Lalaque, across the river.

Brief history

Montauban's origins go back to 1144 when Alphonse Jourdain, count of Toulouse, decided to create a **bastide** here as a bulwark against English and French royal power. Indeed, it is generally regarded as the first *bastide*, the model for the medieval new towns found throughout this region (see page 223). The city has enjoyed various periods of great prosperity (as one can guess from the proliferation of fine houses), mainly based on trade in silk and other textiles. The first followed the suppression of the Cathar heresy and the final submission of the counts of Toulouse in 1229 and was greatly enhanced by the building of the **Pont-Vieux** in 1335, making it the best crossing point on the Tarn for miles. The Hundred Years' War did its share of damage, as did Montauban's opting for the Protestant cause in the Wars of Religion, but by the time of the Revolution it had become once more one of the richest cities in the southwest.

Place Nationale

The grand **place Nationale** is the epicentre of modern Montauban and the city's main social hub. Rebuilt after a fire in the seventeenth century, it is surrounded on all sides by a double row of arcades beneath two- and three-storeyed townhouses, their uniformity tempered by the square's irregular shape.

Église St-Jacques

04 63 66 42 78

The distinctive octagonal belfry of the **Église St-Jacques**, a couple of minutes' walk west of place Nationale, shows above the southwestern rooftops. First built in the thirteenth century on the pilgrim route to Santiago de Compostela, the church bears the scars of Montauban's troubled history, not only in its mix of architectural styles, but in the holes gouged out of the belfry's fortified base by cannonballs during an unsuccessful siege by twenty thousand Catholic troops – held off by just six thousand locals – in 1621.

Musée Ingres Bourdelle

Charge • http://museeingresbourdelle.com

Overlooking the river south of the Église St-Jacques stands a massive half-palace, half-fortress, begun by the counts of Toulouse, then continued by the Black Prince in 1363. He left it unfinished when the English lost control of the town, and so it remained until 1664 when the bishop of Montauban chose this very prominent spot for his residence. Now the **Musée Ingres Bourdelle**, it houses paintings and more than four thousand drawings left to the city by locally born **Jean-Auguste-Dominique Ingres** (1780–1867). The collection includes several of the supremely realistic, luminous portraits of women which are the artist's trademark. It also contains a substantial collection of works by another native, **Émile-Antoine Bourdelle** (1861–1929), the ubiquitous monumental sculptor and student of Rodin, alongside a hotchpotch of other exhibits, from Gallo-Roman mosaics to fifteenth- and sixteenth-century European fine art. In the early days of World War II, the museum hosted more illustrious visitors when the Louvre dispatched over three thousand works of art to Montauban for safe-keeping prior to the German invasion. When southern France was occupied in 1942, however, they were moved again to more remote locations, including the Château de Montal (see page 177).

Cathédrale Notre-Dame

Rue Notre-Dame • Free • 05 63 63 10 23

Providing a stark exception to Montauban's red-brick homogeneity is the **Cathédrale Notre-Dame**, a cold, sore-thumb of a building some ten minutes' walk southeast of the Musée Ingres along rue de l'Hôtel-de-Ville. It was erected on the city's highest spot at the end of the seventeenth century as part of the triumphalist campaign to reassert the Catholic faith, following the defeat and harsh repression of the Protestants. Inside the dazzling white Classical facade lies an echoing nave, whose main point of interest is another Ingres painting, *Le Voeu de Louis XIII*, hanging in the north aisle. Specially commissioned for the cathedral, the vast canvas depicts Louis offering France, symbolized by his crown and sword, to a Virgin and Child, and is strongly influenced by Raphael's romantic style.

ARRIVAL AND DEPARTURE — MONTAUBAN

By plane The nearest airport is Toulouse-Blagnac (08 25 38 00 00, http://toulouse.aeroport.fr), 40km south of Montauban, straight down the A62 *autoroute*.

By train Montauban's *gare SNCF* lles roughly 1km west of the centre across the Pont-Vieux at the far end of avenue Mayenne. A city bus runs from the train station to the centre (line A), stopping on allée de l'Empereur near place Prax-Paris, on the northeast side of town; tickets can be bought on the bus.

Destinations Agen (up to 20 daily; 35–50min); Brive (2–8 daily; 1hr 50min); Cahors (up to 17 daily; 40min–1hr 20min); Moissac (up to 11 daily 20–30min); Toulouse (every 30min; 25min).

By bus While there are buses from Montauban to Bruniquel, Laguépie, Montricoux and St-Antonin-Noble-Val, these are primarily aimed at schoolchildren to coincide with pickups and drop-offs during term time; as such they're not much use for visitors.

By car The most convenient car park is the underground pay parking on place Prax-Paris or place Roosevelt. Free parking is available along the riverbanks beneath the Pont-Vieux and north of the theatre on rue de la Mandoune.

GETTING AROUND AND INFORMATION

Car rental Near the train station, try Avis, 23 av Mayenne (http://avis.fr); or Europcar, 382 av de Toulouse (http://europcar.fr).

Taxis There are taxi stands at the station and the north end of allée de l'Empereur, or contact Taxis Montalbanais (05 63 66 99 99, http://taxis-montauban.com).

Tourist office Rue du Collège (July & Aug Mon–Sat 9am–6.30pm, Sun 10am–12.30pm; May, June, Sept & Oct Mon–Sat 9.30am–12.30pm & 2–6.30pm; Nov–April Mon–Sat 9.30am–12.30pm & 1.30–6pm; 05 63 63 60 60, http://montauban-tourisme.com).

ACCOMMODATION — SEE MAP PAGE 247

★ **Abbaye des Capucins** 6–8 quai de Verdun, http://abbayedescapucins.fr. A large and beautifully renovated hotel in a seventeenth-century monastery with a Michelin-starred restaurant attached, this is the last word in urban luxury. Rooms are spacious and well appointed, and there is a spa, a pool, bike rental and a great bistro. €€

★ **Château Mezger** 105 chemin du Bois Vieux de Bernoye, Pignes, http://chateaumezger.fr. An exquisite *chambre d'hôte* in a lovely county manor house just a 10min drive from Montauban. The three huge rooms each have wooden floors, chandeliers and Egyptian cotton sheets, with views over the ample gardens. There's also a spring-fed swimming pool, a home-made breakfast included and a four-course dinner *menu* available. €

Du Commerce 9 place Roosevelt, http://hotel-commerce-montauban.com. Charming pops of colour and thoughtful furnishings make good use of the space at this central hotel, making it the best deal for those wanting to be in the thick of it. Parking is extra. €

Mercure 12 rue Notre-Dame, http://all.accor.com . Part of the nationwide *Mercure* chain of hotels, this is nevertheless a very good option as it's housed in an attractive eighteenth-century building right in the town centre. It boasts modern, reasonably spacious rooms and a good restaurant. €€

EATING — SEE MAP PAGE 247

Montauban has a surprisingly varied selection of **restaurants**, with options for all budgets. Keep an eye open for the local speciality, **montauriols**, a chocolate-coated cherry preserved in armagnac; you'll find them at *pâtisseries* all over town.

Le Bistro des Capucins 6–8 quai de Verdun, http://abbayedescapucins.fr. The renowned restaurant attached to *Abbaye des Capucins* is worth a detour even for non-guests. Sample quintessential French specialities like pan-fried frogs' legs or tuck into delicious truffle risotto. €€€

★ **La Cave Ô Délices** 10 place Roosevelt, http://cave-o-delices.fr. A local favourite housed in an atmospheric stone cellar and offering lunchtime *formules* and evening *menus*. Opt for the fish, followed by the divine basil and forest fruits sorbet. €€

Da Nang 344 av Jean Moulin, 09 54 56 12 78. Chinese and Vietnamese food done extremely well, with plenty of choice – rice dishes, noodles, meat, fish and plenty of vegetarian options too. Go to town on the starters; the spring rolls are particularly good. €

L'Estanquet 16 rue du Général Sarrail, http://restaurantlestanquet.com. Mismatched furniture and quirky decor set the scene at this hip restaurant on the west bank of the Tarn. Expect well-presented dishes, including casseroles and grills, plus some truly decadent desserts. *Menus* are generally buffet-style. €€

Le Ventadour 23 quai Villebourbon, http://le-ventadour.com. Magnificently sited in an old house on the west bank near the Pont-Vieux, this upmarket restaurant serves up dishes like oven-baked sea bream, salmon carpaccio and apricot panna cotta. €€

DRINKING AND NIGHTLIFE   SEE MAP PAGE 247

Le Caï 8 quai Montmurat, 05 63 91 99 09. With its huge red sign right on the waterfront, it's impossible to miss this hip nightclub, usually teeming with revellers. It's also linked by an underground passageway from nearby sister bar *Le Santa Maria*.

Le Flamand 8 rue de la République, 05 63 66 12 20. This lively bar-café is the place to go for a beer – they serve a huge selection, including an impressive number of Belgian brews, both on tap and bottled. There's plenty of choice for hungry drinkers too: the extensive menu offers pizzas, grills and salads as well as more local fare such as *tartiflette* (potato gratin with lardons and cheese) and *cassoulet*.

Le Santa Maria 2 place Léon-Bourjade, 05 63 91 99 09. The shabby exterior does nothing to deter Montauban's youth from descending on *Le Santa Maria* en masse come the evening. As well as an ample cocktail menu, it also serves numerous tapas and more substantial Tex Mex meals, including wine.

DIRECTORY

Hospital Centre Hospitalier, rue Léon-Cladel, to the north of the old quarter (05 63 92 82 82).
Police Commissariat de Police, 50 bd Alsace-Lorraine (05 63 21 54 00), northeast of the centre.
Post office Allée de l'Empereur.

The Gorges de l'Aveyron and around

In its lower course the Aveyron glides across the dull flood plain surrounding Montauban, offering little reason to stop other than the village of **Montricoux**, with its museum dedicated to a forgotten artist. The scenery becomes more interesting, however, about 30km east of Montauban where the river has sliced a narrow defile through the hills. The entrance to the **Gorges de l'Aveyron** is guarded by the fortress village of **Bruniquel**, its ancient houses assembled higgledy-piggledy on steep cobbled streets, while further east **Penne** perches beneath a crumbling castle. From here on the gorge gets increasingly dramatic as you work your way upriver to **St-Antonin-Noble-Val**, an excellent base for exploring the gorge and surrounding sights. The most compelling of these is the partially ruined **Abbaye de Beaulieu-en-Rouergue**, located 14km northwest, where the Gothic church has been converted into a contemporary art gallery. Beyond St-Antonin, **Laguépie** is less interesting but provides another possible base, from where you can hop south to the beguiling – if very touristy – hilltop town of **Cordes-sur-Ciel**. At Laguépie the Aveyron valley turns abruptly north, and its sides close in again to form a second, increasingly deep, thickly wooded gorge, dominated by the ruins of **Najac**'s mighty fortress. This stands guard over the frontier of the former province of Rouergue, now the Aveyron *département*, and the southern approach to the refreshingly unprettified *bastide* of **Villefranche-de-Rouergue**.

GETTING AROUND   THE GORGES DE L'AVEYRON

By car With bus services sparse and aimed at schoolchildren, you'll need your own transport to get between Montricoux, Bruniquel, Penne, St-Antonin-Noble-Val and Varen.

By train The best way of travelling between Laguépie, Najac and Villefranche is the Toulouse–Brive train line; these trains also stop at Cordes-sur-Ciel, further south.

Montricoux

Just before you leave the flat alluvial plains, 25km west of Montauban, **MONTRICOUX** would hardly be worth the stop if it weren't for its intriguing art museum dedicated to **Marcel Lenoir**, a prolific local artist who, like Ingres, was born in Montauban in 1872; he died in Montricoux in 1931. Lenoir was much fêted during his early years, when he was at the forefront of Pointillism and Cubism, and he even presaged Art Deco as he searched for new means of expression; but he was also an irascible character and managed to offend so many critics, dealers and galleries that he was eventually cast into oblivion. And there he stays, despite the best efforts of the owner of the museum's collection.

Musée Marcel-Lenoir
56 Grand Rue • Charge • http://marcel-lenoir.com

On the west side of Montricoux, the collection at the **Musée Marcel-Lenoir** comprises 140 works spanning Lenoir's whole career. One of the most revealing is the *Kiss of Judas*, in which you see Picasso profiled in blue and Van Gogh cutting off Gauguin's ear, while Judas is portrayed as a well-known art critic of the time.

ACCOMMODATION AND EATING

Aici sèm pla http://aicisempla.com. A delightfully friendly campsite on a farm in Revel, 2km from the village of Vaïssac and 5km southwest of Montricoux. Facilities include a communal BBQ, *boules* court, bike hire and free wi-fi throughout the site, plus mobile homes for rent (weekly only) and glamping tents. Discounted weekly camping rates available. Closed mid- to late-Dec. €

Chez Terrassier Le Bourg, Vaïssac. For comfortable accommodation, head 8km southwest of Montricoux to this pretty, modern place in the middle of Vaïssac; there's a pool, and a restaurant. €

Les Gorges de l'Aveyron Le Bugarel, http://lesgorges aveyron.com. As you walk into Montricoux village, you'll pass the entrance to this very swish riverside hotel-restaurant along a lane beside the bridge. It's as good as it looks, with beautifully decorated rooms, a swimming pool, leafy gardens and a high-end restaurant. €€€

Bruniquel

Around 5km east of Montricoux, **BRUNIQUEL** shelters in the lee of its château and has an interesting museum. Once a Protestant stronghold, today it's better known for its striking location, and the drive over from Montricoux is stunning, winding through the hills of the Gorges de l'Aveyron, where fortified villages cling to the rocky crags.

Château de Bruniquel
Charge • http://bruniquel.fr

The **Château de Bruniquel** teeters on the edge of a 100m-high cliff at the north side of town. The medieval ruins are actually the remains of two adjacent castles, since the original twelfth-century fortress was divided between rival cousins in 1484. Both are rather knocked about, although there is an impressive carved wooden fireplace in the larger of the two.

Maison des Comtes de Payrol
Place des Monges • Charge • 05 63 67 26 42

To the west of the castle entrance, and a little more engaging, is the **Maison des Comtes de Payrol**. The thirteenth-century home of a wealthy merchant family, its vaulted cellars and panelled and frescoed rooms now house an unusually good local history **museum**, including an interesting collection of oil lamps and candle holders.

INFORMATION — BRUNIQUEL

Tourist office At the entrance to the village (March–June, Sept & Oct Tues–Sat 10am–1pm & 2–6pm; July & Aug daily 10am–7pm; Nov–Feb Wed–Sat 10am–1pm & 2–5pm; 05 63 67 29 84, http://bruniquel.fr). All practical information, including accommodation details, is listed on noticeboards outside.

ACCOMMODATION

Cornelia Promenade du Ravelin – rue d'Albi, 06 16 04 90 69. The swanky, Dutch-run *Cornelia*, 200m from the tourist office, has four rooms, including the hammock-strewn attic. Meals are available (guests-only, booking needed). €

L'Étape du Château Promenade du Ravelin, 05 63 67 25 00. The five rooms at this upmarket *gîte d'étape* are decorated in a different scheme, plus there's a sauna and spa. Meals available for guests by advance booking. €

Penne

Six kilometres upriver from Bruniquel lies the even more beautiful ridge-top village of **PENNE**, once a Cathar stronghold, with its ruined castle perched on an impregnable pinnacle. Everything is old and leaning and bulging, but holding together nonetheless, with a harmony that would be impossible to create purposely. There's just one cobbled street leading from an arch under the church belfry and through a second gate – where ancient grain measures are cut into the wall – to a footpath scrambling among the **castle ruins**. There's not much left, although restoration work is being undertaken, and it's an atmospheric spot, the piles of stones overrun with dog-roses, clematis and honeysuckle, with a panorama taking in the village roofs and the wooded country beyond.

EATING — PENNE

La Terrasse 13 rue Peyragude, 05 63 56 35 03. Grills cooked over an open fire are the speciality here, but the real star is the location – the terrace offers a spectacular view of Penne's castle and the Aveyron gorges. €€

The Corniche

Beyond Penne the Aveyron gorge becomes deeper and more dramatic. To appreciate it at its best, turn off the main road just after Cazals, 6km from Penne, following signs for the **Corniche**, a single-track road that climbs steeply for a kilometre or so up to the cliff's edge. You'll be rewarded with tremendous views, and six kilometres later, you drop down to the river again to the west of St-Antonin-Noble-Val.

St-Antonin-Noble-Val

The finest and most substantial town in the lower stretch of the Aveyron valley is **ST-ANTONIN-NOBLE-VAL**, 16km northeast of Penne. It sits on the river's north bank beneath the beetling white cliffs of the **Roc d'Anglars**, where it developed in the ninth century around an abbey said to house the remains of the evangelizing **St Antonin**. According to legend, his body was carried here in a boat guided by two white eagles from Pamiers, in the Ariège, where the saint met his death. Since then the town has endured all the vicissitudes of this region's history: it sided with the Cathars, then the Protestants and each time was walloped by the alien power of the kings from the north, until it eventually sank into oblivion after the seventeenth century. Yet, in spite of it all, a marvellous heritage of houses endowed by wealthy merchants remains from its medieval glory days, when St-Antonin was an important commercial centre, manufacturing linen and leather goods.

The easiest landmark to head for is the spire of the large but uninteresting Neo-Gothic **church**, towards the town's southeast corner. Along the church's west wall rue du Pont-de-l'Aveyron leads south to the bridge, while rue Guilhelm-Peyre curves northeast to **place de la Halle**. This square is St-Antonin at its most picturesque, with its cafés and pint-sized *halle*, and the focus of an important Sunday-morning **market**.

Musée du Vieux St-Antonin
Place de la Halle • Charge • 05 63 30 63 47

The finest building in St-Antonin-Noble-Val is the **Maison des Consuls**, whose origins go back to 1125. The facade is pierced with arcades, pairs of colonnaded openings and a contrastingly severe oblong window on the first floor, on one pillar of which Adam and Eve hide their modesty; the old man on the pillar to the left, holding some books and a staff, is Emperor Justinian (483–565), who codified Roman law.

The building's most striking feature, however, is the tower with its top-heavy loggia and too-perfect machicolations added by the nineteenth-century architect Viollet-le-Duc – though he did save the building from collapse. It now houses the **Musée du Vieux St-Antonin**, with an uninspiring collection of objects to do with the former life of the place, including various prehistoric finds.

INFORMATION AND ACTIVITIES ST-ANTONIN-NOBLE-VAL

Tourist office In the *mairie* next to the church (March & Oct Mon 2–5.30pm, Tues–Sat 10am–12.30pm & 2–5.30pm, Sun 10am–1pm; April 9.30am–12.30pm & 2–6pm & Sun 9.30am–1pm; May, June & Sept Mon–Sat 9.30am–12.30am & 2–6pm, Sun 9.30am–1pm 2–5pm; July & Aug daily 9.30am–12.30pm & 2–7pm; Nov–Feb Mon & Sat 2–5pm, Tues–Fri 10am–12.30pm & 2–5pm; 05 63 30 63 47, http://tourisme-saint-antonin-noble-val.com).

Outdoor activities St-Antonin is the starting point for canoeing down this lower stretch of the Aveyron. Variation La Plage (http://variationsportnature.com) offers canoe rental, stand-up paddleboarding and a tree-top adventure park.

ACCOMMODATION AND EATING

Le Festin de Babette 1 rue de Marsac, 05 63 31 69 03. Don't judge a book by its cover; it may look like a 1970s motel, but this is the best restaurant in town. Menus generally consist of three main dishes: meat, fish and vegetarian. Desserts are a work of art, and surprisingly copious. €€

Gorges de l'Aveyron http://camping-gorges-aveyron.com. About 1.5km out of town on the Marsac road, this friendly campsite is situated next to the river, overlooked by the cliffs. Facilities include a pool, bar, restaurant and children's play area; they will also lend out BBQs. €

Le Ponget Ponget, 05 63 68 21 13. Just out of town on the Caylus road, you'll find this simple but peaceful and well-kept municipal campsite with great views of the cliffs and river. €

La Résidence 37 rue Droite, http://laresidence-france.com. Smart Dutch/German-run *chambre d'hôte* on the road leading northwest out of place de la Halle. The five en-suite rooms are large and colourfully decorated – one even has its own roof terrace. €€

Les Trois Cantons http://3cantons.fr. Some 6km north up onto the *causse* from St-Antonin, this spacious and well-organized campsite offers three-star facilities including a heated pool, shop and snack bar. €

Abbaye de Beaulieu-en-Rouergue

Free • http://art-beaulieu-rouergue.com

Some 14km northwest of St-Antonin, the beautiful Cistercian **Abbaye de Beaulieu-en-Rouergue** lies deep among wooded hills. The abbey was founded in 1144, though the present buildings date from the thirteenth century, and are remarkably unscathed considering it was sacked and burnt during the Wars of Religion, looted again during the Revolution and then used as a barn until the late 1950s; in 1844 Viollet-le-Duc even wanted to rebuild the whole caboodle in St-Antonin but had to give up through lack of funds. The present owners have now restored the church to create a superb exhibition space for their collection of **contemporary art**; displays change several times a year, in combination with temporary exhibitions. The high, light nave with its clean lines and lack of ornamentation, save for the delicate rose windows and a few sculpted capitals, provides the perfect foil for works by Jean Dubuffet, Simon Hantaï and Henri Michaux, among others.

Varen

Upstream from St-Antonin, the Aveyron valley widens out for a while and is spoilt by stone quarries. The only reason to stop is the village of **VAREN**, 16km from St-Antonin on the river's north bank. Its Romanesque **Église St-Pierre** and tiny area of old streets repay a quick wander, but the prime attraction is another excellent though fairly upmarket **restaurant** (see below).

EATING — VAREN

Moulin de Varen http://lemoulindevaren.fr. An authentic country restaurant housed in an old stone mill, *Moulin de Varen* offers a surprisingly wide menu, paired with a carefully selected wine list. Snag a seat on the garden terrace overlooking the River Aveyron and dig into traditional cuisine; don't miss the zesty lemon-vodka sorbet for dessert. Reservations recommended. €€

Laguépie

LAGUÉPIE, 9km east of Varen, where the cliffs begin to close in again, guards the confluence of the Viaur and Aveyron rivers. The village has nothing in the way of sights, but is pretty enough and provides a useful base, served both by occasional buses from Montauban and by trains on the Toulouse–Brive line. The **church** pinpoints the village centre, occupying a spit of land between the two rivers, while a short stroll southwest is the place du Foirail, where the covered *halle* hosts a fresh produce **market** on Wednesday and Sundays.

ARRIVAL AND INFORMATION — LAGUÉPIE

By train The *gare SNCF* lies 500m northwest on the north bank of the Aveyron.
Destinations Cordes-sur-Ciel (4–8 daily; 20min); Figeac (4–8 daily; 1hr); Najac (4–6 daily; 10min); Toulouse (3–8 daily; 1hr 20min); Villefranche-de-Rouergue (4–8 daily; 25min).

Tourist office 2 place Henri-Granier (July & Aug daily 9.30am–12.30pm & 2.30–6pm; April–June, Sept & Oct Wed, Fri, & Sat 10am–12.30 & 2–5pm; Nov–March Tues & Fri 10am–12.30pm & 2–5pm, Sat 10am–12.30pm; 05 63 30 20 34, http://laguepie-en-rouergue.fr).

ACCOMMODATION AND EATING

La Ferme Parrinet http://lafermeparrinet.com. Set amid 10 hectares of countryside and woodland, this farmhouse *maison d'hôte* has three rooms and a *gîte* in idyllic surroundings, and an outdoor pool. A great place to get away from it all. €€
Les Tilleuls http://camping-lestilleuls-laguepie82.fr. Municipal campsite in a shady spot beside the Viaur river, roughly 1km to the east of Laguépie. There are chalets available for rent by the week, plus tennis courts, ping-pong tables, a snack bar, a small swimming pool and children's play areas. €

Cordes-sur-Ciel

The traveller who, from the terrace of Cordes, watches the summer night knows that he has no need to go further and that, if he so wishes, the beauty of this place, day after day, will lift him from all solitude.

Albert Camus

The spotlight has been shining on **CORDES-SUR-CIEL** since it was honoured with the title of Village Préféré des Français ("France's favourite village") back in 2014, and visitors have long frequented this spectacularly situated fortified town, perched high above the Cérou valley – it's easy to see how it earned its suffix of *sur-ciel* ("in the sky"). Located 15km south of Laguépie on the D922 (and also accessible by train), Cordes is a tourist magnet in July and August, when streets swell with crowds and the growing community of artisans do a roaring trade. Take time to explore away from the main drag and you'll find a tangle of steep cobblestone lanes and impossibly narrow alleyways, where the medieval houses, flower-filled windowboxes and stone arches offer endless inspiration for photographers.

Founded in 1222 by Count Raymond VII of Toulouse, Cordes grew rich on **leatherworking** and in the following century its walls had to be enlarged no fewer than seven times to contain the expanding population. Things took a downturn, however, with the arrival of the plague in the fifteenth century, but Cordes later recovered, and developed a notable **lace industry** in the nineteenth century. However, its real renaissance came in the 1970s, when hippies, including the **craftspeople** and

artisans whose studios now cram the old town, arrived to put Cordes back on the map, attracted by its beauty and abandon.

Camus' words give some idea of the town's allure, and hard though it may be to achieve such a placid state when the streets are packed during summer days, in the evening or out of season the romance of Cordes returns. It's worth rising early to view the sunrise from the ramparts, and with every other building a medieval mansion, walking the town before the crowds arrive is a delight. Its layout is simple: the old citadelle – known as the **haute cité** – runs along and down the sides of the long and narrow ridge which juts up from the plain, while the modern part consists of a clump of streets at the foot of the old town's eastern tip. The best route to the *haute cité* is the knee-cracking **Grand Rue de l'Horloge** ascending from the tourist office, although at busy times it is more pleasant to take one of the picturesque but less crowded side streets. At the town's eastern limit, place de la Bouteillerie hosts a lively **market** each Saturday, selling produce from around the region.

You'll need good shoes and plenty of stamina to scale the steep streets on foot, but if you get tired, you can hop onto a **petit train** which makes frequent trips from outside the tourist office.

Maison de l'Art du Sucre et du Chocolat
33 Grand Rue Raimond-VII • Charge • http://yvesthuries.com

Heading straight up the Grand Rue Raimond-VII from the tourist office, you'll pass through progressively older gateways towards the heart of the *haute cité*. En route, you'll come across the **Maison de l'Art du Sucre et du Chocolat**, an exhibition of sculptures made entirely out of sugar or chocolate. It has a couple on display in the shop, so it's worth sticking your head round the door even if you don't want to see the full museum. Visits include a chocolate tasting.

Musée d'Art Moderne et Contemporain
Grand Rue Raimond-VII • Charge • http://mamc.cordessurciel.fr

About halfway along Grand Rue Raimond-VII, the elegant and symmetrical arcaded face of the fourteenth-century **Maison du Grand Fauconnier** conceals the **Musée d'Art Moderne et Contemporain**, which features works by the figurative painter Yves Brayer, who lived in Cordes from 1940, as well as a French-only audio presentation explaining the town's lacemaking tradition and a motley collection of modern art, including minor pieces by Picasso, Miró and Klee.

Grand Rue Raimond-VII
Grand Rue Raimond-VII holds some of Cordes' most remarkable buildings. Be sure to take in the facade of the **Maison du Grand Veneur** ("House of the Great Hunter"), a wonderful Gothic pile whose otherwise plain stone face is festooned with amusingly sculpted and extremely well-preserved medieval caricatures of beasts and hunters. A few doors down, the former **palace** of Raymond of Toulouse boasts an impressively carved frontage.

Musée Charles Portal
1 rue St-Michel • Charge • http://museecharlesportal.fr • The official entrance to the museum is off rue St-Michel

At the meeting point of Grand Rue Raimond-VII and rue St-Michel, close to the **Porte des Ormeaux** ("Gate of the Elms"), is the **Musée Charles Portal**. Inside, the small exhibition rooms house a display on the medieval wells that riddle the town, and which were used in times of siege for water supply or to store grain. If you want to take a closer look, one of the most easily accessible wells lies in the ancient covered market, opposite the Musée d'Art Moderne et Contemporain.

ARRIVAL AND INFORMATION CORDES-SUR-CIEL

By train Trains stop 5km to the west of Cordes at Vindrac (05 63 56 05 64), from where it's a pleasant hour-long walk

or short taxi ride costing about €5 – taxis are easy to find in July and Aug, otherwise you can call one (05 63 56 14 80).
Destinations (Cordes-Vindrac) to: Figeac (4–8 daily; 1hr 20min); Laguépie (4–8 daily; 20min); Najac (4–6 daily; 30min); Toulouse (4–8 daily; 1hr); Villefranche-de-Rouergue (4–8 daily; 50min).

By bus Buses from Albi (40min–1hr) stop near the tourist office in the lower town.

By car Parking can be a challenge – in the summer months, the area a few metres east of the tourist office soon fills up and cars line the roads leading into town. Don't be tempted to drive into the *haute cité*, better to park at the bottom and walk or take the tourist train (see below).

Tourist office 38–42 Grand Rue Raimond-VII (April & Oct Mon–Sat 10.30am–12.30pm & 2–6pm, Sun 10.30am–12.30pm & 2–5pm; July & Aug Mon–Sat 9.30am–1pm & 2–6.30pm, Sun 10am–1pm & 2–6pm; May, June & Sept Mon–Sat 10am–12.30pm & 2–6pm, Sun 10.30am–12.30pm & 2–5pm; 05 63 56 00 52, http://cordessurciel.fr).

GETTING AROUND

Le Petit Train Trains run every 10min from place de la Bouteillerie to Porte de la Jane. In July and Aug 45min tours with commentary are also available, departing hourly on the hour.

ACCOMMODATION

L'Escuelle des Chevaliers 87 Grand Rue Raimond-VII http://lescuelledeschevaliers.fr. Housed in a fourteenth-century building and adorned with heraldic tapestries, suits of armour and ancient swords, this medieval-themed *chambre d'hôte* has rooms equipped with four-poster beds and wrought-iron chandeliers, and a restaurant where you can even dress up and dine in medieval costume. Dishes include date-stuffed chicken, roasted chestnuts and suckling pig. €€

Logis sur Ciel 18 Grand Rue Raimond-VII, 05 63 56 25 87. Behind the authentic thirteenth-century façade, this charming *chambre d'hôte* is a maze of stone arches and narrow stairwells. The five rooms are all comfortable and modern, but for the best views, book the top-floor "Estela", which has a huge terrace overlooking the valley and an ingenious pulley system to transport your luggage for you. €€

★ **Le Secret du Chat** 16 le Planol, http://lesecretduchat.com. Effortlessly walking the line between luxurious and homely, *Le Secret du Chat* is a cut above most other *chambres d'hôtes*. The five rooms each boast a countrified elegance, with original beams, polished wood floors and antique furnishings, jazzed up with patterned bedlinen. The restaurant is equally impressive, with regional cuisine paired with local Gaillac wines, served in the old cellar. €€

Le Vieux Cordes 21 rue Saint-Michel, Haute Cité, 05 63 53 79 20. Original brickwork, spiral staircases and restored wooden beams lend this *hostellerie* a rustic elegance, while the rooms offer big comfy beds, spotless bathrooms and all the mod-cons. Downstairs, the restaurant serves *menus*; in summer you can eat in the ancient, cobbled courtyard under a canopy of wisteria. Don't miss out on the desserts, which include perfectly scorched crème brûlée and delicious profiteroles. €€

EATING

There are numerous options for eating in Cordes. The best **restaurants** are in the town's hotels, but there are plenty of cheaper options around the central place de la Halle and adjacent place de la Bride – some also offer magnificent views over the valley.

Le Cayrols Le Cayrols, http://lecayrols.com. For a change of pace from the busy tourist haunts of the *cité*, head up the road to *Le Cayrols*, where dinner is served in a pretty sculpture garden. Choices are limited but dishes like the goat's cheese and vegetable millefeuille and orange-glazed scallops leave a lasting impression. €€

La Table d'Yvonne 1 place de la Halle, 05 63 56 92 09. The foie gras made in-house by artisan Michel Monteil is the signature dish at this busy restaurant. Most popular is the tagliatelle with foie gras, preceded by a complimentary apéritif. You can also buy a range of artisan products at the adjoining boutique. Reservations recommended. €€€€

SHOPPING

There are more than forty **boutiques** in Cordes, selling artisan foods, local wines, art and handicrafts including leather- and metalwork. Many shops are touted as "museums" and the artisans are often happy to discuss their work or perform demonstrations. Pick up the free *Guide des Artistes et Artisans* booklet from the tourist office for a full rundown of outlets. Be aware that most shops don't accept cards, so it's best to carry cash or check before you buy.

La Cave St-Michel Place Saint-Michel, 05 63 56 92 07. The place to buy regional wines, apéritifs, whiskies and Eau de Vie, with a huge range available and free wine tasting daily in July & Aug (and rest of the year on request).

Éditions Larroque Place de la Halle, http://editionslarroque.fr. Specializing in exquisite hand-bound books, tapestry book covers, calligraphy art and medieval-style books.

La Fabrique des Petites Mains 3 grande rue de la Barbacane, 05 63 53 96 94. Showcasing the artistic endeavours of twelve female artists, this boutique is the place to find unique gifts with a feminine touch: think hand-crafted leather purses, jewellery, baby clothes and beautiful origami fairy lights.

Najac

At Laguépie (see page 254), the Aveyron valley heads northwards and the river flows through a wooded defile. The most picturesque route along the valley bottom is either the train or the GR36 footpath, while road users should take the D106 and D594 along the western line of hills. Either way, you eventually arrive at a bridge – 15km by road and slightly less on foot – beneath the brooding towers of the semi-ruined **Château de Najac**.

The castle occupies an extraordinary site on the peak of a conical hill isolated in the river's wide meander – a spot chosen in the mid-1200s by **Alphonse de Poitiers**, who wanted to bring the area's Cathar sympathizers to heel. He enlarged the original fortress and laid out a new town to the east in an elongated version of a *bastide* with its arcades and central market square. For a short while Najac prospered as the region's capital, but the site proved too restrictive and by the end of the thirteenth century it had lost out to Villefranche-de-Rouergue (see page 258), leaving the castle to be fought over endlessly in the conflicts that ensued. The Protestants pillaged it in 1572 and the revolutionaries had their turn in 1793, but, in spite of all this, Najac survived.

The heart of modern Najac consists of a big, open square lying to the east of the medieval village, where grey-tiled houses tail out westwards in a single street along the narrow spur connecting the valley side to the castle hill.

Château de Najac
Charge • 05 65 29 71 65

Entering Najac from the east you come first to the **faubourg**, the elongated market square bordered by houses raised on pillars. It slopes gently downhill towards a cobbled street, overlooked by more ancient houses, which leads past a fountain to the **Château de Najac**. The castle is a model of medieval defensive architecture: its curtain walls reach to over 20m in places, within which five round towers supplement the square twelfth-century turret, and the castle is equipped with unusual multi-storey loopholes for archers.

However, the main reason to visit is for the magnificent all-round **view** from the top of the keep, a full 200m above the river.

Église St-Jean
Rue de l'Église • Free

Just below Najac's castle, in what was the original medieval village, stands the huge, very solid-looking and austere **Église St-Jean**, which the villagers were forced to build at their own expense in 1258 as a punishment for their conversion to Catharism. In addition to a collection of reliquaries and an extraordinary iron cage for holding candles, the church has one architectural oddity: its windows are solid panels of stone from which the lights have been cut out in trefoil form.

Below the church, a surviving Roman road leads downhill to where a thirteenth-century bridge spans the Aveyron.

ARRIVAL AND INFORMATION — NAJAC

By train The *gare SNCF* is 2km by road from the village. Taxis often wait outside the station, or call 05 65 81 12 92.
Destinations Cordes-sur-Ciel (4–8 daily; 30min); Figeac (4–8 daily; 50min); Laguépie (4–8 daily; 10min); Toulouse (3–8 daily; 1hr 30min); Villefranche-de-Rouergue (4–8 daily; 15min).

Tourist office On the south side of the *faubourg* (May, June & Sept Mon–Sat 10.30am–12.30pm & 2–5.30pm Sun 9.30–12.30pm; July & Aug daily 10am–6.30pm; March, April & Oct Tues–Sat 2–5.30pm, Wed & Sat 10am–12.30pm; Nov–Feb Wed 10am–12.30pm & 2–5pm; 05 65 29 72 05, http://tourisme-villefranche-najac.com).

ACCOMMODATION AND EATING

Le Belle Rive http://le-belle-rive.fr. This charmingly old-fashioned hotel occupies a lovely riverside position near the train station. Rooms are well-sized and comfortable, there's a large pool and the garden offers views of the castle perched high on the hilltop. It also runs an excellent restaurant serving good-value regional cooking. €

Gîte d'Étape 05 65 29 73 94, http://aagac.com. Budget accommodation situated at the leisure centre adjacent to the campsite. Sparse but clean rooms have 2–6 beds, and there's a communal kitchen and dining area. Reservations essential. €

L'Oustal del Barry 2 place Sol del Barry, http://oustaldelbarry.com. A taste of the country right in the heart of town, with bright, spacious rooms and a leafy terrace with views of the castle. It's worth opting for half-board, as the hotel restaurant is renowned for its subtle and inventive cuisine. Reservations essential. €€

Le Païsserou http://camping-aveyron-najac.com. Najac's four-star riverside campsite, to the southwest of the old bridge, is spacious and very well equipped. Facilities include a restaurant/snack bar and large pool. €

★ **Relais Mont Le Viaur** St-André-de-Najac, http://montleviaur.fr. Lovely stone building, some 1km east of Najac, boasting sunny, well-furnished rooms with en-suite bathrooms and air-conditioning. The highlight is its wonderful restaurant – *the* place to eat in the area. They serve beautifully presented food, combining traditional and modern cuisine. All products are market-fresh and reservations are essential. €

Villefranche-de-Rouergue

The second stretch of the Aveyron gorge peters out about 10km north of Najac, but it's worth continuing upstream to the laidback market town of **VILLEFRANCHE-DE-ROUERGUE**, which boasts one of the most atmospheric central squares in the whole region. As its regular form and the die-straight streets indicate, this is a *bastide*, founded in 1252 by the ubiquitous **Alphonse de Poitiers**, as part of the royal policy of extending control over the recalcitrant lands of the south. A prosperous town thanks to its copper-rich mines, Villefranche was also made the seat of the seneschal, the king's representative, in 1369, with the right to mint money. While its wealthy merchants built the ornate houses that grace the cobbled streets to this day, conditions in the surrounding countryside were so desperate that in 1643, more than ten thousand peasants, known as **Croquants**, besieged the town for a week. As elsewhere, the rebellion was harshly put down and the leaders strung up in the market square.

The medieval quarter

Villefranche's **medieval quarter** lies on the north bank of the Aveyron, accessed by a modern road-bridge beside its pedestrian fourteenth-century counterpart. From the old bridge, the town's main street, pedestrianized **rue de la République**, runs northwards up a gentle incline into the heart of the *bastide*. It is attractive enough, but no preparation for the central square you come out into, **place Notre-Dame**. The square, too, is built on a slope and is surrounded by unusually tall houses, arcaded at ground-floor level, some with elaborate window surrounds. If possible, visit on a Thursday morning when local merchants and farmers spread out their produce at the weekly **market**, presided over by the colossal porch and bell tower – nearly 60m high and fortified – of the **Collégiale Notre-Dame**. The church was started in 1260 but wars and fires intervened and it was not completed until 1519. Behind the altar are two fine mid-fifteenth-century stained-glass windows: the one on the left depicts the Creation; that on the right portrays sixteen characters from the Old and New Testaments. Also note the oak choir stalls alive with a superb array of beasts and demons, as well as scenes from daily life – they took the craftsman, André Sulpice, fifteen years to complete in the late fifteenth century.

Chapelle des Pénitents-Noirs
Charge • 05 65 45 13 18

On boulevard Haute Guyenne, which forms the northern limit of the old town, the seventeenth-century **Chapelle des Pénitents-Noirs** boasts a splendidly Baroque painted ceiling and an enormous gilded retable – resplendent after its extensive renovations.

Chartreuse St-Sauveur

Charge • 05 65 45 13 18 • The site is in the grounds of a hospital about 1km south of town on the main D922 to Najac and Laguépie

Worth the slight detour from central Villefranche, the **Chartreuse St-Sauveur** was completed in the space of ten years from 1450, giving it a singular architectural harmony. The highlight is the second of the two cloisters, a minuscule quadrangle of white, sculpted stone, while the church itself contains more examples of André Sulpice's craftsmanship on the screen and choir stalls.

ARRIVAL AND INFORMATION   VILLEFRANCHE-DE-ROUERGUE

By train The *gare SNCF* is located a couple of minutes' walk south across the Aveyron from the old centre.
Destinations Cordes-sur-Ciel (4–8 daily; 50min); Figeac (4–8 daily; 45min); Laguépie (4–8 daily; 25min); Najac (4–8 daily; 15min); Toulouse (3–8 daily; 1hr 40min).
By bus Raynal Voyages (05 65 23 28 28) runs buses to Cahors; pick up the timetable, *Les Bus du Lot*, from the tourist office, or book in advance if travelling outside of school terms. They stop in place de la Liberté and at the *gare routière*, next to the *gare SNCF* on the southern side of the river.
Tourist office Promenade du Giraudet (May, June & Sept Mon–Sat 9.30am–12.30pm & 2–6pm, Sun 10am–12.30pm; July & Aug Mon–Sat 9.30am–6.30pm & 2–7pm, Sun 10am–1pm & 2–5pm; March, April & Oct Mon–Fri 10am–noon & 2–5pm, Sat 9am–noon; Nov–Feb Mon–Fri 10am–noon & 2–5pm, Sat 10am–noon; 05 65 45 13 18, http://tourisme-villefranche-najac.com).

ACCOMMODATION

Camping du Rouergue http://campingdurouergue.com. Huge but friendly three-star municipal campsite, 1.5km to the south of Villefranche, signed off the D47 to Monteils. Facilities include a pool, table tennis and a summer-only bar. Closed Sept–April. €
Les Fleurines 17 bd Haute Guyenne, 05 65 45 86 90, http://lesfleurines.com. Ideally situated opposite the Chapelle des Pénitents-Noirs, *Les Fleurines* has a range of great-value rooms. Rooms are smart, well-furnished and spotless, embellished with some contemporary touches like circular beds and faux-fur scatter cushions. There's a coworking space too. €€
Relais de Farrou Rue de Figeac, http://relaisdefarrou.com. Smart, ultra-modern hotel about a 20min drive out of town on the Figeac road. Guests have use of a small spa, gym and an outdoor pool, while the hotel also provides bicycles and other activities, and there's a restaurant. €€

EATING

L'Atelier 5 place Louis Fontanges, http://latelier-restaurant.fr. Surely not far off a Michelin star, the chef that runs *L'Atelier* trained under Alain Ducasse in Paris. Dishes are served with flair, and the presentation is exquisite. €€€€
La Gabelle 10 rue Belle-Isle, 05 65 45 57 13. Well-run restaurant one block south of the church, where you'll find cheerful staff and an extensive menu of pizzas, home-made pastas and grills, as well as some more adventurous options like frogs' legs. €
Gaya Place Lescure, 05 65 45 25 95. A heavy emphasis on seafood, and excellent *tartines* for lunch. Dishes are so colourful that you'll get your five a day on one plate. There's a varied selection of local wines. €€
Jacques a Dit 54 rue de la République, 05 65 45 37 26. Bistro serving a fixed *menu* with three choices of dish for each course. For the adventurous, there's 'typical' French fare such as *tête de veau* (calf's head). €€

SUNRISE OVER A VINEYARD NEAR BERGERAC

Contexts

261 History

279 Books

281 French

289 Glossary

History

The history of the Dordogne and Lot region is a fascinating illustration of how the political entity that is now a unified France in fact consists of numerous components of entirely distinct historical character. The southwest's vigorously independent cultural identity was forged millennia ago in the artistic endeavours of mysterious but highly gifted cave-dwellers, and hundreds of years ago in the influence of English rule and in the poetry of the troubadours, written in a language now virtually extinct. Even from the fifteenth century onwards, when the region was officially part of metropolitan France, it remained a distant territory, at least a week's travel from Paris, and one where local interests and powerful families held far more sway than the voice of the king. To this political detachment must be added the entirely secluded nature of the life led by the vast majority of the region's population, barely 15 percent of whom lived in towns even as late as 1910. Communicating in myriad local dialects, worshipping the gods of local folklore and working on the land in the same manner as their ancestors had for centuries, the rural poor of the Dordogne and Lot, largely oblivious to the causes – though certainly not the devastating consequences – of the political and religious conflicts going on around them, were only dragged into the familiar historical timeline during the twentieth century.

The beginnings

Primitive flint tools found in the Dordogne indicate human presence dating back at least 400,000 years. However, the region's archeological treasure-trove really gets going with the **Neanderthal** people, who arrived on the scene some 100,000 years ago. Despite their brutish image, evidence now suggests that Neanderthals were surprisingly sophisticated. They developed not only an increasingly elaborate range of stone tools but also complex burial rituals. This didn't, however, equip them to compete with the next wave of immigrants sweeping across Europe between 30,000 and 40,000 years ago, and Neanderthals gradually died out.

Early archeologists named the newcomers **Cro-Magnon** after a rock shelter near Les Eyzies where the first skeletons were identified. Now they are better known as *Homo sapiens sapiens* – in other words, our direct ancestors. While Cro-Magnons developed ever more sophisticated tools, they also began to scratch fertility symbols into the rock, made various pigments and then took the great leap into abstraction that led to drawing, painting and carving. The earliest evidence of **prehistoric art** dates from

400,000 BC	c.30,000 BC	200 BC	51 BC
Evidence of human presence in the Dordogne	Cro-Magnons create the earliest cave art near Les Eyzies	Romans begin to colonize southern France	Julius Caesar wins the battle of Uxullodunum (Puy d'Issolud), crushing tribal rule in the area

around 30,000 years ago, but reached its apogee during the Magdalenian era (10,000–17,000 years ago), also named after a shelter in the Dordogne's Vézère valley. It was during this era that Cro-Magnon people covered the walls and ceilings of the region's caves with art of a quality that would not be seen again for several millennia.

Around 10,000 BC the all-important reindeer herds, the Cro-Magnons' one-stop source of meat, fat, skin, bone and sinew, began to move north as the climate grew warmer and wetter. Over the next three thousand years these nomadic hunter-gatherers were gradually replaced by settled **farming and pastoral communities** who left hundreds of **dolmens** (megalithic stone tombs) scattered over the region. This Neolithic era in its turn made way for the great metal-working cultures, culminating in the Iron Age, from around 700 BC. About the same time **Celtic** people began to spread into the region from north and central Europe, establishing trade routes and building towns and hilltop fortresses. They were skilled manufacturers and had their own coinage, but instead of a cohesive entity, they comprised individual or loosely allied clans which were continuously fighting among themselves. It was these disunited tribes that the Roman legions encountered when they arrived in what they called **Gaul** – roughly equivalent to modern France – in the second century BC.

The Roman occupation

At first the **Romans** contented themselves with a colony along the Mediterranean coast, but in 59 BC the threat of a Germanic invasion and various Celtic uprisings prompted **Julius Caesar** to subjugate the entire area. It took him just eight years. By 56 BC he had pacified southwest Gaul and the only real opposition came from a young Arvenien (modern-day Auvergne) chieftain called **Vercingétorix**, who managed to rally a united Gaulish opposition in 52 BC. The Gauls had some initial victories, but in the end were no match for Caesar's disciplined armies. Vercingetorix was taken back to Rome in chains in 52 BC and the following year the Gauls staged their final stand at **Uxellodunum**, under the command of Lucterius, leader of the Cadurci. Caesar himself took command of the siege and eventually cut off their water supply thus forcing the surrender. **Uxellodunum** is generally believed to be at Puy d'Issolud, to the east of Martel.

The battle was one of the major turning points in the region's history. In 16 AD Emperor Augustus established the new Gallo-Roman province of **Aquitania**, stretching from Poitiers south to the Pyrenees. Its capital was Burdigala (Bordeaux), and regional administrative centres were set up in Vesunna (Périgueux) and Divona Cadurcorum (Cahors), each with its forum, amphitheatre, law courts and temples. During more than three centuries of peace – the **Pax Romana** – that followed, the Romans built roads, introduced new technologies, traded, planted vineyards and established an urbanized society administered by an educated, Latin-speaking elite. Today, the physical traces of this practically and culturally sophisticated society are most visible in the Roman ruins in Périgueux and Cahors. Just as durable, though, has been the linguistic impact: as well as being the language of the rulers, Latin penetrated rural areas and eventually fused with the local Celtic dialects to form two broad new language groups: the *langue d'Oïl* (where "yes" is *oïl* – later, *oui*), spoken north of the Loire, and the *langue d'Oc*, or *Occitan* (where "yes" is *oc*), to the south.

c.15 AD	**16 AD**	**360 AD**	**507 AD**
Administrative centres created at Divona Cadurcorum (Cahors) and Vesunna (Périgueux)	Emperor Augustus establishes the Gallo-Roman province of Aquitania	Frankish tribes invade from the north	Clovis, king of the Franks, founds the Merovingian dynasty

By the third century AD, Roman authority was starting to crack. Oppressive aristocratic rule and an economic crisis turned the destitute peasantry into gangs of marauding brigands, who were particularly rampant in the southwest. But more devastating were the incursions across the Rhine by various restless **Germanic tribes**, starting with the Alemanni and Franks, who pushed down as far as Spain, ravaging farmland and looting towns along the way. In response, urban centres such as Périgueux were hurriedly fortified while the nobles hot-footed it to their country villas, which became increasingly self-sufficient – economically, administratively and militarily.

The crunch came, however, in the fifth century when first the Vandals and then the **Visigoths** stormed through the region as the Roman empire crumbled. For nearly a hundred years the Visigoths ruled a huge territory extending across southern France and into Spain, with its capital at Toulouse.

Christianity and independence

The Visigoths' destructive and mercenary temperament was not conducive to sustained rule, and in 507 AD they were driven out of the region by the **Franks**, a northern tribe who gave their name to modern France. The end of the Visigoths marked the beginning of a long period of relative independence for Aquitaine and the southwest. Although the Frankish king, Clovis, was to found the **Merovingian dynasty** whose power technically extended to this region, he failed to re-establish the same over-arching authority as the Romans had acheived.

The power vacuum had been filled, in part, by representatives of the early Church. **Christianity** had arrived from Rome in the early fourth century and was spreading slowly through France, but the invasion of the Vandals and Visigoths had put its advance on hold. It fell to **bishop Chronope**, active in the region between 506 and 533 AD, to re-establish the faith by a prolific programme of church building, most notably the first cathedral of St-Etienne in Périgueux. Chronope is also thought to have played a role in the creation of the legend of St-Front, after whom Périgueux's modern cathedral is named. Clovis himself had embraced Christianity around 500 AD and thereafter was happy to devolve a great deal of everyday administration to local bishops, such as those at Cahors.

The Merovingian empire began to disintegrate in the late seventh century, leaving the way clear for their chancellors, the Pepin family, to take control. One of their most dynamic scions, **Charles Martel**, defeated the Spanish Moors when they swept up through the southwest as far as Poitiers in 732. His grandson, **Charlemagne**, continued the expansionist policy of the **Carolingian** dynasty – so called for their fondness for the name Charles, or "Carolus" – to create an empire which eventually stretched from the Baltic to the Pyrenees.

Charlemagne and his descendants, however, had no more genuine control over the southwest region than the Merovingians had, preferring, like them, to rule from a distance. In 781 Charlemagne created the quasi-independent **kingdom** of Aquitaine – an area extending from the Loire to the Cévennes and from the Rhône to the Pyrenees. Within the kingdom, the Carolingians delegated administrative power to royally appointed bishops, now joined by a growing number of counts – Quercy and Périgord for example – who had been awarded territory in exchange for their loyalty. In theory,

c.650	c.732	781	814	844
St Didier, bishop of Cahors, founds the abbey of St-Pierre at Moissac	Charles Martel defeats the invading Moors and founds the Carolingian dynasty	Charlemagne creates the quasi-independent kingdom of Aquitaine	Death of Charlemagne	Plundering Vikings sail up the Lot, Garonne, Dordogne and Isle rivers

> ## THE WAY OF ST JAMES
>
> According to the Bible, **St James the Apostle** was decapitated in Jerusalem in 44 AD. There is nothing to suggest how his remains came to be buried in northwest Spain, but in 820 it was declared that they had been discovered there, and during the fervent religious revival of the Middle Ages millions of pilgrims began flocking to his supposed tomb in **Santiago de Compostela**. The route took on a life of its own: monasteries, churches and hospitals were founded and villages grew up along the way to cater for the pilgrims wearing their distinctive cockleshell badge.
>
> The pilgrimage faded out during the sixteenth century, partly because of the wars sweeping France and partly because the cathedral canons rather carelessly lost the saint's remains; the relics were allegedly hidden to keep them out of the hands of Sir Francis Drake, who was then sniffing around Galicia, but later no one could remember where they'd put them. By another "miracle" they were rediscovered by archeologists in 1879, declared by the pope to be the genuine article, and the pilgrimage revived, though on a far more modest scale.
>
> In 1998 the whole system of paths and associated buildings was inscribed on the UNESCO World Heritage list. As a result, to walk the **chemin de St-Jacques** (Way of St James) – or at least some of it – has become popular again, partly as a spiritual quest, but also simply as a walking holiday. Three of the four main routes – from Vézelay, Le Puy-en-Velay and Arles – have been waymarked as long-distance footpaths (*grandes randonnées*, or GRs). Of these the GR654 from Vézelay and the GR65 from Le Puy pass through the Dordogne and Lot region; booklets outlining the routes are available in the Topo-guide series (see page 280).

the king retained feudal authority, but in reality the bishops and counts did largely as they pleased.

The royal position became weaker still in the ninth century, in part due to a long-drawn-out **battle of succession** following Charlemagne's death in 814, but also thanks to a series of extravagantly destructive raids by the **Vikings**, who sailed their longboats down from Scandinavia. They had been raiding coastal areas for decades, but in 844 they penetrated deep inland along the Garonne, Dordogne, Isle and Lot rivers, plundering towns and churches. Périgueux was razed in 849: the annals of one monastery recount matter-of-factly, "the devastating Normans put fire to Périgueux and, without further ado, got back on their boats."

In the face of these destabilizing invasions the Carolingians were obliged to delegate ever more autonomy to the provincial governors until these eventually grew more powerful than the king. So it was that when **Hugues Capet** succeeded to the French throne in 987, founding a 400-year dynasty that in theory ruled the whole of France, he in practice had authority only over a small area near Paris. Around the turn of the millennium, Aldebert I, one of the counts of Périgord, is supposed to have rebuked a royal demand for payment of feudal dues with the withering question "*Qui vous a fait roi?*" – "Who made you king, then?" By this point, the local aristocratic families were more embroiled in jostling for power with one another than with the king. In the tenth century Périgord was carved up into four **baronies** (Beynac, Mareuil, Bourdeilles and Biron), while Quercy was divided between five powerful families (Turenne, Gourdon, Cardaillac, Castelnau and St-Sulpice). At the same time, the counts of Poitou (based at

849	987	c.990	1122	1137
Vikings raze Périgueux	Hugues Capet crowned king of France and founds the Capetian dynasty	Counts of Poitou take control of Aquitaine and begin construction of the Romanesque churches	Birth of Eleanor of Aquitaine	Eleanor becomes duchess of Aquitaine at the age of 15

Poitiers) and Toulouse were fighting for control of what was once again the **Duchy of Aquitaine**. The former emerged victorious, thus creating a vast territory that by the twelfth century reached from the Loire to the Pyrenees. The Poitou counts also ushered in a period of relative peace, rapid economic growth and renewed religious vigour, demonstrated in a wave of church building. To them we owe the lovely Romanesque churches (see page 270) seen throughout the region to this day. At least some of this building activity was spurred and financed by the great procession of **pilgrims** passing along the route to Santiago de Compostela in Spain (see box).

English rule

It was the huge kingdom created by the amalgamation of the territories of the counts of Poitou and the dukes of Aquitaine that indirectly allowed the whole of the Dordogne and Lot region to fall into the hands of the **English Crown**. The cause of this catastrophe for the French royal family, the Capetian dynasty, was the strong-willed **Eleanor of Aquitaine** (1122–1204; see box), who inherited the domains of Aquitaine and Poitou in 1137 at the tender age of 15. Fifteen years later, she ditched her first husband, the French king, to marry **Henry of Anjou**, thereby creating an empire comprising Anjou and Normandy in addition to Eleanor's possessions. This in itself was a disastrous blow to the Capetians, but it was compounded in 1154 when Henry succeeded to the English throne (as Henry II). As a result, almost half of France fell under English rule. Much of it would remain so for the next three hundred years.

For the southwest region itself, however, English rule ushered in a period of peace, stability and impressive economic progress. With the major exception of **Richard the Lionheart** (Richard Coeur de Lion), Eleanor's third son, who plundered the area ruthlessly, the **English overlords** proved to be popular. For the most part they ruled from a distance, often preferring to stay put in England, and ensured the loyalty of their southern subjects by granting a large degree of independence to many of Aquitaine's rapidly growing towns and their local lords. Peasants lived under relatively privileged feudal conditions, helped by the fact that local lords were often in competition for their services. An important factor here was the building of dozens of **new towns**, the *bastides*, designed to secure border areas and accommodate the rapidly expanding population. In order to attract peasants to inhabit the new towns and cultivate the surrounding land, feudal lords had to offer enticing terms and considerable freedom.

The region continued to produce wheat and oats, but the real sensation of the era of English rule was the transformation of **wine** production into a lucrative and international industry. Merchants exporting the claret beloved of the English to London and other British ports grew wealthy, and the proceeds filtered through to the whole region. **Urban life**, too, began to take off, with the towns of Périgueux, Bergerac and Sarlat growing to populations of around five thousand each.

As English rule was delivered from across the Channel and therefore somewhat removed, it did not mean any perceptible invasion by the English language. On the contrary, independence from northern France allowed local language and culture to flourish, creating perfect conditions for the high-culture phenomenon of the **troubadours** (see box).

c.1140	1152	1154
The fortified Château de Beynac is constructed at Beynac-et-Cazenac	Henry Plantagenet, Duke of Anjou and Normandy, later Henry II, marries Eleanor of Aquitaine in Poitiers cathedral	Henry Plantagenet succeeds to the English throne and the region comes under English rule, ushering in a golden age of prosperity

ELEANOR OF AQUITAINE

The life of **Eleanor of Aquitaine** (1122–1204) is an incredible tale of romance and tragedy, of high farce and low intrigue that rivals any modern-day pot-boiler. As duchess of Aquitaine and countess of Poitou she was already a key figure in twelfth-century Europe. She then married two kings and gave birth to two more, effectively ruled England for a time and died at the grand old age of 82.

In 1137, at the age of just 15, Eleanor inherited the domains of Aquitaine and Poitou. These assets, combined with her intelligence and beauty, gave her a healthy list of suitors, at the head of which was the future King Louis VII of France. They were married in Bordeaux's St-André cathedral, and just a week later, the death of Louis VI made the young couple king and queen of France. The marriage, however, was not a success: it bore no male heirs, and the vivacious Eleanor found her attentions wandering elsewhere. In March 1152, they were divorced.

Just two months later, Eleanor married the handsome, charismatic and extremely ambitious **Henry of Anjou**, who was eleven years her junior, but far closer in temperament. The following year she bore him the all-important heir, and, when Henry II succeeded to the English throne in 1154, Eleanor found herself queen of England.

Although Eleanor spent much of her time in France, she and Henry produced at least eight children. Of these both Richard and John became kings of England, while only two, John and Eleanor, outlived her. In the meantime, since Henry proved reluctant to delegate power, his sons rebelled against him in 1173, supported by both Eleanor and her former husband, Louis VII; the latter hoped to put a more compliant neighbour on the English throne – and was possibly also out for a spot of revenge.

But the rebellion soon collapsed, and Henry placed his wife under house arrest. She remained closely guarded until his death in 1189, but her problems had by no means ended. Richard I (the Lionheart), Eleanor's favourite son, was next in line. All went well until he was captured in 1192 while returning from the Third Crusade. The indomitable seventy-year-old waded in as unofficial regent, while also keeping her French possessions under control, for the next two years.

Eleanor withdrew from public life after Richard's release, and even more so after his death in 1199. She retired to the abbey of Fontevraud, in the Loire valley, where she died almost unnoticed in 1204, to be remembered as a popular, shrewd and effective ruler, well able to control her notoriously hot-blooded southern vassals.

The Cathar crusades

While the English ruled in Aquitaine, an audacious bid for independence from the political and religious dictats of the French Crown was also being made over to the east, by the powerful **counts of Toulouse**. From the mid-twelfth century on, the so-called **Cathars** (also known as Albigensians) had won a great deal of support in the area, which extended as far as the Dordogne valley, by preaching that the material world was created by the Devil and the spiritual world by a benevolent God. They also believed in reincarnation and that the only way to escape the mortal coil was to lead a life of saintly self-denial – all of which completely undermined the role of the clergy. To put an end to such **heresy**, Pope Innocent III unleashed a **crusade** against the Cathars in

1166	1183	Mid-12th century
A perfectly preserved body discovered in a cave in the Quercy is declared to be St Amadour. Rocamadour sanctuary is built around it	Henry the Young King dies at Martel, days after ransacking the holy shrines at Rocamadour	Cathars begin to spread through the region

1209, starting off with a particularly murderous attack led by **Simon de Montfort** in which the entire population of the Mediterranean town of Béziers, estimated at twenty thousand people, was slaughtered; the papal legate in charge of the assault is famously supposed to have proclaimed, "Kill them all. God will know his own."

A series of crusading armies, composed largely of land-hungry northern nobles, then proceeded to rampage through the region on and off for the next twenty years. This was followed by an equally vicious **inquisition** designed to mop up any remaining Cathars, which culminated in the siege of Montségur, in the eastern foothills of the Pyrenees, in 1244, when two hundred people were burnt alive.

As a result of the Cathar crusades, the French Crown now held sway over the whole of southwestern France, including Toulouse. The new count of Toulouse was **Alphonse de Poitiers**, brother of the future Louis IX, whose lands stretched north through Quercy into Périgord, and west along the Garonne as far as Agen. Like his English neighbours, Alphonse started establishing a rash of *bastides* in order to impose his authority over his new domains.

The Hundred Years' War

Though the English had lost their possessions north of the Loire by the mid-thirteenth century, they remained a perpetual thorn in the side of the French kings thanks to their grip on Aquitaine. Skirmishes took place throughout the century, followed by various peace treaties, one of which, in 1259, took Quercy and Périgord back into the English domain. But the spark that ignited the ruinous – and misnamed – **Hundred Years' War** (1337–1453) was a Capetian succession crisis. When the last of the line, Charles IV, died without an heir in 1328, the English king, **Edward III**, leapt to claim the throne of France for himself. It went instead to Charles's cousin, **Philippe de Valois**. Edward acquiesced for a time, but when Philippe began whittling away at English possessions in Aquitaine, Edward renewed his claim and embarked on a war.

The major battles of the war were almost all fought in the northern half of the country, where Edward won an outright victory at **Crécy**, before his son, the **Black Prince**, took the French king, Jean le Bon, prisoner at the Battle of Poitiers in 1356 and established a capital at Bordeaux. The resulting treaty appeared to give the English victory, but the French fought back, banishing the English entirely but for a toehold in Bordeaux. In 1415, though, the tables turned again as Henry V inflicted a crushing defeat on the French army, against all odds, at the legendary battle of **Agincourt**. Once again, France seemed on the verge of unravelling at the seams, until **Jeanne d'Arc** (Joan of Arc) arrived on the scene. In 1429 she rallied the demoralized French troops, broke the English siege at Orléans and tipped the scales against the invaders. The English were slowly but surely driven back to their southwest heartland until even that was lost at the **Battle of Castillon** in 1453. Within months, the English surrendered Bordeaux, and their centuries-long adventure in France came to an end.

Although Castillon was the only major battle fought in the southwest, the region did not spare itself from **bloodshed**. The region's powerful families, operating from their fortified bases (see box), sought to take advantage of the general chaos by attacking their neighbours and trying to strengthen their own hands. Many nobles swapped sides repeatedly, fighting under English or French colours as it suited them. **Raymond de**

1209	1244	1250
Simon de Montfort leads the first crusade against the Cathars	The siege and surrender of the last Cathar stronghold at Montségur sees 200 people burnt alive	Alphonse de Poitiers, count of Toulouse, begins a massive *bastide*-building programme, including Monflanquin, Cordes, Najac and Ste-Foy-la-Grande

Montaut, for example, a powerful baron based in Mussidan, initially swore allegiance to the French Crown, but then fought with the English in the sieges of Bourdeilles (1369) and Limoges (1370). Only when he was captured by the French did he conveniently rediscover his patriotic sentiment and transfer his allegiance back. Most towns and castles were attacked at some point and many changed hands on numerous occasions, either by treaty or force. By the end of the war, farms and villages lay abandoned and roving bands of **brigands** terrorized the countryside, having abandoned all pretence of fighting for one side or the other. The population had been reduced by roughly a half to under twelve million, partly by warfare, but largely through famine and disease; millions died as the bubonic **plague** repeatedly swept through France during the fourteenth and fifteenth centuries.

Gradually the nightmare ended. Though the south now had to kow-tow to the hated northerners – the counts of Périgord were particularly big losers, having their land and privileges confiscated by the Crown – Louis XI proved to be an astute ruler who allowed some of the privileges granted by the English to remain. Trade – particularly in wine – began to revive, towns were rebuilt and land brought back into production.

The Wars of Religion

In the early sixteenth century the ideas, art and architecture of the **Renaissance** began to penetrate France. As elsewhere in Europe, the Renaissance had a profound influence on every aspect of life, engendering a new optimism and spirit of enquiry that appealed in particular to the new class of wealthy merchants. At the same time, increased trade and improved communications, including the invention of the printing press, helped disseminate ideas throughout Europe. Among them came the new **Protestant** message espoused by Martin Luther and John Calvin that the individual was responsible to God alone and not to the Church.

Such ideas gained widespread adherence throughout France, partly feeding on resentment toward a Catholic clergy who were often seen as closely linked to the oppressive feudal regime, but mainly because a handful of powerful families converted and, where the feudal overlord led, his subjects were bound to follow. On the national scale, the most significant families to convert were those of the **Bourbon-d'Albret** royal dynasty. In the southwest, the first Protestant (also known as **Huguenot**) enclaves were at Ste-Foy-la-Grande and Bergerac in the 1540s, followed soon after by Nérac, the fief of the **d'Albret** family. As the Protestant faith took hold and Catholics felt increasingly threatened, the sporadic brutal attempts to stamp out Protestantism, such as a massacre in Cahors in 1560, erupted two years later into a series of bitter civil wars. Interspersed with ineffective truces and accords, the **Wars of Religion** lasted for the next thirty years.

On the Catholic side, a powerful lobbying group of traditionalists, organized mainly by the **de Guise** family, led an army against the Huguenots, who were in turn marshalled by **Admiral de Coligny**. The two armies toured northern France, occasionally clashing directly, but more often capturing and converting towns that had taken one side or the other. The duc de Guise was murdered in 1563, an act for which his allies held Coligny responsible. And in 1572, Coligny was among the victims of the war's bloodiest and most notorious date: the **St Bartholomew's Day Massacre**, when some

1308	**1332**	**1415**
Construction of the Pont Valentré begins in Cahors	Edward III of England claims the French throne and sparks the Hundred Years' War	Henry V of England inflicts a crushing defeat on the French army at Agincourt

THE LANGUAGE OF LOVE

The **troubadours**, poets and musicians of the twelfth century, were early pioneers of Western Europe's cultural renaissance. Their love poetry, written in **Occitan**, elevated the vernacular of the rural peasantry to the status of high culture and, for the first time since Roman occupation, language was used for something other than essential, practical communication. Troubadour poems focus on courtly love, an idealized, noble emotion which might be romantic, tender, familiar, feudal, patriotic – or, in the best poems, a combination of all these. Thus, the Troubadours not only reintroduced art to the region, they also gave it a linguistic and cultural identity – when troubadours talk about their *pays*, they do not mean France as a whole, just the southwest.

The aggressive campaign of unification and standardization waged by the state following the 1789 revolution outlawed the everyday use of the Occitan **language**, causing its gradual disappearance as a native tongue. It continued to inspire poets, however, most notably **Frédéric Mistral**, an early winner of the Nobel Prize for literature, who wrote in Occitan. Today, the language described in 1900 by the visionary politician Jean Jaurès as "a noble language of courtship, poetry and art", is being revived. Basing their strategy on the models for the revival of the Welsh and Irish languages, regional authorities have established a number of Occitan-speaking **schools**, known as *Calandretas*, including one in Périgueux, while local *collèges* (roughly equivalent to an English secondary school) also offer Occitan as one of their language options. The Toulouse-based newspaper *Dépêche du Midi* prints a regular column in Occitan.

---

three thousand Protestants, gathered in Paris for the wedding of Protestant **Henri d'Albret** to Marguerite de Valois, the sister of Henry III of France, were slaughtered.

Just as in earlier conflicts, the nationwide dispute was used as a pretext by **powerful families** in the southwest to consolidate their positions. Once again, private armies roamed the region, vying with each other in their savagery, but with only vaguely religious motives. Before his death, Coligny famously complained of Huguenot generals in the southwest who took no interest in the wider struggle and "refused to fight unless they could turn around and see their own chimney". One such general was the impulsive and ingenious **Geoffroi de Vivans**, who even succeeded in briefly capturing the staunchly Catholic towns of Sarlat and Périgueux. One of his most daring exploits, in 1588, involved hiding out in the caves beneath the hilltop town of Domme before scaling the formidable cliffs at dawn and taking the town with only a handful of men.

Some towns were attacked and changed hands repeatedly, either through violence or as a result of various **truces**, by which they were nominally declared either Catholic or Protestant. In reality, the majority of ordinary people, though cruelly affected by the fighting, saw little impact on their **notions of religion**, which remained a hotch-potch of rural paganism and local folklore, with only hints of orthodox Christianity, until several centuries later.

A twist of fate signalled the beginning of the end of the conflicts, when Henri d'Albret – king of Navarre and leader of the Protestant army – became heir to the French throne when Henry III's son died in 1584. Five years later, Henry III himself

1429	1453	1533
Jeanne d'Arc, the maid of Orléans, rallies the French troops	The crucial battle of Castillon effectively ends the Hundred Years' War and with it English rule in southwest France	Michel de Montaigne, influential "Father of the Essay", is born in the Dordogne region

> ### CHURCHES AND CASTLES: THE VIEILLES PIERRES OF PÉRIGORD
>
> In spite of the many conflicts that have ravaged the countryside since the Middle Ages, the Dordogne and Lot region has preserved an impressive wealth of medieval **churches**, at the heart of almost every village in some areas; while the many **castles** (aka **châteaux**) seem to crown the crest of every hill, especially along the golden stretch of the Dordogne valley.
>
> #### CHURCHES
>
> Few traces now remain of the earliest churches, one exception being in St-Front in Périgueux, where the enthusiastic nineteenth-century restoration conceals traces of the original chapel built by bishop Chronope (see page 263) in the early sixth century. The region's golden age for church-building, however, came in the twelfth and thirteenth centuries, when the style of architecture and sculpture known as **Romanesque** (or sometimes Norman, in England) was dominant. In terms of architecture, these churches are characterized by round arches, sometimes domes (particularly in the Périgord region) and simple, graceful lines, but the highlights are often the sculptures that adorn the key structural points: the tympanum above the main entrance, the capitals at the top of supporting pillars, the keystones in their vaults – these all formed a blank canvas for craftsmen to forge the most beautifully humane and unglorified depictions of saints, prophets and biblical stories. In no other architectural style are religious teachings so organically integrated into the physical structure of the church. The best examples include the churches in Souillac and Beaulieu, in the upper reaches of the Dordogne, and the world-famous cloister at Moissac in the Tarn valley, but it's the range and variety of styles, from the Byzantine touches in Périgueux and Souillac to the unembellished purity, almost austerity, of the church at Cadouin, which make the region such a goldmine.

was dead, leaving a tricky problem, since a Protestant could not be king. After trying to seize the crown by force, Henri d'Albret eventually abjured his faith and became **Henry IV** of France. "Paris is worth a Mass," he is reputed to have said.

Once on the throne, Henry IV set about reconstructing and reconciling his kingdom. Under the visionary **Edict of Nantes** of 1598 the Protestants were accorded freedom of conscience, freedom of worship in specified places, the right to attend the same schools and hold the same offices as Catholics, their own courts and the possession of a number of fortresses, including Montauban, as a guarantee against renewed attack.

The stirrings of discontent

The Dordogne and Lot region had barely drawn breath after the end of the Wars of Religion when a different type of conflict erupted – this time one whose causes the ordinary peasantry could identify with all too easily. The countryside lay in ruins and the cost of the wars and rebuilding fell squarely on their shoulders. Ruinous taxes, a series of bad harvests, high prices and yet more outbreaks of the plague combined to push them over the edge in the late sixteenth century. There were **peasant rebellions** in Normandy and Brittany, but the worst of the "**Croquants**" (yokels')

1572	1589	1637	1643
The St Bartholomew's Day massacre sees some 3000 people killed in Paris	Protestant Henri Bourbon d'Albret abjures his faith and is crowned Henry IV of France	A crushing defeat at Sauvetat-du-Dropt leads to the execution of peasant leaders	Louis XIV, the Sun King, begins his long reign, exerting increasing control over the southwest

Rarer, but of all the more interest for that, are the region's **Gothic** edifices. While in Romanesque architecture the charm lies in the detail, evoking a humble down-to-earth spirituality, in Gothic buildings it's the soaring, awe-inspiring ensemble that appeals, embodying a sense of elevation to a higher realm.

CASTLES

While the Hundred Years' War was raging, it was said that "towns were loyal to the king; castles were a law unto themselves." In both the conflict between the French and English and the later religious wars, the region's powerful families sought to strengthen their own positions and independence by fortifying their residences into grand châteaux.

Invariably built on high ground, for strategic reasons, many castles would originally have covered a large area, with entire villages enclosed within their walls. In most cases, they were destroyed or dismantled when captured during various wars, so today it is often just a ruined keep that remains. From a military perspective, two of the most satisfying are those at Beynac and Castelnaud, squaring up to each other across the Dordogne river and offering commanding views over the surrounding countryside. For romance, it's hard to beat the rugged keep of Najac rising above the village, shrouded in mist. In more peaceful centuries, the region's aristocracy set about making their residences more comfortable, and places like the Château de Hautefort combined impregnability with stately grandeur, lavish furnishings and extravagant interior design.

In many cases, buildings were designed to serve both a religious purpose and a military one. The churches at Rocamadour, St-Amand-de-Coly and Beaumont, to name just three, are notable for their imposing, fortified walls and slit windows, revealing them as buildings designed not just for worship, but also to be defended.

---

uprisings broke out in the southwest. The first major revolt occurred in the winter of 1593, when a number of towns and castles, including Monpazier, Excideuil and Puy-l'Évêque, were attacked. After two years of skirmishes, nobles pulled together an army in 1595 and the rebellion was quickly and savagely put down by the allied forces of the local nobility. The same grievances resurfaced in more uprisings in May 1637, however, no doubt nourished in part by tales of the earlier failed rebellion, passed down by word of mouth from generation to generation. This time, the revolt was altogether more serious. In the face of one tax demand too many, a ten-thousand-strong **peasant army** tried unsuccessfully to seize Périgueux. Instead, they took Bergerac and then marched on Bordeaux. They were stopped, however, at Ste-Foy-la-Grande and the final show-down took place soon after against 3400 royal troops at La Sauvetat-du-Dropt, south of Bergerac, leaving at least a thousand Croquants dead. The leaders were executed, one in Monpazier, while the surviving rebels returned to the land.

Thereafter, the long reign of **Louis XIV** (1643–1715) saw the French Crown and Catholic religion begin to reassert control over the southwest. With the exception of the **Frondes** (of 1648–52), when aristocrats joined the lower classes in rebelling against royal taxes and when the army had to be brought in to crush demonstrations in Bordeaux, the state successfully reinstated military and feudal control. At the

1789	**1790**	**1792**	**1799**
Storming of the Bastille in Paris sows the seeds of Revolution	Creation of the modern *départements* of Dordogne, Lot and Tarn and Garonne, named after their major rivers	Declaration of the First Republic	Napoleon Bonaparte seizes power, declaring himself emperor in 1804

same time, the bishops of Sarlat and Périgueux set about the "Vendange des Âmes", the **Harvesting of Souls**, an aggressive campaign designed to eradicate strongholds of the Protestant faith. Protestant towns such as Bergerac were seized by the Catholics and Protestant rights were gradually eroded until in 1685 Louis revoked the Edict of Nantes, forbade Protestant worship and set about trying to eliminate the faith completely. Orders were given for the destruction of Protestant churches and of the castles of its most fervent supporters. Thousands of Protestants fled the southwest for the safety of the Netherlands, Germany and England.

At the same time, France began to establish a **colonial empire** in North America, Africa, India and the Caribbean, and, as trade from these places started to grow in the early eighteenth century, so Bordeaux and the other Atlantic ports prospered, in a so-called **golden age**.

Revolution

For the majority of people, however, little had changed. The gap between rich and poor grew ever wider as the clergy and aristocracy clung onto their privileges and the peasants were squeezed for higher taxes. Their general misery was exacerbated by a catastrophic harvest in 1788, followed by a particularly severe winter. Bread prices rocketed and on July 14, 1789, a mob stormed the **Bastille** in Paris, a hated symbol of the oppressive regime. As the **Revolution** spread, similar insurrections occurred throughout the country, accompanied by widespread peasant attacks on landowners' châteaux and the destruction of tax and rent records. In August the new National Assembly abolished the feudal rights and privileges of the nobility and then went on to nationalize Church lands.

In these early stages the general population of the southwest supported the Revolution. However, as the Parisian revolutionaries grew increasingly radical and proposed ever more centralization of power, they found themselves in bitter opposition. Towards the end of 1792, as the **First Republic** was being declared, they finally lost out to the extremists and in October the following year **the Terror** was unleashed as mass executions took place throughout France; estimates run to three thousand in Paris and 14,000 in the regions.

Though revolutionary bands wrought a fair amount of havoc in the southwest, looting and burning castles and churches, hacking away at coats of arms and religious statuary, on the whole the region escaped fairly lightly; many aristocrats simply fled and their possessions were sold off at knock-down prices. Among many administrative changes following the Revolution, one of the most significant was the creation of **départements** in 1790 to replace the old provinces. Thus began yet another attempt at national unification, accompanied by efforts to draw the traditionally independent southwest into mainstream France. The campaign continued in the nineteenth century with moves to stamp out Occitan and other regional dialects (see page 269).

From Napoleon I to the Third Republic

By the end of 1794, more moderate forces were in charge in Paris. However, continuous infighting left the way open for **Napoleon Bonaparte**, who had made a

1808	1815	1822	1852
Napoleon invades Spain, sparking the Peninsular War	Napoleon is narrowly defeated by Wellington in the Battle of Waterloo	Jean-François Champollion translates the hieroglyphs on the Rosetta Stone	The Garonne Canal is opened. Napoléon III is declared emperor

name for himself as commander of the Revolutionary armies in Italy and Egypt, to seize power in a coup d'état in 1799. Napoleon quickly restored order and continued the process of centralization, replacing the power of local institutions by appointing a *préfet* to each *département* answerable only to the **emperor**, as Napoleon declared himself in 1804. Nevertheless, the Dordogne and Lot *départements* supported the new regime by providing many military leaders – and more lowly troops – for Bonaparte's armies: the most notable examples were Périgueux's Baron Pierre Daumesnil and Joachim Murat (1767–1815), the son of a village innkeeper near Cahors, who was proclaimed king of Naples in reward for his numerous military successes. As elsewhere, however, it was the burden of the unceasing **Napoleonic wars** that cost the emperor his support. The economy of Bordeaux in particular and the southwest in general was hard hit when Napoleon banned commerce with Britain, to which Britain responded by blockading French ports in 1807.

Few tears were shed in the region when Napoleon was finally defeated in 1815 at the **Battle of Waterloo**. The subsequent restoration of the **monarchy**, on the other hand, saw opinions divided along predictable lines: the aristocracy and the emerging *bourgeoisie* (the middle classes) rallied to the king, while the working population supported the uprising in 1848 – a shorter and less virulent reprise of the 1789 Revolution – which ended in the declaration of the **Second Republic**. The new government started off well by setting up national workshops to relieve unemployment and extending the vote to all adult males – an unprecedented move for its time. But in elections held later in 1848 the largely conservative vote of the newly enfranchised peasants was sufficient to outweigh the urban, working-class radicals. To everyone's surprise, Louis-Napoléon, nephew of the former emperor, romped home. In spite of his liberal reputation, he restricted the vote again, censored the press and pandered to the Catholic Church. In 1852, following a coup and further street fighting, he had himself proclaimed **Emperor Napoléon III**.

Like his uncle, Napoléon III pursued an expansionist military policy, both in France's colonial empire and in Europe. And also like his uncle, this brought about his downfall. Napoléon III declared war on Prussia in 1870 and was quickly and roundly defeated by the far superior Prussian army. When Napoléon was taken prisoner the politicians in Paris – Cahors' Léon Gambetta among them – quickly proclaimed the **Third Republic**. Though it experienced a difficult birth, the Third Republic survived until 1940.

Into the twentieth century

Napoléon was more successful on the economic front, however. From the 1850s on, France experienced rapid **industrial growth**, while foreign trade trebled. The effect on the Dordogne and Lot region, however, was mixed.

The towns along the region's great rivers benefited most from the economic recovery. Although the region had no coal or mineral resources to stimulate large-scale industrialization (beyond metalworking around Fumel), industries were established along the navigable rivers – tanneries, paper mills, textile and glass industries. At the same time, agricultural areas within easy access of the rivers grew wealthy from exporting wheat, wine and tobacco. Many towns were given a facelift, with their

1870	1870–85	1914	1926
Cahors-born statesman, Léon Gambetta, crafts the Third Republic	Phylloxera wipes out vast swathes of the region's vine stock	Outbreak of WWI. Thousands of youths from the southwest march north to battle, losing their lives in Flanders fields	The caves of Pech-Merle open to the public

ramparts torn down, wide avenues sliced through the cramped medieval quarters and a start made on improving sanitation and water supply. Transport was also modernized, although the **railways** came late to the Dordogne and Lot and were never very extensive. The region's first railway, the Bordeaux–Paris line, was completed in 1851, while the following year saw the opening of the **Canal latéral** (now the Garonne Canal), linking the Garonne with the Canal du Midi and thus the Mediterranean.

All this created pockets of economic growth, but the **rural areas** in between became increasingly marginalized. Local industries dwindled in the face of competition from cheap manufactured goods and imports, while the railways simply provided the means for people to quit the country for the cities.

But by far the biggest single crisis to hit the area's rural economy in the late nineteenth century was **phylloxera**. The parasite, which attacks the roots of vines, wiped out almost one-third of the region's vineyards in the 1870s and 1880s. For a while growers tried all sorts of remedies, from flooding the fields to chemical fumigation, before it was discovered that vines in America, where phylloxera originated, were immune and that by grafting French vines onto American root-stock it was possible to produce resistant plants. The vineyards were slowly re-established, but over a much smaller area. Many farmers turned to alternative crops, such as tobacco around Bergerac and sheep-rearing on the *causse* above Cahors.

The world wars

Such problems paled into insignificance, however, when German troops marched into northern France following the outbreak of **World War I** in 1914. The French government fled south to Bordeaux while thousands of southern men trekked north to lose their lives in the mud and horror of Verdun and the Somme battlefields. By the time the Germans were forced to surrender in 1918, the cost to France was 1.3 million dead, a quarter of whom were under 25 years of age, and three million wounded. Every town and village in the Dordogne and Lot, as elsewhere in France, has its sad war memorial recording the loss of this generation of young men.

In the aftermath of the war, agricultural and industrial production declined and the birth rate plummeted, although this was offset to some extent in the southwest by an influx of land-hungry refugees from Spain in the late nineteenth century and from Italy in the first decades of the twentieth. The French government lurched from crisis to crisis while events across the border in Germany became increasingly menacing.

In April 1940, eight months after the outbreak of **World War II**, Hitler's western offensive began as he overran Belgium, Denmark and Holland. In June the French government retreated to Bordeaux again and millions of refugees poured south as Paris fell to the Germans. **Maréchal Pétain**, a conservative 84-year-old veteran of World War I, emerged from retirement to sign an armistice with Hitler and head the collaborationist **Vichy government**, based in the spa town of Vichy in the northern foothills of the Massif Central. France was now split in two. The Germans occupied the strategic regions north of the Loire and all along the Atlantic coast, including Bordeaux, while Vichy ostensibly governed the "Free Zone" comprising the majority of southern France. The frontier, with its customs points and guardposts, ran from the Pyrenees north through Langon and Castillon-la-Bataille to just south of Tours,

1939	1940	1956	1961
Outbreak of WWII	Josephine Baker moves to Château Milandes in the Dordogne. The prehistoric cave paintings at Lascaux are discovered by four teenagers	Severe and prolonged frost devastates Cahors vineyards, necessitating a mass replanting	After centuries of mixed produce and livestock, the first market exclusively for truffles is established in Lalbenque

and from there cut east to Geneva. Then, in 1942, German troops moved south to occupy the whole of France until they were driven out by Britain, America and their allies after 1944.

Resistance to the German occupation didn't really get going until 1943 when **Général de Gaulle**, exiled leader of the "Free French", sent **Jean Moulin** to unify the disparate and often ideologically opposed Resistance groups. Moulin was soon captured by the Gestapo and tortured to death by Klaus Barbie – the infamous "Butcher of Lyon", who was convicted as recently as 1987 for his war crimes – but the network Moulin established became increasingly effective. Its members provided information to the Allies and blew up train tracks, bridges and factories. They undertook daring raids into enemy-held towns; and the high, empty uplands of the Dordogne and Lot *départements* afforded safe bases for many Resistance fighters. But for every action, the Germans hit back with savage **reprisals**. In May 1944 the SS Das Reich division, based at Montauban, set out to break the local resistance by massacring civilians and torching houses in some twenty towns and villages; the worst atrocities took place in Terrasson-la-Villedieu, Montpezat-de-Quercy, Mussidan and Frayssinet-le-Gélat.

Soon afterwards the Germans were being driven out, but the fighting didn't stop there. In the weeks following **liberation** thousands of **collaborators** were executed or publicly humiliated – women accused of consorting with the enemy had their heads shaved and were sometimes paraded naked through the streets. Not surprisingly, the issue of collaboration left deep scars in rural communities throughout the region, a bitterness which occasionally surfaces to this day in local disputes.

Into the new millennium

The issues that have dominated the past fifty years continue to remain paramount in the Dordogne and Lot. One of the main themes, as in much of rural France, has been that of **depopulation**. On average there are now 25 percent fewer people living on the land than at the end of the nineteenth century, rising to thirty percent or more in the worst-hit areas, such as parts of Lot-et-Garonne. Once again this has been partly offset by immigration, in this case by *pieds noirs* – French colonialists forced to flee Algeria after independence in 1962 – many of whom settled on farms in the southwest; and by north Europeans in search of the good life. Agricultural production is in slow decline as the younger generation leave the land, though this has partly been offset by a massive push towards mechanization and the amalgamation of small farms into larger, more efficient holdings – albeit often propped up by subsidies from the European Union.

Agriculture remains the backbone of the region's economy, notably wine production but also poultry, maize, fruit, tobacco, fishing and forestry. Cahors alone has 42 square kilometres planted with AOP (recently changed from the old AOC status) vines. Agen is also known for pharmaceuticals, while other main towns such as Périgueux, Figeac, Montauban, Fumel and Villeneuve-sur-Lot boast modest industrial sectors.

Besides agriculture and industry, **tourism** plays an increasingly important role in the regional economy. In recent years an enormous effort has gone into improving facilities and marketing the region, not just the honeypot attractions of Sarlat, Les Eyzies and the Dordogne valley châteaux, but also in the successful promotion of "green holidays",

1971	**1992**	**2004**	**2007**
Cahors wine is awarded AOC status	Treaty of Maastricht; the European Union is born	Musée National de la Préhistoire opens in Les Eyzies	Nicolas Sarkozy elected president of France

tempting people away from the Mediterranean and Atlantic coasts to discover all that the countryside has to offer. One of the largest such projects was the reopening of the River Lot and the Garonne Canal to navigation, but at a local level almost every town and village now puts on a programme of summer events to lure visitors.

Across France, however, the economy continues to be hampered by the seemingly perpetual stand-off between advocates of economic reform to liberalize markets and stimulate growth, and uncompromising defenders of the "**French Model**", with generous social allowances and high job security. Almost every section of society seems to have seen this debate come its way in recent years: from teachers to car manufacturers, employees in all industries have taken action to block any reforms which might erode their privileges. Perhaps most emblematic of the battle lines was the controversy in 2006 surrounding the government's attempt to introduce the **CPE** or "First Employment Contract", aimed at encouraging the employment of young people by making them less costly to hire/employ (with fewer social security benefits and no guarantee that they would be kept on after two years). The intended beneficiaries, however, were less than grateful, and took to the streets in their thousands to protest against the new contract, arguing that it was the first step towards the hire-and-fire culture reviled in left-wing French circles.

In the **2007 presidential election**, it seemed as though momentum was swinging behind the arguments of the economic reformers, as former interior minister **Nicolas Sarkozy**, a member of the centre-right UMP party, was elected president having campaigned for a hard-line "rupture" with the French Model. In power, however, he only fitfully pursued a free-market agenda.

Economic crisis and political swing

The **financial crisis** of 2008–09 hit manufacturing across France badly, and its effect in the Dordogne and Lot region was most strongly felt in the wine industry, with a partial collapse of prices and plummeting export sales. House prices took a nosedive too, sending many estate agents to the wall. In the light of the general discrediting of liberal capitalism, Sarkozy shrewdly abandoned his rupturist rhetoric in favour of a new-found pride in the traditional French system. This impeccable tactical U-turn left the Socialist opposition lost for words and floundering in the polls: the **2009 European elections** saw Sarkozy's party come out on top with 28 percent of the vote, while across France, including in the southwest region, the Socialists were pushed into third place behind a green alliance – "Europe Écologie" – led by Daniel Cohn-Bendit, familiar as the youthful leader of the 1968 student uprising. By 2012, however, the power pendulum had swung the other way, with the Socialists once again claiming massive victories in the polls, especially in the southwest. **François Hollande** was elected president, promising to beat the recession by taxing wealthier citizens and larger corporations while separating risky investment-banking enterprises from retail.

As Hollande neared the end of his term, however, many felt his government had largely failed to deliver on its pledges – and by the middle of 2016, Hollande could only scrape up seventeen percent approval ratings in the polls, making him the most unpopular president in modern French history. In the 2017 **presidential elections**, the Socialists took a nose-dive and the battle for the presidency was fought between

2008	2012	2012	2015–2016
Financial crisis hits the region, property prices drop and exchange rates fluctuate, forcing many British residents to return to the UK	François Hollande elected president of France	The Dordogne valley named a UNESCO biosphere reserve	Three terror attacks hit France and tourism is badly affected

Marine le Pen of the far-right **Front National** party and centrist **Emmanuel Macron** and his new **En Marche!** party. Macron won with just over 61 percent of the vote.

Into the future

After an economically rough few years, things had started to look a little brighter by 2015, with tourism in the Dordogne and Lot on the rebound. Then, between January 2015 and July 2016, three Islamic **terrorist strikes** (and a fourth in neighbouring Belgium) hit France. Although the atrocities were geographically remote from the Dordogne and Lot, the impact on tourism was immediate and hoteliers reported significant dips in bookings across the region.

The world's economic woes also complicated the situation of the thousands of **British residents** in the Dordogne and Lot. Since the 1960s, low property prices, coupled with beautiful scenery and an enviable lifestyle, have attracted Brits, Dutch and other northern Europeans to settle here. However, volatile exchange rates and devalued savings and investments have caused what some call the biggest British exodus from France since Dunkirk.

The situation was further compounded by the June 2016 **Brexit** vote, which has had a mixed impact in the Dordogne and Lot. The initial fear was that with the heightened bureaucracy of living in France as a non-EU citizen, alongside the falling value of the pound against the euro and the resultant hike in costs for those reliant on UK-based salaries or pensions, many more expats would be forced to sell up and return to the UK. This departure of British residents could have a significant economic impact upon the numerous villages in the Dordogne and Lot which have been revitalized by the expat community. However, the region has also seen a surprising number of Britons looking to purchase property and seek French residency. Only time will tell what long-term effect this will have on the region's expat community.

France has also suffered its own political troubles in recent years. Since the 2017 election of Emmanuel Macron, a number of political and economic reforms have led to some improvements in France's economy and unemployment numbers. However, these reforms have been met with widespread resistance, leading to some of the country's largest ever demonstrations and protests. The gilets jaunes (yellow vest) movement swept across France in late 2018, with tens of thousands of protesters taking to the streets all over the country, and reports of violent protests and police brutality making the headlines around the world. Although initially sparked by the proposal of a carbon tax, the protests revealed the growing dissonance between the French government and the people, particularly those in rural areas, who felt that increased taxes and decreased opportunities disproportionately affected them, further compounding the divide between France's working and middle class and the elite. As a region with a large rural population, the Dordogne saw a large number of protests and strikes take place, which continued into 2019 and 2020. Despite these political tensions, the region today retains its strong sense of identity and a deep-burning pride in the land, its produce and its traditions, which will doubtless continue unabated.

In January 2020, the first case of Covid-19 was confirmed in a patient in Bordeaux. Less than two months later, France was in its first state of lockdown. By May, cases had dropped significantly, but in line with much of Europe, a second lockdown

2016	**2017**	**2018**
The high-tech Lascaux VI complex opens close to the original caves	Emmanuel Macron elected president of France	France wins the FIFA World Cup for the second time. Anti-austerity *gilets jaunes* (yellow vests) movement organises countrywide protests and demonstrations

followed in November, followed by a third in April 2021. The global pandemic hit France hard, and had a significant impact on the tourism industry, particularly in rural areas where a considerable amount of their revenue comes from foreign tourism, such as Dordogne and the Lot. Many hotels and restaurants permanently closed their doors.

In 2024, the far right came out on top in France during the European elections, prompting Macron to call a snap general election. Parties on the left created an alliance to form the Nouveau Front Populaire to block the Rassemblement National, headed by Jordan Bardella (although the infamous Marine Le Pen remains a prominent figure within the party), from gaining the absolute majority. Nevertheless, in many rural areas (and in a significant part of Dordogne and the Lot), Bardella's Rassemblement National topped the polls. With no party currently holding the majority, at the time of writing the French government was in a state of flux.

2020–2021

The Covid-19 pandemic sweeps France in successive waves, causing thousands of deaths

2024

Paris holds the Olympic Games, with cities from Lille to Bordeaux hosting events. Following an unprecedented rise in support for the far right during the European elections, Macron calls a snap general election, which leaves no party with an absolute majority

Books

There are few English-language history books specifically devoted to the Dordogne and Lot region, and a bit of a dearth of novels, whether in French or in translation. A few of those that do exist – and are worth recommending – are detailed below, along with a number of general history books and classic texts which provide the background to events that have occurred in the region. The best books in this selection are marked by a ★ symbol.

HISTORY & BIOGRAPHY

Marc Bloch *Strange Defeat*. Moving personal study of the reasons for France's defeat in 1940 and subsequent caving-in to Fascism. Found among the papers of this Sorbonne historian after his death at the hands of the Gestapo in 1942.

Lynn Haney *Naked at the Feast*. A lively warts-and-all biography of the cabaret star Josephine Baker, which traces the many setbacks and comebacks of her rags-to-riches tale, getting across her amazing charisma and just why France took her to its heart.

Colin Jones *The Cambridge Illustrated History of France*. A political and social history of France from prehistoric times to the mid-1990s, concentrating on issues of regionalism, gender, race and class. Good illustrations and an easy, unacademic writing style.

★ **Don and Petie Kladstrup** *Wine & War*. The role of wine in World War II and the often courageous and ingenious strategies used to prevent the best wines from being plundered by the German army; fascinating reading.

Marion Meade *Eleanor of Aquitaine*. Highly accessible biography of one of the key characters in twelfth-century Europe. The author fleshes out the documented events until they read more like a historical novel.

Ian Ousby *Occupation: The Ordeal of France 1940–1944*. Somewhat revisionist 1997 account looking at how widespread collaboration was and why it took so long for the Resistance to get organized.

★ **Graham Robb** *The Discovery of France*. A fascinating alternative history of France, in which Robb goes in search of the reality of life for the provincial, rural majority ignored by the currents of history, before recounting the way in which the nineteenth century saw this other France gradually discovered and "civilized". Contains some excellent sections on the southwest.

Anne-Marie Walters *Moondrop to Gascony*. An absorbing and spine-tingling account of the real life of a secret agent in World War II; written in the immediate aftermath of the war, it reveals the naked courage of the French Resistance.

★ **Alison Weir** *Eleanor of Aquitaine: By the wrath of God, Queen of England*. A magnificent medieval pot pourri of romantic events that vividly chronicles the extraordinary life of this fascinating woman. Contains some interesting photographs, including one of the effigy on Eleanor's tomb at Fontevraud abbey, the only verifiable image of her still in existence.

★ **Theodore Zeldin** *The French*. Urbane and witty survey of the French world view – chapter titles include "How to be chic" and "How to appreciate a grandmother".

TRAVEL, ART AND LITERATURE

Patricia Atkinson *The Ripening Sun*. The ultimately uplifting tale of an Englishwoman who struggles against all kinds of adversity to establish a well-respected vineyard near Bergerac.

★ **Michael Brown** *Down the Dordogne*. In the late 1980s, Michael Brown fulfilled a long-held ambition to follow the Dordogne from its source in the Massif Central to the Gironde estuary. The story of his journey – on foot, by canoe and bicycle – provides a lyrical introduction to the region.

Elizabeth Chadwick *Daughters of the Grail*. This compelling novel offers an insightful glimpse into the little-known world of the much persecuted Cathars. Set in thirteenth-century southwest France the succession of heroines battle with their beliefs, Catholic prejudice and eventually with the merciless Simon de Montfort.

★ **André Chastel** *French Art*. Authoritative three-volume study by one of France's leading art historians. Discusses individual works of art – from architecture to tapestry, as well as painting – in detail in an attempt to locate the Frenchness of French art. With glossy photographs and serious-minded but readable text.

Angela Clarke *Dark Secrets of the Dordogne*. Easy to read, satirical take on the British expat life in southwest France, but with the added twist of a murder-mystery tale.

★ **Arthur Conan-Doyle** *The White Company*. A far cry from Sherlock Holmes, here Conan-Doyle turns his talents to historical fiction, depicting a Hundred Years' War where the English have hearts of gold and all the rest are jolly rotters.

Eugène Le Roy *Jacquou le Croquant*. This novel is one of the most important chronicles of the hardship of rural life in nineteenth-century France. The action takes place in the forest and villages around Montignac, home of the hero Jacquou who leads a vengeful revolt against the tyrannical local feudal lord.

Christian Signol *La Rivière Espérance*. Set in the 1830s, this French novel – which was made into a hugely successful TV film – follows the adventures of a young sailor working the *gabares* that then plied the Dordogne. This nostalgic tale commemorates the end of an era as the railways relentlessly destroy the romanticized river life.

★ **Ruth Silvestre** *A House in the Sunflowers*. There are any number of books about Brits upping sticks and moving to France to renovate a ruin. Most are none-too impressive but this is a cut above the rest. Set in the Lot and Garonne, it's the first in a trilogy that also includes *A Harvest of Sunflowers* and *Reflections of Sunflowers*.

Peter Strafford *Romanesque Churches of France*. This scholarly guide to a handful of France's best churches contains a healthy section on those of the southwest, with several pages devoted to Moissac and Souillac alone. Strafford gives a somewhat dry but detailed account of the architecture and history of the churches featured, and an almost stone-by-stone description of some of the most important sculpture.

GUIDES

Tanja Bulatovic *Living in France Made Simple*. An invaluable guide, packed with ideas and advice on everything from job-hunting, tax and bureaucracy to healthcare.

Cicerone Walking Guides Neat, durable guides, with detailed route descriptions. Titles include *The Way of Saint James; A Walker's Guide* and *The Way of Saint James; A Cyclist's Guide*, both of which follow the route from Le Puy to Santiago (GR65), and *Walking in the Dordogne*.

Peter Knowles *White Water: Massif Central*. Out of print and fairly hard to find but worth tracking down, this guide covers rivers suitable for a spot of gentle family canoeing and canoe touring, including parts of the Dordogne, Lot, Tarn, Vézère, Célé and Aveyron. Packed with good, practical advice.

★ **Joy Law** *Dordogne*. Erudite and accessible thematic guide-cum-history text written by a long-time resident of the *département*, packed with interesting anecdotes and local colour.

Helen Martin *Lot: Travels Through a Limestone Landscape in Southwest France*. It's well worth investing in this updated and expanded edition of Helen Martin's classic book about the Lot if you're going to be spending much time in the *département*. Her passion for the area, which she has known for more than forty years, comes across loud and clear.

Alain Roussot *Discovering Périgord Prehistory*. Translated into English, this guide provides a solid introduction to the prehistoric caves of the Périgord. It covers the most significant caves in chronological order, while the illustrations give a taste of what's on offer.

Mark Sampson *Essential Questions to Ask When Buying a House in France*. Published in 2014 and, as the name suggests, full of vital advice for those taking the plunge.

Topo-guides The best of the walking guides covering the long-distance paths, Topo-guides are widely available in France and not hard to follow with a working knowledge of French. The series includes guides to the GR65 St-Jacques pilgrimage routes, the *Tour des Gorges de l'Aveyron* (Topo-guide #323), the *Traversée du Périgord* (#321) and, for shorter walks, *Dordogne à Pied* (#D024) and *Lot à Pied* (#D046).

FOOD AND DRINK

Stephanie Alexander *Cooking and Travelling in South-West France*. Inspiring and lavishly illustrated, this is a book for foodies. Alexander is a well-known Australian cookery writer whose deep-rooted passion for this region's food is practically palpable on every page.

Elisabeth Luard *Truffle*. Of all the gourmet treats available in the southwest, a truffle must surely be the ultimate prize. Luard demystifies this unprepossessing but delicious lump of fungus, showing you not only where to buy it, but exactly what to do with it when you get it home.

Orlando Murrin *A Table in the Tarn*. Out of print but worth tracking down, this is a beautifully presented celebration of southern cuisine; the first half of this coffee-table book describes the author's move to a run-down manor and the subsequent transformation to luxury *chambres d'hôtes*. The second half is a rich hoard of recipes that will have you racing to the kitchen, book in hand.

Jeanne Strang *Goose Fat and Garlic, Country Recipes from South-West France*. A huge store of traditional gastronomy from the old southwest. Strang lived and worked in the area for more than forty years and shares her profound knowledge in this book, which is perhaps a little thin on illustrations but makes up for the lack with recipes that you will find nowhere else.

Paul Strang *Wines of South-West France*. A bit dated now, but surprisingly still one of the few English-language guides to the region's wines. In addition to the history of viticulture and brief reviews of recommended producers in all the wine-producing areas from Figeac to Bergerac, the book gives a glimpse into local culture and traditions.

French

French can be a deceptively familiar language because of the number of words and structures it shares with English. Despite this, it's far from easy, though the bare essentials are not difficult to master and can make all the difference. Even just saying "Bonjour Madame/Monsieur" and then gesticulating will usually get you a smile and helpful service. People working in tourist offices, hotels and so on, almost always speak English, though, and tend to use it when you're struggling to speak French – be grateful, not insulted.

Pronunciation

One easy rule to remember is that consonants at the ends of words are usually silent. *Pas plus tard* (not later) is thus pronounced "pa-plu-tarr". But when the following word begins with a vowel, you run the two together: *les oranges* (the oranges) becomes "layzoronge". Vowels are the hardest sounds to get right. Roughly:

a as in hat
e as in get
é between get and gate
è between get and gut
eu like the u in hurt

i as in machine
o as in hot
ô, au as in over
ou as in food
u as in a pursed-lip version of use

More awkward are the combinations *in/im*, *en/em*, *an/am*, *on/om*, *un/um* at the beginning and end of words, or followed by consonants other than *n* or *m*. Again, roughly:

in/im like the an in anxious
an/am like the don in
en/em Doncaster when said with a nasal accent

on/om like the don in Doncaster said by someone with a heavy cold
un/um like the u in understand

Consonants are much as in English, except that: *ch* is always "sh", *h* is silent, *th* is the same as "t", *ll* is often like the "y" in yes, *w* is "v", and *r* is growled.

BASIC WORDS AND PHRASES

French nouns are divided into **masculine** and **feminine**. This causes difficulties with adjectives, whose endings have to change to suit the gender of the nouns they qualify. If you know some grammar, you will know what to do. If not, stick to the masculine form, which is the simplest – it's what we have done in this glossary.

BASICS

hello (morning or afternoon) bonjour
hello (evening) bonsoir
goodnight bonne nuit
goodbye au revoir
yes oui

no non
thank you merci
please s'il vous plaît
sorry pardon/je m'excuse
excuse me pardon
ok/agreed d'accord
help! au secours!
here ici
there là
this one ceci
that one cela
open ouvert
closed fermé

PHRASEBOOKS AND COURSES

Rough Guide French Phrasebook Mini dictionary-style phrasebook with both English–French and French–English sections, along with cultural tips, a menu reader and downloadable scenarios read by native speakers.

big grand
small petit
more plus
less moins
a little un peu
a lot beaucoup
cheap bon marché, pas cher
expensive cher
good bon
bad mauvais
hot chaud
cold froid
with avec
without sans
man un homme
woman une femme

NUMBERS

1 un
2 deux
3 trois
4 quatre
5 cinq
6 six
7 sept
8 huit
9 neuf
10 dix
11 onze
12 douze
13 treize
14 quatorze
15 quinze
16 seize
17 dix-sept
18 dix-huit
19 dix-neuf
20 vingt
21 vingt-et-un
22 vingt-deux
30 trente
40 quarante
50 cinquante
60 soixante
70 soixante-dix
75 soixante-quinze
80 quatre-vingts
90 quatre-vingt-dix
95 quatre-vingt-quinze
100 cent
101 cent-et-un
200 deux cents
300 trois cents
500 cinq cents
1000 mille
2000 deux mille
5000 cinq mille
1,000,000 un million

DAYS AND DATES

January janvier
February février
March mars
April avril
May mai
June juin
July juillet
August août
September septembre
October octobre
November novembre
December décembre
Sunday dimanche
Monday lundi
Tuesday mardi
Wednesday mercredi
Thursday jeudi
Friday vendredi
Saturday samedi
August 1 le premier août
March 2 le deux mars
July 14 le quatorze juillet
November 23 le vingt-trois novembre
2020 deux mille vingt

TIME

today aujourd'hui
yesterday hier
tomorrow demain
in the morning le matin
in the afternoon l'après-midi
in the evening le soir
now maintenant
later plus tard
at one o'clock à une heure
at three o'clock à trois heures
at ten-thirty à dix heures et demie
at midday à midi

TALKING TO PEOPLE

When addressing people you should always use *Monsieur* for a man, *Madame* for a woman, *Mademoiselle* for a young woman or girl. Plain *bonjour* by itself is not enough. This isn't as formal as it seems, and it has its uses when you've forgotten someone's name or want to attract someone's attention.
Do you speak English? Parlez-vous anglais?
How do you say it in French? Comment ça se dit en français?

What's your name? Comment vous appelez-vous?
My name is… Je m'appelle…
I'm Je suis
…English …anglais[e]
…Irish …irlandais[e]
…Scottish …écossais[e]
…Welsh …gallois[e]
…American …américain[e]
…Canadian …canadien[ne]
…Australian …australien[ne]
…a New Zealander …néo-zélandais[e]
I understand Je comprends
I don't understand Je ne comprends pas
Can you speak more slowly? S'il vous plaît, parlez moins vite
How are you? Comment allez-vous?/Ça va?
fine, thanks Très bien, merci
I don't know Je ne sais pas
Let's go Allons-y
See you tomorrow À demain
See you later À plus tard or À toute à l'heure
See you soon À bientôt
Leave me alone! (aggressive) Fichez-moi la paix!
Please help me Aidez-moi, s'il vous plaît

QUESTIONS AND REQUESTS

The simplest way of asking a question is to start with *s'il vous plaît* (please), then name the thing you want in an interrogative tone of voice. For example:
Where is there a bakery? S'il vous plaît, la boulangerie?
Which way is it to Cahors? S'il vous plaît, la route pour Cahors?
Can we have a room for two? S'il vous plaît, une chambre pour deux?
Can I have a kilo of oranges? S'il vous plaît, un kilo d'oranges?
where? Où?
how? Comment?
how many/how much? Combien?
when? Quand?
why? Pourquoi?
at what time? À quelle heure?
what is/which is? Quel est?

GETTING AROUND

bus autobus/bus/car
bus station gare routière
bus stop arrêt de bus
train/taxi/ferry train/taxi/ferry
boat bâteau
plane avion
train station gare (SNCF)
platform quai
What time does it leave? Il part à quelle heure?
What time does it arrive? Il arrive à quelle heure?
a ticket to… un billet pour…
single ticket aller-simple
return ticket aller-retour
validate your ticket compostez votre billet
valid for valable pour
ticket office vente de billets
how many kilometres? combien de kilomètres?
how many hours? combien d'heures?
hitchhiking autostop
on foot à pied
Where are you going? Vous allez où?
I'm going to… Je vais à…
I want to get off at the Je voudrais descendre à la
road to… route pour…
…near …près/pas loin
far loin
left à gauche
right à droite
straight on tout droit
on the other side of de l'autre côté de
on the corner of à l'angle de
next to à côté de
behind derrière
in front of devant
before avant
after après
under sous
to cross traverser
bridge pont

ACCOMMODATION

a room for one/two people une chambre pour une/deux personne(s)
a twin room une chambre à deux lits
a double bed un grand lit
a room with a shower une chambre avec douche
a room with a bath une chambre avec salle de bains
for one/two/three nights pour une/deux/trios nuits
Can I see it? Je peux la voir?
a room on the courtyard une chambre sur la cour
a room over the street une chambre sur la rue
first floor premier étage
second floor deuxième étage
with a view avec vue
key clef
to iron repasser
do laundry faire la lessive
sheets draps
blankets couvertures
quiet calme
noisy bruyant
hot water eau chaude
cold water eau froide

Is breakfast included? Est-ce que le petit déjeuner est compris?
I would like breakfast Je voudrais prendre le petit déjeuner
I don't want breakfast Je ne veux pas de petit déjeuner
Can we camp here? On peut camper ici?
campsite un camping/terrain de camping
tent une tente
tent space un emplacement
youth hostel auberge de jeunesse

DRIVING

car voiture
service station garage
service révision
to park the car garer la voiture
car park un parking
no parking défense de stationner/stationnement interdit
petrol station station service
petrol essence
diesel gazole/gasoil
(to) fill it up faire le plein
oil huile
air line ligne à air
put air in the tyres gonfler les pneus
battery batterie
the battery is dead la batterie est morte
plugs bougies
to break down tomber en panne
gas can bidon
insurance assurance
green card carte verte
traffic lights feux

red light feu rouge
green light feu vert

HEALTH MATTERS

doctor médecin
dentist dentiste
I don't feel well Je ne me sens pas bien
medicines médicaments
prescription ordonnance
I feel sick Je suis malade
I have a headache J'ai mal à la tête
stomach ache mal à l'estomac
period règles
pain douleur
it hurts ça fait mal
chemist pharmacie
hospital hôpital

OTHER NEEDS

bakery boulangerie
food shop alimentation
supermarket supermarché
to eat manger
to drink boire
camping gas camping gaz
stamps timbres
bank banque
money argent
toilets toilettes
police police
telephone téléphone
cinema cinéma
theatre théâtre
to reserve/book réserver

FOOD AND DISHES

BASIC TERMS

l'addition bill/check
beurre butter
bouteille bottle
chauffé heated
couteau knife
cru raw
cuillère spoon
cuit cooked
à emporter takeaway
formule lunchtime set menu
fourchette fork
fumé smoked
huile oil
lait milk
le menu set menu
moutarde mustard

oeuf egg
offert free
pain bread
poivre pepper
salé salted/savoury
sel salt
sucre sugar
sucré sweet
table table
tisane a flower or herb infusion or tea
verre glass
vinaigre vinegar

SNACKS AND STARTERS

un sandwich/une baguette a sandwich
...au jambon ...with ham
...au fromage ...with cheese

...au saucisson ...with salami
...au poivre ...with pepper
...au pâté (de campagne) ...with pâté (country style)
croque-monsieur grilled cheese and ham sandwich
croque-madame grilled cheese and ham sandwich topped with an egg
panini toasted Italian sandwich
tartine buttered bread or open sandwich
crudités raw vegetables with dressings
hors d'oeuvres combination of charcuterie, crudités, smoked fish and other cold starters
charcuterie pâté and cold meats
oeufs eggs
...au plat ...fried
...à la coque ...boiled
...durs ...hard-boiled
...brouillés ...scrambled
...pochés ...poached
omelette omelette
...nature ...plain
...aux fines herbes ...with herbs
...au fromage ...with cheese
...aux truffes ...with truffles

PASTA (PÂTES), PANCAKES (CRÊPES) AND FLANS (TARTES)

nouilles noodles
pâtes fraîches fresh pasta
crêpe au sucre/aux oeufs pancake with sugar/eggs
galette (de sarrasin) buckwheat pancake
pissaladière tart of fried onions with anchovies and black olives
tarte flambée thin pizza-like pastry topped with onion, cream and bacon or other combinations

SOUPS (SOUPES)

bisque shellfish soup
bouillabaisse Mediterranean fish soup
bouillon broth or stock
consommé clear soup
garbure potato, cabbage and meat soup
miques dumplings of maize or wheat flour served in a thick soup; or as a large, sliced dumpling in a stew
potage thick soup, usually vegetable
potée thick vegetable and meat soup
soupe à l'oignon onion soup with a chunk of toasted bread and melted cheese topping
tourain, tourin garlic soup made with duck or goose fat served over bread topped with cheese

FISH (POISSON), SEAFOOD (FRUITS DE MER) AND SHELLFISH (CRUSTACÉS OR COQUILLAGES)

alose shad
anchois anchovies
anguilles eels
bigorneaux periwinkles
brandade de morue puréed, salted cod with oil, milk, garlic and mashed potato
brème bream
brochet pike
bulot whelk
cabillaud cod
calmar squid
carrelet plaice
colin hake
coques cockles
coquilles St-Jacques scallops
crabe crab
crevettes grises shrimp
crevettes roses prawns
daurade sea bream
écrevisses freshwater crayfish
éperlan smelt
escargots snails
esturgeon sturgeon
flétan halibut
gambas king prawns
hareng herring
homard lobster
huîtres oysters
lamproie lamprey
langoustines saltwater crayfish
limande lemon sole
lotte de mer monkfish
loup de mer sea bass
maquereau mackerel
merlan whiting
moules (marinières) mussels (with shallots in white wine sauce)
raie skate
rascasse scorpion fish
rouget red mullet
saumon salmon
sole sole
thon tuna
truite trout
turbot turbot

FISH DISHES AND TERMS

aïoli garlic mayonnaise served with salt cod and other fish
arête fish bone
beignet fritter
darne fillet or steak
la douzaine a dozen
frit fried
friture deep-fried small fish

fumé smoked
grillé grilled
hollandaise butter and vinegar sauce
à la meunière in a butter, lemon and parsley sauce
mousse/mousseline mousse
pané breaded
quenelles light dumplings
thermidor lobster grilled in its shell with cream sauce

MEAT (VIANDE) AND POULTRY (VOLAILLE)

agneau (de pré-salé) lamb (grazed on salt marshes)
andouille/andouillette tripe sausage
boeuf beef
boudin blanc sausage of white meats
boudin noir black pudding
caille quail
canard duck
caneton duckling
contrefilet sirloin roast
dinde, dindon turkey
entrecôte rib steak
faux filet sirloin steak
foie liver
foie gras duck/goose liver
gibier game
gigot (d'agneau) leg (of lamb)
grenouilles (cuisses de) frogs (legs)
grillade grilled meat
hâchis chopped meat or mince hamburger
langue tongue
lapin/lapereau rabbit/young rabbit
lard/lardons bacon/diced bacon
lièvre hare
merguez spicy sausage
mouton mutton
oie goose
onglet cut of beef
os bone
poitrine breast
porc pork
poulet chicken
ris sweetbreads
rognons kidneys (usually lambs')
sanglier wild boar
steak steak
tête de veau calf's head (in jelly)
tournedos thick slices of fillet
tripes tripe
tripoux mutton tripe
veau veal
venaison venison
volaille poultry

MEAT AND POULTRY DISHES AND TERMS

aiguillettes de canard thin, tender pieces of duck
au feu de bois cooked over wood fire
au four baked
blanquette, daube, estouffade, navarin, ragoût types of stew
blanquette de veau veal in cream and mushroom sauce
boeuf bourguignon beef stew with Burgundy, onions and mushrooms
brochette kebab
canard périgourdin roast duck with prunes, foie gras and truffles
carré best end of neck, chop or cutlet
choucroute pickled cabbage with peppercorns, sausages, bacon and salami
civet game stew
confit meat preserve
coq au vin chicken cooked with wine, onions and mushrooms
côte chop, cutlet or rib
cou neck
cuisse thigh or leg
en croûte in pastry
épaule shoulder
farci stuffed
garni with vegetables
gésier gizzard
gigot (d'agneau) leg (of lamb)
grillé grilled
magret de canard duck breast
marmite casserole
médaillon round piece
noisettes small, round fillets
pavé thick slice
poêlé pan-fried
poule au pot chicken simmered with vegetables
rôti roast
sauté lightly cooked in butter
steak au poivre (vert/rouge) steak in a black, green or red peppercorn sauce
steak tartare raw chopped beef, topped with a raw egg yolk
tournedos rossini beef fillet with foie gras and truffles
viennoise fried in egg and breadcrumbs

TERMS FOR STEAKS

bleu almost raw
saignant rare
à point medium
bien cuit well done
très bien cuit very well done

GARNISHES AND SAUCES

américaine white wine, cognac and tomato

au porto in port
béarnaise sauce of egg yolks, white wine, shallots and vinegar
beurre blanc sauce of white wine and shallots, with butter
bonne femme with mushroom, bacon, potato and onions
bordelaise red wine, shallot and bone-marrow sauce
chasseur with white wine, mushrooms and shallots
diable strong mustard seasoning
forestière with bacon and mushroom
fricassée rich, creamy sauce
mornay cheese sauce
périgourdine/périgueux rich wine sauce, possibly with truffles
provençale tomatoes, garlic, olive oil and herbs
rouille a mayonnaise of chillies and garlic
savoyarde with Gruyère cheese

VEGETABLES (LÉGUMES), HERBS (HERBES) AND SPICES (ÉPICES)

ail garlic
artichaut artichoke
asperge asparagus
avocat avocado
basilic basil
betterave beetroot
câpre caper
carotte carrot
céleri celery
champignon, cèpe, chanterelle, girolle, morille types of mushrooms
chou (rouge) (red) cabbage
choufleur cauliflower
ciboulette chives
concombre cucumber
cornichon gherkin
échalotes shallots
endive chicory
épinards spinach
estragon tarragon
fenouil fennel
fèves broad beans
flageolets white beans
haricots (verts, rouges, beurres) beans (French, string, kidney, butter)
lentilles lentils
mange-tout snow peas
menthe mint
moutarde mustard
oignon onion
persil parsley
piment pimento
poireau leek
pois, petits pois peas
poivron vert/rouge green/red sweet pepper
pommes de terre potatoes
radis radish
riz rice
salade verte green salad
tomate tomato
truffes truffles

VEGETABLE DISHES AND TERMS

à l'anglaise/à l'eau boiled
beignet fritter
biologique organic
duxelles fried mushrooms and shallots with cream
farci stuffed
feuille leaf
fines herbes mixture of tarragon, parsley and chives
garni served with vegetables
gratiné browned with cheese or butter
à la grecque cooked in oil and lemon
jardinière with mixed diced vegetables
mousseline mashed potato with cream and eggs
parmentier with potatoes
pimenté peppery hot
piquant spicy
pistou ground basil, olive oil, garlic and parmesan
râpée grated or shredded
sauté lightly fried in butter
à la vapeur steamed

FRUIT (FRUITS) AND NUTS (NOIX)

abricot apricot
amande almond
ananas pineapple
banane banana
brugnon, nectarine nectarine
cacahouète peanut
cassis blackcurrant
cerise cherry
citron lemon
citron vert lime
figue fig
fraise (des bois) strawberry (wild)
framboise raspberry
fruit de la passion passion fruit
grenade pomegranate
groseille rouge/blanche red/white currant
kaki persimmon
mangue mango
marron chestnut
melon melon
mirabelle small yellow plum
mûre blackberry
myrtille blueberry

noisette hazelnut
noix nuts, walnuts
orange orange
pamplemousse grapefruit
pastèque watermelon
pêche peach
pistache pistachio
poire pear
pomme apple
prune plum
pruneau prune
raisin grape
reine-claude greengage

FRUIT DISHES AND TERMS

beignet fritter or doughnut
compote stewed fruit
coulis sauce of puréed fruit
crème de marrons chestnut purée
flambé set aflame in alcohol
frappé iced
macédoine fruit salad

DESSERTS (DESSERTS OR ENTREMETS), PASTRIES (PÂTISSERIE) AND RELATED TERMS

bavarois refers to the mould, could be a mousse or custard
bombe moulded ice-cream dessert
brioche sweet, high-yeast breakfast roll
charlotte custard and fruit in lining of almond fingers
clafoutis cake-like fruit tart
coupe/boule a serving of ice cream
crème anglaise custard
crème Chantilly vanilla-flavoured and sweetened whipped cream
crème fraîche sour cream
crème pâtissière thick, eggy pastry-filling
crêpe pancake
crêpe suzette thin pancake with orange juice and liqueur
fromage blanc cream cheese
gaufre waffle
génoise rich sponge cake
glace ice cream
île flottante/oeufs à la neige soft meringues floating on custard
macaron macaroon
madeleine small sponge cake
mousse au chocolat chocolate mousse
omelette norvégienne parfait baked Alaska frozen mousse; sometimes ice cream
pâte pastry or dough
petit-suisse a smooth mixture of cream and curds
poires belle-hélène pears and ice cream in chocolate sauce
sablé shortbread biscuit
savarin a filled, ring-shaped cake
tarte tart
tartelette small tart
tarte tatin upside-down apple tart
yaourt, yogourt yogurt

WINE TERMS (VIN)

barrique oak barrel for maturing wine
blanc white
cave wineshop/cellar
cépage grape variety (e.g. Merlot, Pinot noir)
chais wine cellars
corsé full-bodied
cuvé vat for fermenting wine
cuvée a specially blended wine
dégustation tasting
doux/moelleux sweet
fin delicate
fort strong
léger light
millésime vintage
mousseux sparkling
riche rich
rosé rosé
rouge red
sec dry
vendange harvest
vignes vines
vignoble vineyard

Glossary

GENERAL VOCABULARY AND TERMS

abbaye abbey
abri prehistoric rock shelter
appellation AOP (*appellation d'origine protégée*) wine classification indicating that the wine meets strict requirements regarding its provenance and methods of production
auberge country inn, frequently offering accommodation
auberge de jeunesse youth hostel
autoroute motorway
bastide new town founded in the thirteenth and fourteenth centuries, built on a grid plan around an arcaded market square (see page)
boules popular French game played with steel balls
cabane, borie *or* **gariotte** dry-stone hut, probably used by shepherds
Capétien Capetian royal dynasty founded by Hugh Capet, which ruled France from 987 to 1328
causse limestone plateau extending from Dordogne *département* south through Lot and into Aveyron
chambre d'hôte bed-and-breakfast accommodation in a private house
chartreuse one-storey building typical of the Bordeaux wine region, slightly raised up and built on top of a half-buried *chai*; also a Carthusian monastery
château castle, mansion, stately home
château fort castle built for a specifically military purpose
collégiale church that shelters a community of priests
colombage traditional building style consisting of a timber frame filled with earth and straw or bricks
commune the basic administrative region, each under a mayor
confiserie confectioner's (shop)
dégustation tasting (wine or food)
département mid-level administrative unit run by a local council – the equivalent of a county in Britain
dolmen Neolithic stone structure, generally held to be a tomb, consisting of two or more upright slabs supporting a horizontal stone
donjon castle keep
église church
falaise cliff

ferme-auberge farm licensed to provide meals in which the majority of the produce must come from the farm itself
foire large market held once or twice monthly in some country towns
formule restaurant menu with two courses, usually comprising a choice of starter and main course or main and dessert
fouille archeological excavation
gabare *or* **gabarre** traditional wooden boat used to transport goods on the Dordogne and Lot rivers up until the late nineteenth century
gavage process of force-feeding ducks and geese to make foie gras
gisement deposit, stratified layers of an archeological excavation
gîte self-catering accommodation
gîte d'étape basic accommodation, usually restricted to walkers, pilgrims and cyclists
gouffre limestone chasm or sinkhole
grotte cave
halle(s) covered market (hall)
hôtel hotel, but also an aristocratic townhouse or mansion
lauze small limestone slabs, a traditional roof covering in the Périgord
navette shuttle-bus, for example connecting a town with its airport
Occitan language (and associated culture) formerly spoken throughout most of south and southwest France
pétanque variation of the game of *boules*
pigeonnier dovecote, often built on stilts and used to collect droppings for fertilizer
pisé traditional Périgordin floor made out of small limestone slabs inserted upright into a bed of clay or lime
porte gateway
retable altarpiece
seneschal chief administrator and justice in medieval times, the representative of the king
table d'hôte meals served to residents of a *chambre d'hôte*. Also, a set menu with choices, at a fixed price.
tour tower
version originale (VO) film shown in its original language and subtitled in French

ARCHITECTURAL TERMS

ambulatory passage around the outer edge of the choir of a church

apse semicircular or polygonal termination at the east end of a church

Baroque High Renaissance period of art and architecture, distinguished by extreme ornateness

chevet east end of a church

Classical architectural style incorporating Greek and Roman elements: pillars, domes, colonnades, etc, at its height in France in the seventeenth century and revived in the nineteenth century as Neoclassical

flamboyant very ornate form of Gothic

fresco painting in watercolour on a wall or ceiling while the plaster is still wet

Gallo-Roman period and culture of Roman occupation of Gaul (1st century BC to 4th century AD)

Gothic architectural style prevalent from the twelfth to sixteenth century, characterized by pointed arches and ribbed vaulting

machicolations parapet on a castle, fortified church, gateway, etc, with openings for dropping stones and so forth on attackers

Merovingian dynasty (and art, etc) ruling France and parts of Germany from the sixth to mid-eighth century

narthex entrance hall of church

nave main body of a church

Renaissance architectural and artistic style developed in fifteenth-century Italy and imported to France in the sixteenth century by King François Ier

Romanesque early medieval architecture distinguished by squat, rounded forms and naive sculpture, called *Roman* in French (not to be confused with *Romain* – Roman)

stucco plaster used to embellish ceilings, etc

transept transverse arm of a church, at right angles to the nave

tympanum semicircular panel above the door of a Romanesque church, usually with sculpture

REGIONAL NAMES

Aquitaine Originally a Roman administrative region extending from Poitiers and Limoges south to the Pyrenees. It later became a duchy, which, at its apogee in the twelfth century, covered roughly the same area, though it fluctuated enormously. In the 1960s the name was resurrected with the creation of regional administrative units. Modern Aquitaine is based around Bordeaux and comprises the *départements* of Dordogne, Gironde and Lot-et-Garonne, among others

Gascony The region to the west and south of the River Garonne, named after a Celtic tribe (the Vascons). In the early tenth century it became an independent duchy but was soon subsumed into the duchy of Aquitaine, though still retained its own identity

Guyenne A corruption of the name "Aquitaine" originating during the period of English rule. Prior to the Revolution, the province of Guyenne extended from Gironde to Aveyron. Nowadays, it is occasionally used to refer to an area roughly encompassing Entre-Deux-Mers and St-Émilion, although there is no strict demarcation

Occitanie The administrative region created in 2016 to the east of Aquitaine, which incorporates the former regions of Languedoc-Roussillon and Midi-Pyrénées

Périgord The confines of Périgord have changed little since pre-Roman times, when it was the home of the Gaulish tribe, the Petrocori. In the eighth century Périgord became a county, and then a province of France until the name was officially changed to Dordogne when *départements* were created in 1790 (each *département* was named after its principal river). However, Périgord is still used frequently, especially in tourist literature. These days it is often subdivided into Périgord Vert (Green Périgord; the *département's* northern sector); Périgord Blanc (White; the central strip along the Isle valley including Périgueux); Périgord Pourpre (Purple; the southwest corner around Bergerac); and Périgord Noir (Black; the southeast, including Sarlat and the Vézère valley)

Quercy Former province roughly equivalent to the modern *départements* of the Lot and the north part of the Tarn-et-Garonne. The latter is often referred to as Bas-Quercy, while Haut-Quercy comprises the Lot's northern region. Like the Périgord, the Quercy was originally named after its Gaulish settlers, the Cadurci tribe. The name is still in regular use today and the sense of burning pride remains. A native of Cahors is still referred to as a Cadurcien

Small print and index

292 About the author
294 Index
304 Map symbols

A ROUGH GUIDE TO ROUGH GUIDES

Published in 1982, the first Rough Guide – to Greece – was a student scheme that became a publishing phenomenon. Mark Ellingham, a recent graduate in English from Bristol University, had been travelling in Greece the previous summer and couldn't find the right guidebook. With a small group of friends he wrote his own guide, combining a contemporary, journalistic style with a thoroughly practical approach to travellers' needs.

The immediate success of the book spawned a series that rapidly covered dozens of destinations. And, in addition to impecunious backpackers, Rough Guides soon acquired a much broader readership that relished the guides' wit and inquisitiveness as much as their enthusiastic, critical approach and value-for-money ethos. These days, Rough Guides include recommendations from budget to luxury and cover more than 120 destinations around the globe, from Amsterdam to Zanzibar, all regularly updated by our team of roaming writers.

Browse all our latest guides, read inspirational features and book your trip at **roughguides.com**.

Rough Guide credits

Editor: Joanna Reeves
Cartography: Katie Bennett
Picture editor: Piotr Kala
Picture Manager: Tom Smyth
Layout: Katie Bennett
Head of DTP and Pre-Press: Rebeka Davies
Head of Publishing: Sarah Clark

Publishing information

Eighth edition 2025

Distribution

UK, Ireland and Europe
Apa Publications (UK) Ltd; sales@roughguides.com
United States and Canada
Ingram Publisher Services; ips@ingramcontent.com
Australia and New Zealand
Booktopia; retailer@booktopia.com.au
Worldwide
Apa Publications (UK) Ltd; sales@roughguides.com

Special Sales, Content Licensing and CoPublishing
Rough Guides can be purchased in bulk quantities at discounted prices. We can create special editions, personalised jackets and corporate imprints tailored to your needs. sales@roughguides.com.
roughguides.com

Printed in China

This book was produced using **Typefi** automated publishing software.

All rights reserved
© 2025 Apa Digital AG
License edition © Apa Publications Ltd UK

All rights reserved. No part of this publication may be reproduced, stored in or introduced into a retrieval system, or transmitted in any form, or by any means (electronic, mechanical, photocopying, recording or otherwise) without the prior written permission of the copyright owner.

A catalogue record for this book is available from the British Library

The publishers and authors have done their best to ensure the accuracy and currency of all the information in **The Rough Guide to Dordogne and the Lot**, however, they can accept no responsibility for any loss, injury, or inconvenience sustained by any traveller as a result of information or advice contained in the guide.

Help us update

We've gone to a lot of effort to ensure that this edition of **The Rough Guide to Dordogne and the Lot** is accurate and up-to-date. However, things change – places get "discovered", transport routes are altered, restaurants and hotels raise prices or lower standards, and businesses cease trading. If you feel we've got it wrong or left something out, we'd like to know, and if you can direct us to the web address, so much the better.

Please send your comments with the subject line "**Rough Guide Dordogne and the Lot Update**" to mail@uk.roughguides.com. We'll acknowledge all contributions and send a copy of the next edition (or any other Rough Guide if you prefer) for the very best emails.

Acknowledgements

Thanks to Stéphanie Gombert, Sophie Nadin, Joanne Bond and Justine Quétier from the Dordogne Tourism Board.

ABOUT THE AUTHOR

Anna Richards lives in Lyon and must be the most insular travel writer out there (she only writes about France). Although the Auvergne-Rhône-Alpes is her base, she spends much of her time haring across the country in every direction, often with a badly-behaved French dog in tow. She's won several awards for her work, which has been featured (online and in print) in the BBC, Condé Nast Traveller, National Geographic and many others. She's the award-winning author of *Paddling France* for Bradt Guides, and she has also written for the *Rough Guide to Brittany and Normandy*.

SMALL PRINT

Photo credits
(Key: T-top; C-centre; B-bottom; L-left; R-right)

All images **Shutterstock** except:
D. Butaeye/SES de Padirac 157
Dreamstime 13TC

iStock 4, 11T, 12, 14T, 14C, 15T, 154/155, 180/181, 260
JGS25/Wikimedia Commons under CC BY-SA 4.0 license
16T

Cover: Chateau de Castelnaud, Dordogne **Peter Adams Photography/Shutterstock**

Index

A

Abri de Laugerie Basse 130
Abri du Cap Blanc 129
Abri du Poisson 130
Accessible travel 36
accommodation 28
activities, outdoor 25, 34, 60. *See also* activities by name
Agen 228
agriculture 275
Aiguillon 222
Airbnb 29
Albas 214
Allemans-du-Dropt 98
Alphonse de Poitiers 223
Aquarium du Périgord Noir 132
Aquitania 262
Argentat 175
Arnac-Pompadour 78
Assier 207
Aubeterre-sur-Dronne 64
Autoire 178
Auvillar 242
Aveyron River 250

B

Baïse, River 28
Baker, Josephine 152
bastides 223
   Bergerac and around 104
   Bretenoux 172
   Lot Valley 211, 214, 217, 219, 222, 225
   Perigord Noir 151
   south of the River Lot 258
   South of the River Lot 241, 243, 246, 250
Bastille Day 33
Beaulieu-en-Rouergue, Abbaye de 253
Beaulieu-sur-Dordogne 174
Beaumont 107
beer 32
Bélaye 215
Belvès 143
Bergerac 84
   accommodation 91
   airport 91
   arrival and departure 91
   bike rental 91
   bus terminus 91
   car rental 91
   Cloître des Récollets 89
   drinking 93
   eating 92
   Église Notre-Dame 90
   Église St-Jacques 90
   Espace Vin 90
   history 88
   hospital 93
   hotels 91
   information 91
   market square 90
   Musée du Tabac 89
   parking 91
   Place de la Myrpe 90
   police 93
   post office 93
   Quai Cyrano 90
   restaurants 92
   river trips 91
   Rue St-James 90
   shopping 93
   taxis 91
   tourist office 91
   tours 91
   train station 91
   wine trade 88
Bergerac, Cyrano de 89
Bergerac wine region 92
Bernard of Clairvaux 116
Bessières, Maréchal 215
Beynac-et-Cazenac 145
bicycles 27
bike rentals 28, 60
boating 28, 62, 195
boat rentals 28. *See also* canoe rentals
boat trips 60, 91, 147, 150, 172, 174, 231, 237
books 279
bories 122, 123
Boschaud, Abbaye de 68
boules 35
Bourdeilles 61
Bouriane 211
Bouziès 195
Brantôme 58
breakfast 30
Bretenoux 172
Brexit 277
Brive-la-Gaillarde 74
Bruniquel 251
Buddhist retreats 97
buses 26
Buzet-sur-Baïse 237

C

Cabanes du Breuil 122
Cabrerets 200
Cadouin 109
Cadouin, Abbaye de 109
Caesar, Julius 262
Cahors 184
   accommodation 192
   arrival and departure 191
   bike rental 191
   boat rental 191, 192
   boat trips 192
   bus terminus 191
   Cahors Plage 191
   canoe tours 192
   car rental 191
   Cathédrale St-Étienne 188
   drinking 193
   eating 192
   entertainment 194
   history 185
   hospital 194
   information 192
   Jardins Secrets 191
   kayak rental 191
   Maison de l'Eau 190
   Mont St-Cyr 191
   Musée de la Résistance 189
   Musée Henri Martin 190
   nightlife 193
   parking 191
   Place Jean-Jacques Chapou 189
   police 194
   Pont Valentré 190
   taxis 191
   tourist office 192
   tours 192
   train station 191
   wines 193
Cajarc 197
Calès 162
camping 30
Canal de Garonne 231
canoeing 34, 59, 105, 126, 147, 195
   La Voie Bleue 55
   Périgueux and the North 60
canoe rentals
   Bergerac and around 100, 106
   Périgueux and the North 63, 64
   Sarlat and the Périgord Noir 119, 126, 132, 136, 149, 150, 152
   Upper Dordogne 160, 170, 171, 172

Cap Cauderoue 237
Capdenac 198
Carennac 171
car rental 27
Carsac-Aillac 153
Castelfranc 214
Castel-Merle 136
Castelnau, Château de 173
Castelnaud-la-Chapelle 148
Castelnau-Montratier 245
Castillon-la-Bataille 33
castles 271. *See also* châteaux
Cathars 266
Causse de Gramat 207
Causses du Quercy 8
caves 112, 124. *See also* prehistoric art
   Combarelles 128
   Cougnac 211
   Cussac 106
   de l'Abbaye de Brantôme 59
   Domme 151
   Foissac 199
   Font-de-Gaume 127
   Gouffre de Proumeyssac 133
   Grand Roc, Grotte du 130
   Lacave 161
   Lascaux 139
   Maxange 107
   Pech-Merle 200
   Presque 178
   Rouffignac 130
   Sorcier 133
   Tourtoirac 74
   Villars 68
caving 35
Cazals 211
Célé valley 200
cellphones 41
Celtic people 262
Cénac 152
chambres d'hôtes 29
Champollion, Jean-François 202, 204
Channel Tunnel 23, 24
Chapelle St-Martin 106
Charlemagne 263
châteaux
   Assier 207
   Beynac 146
   Biron 224
   Bonaguil 217
   Bridoire 94
   Bruniquel 251
   Castelnau 173
   Castelnaud 148
   Cénevières 197
   Commarque 129
   Doyens 171
   Ducs de Duras 99
   Fénelon 153
   Hautefort 72
   Herm 131
   Jaubertie 94
   Jumilhac 70
   Lanquais 103
   Losse 137
   Marqueyssac 147
   Milandes 149, 152
   Monbazillac 93
   Montaigne 101
   Montal 177
   Najac 257
   Nérac 236
   Pompadour 78
   Puyguilhem 67
   Puymartin 121
   Rocamadour 165
   St-Cirq 196
   St-Laurent-les-Tours 175
   Tiregand 95
   Turenne 80
children, travelling with 36
Chocolaterie Lamy 76
churches 270
Cirque d'Autoire 178
Cirque de Montvalent 171
climate 10
coffee 33
Collonges-la-Rouge 81
Colombier 94
Combarelles Grotte des 128
Cordes-sur-Ciel 254
Corniche, the 252
costs 37
Cougnac, Grottes de 211
Couze-et-St-Front 103
Couze valley 107
Creysse 170
crime and personal safety 37
Cro-Magnon 261
Cro-Magnon people 128
Croquants 270
currency 40
Cussac Grotte de 106
customs 8
cycling 27, 34, 60
   Voie Verte 66

D

dark skies 8
Daumesnil, Baron Pierre 53
de Gaulle, General 275
Denoix Distillery 76
discounts 37
Domme 151
Domme, Grotte de 151
Dordogne River 8
Dordogne Valley 102, 141
drinks 5, 30, 32, 76. *See also* wine
driving 26
driving from the UK 24
Dronne River 59
Dronne valley 61
drugs 38
Duèze, Jacques 188
Duras 98
Duravel 217

E

Échourgnac 65
Eco-musée de la Noix du Périgord 148
economy 8, 276, 277
Edward I of England 223, 225
Église Saint-Eutrope 98
Eleanor of Aquitaine 109, 265, 266
electricity 38
emergency numbers 37
English rule 265
entry requirements 38
Espagnac-Ste-Eulalie 202
Étang de la Jemaye 65
European Health Insurance Card 38
Eurostar 20, 23
Eurotunnel 25
Excideuil 71
Eymet 97

F

fact file 8
faïence 68
Félibrée 33
Ferme du Parcot 66
ferries 23
   from Ireland 24
   from the UK 24
festivals 33, 158, 233
   Bergerac and around 87
   Lot valley 186, 197, 198
   Perigueux and the North 49
   Sarlat and the Perigord Noir 115
Fête de la Musique 33
Figeac 202
   accommodation 206
   arrival and departure 205
   bike rental 205
   bus terminus 205
   camping 206
   car rental 206
   drinking 206
   eating 206
   Église Notre-Dame-du-Puy 205

INDEX

Église St-Sauveur 204
history 202
hospital 207
market 204
Musée Champollion 205
parking 205
Place Carnot 204
Place Champollion 205
Place des Écritures 205
Place Vival 204
police 207
restaurants 206
taxis 206
tourist office 206
train station 205
Filature de Belvès 144
flights 23
  from Australia 23
  from Canada 23
  from Ireland 23
  from New Zealand 23
  from South Africa 23
  from the UK 23
  from the US 23
foie gras 69
Foissac, Grotte de 199
Font-de-Gaume, Grotte de 127
food 5, 30, 69
foyers 29
Franks 263
French Air Force 8
Fronde rebellion 271
Fumel 218

G

Gambetta, Léon 188, 189, 190
Garonne Canal 28
Garonne River 228
gîtes 29
gîtes d'étape 29
glossary 289
Gluges 170
gold 70
Gorges de l'Aveyron 250
Gouffre de Padirac 172
Gouffre de Proumeyssac 133
Goujounac 212
Gourdon 209
GR6 long-distance footpath 161
GR36 long-distance footpath 195
Gramat 208
Grand Roc, Grotte du 130
Grézels 215

H

Hautefort 72

Hautefort, Louise de 70
Haut-Quercy 156
health 38
Henry III 88
Henry II of England (Henry of Anjou) 265
Henry IV (Henry of Navarre) 97, 187, 197, 236
Henry, the Young King 168, 169
hiking 126
history 261
history timeline 261
Hollande, François 276
horse racing 78. *See also* National Stud
horseriding 35, 106, 132
hostels 29
hot-air ballooning 147
hot chocolate 33
hotels 28
Hundred Years' War 51, 267

I

insurance 39
internet 39
Isle, River 55
Issigeac 96
itineraries 18

J

jam 8, 174
Jardins de Sardy 101
Jardins du Grand Couvent 209
Jardins Panoramiques de Limeuil 105
Jardins Suspendus de Marqueyssac 147
Jumilhac-le-Grand 70

K

kayaking 34, 59, 60, 105

L

La Boétie, Étienne de 116
Labyrinthe Préhistorique 132
Lacave 161
Lacave, Grottes de 161
La Double 65
Laguépie 254
Lalbenque 245
Lalinde 104
La Madeleine 134

language 281
La Roque-Gageac 149
La Roque St-Christophe 136
Lascaux II 139
Lascaux IV 139
laundry 39
Lauzerte 243
lauzes 122, 123
Le Bugue 131
Le Buisson-de-Cadouin 107
Le Conquil 136
Lenoir, Marcel 251
Les Arques 211
Les Eyzies-de-Tayac 123
Les Jardins de l'Imaginaire 141
Les Milandes 149
Le Thot 137
LGBTQ+ travellers 39
Limeuil 105
Limeuil, Isabeau de 103
liqueurs 32, 76
Lot, River 28
Lot valley 194
Loubressac 179
Louis IX 109
Louis XIV 271
lunch 31
Lurçat, Jean 176
Luzech 213

M

Macron, Emmanuel 277
Magdalenian era 262
mail 40
Maison Forte de Reignac 135
Malraux, André 116
Manoir d'Eyrignac 121
maps 40
  Agen 232
  Bergerac 88
  Bergerac and around 86
  Brive la Gaillarde 75
  Cahors 187
  Central Périgueux 54
  Figeac 203
  Itineraries 19
  Moissac 239
  Montauban 247
  Périgueux 50
  Périgueux and the north 48
  Rocamadour 162
  Sarlat and the Périgord Noir 114
  Sarlat la Caneda 117
  South of the River Lot 230
  The Dordogne & the Lot 6
  The Lot valley and around 184
  The middle Dordogne valley 144

INDEX

The Upper Dordogne valley and Rocamadour 156
The Vezere valley 124
Villeneuve sur Lot 220
Marcilhac 201
markets 8, 35, 100
  Bergerac and around 87, 93
  Lot Valley 186, 197, 208, 211, 216, 218, 222
  Périgueux and The North 49, 58, 72, 78
  Sarlat and the Périgord Noir 115, 116, 131, 142
  south of the River Lot 233, 235, 238, 245, 252, 254
  Upper Dordogne and Rocamadour 158, 173, 175
Martel 168
Martignac 216
Maxange, Grottes de 107
Meyronne 169
mobile phones 41
Moissac 238
Monbazillac 92, 93
money 40
Monflanquin 222
Monkey's Leap, legend of 199
Monpazier 225
Montaigne, Michel de 102
Montauban 246
Montcabrier 217
Montcuq 244
Montcuq Monopoly 244
Montferrand-du-Périgord 108
Montignac 137
Montpezat-de-Quercy 245
Montricoux 251
Mont St-Cyr 191
Mouliérat, Jean 173
Moulin de Cocussotte 99
Moulin de Cougnaguet 159, 162
Moulin de la Rouzique 103
Moulin, Jean 275
Musée de l'Abri Pataud 125
Musée de l'Insolite 201
Musée du Corbillard et de l'Attelage 243
Musée National de la Préhistoire 123

N

Najac 257
Napoleon Bonaparte 272
Napoléon III 273
National Stud 79
Nérac 236
newspapers 40

O

Occitan 269
opening hours 40
outdoor activities 25, 34

P

Parc Animalier de Gramat 209
Pécharmant 92, 95
Pech-Merle, Grotte de 200
Penne 252
Penne-d'Agenais 218
perched villages 10
Périgord Pourpre 84
Périgord Vert 66
Périgueux 49
  accommodation 57
  arrival and departure 56
  car rental 56
  Cathédrale St-Front 53
  cinema 58
  drinking 58
  eating 57
  history 51
  hospital 58
  information 56
  Jardin des Arènes 55
  La Cité 51, 55
  Le Puy-St-Front 51, 52
  Maison des dames de la Foi 52
  markets 53, 58
  Musée d'Art et d'Archéologie du Périgord 54
  Musée Gallo-Romain Vesunna 56
  Musée Militaire 52
  place de la Clautre 52
  police 58
  post office 58
  Rue de l'Aubergerie 52
  Rue St-Roch 52
  shopping 58
  St-Étienne-de-la-Cité 55
  swimming pool 58
  taxis 56
  theatre 58
  Tour de Vésone 56
  tourist office 56
Périgueux and the north 46
Peyrusse-le-Roc 199
pharmacies 38
phones 41
phylloxera 274
Piaf, Edith 170
pigeonniers 8
Plum Village 97
Pôle International de la Préhistoire 123
police 37

politics 276
post offices 40
Prayssac 215
Préhisto-parc 135
prehistoric art 68, 106, 112, 123, 127, 128, 130, 133, 137, 139, 200, 211, 261
prehistoric rock shelters
  Cap Blanc, Abri du 129
  Castel-Merle 136
  La Madeleine 134
  La Roque St-Christophe 135
  Laugerie Basse, Abri de 130
  Le Conquil 136
  Pataud, Abri 125
  Poisson, Abri du 130
Presque Grottes de 178
Pruneaux d'Agen 234
prunes 230, 234
public holidays 40
Pujols 221
Puyguilhem, Château de 67
Puy-l'Évêque 216

Q

Quercy 198
Quercy Blanc 242

R

radio 40
rail passes 24
rail travel 25. *See also* trains
Rainbow Tribe 152
rainfall 10
Rampoux 211
restaurants 31
Revolution 272
Ribérac 62
Richard the Lionheart 106, 109, 169, 218, 241, 265, 266
River Baïse 28
River Dronne 59
River Isle 55
River Lot 28, 212
River Lot, South of 228
Rocamadour 163
  accommodation 166
  arrival 166
  Basilique St-Sauveur 164
  Borie d'Imbert, La 166
  Chapelle Notre-Dame 164
  Chapelle St-Michel 165
  Château de Rocamadour 165
  Cité Religieuse 164
  eating 167
  Forêt des Singes 165

funicular 166
history 104
information 166
L'Hospitalet 165
lift 166
parking 166
Petit Train 166
restaurants 167
Rocher des Aigles 165
tourist offices 166
train station 166
Roc de Cazelle 129
rock climbing 35
Roman occupation 262
Rosetta Stone 204
Rostand Edmond 89
Rouffignac 131
Rouffignac, Grotte de 130
rugby 35, 76
rules of the road 27

S

saffron 197, 198
Salviac 211
Sarkozy, Nicolas 276
Sarlat and the Périgord Noir 112
Sarlat-la-Canéda 115
   accommodation 119
   activities 119
   arrival and departure 119
   Ascenseur Panoramique 118
   bike rental 119
   bus terminus 119
   car rental 119
   Cathédrale St-Sacerdos 117
   driving 119
   eating 120
   Gorodka 118
   history 116
   hospital 121
   Hôtel de Maleville 116
   information 119
   Maison de La Boétie 116
   Manoir de Gisson 118
   parking 119
   Place de la Liberté 116
   police 121
   post office 121
   restaurants 120
   shopping 121
   taxis 119
   tourist office 119
   tours 119
   train station 119
Saut de la Mounine 199
self-catering 29
service charges 31
Shasmoukine, Pierre 118

shopping 35
smoking 41
SNCF 25
soft drinks 33
Sorcier Grotte du 133
Souillac 159
speed limits 27
spirits 32
sports 34
St Amadour 164, 201
St-Amand-de-Coly 140
St Antonin 252
St-Antonin-Noble-Val 252
St-Avit-Sénieur 108
St-Céré 175
St-Cirq Lapopie 195
St-Cyprien 142
Ste-Foy-la-Grande 100
Ste Spérie 176
St Front 51
St-Geniès 121
St James, Way of 264
St-Jean-de-Côle 66
St-Léon-sur-Vézère 135
St-Médard 212
St Namphaise 208
St-Nicolas-de-la-Grave 241
studying in the Dordogne and Lot 42
sustainable travel 20
swimming 35

T

Tarn River 228
taxes 37
tea 33
telephone codes, international 41
telephones 41
temperatures 10
Terrasson-la-Villedieu 141
Thénac 97
Thiviers 68
time zone 41
tipping 31
tourism 275, 277
tourist information 41
tourist offices 42
tour operators 25
Tourtoirac, Abbaye de 74
Tourtoirac, Grotte de 74
trains 24
   Eurostar 23, 24
   fares 26
   from the UK 23, 24
   rail passes 24
   TGV 25
transport 25
travel agents 25

travel essentials 36
Trémolat 104
Troglodyte houses 111
troubadours 269
truffles 72, 245
Turenne 80
Tursac 134

U

Upper Dordogne valley and Rocamadour 156
Uxellodunum 262

V

Varen 253
VAT (TVA) 37
vegan food 32
vegetarian food 32
Vercingétorix 262
Vers 194
Vézère valley 122
Vikings 264
Villa Gallo-Romaine de Montcaret 101
Village du Bournat 132
Villars, Grotte de 68
Villefranche-de-Rouergue 258
Villeneuve-sur-Lot 219
vineyards 8, 32, 92, 193, 274. *See also* wine producers
visas 38
Visigoths 263
Voie Bleue, La 55
Voie Verte, La 55, 66

W

walking 34
   chemin de halage 195
   GR6 Lacave to Rocamadour 161
   GR36 long-distance footpath 195
   La Voie Verte 55
   Sarlat and the Périgord Noir 147
   Transhumance (Rocamadour) 166
   Voie Verte 66
walnuts 150
Wars of Religion 187, 225, 268
weather 10
wi-fi 39
wine 31, 32, 265
   Bergerac 92
   Châteauneuf-du-Pape 188
   wines of Cahors 193
wine festivals 34
wine producers 32

Ancienne Cure, Domaine de l' 94
Côtes d'Olt 193
Haut-Pécharmant, Domaine du 95
Lagrézette, Château 193
Les Vignerons de Buzet 237

working in the Dordogne and Lot 42
World Heritage Sites 8
World War I 274
World War II 203, 274

Z

Zadkine, Ossip 212

NOTES

NOTES

YOUR TAILOR-MADE TRIP
STARTS HERE

Tailor-made trips and unique adventures crafted by local experts

Rough Guides has been inspiring travellers with lively and thought-provoking guidebooks for more than 35 years. Now we're linking you up with selected local experts to craft your dream trip. They will put together your perfect itinerary and book it at local rates.

Don't follow the crowd – find your own path.

HOW ROUGHGUIDES.COM/TRIPS WORKS

STEP 1

Pick your dream destination, tell us what you want and submit an enquiry.

STEP 2

Fill in a short form to tell your local expert about your dream trip and preferences.

STEP 3

Our local expert will craft your tailor-made itinerary. You'll be able to tweak and refine it until you're completely satisfied.

STEP 4

Book online with ease, pack your bags and enjoy the trip! Our local expert will be on hand 24/7 while you're on the road.

BENEFITS OF PLANNING AND BOOKING AT ROUGHGUIDES.COM/TRIPS

PLAN YOUR ADVENTURE WITH LOCAL EXPERTS

Rough Guides' English-speaking local experts are hand-picked, based on their experience in the travel industry and their impeccable standards of customer service.

SAVE TIME AND GET ACCESS TO LOCAL KNOWLEDGE

When a local expert plans your trip, you save time and money when you book, even during high season. You won't be charged for using a credit card either.

MAKE TRAVEL A BREEZE: BOOK WITH PEACE OF MIND

Enjoy stress-free travel when you use Rough Guides' secure online booking platform. All bookings come with a money-back guarantee.

WHAT DO OTHER TRAVELLERS THINK ABOUT ROUGH GUIDES TRIPS?

Trip to Spain

This Spain tour company did a fantastic job to make our dream trip perfect. We gave them our travel budget, told them where we would like to go, and they did all of the planning. Our drivers and tour guides were always on time and very knowledgable. The hotel accommodations were better than we would have found on our own. Only one time did we end up in a location that we had not intended to be in. We called the 24 hour phone number, and they immediately fixed the situation.

Don A, USA

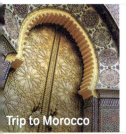

Trip to Morocco

Our trip was fantastic! Transportation, accommodations, guides – all were well chosen! The hotels were well situated, well appointed and had helpful, friendly staff. All of the guides we had were very knowledgeable, patient, and flexible with our varied interests in the different sites. We particularly enjoyed the side trip to Tangier! Well done! The itinerary you arranged for us allowed maximum coverage of the country with time in each city for seeing the important places.

Sharon, USA

PLAN AND BOOK YOUR TRIP AT ROUGHGUIDES.COM/TRIPS

Map symbols

The symbols below are used on maps throughout the book

Listings key

- Accommodation
- Eating
- Drinking/nightlife
- Shopping